The Cambridge Companion to Chopin

1836,   watercolour by Maria Wodzińska,
painted in Marienbad

1838,   detail from a portrait by Eugène
Delacroix, Musée du Louvre, Paris

1847,   pencil drawing by F. X. Winterhalter

1849,   from a photograph by L. A. Bisson

The Cambridge Companion to Chopin

edited by Jim Samson

CAMBRIDGE
UNIVERSITY PRESS

HOUSTON PUBLIC LIBRARY

Published by the Press Syndicate of the University of Cambridge
The Pitt Building, Trumpington Street, Cambridge CB2 1RP
40 West 20th Street, New York NY 10011–4211, USA
10 Stamford Road, Oakleigh, Victoria 3166, Australia

First published 1992

Printed in Great Britain by
Redwood Press Limited, Melksham, Wiltshire

A catalogue record for this book is available from the British Library

Library of Congress cataloguing in publication data

The Cambridge Companion to Chopin/edited by Jim Samson.
   p.   cm.
Includes bibliographical references and index.
ISBN 0 521 40490 8 (hardback)
1. Chopin, Frédéric, 1810–1849 — Criticism and interpretation.
2. Chopin, Frédéric, 1810–1849. Piano music. I. Samson, Jim.
ML410.C54C2   1992
786.2′092 – dc20   91–24533   CIP   MN

ISBN 0 521 40490 8 hardback

ME

Contents

Chronology

	Biography	Music and musicians
1810	Chopin born, 1 March, in Żelazowa Wola, son of Nicolas Chopin and Justyna Krzyzanowska. The family moves to Warsaw in October.	Beethoven: music of *Egmont*.
1811		Beethoven's Fifth Piano Concerto performed, Leipzig. Weber's *Abu Hassan* given, Munich. Liszt born.
1812		Field's first nocturnes published, Moscow. Thalberg born.
1813		Rossini's *L'italiana in Algeri* given, Venice. The Philharmonic Society formed, London. Verdi and Wagner born.
1814		Final version of Beethoven's *Fidelio* given, Vienna.
1815		Schubert: *Erlkönig*. Maelzel invents the metronome.
1816	Begins to take piano lessons from Adalbert Żywny.	Schubert: Fifth Symphony. Rossini's *Il barbiere di Siviglia* given, Rome.
1817	Polonaise in G minor published.	Weber appointed Kapellmeister, Dresden. Part I of Clementi's *Gradus ad Parnassum* published.
1818	Plays at a charity concert in Warsaw, followed by numerous invitations to aristocratic homes.	Beethoven: 'Hammerklavier' Sonata.
1819		Schubert: 'Trout' Quintet. Offenbach born.

1820   Hears the singer Angelica Catalani, who gives him a gold watch. Plays for the Grand Duke Constantin.

Metal piano frames first used. Moniuszko born.

1821   Dedicates his A♭ Polonaise to Żywny.

Weber's *Der Freischütz* given, Berlin. Beethoven: Piano Sonatas Opp. 110–11.

1822   Has composition lessons from Józef Elsner. Composes the G♯ minor Polonaise.

Schubert: 'Unfinished' Symphony. Franck born. Royal Academy of Music founded, London.

1823

Beethoven begins the composition of his late string quartets. Spohr's *Jessonda* given, Kassel.

1824   Enrols at the Warsaw Lyceum, where his father teaches.

Beethoven's 'Choral' Symphony performed in Vienna, and his *Missa Solemnis* in St. Petersburg. Schubert: *Die Schöne Müllerin*. Rossini director of the Théâtre-Italien, Paris.

1825   Edits (with his sister) the holiday diary *Szafarnia Courier*. Plays to Czar Alexander I. Rondo Op. 1 published.

Schubert: 'Great' C major Symphony. Johann Strauss the elder forms his own orchestra, Vienna. Bruckner, Smetana and Johann Strauss the younger born.

1826   Enters Warsaw Conservatory. Polonaise in B♭ minor. Gives several concerts in Warsaw.

Weber's *Oberon* given, London. He dies there. Mendelssohn: Overture to *A Midsummer Night's Dream*.

1827   His younger sister Emilia dies. Sonata Op. 4, Variations Op. 2. Visits Prince Radziwiłł at Antonin.

Schubert: *Die Winterreise* and two piano trios. Liszt settles in Paris. Beethoven dies, Vienna.

1828   Visits Berlin. *Fantasy on Polish Airs*, Op. 13. *Rondo à la krakowiak*, Op. 14.

Schubert: String Quintet in C and last three piano sonatas. He dies, Vienna. Auber's *La Muette de Portici* given, Paris.

1829   Meets Hummel and hears Paganini in Warsaw. Finishes at the Conservatory and gives two successful concerts in Vienna. Second visit to Antonin, where he writes the Polonaise Op. 3 for cello and piano.

Rossini's *Guillaume Tell* given, Paris. Mendelssohn conducts Bach's St Matthew Passion.

Infatuation for Konstancja
Gładowska.

1830 Plays the two concertos at public
concerts in Vienna. Leaves for
Vienna with Titus Wojciechowski.

1831 Unsuccessful months in Vienna.
Friendship with Dr Malfatti.
Leaves for Munich, where he gives
a concert, then Stuttgart, where he
learns of the failure of the Polish
uprising. The 'Stuttgart Diary'.
Arrives in Paris early October.
Meets Kalkbrenner, Hiller and
Liszt.

1832 First concert in Paris. Friendships
with Mendelssohn and Berlioz.
First publications in Paris and
London. Begins a highly successful
and lucrative teaching career.

1833 Plays with Liszt at a benefit for
Harriet Smithson. Other private
appearances. Friendship with
Bellini. Opp. 8–12 published.

1834 Visits (with Hiller) the Rhenish
Music Festival, where he renews his
acquaintance with Mendelssohn.
Plays at one of the prestigious
Conservatory Concerts in Paris.
Opp. 13–19 published. The
Fantaisie-Impromptu composed.

1835 Travels to Karlsbad to meet his
parents. Visits Dresden and
begins his friendship with Maria
Wodzińska. Visits Leipzig, where
he meets Mendelssohn, Schumann
and Clara Wieck. Seriously ill at
Heidelberg. Opp. 20 and 24
published.

1836 Visits Marienbad to meet the
Wodziński family. Proposes to
Maria, but is pledged to secrecy by

Berlioz: *Symphonie fantastique*.
Mendelssohn: 'Reformation'
Symphony.
Bellini's *La sonnambula* and *Norma*
given, Milan. Meyerbeer's *Robert le
diable* given, Paris. Schumann writes
his early piano music.

Donizetti's *L'elisir d'amore* given,
Milan.

Mendelssohn: 'Italian' Symphony.
Brahms born.

Liszt: *Harmonies poétiques et
religieuses*. Berlioz: 'Harold in Italy'
Symphony. First issue of *Neue
Zeitschrift für Musik* published,
Leipzig. Borodin born.

Donizetti's *Lucia di Lammermoor*
given, Naples. Schumann: *Carnaval*.
Mendelssohn appointed conductor
of the Leipzig Gewandhaus Orchestra. Bellini dies, Paris. Saint-Saëns
born.

Glinka's *A Life for the Tsar* given,
St. Petersburg. Meyerbeer's
Les Huguenots given, Paris.

her mother. Opp. 21–3, 26 and 27 published. First meeting with George Sand.

1837 The Wodzińska engagement is severed by her family. Visits London (with Pleyel) in July. Growing friendship with Sand. Opp. 25 and 29–32 published.

Berlioz: *Grande messe des morts.* Liszt: *24 grandes études.* Field and Hummel die. Balakirev born.

1838 Plays for Louis Philippe and at a concert by Alkan. Goes to Majorca with Sand. Completes the Preludes Op. 28 and the Second Ballade at Valldemosa. Opp. 33–4 published.

Schumann: *Kinderszenen* and *Kreisleriana.* Donizetti settles in Paris. Bizet and Bruch born.

1839 Ill in Valldemosa. Returns to Marseilles in spring and spends summer at Sand's home, Nohant. Completes the B♭ minor Sonata. On return to Paris meets Moscheles, with whom he plays at Saint-Cloud. Op. 28 published.

Berlioz: *Roméo et Juliette* Symphony. Musorgsky born.

1840 Quiet year spent composing in Paris. Opp. 35–42 published.

Schumann marries Clara Wieck and composes over a hundred songs. Paganini dies.

1841 Concert in Paris in April. Summer at Nohant including music-making with Pauline Viardot. On return to Paris joins Sand at Rue Pigalle. Opp. 43–9 published.

Schumann's 'symphonic year'. Chabrier and Dvorak born.

1842 Concert with Viardot and the cellist Franchomme in February. Summer at Nohant, where Delacroix is among the guests. Death of his close friend Jan Matuszyński. Moves to Square d'Orléans. Op. 50 published.

Wagner's *Rienzi* given, Dresden. Verdi's *Nabucco* given, Milan. Glinka's *Ruslan and Lyudmila* given, St. Petersburg. Schumann: Piano Quintet and other chamber works. Meyerbeer appointed Court Musical Director, Berlin.

1843 Summer at Nohant. Opp. 51–4 published.

Wagner's *Der fliegende Holländer* given, Dresden. Donizetti's *Don Pasquale* given, Paris. Berlioz treatise on orchestration published. Leipzig conservatory opens. Grieg born.

1844	Death of Nicolas Chopin. Fryderyk's sister Ludwika visits him in Nohant. Opp. 55–6 published.	Mendelssohn: Violin Concerto. Liszt's connection with Weimar begins. Rimsky-Korsakov born.
1845	Health deteriorates. The beginning of a major rift in his relationship with Sand. Opp. 57–8 published.	Wagner's *Tannhäuser* given, Dresden. Schumann: Piano Concerto. Fauré born.
1846	Quarrels with Sand exacerbated by family difficulties. Publication of Sand's novel *Lucrezia Floriani*, a 'portrait' of her relationship with Chopin. Opp. 59–61 published.	Mendelssohn's *Elijah* performed, Birmingham. Berlioz's *La damnation de Faust* performed, Paris.
1847	Marriage of Sand's daughter Solange to the sculptor Clesinger. Labyrinthine family quarrels resulting in Chopin's break with Sand. Opp. 63–5 published.	Verdi's *Macbeth* given, Florence. Mendelssohn dies.
1848	Last concert in Paris. Visits England and Scotland under the protection of his pupil Jane Stirling. Plays at many functions and gives public concerts in Manchester and Glasgow. Returns to London, very ill, in November and plays at the Guildhall. Returns to Paris.	Glinka: *Kamarinskaya*. Wagner flees to Weimar to escape arrest following the uprising in Dresden. Donizetti dies.
1849	Unable to teach or give concerts. Assisted financially by Stirling. His sister arrives in Paris to nurse him at his final home in Place Vendôme. He dies there on 17 October.	Meyerbeer: *Le prophète*.

Myth and reality: a biographical introduction

JIM SAMSON

Biography is a discipline sufficient to itself, and one which presents formidable intellectual challenges. As a component of art histories, however, its explanatory value needs careful assessment. The traditional 'life and works', much favoured by English writers on music, highlights the difficulties. With notable exceptions it has been a hybrid genre, seldom addressing – except on a rather surface level – just how a composer's life may *explain* his music. More often than not we are given two books in one, even when they are interleaved rather than formally separated. And in writing two books in one, the author will be hard pressed to do justice to either. A worthwhile objective would be to translate the 'life and works' from a hybrid to a compound genre, and the present introduction, biographical in orientation, is programmatic of such an approach.

A key issue is to evaluate the respective roles of 'real' and 'ideal' biographies in the elucidation of a composer's creative output. For the biographer the task is of course clear-cut: to extract the real from the ideal. But for the music historian it is by no means so simple. The real biography bears directly, though in very complicated ways, on 'production' (*poiesis*) and is therefore a primary cause of the music itself. The ideal biography, on the other hand, bears on 'reception' (*aesthesis*), since it influences substantially the several ways in which the music has been 'made concrete'[1] or 'constituted' in the world. Both the real and the ideal biographies are therefore of concern to the music historian.

In the case of Chopin the gap between the two biographies is so wide as to render them at times oppositional. This is well known. A personality wrapped in secrecy made itself available to multiple interpretation, and the process had already started during his lifetime. We need only compare contemporary portraits and drawings with the one surviving photograph to measure something of the distance between myth and reality. Contemporary writing (criticism, letters, memoirs) rendered the myths specific and they were firmed up and validated after his death. Already in the first biography by Liszt (1852) there was a notable economy with the truth, initiating receptional traditions which culminated in the celluloid

1

biography of our own century. Apocryphal stories aside, the truly remarkable aspect of all this is the power of critical discourse to transform a composer of decidedly classical orientation into the archetype of a romantic artist.

In a 'biography' of the biographies[2] Adam Harasowski divided the many studies of Chopin into two categories, those that generated legends and those that set out to destroy them. A worthwhile, though apparently perverse, exercise would invert Harasowski's values, examining the legends positively as part of the 'effective history'[3] of Chopin's music and at the same time questioning the reality portrayed by even the most conscientious and scrupulous biographies. The first part of this exercise would be a study in reception. Through a focus on the history of taste it would tend to deconstruct the musical work by revealing its multiple meanings. The second part of the exercise would examine issues at the heart of biography as a discipline. In particular it would address the single most serious lacuna in Chopin biography, a failure to meet the challenge of his compositions. Their creation, in all its experiential complexity, was after all integral to his life.

We will consider first the myths. Viewed reductively, they might be classifed under three broad headings – the 'salon composer', the 'romantic composer' and the 'slavonic composer'. Each of these set the compass points for a particular reading of the music – embracing a manner of performance, listening and even editing – and for that reason they are a part of its legitimate esthetic property. They are among the constructs that have mediated between Chopin's singular creative activity and the social existence of his music, building plural layers of receptional insight which have influenced the understanding of determinate groups at particular times. The following remarks offer little more than a sketch of Chopin reception, a subject to which I hope to return in the future.

THE 'SALON COMPOSER'

A substantial income from teaching in Paris enabled Chopin to avoid the public concert and to restrict his appearances as a performer mainly to small gatherings of initiates in society drawing-rooms. From his earliest days in Warsaw he had been at ease in such circles, and his playing, with its discriminating sensitivity of touch, was best suited to them. His creative path reflected this. The limitation of medium was in itself an eloquent credo, but within it we may note a progression from public virtuosity (the concert music of the Warsaw years) towards a mature pianism at once more intimate and more powerful. Chopin never rejected the world of the salon, but he was in no sense confined by it. His achievement was to elevate some of its traditions to unsuspected creative heights, where they might yield nothing in stature to more epic and prestigious genres.

His association with the salon generated a number of powerful images which have proved enduring in Chopin reception. One celebrates the near-magical effect of his playing, pointed up in numerous apocryphal stories of his childhood feats (he quietens the restless boys with his playing) and of his hypnotic presence as a performer (he exchanges places with Liszt in a darkened auditorium). A frequent description was the 'ariel of the piano'. In due course such images of Chopin the pianist were transferred to Chopin the composer, promoting notions of inspiration which hardly square with his remarks to Delacroix on counterpoint and form,[4] or indeed with our knowledge (through manuscript sources) of his working methods.

We may mention two further associations with the salon. One is the cult of the feminine, the image of a composer 'for the ladies', reinforced not just in critical writing but in portraits, drawings and pictorial representations on nineteenth-century editions. Again this image was transferred to the music itself, especially the nocturnes, composed for 'a woman's sensitiveness of finger'.[5] The reality was very different. Chopin enjoyed elegant feminine company, but he had harsh views on the fawning of his 'adoring women'. He himself used the phrase 'music for the ladies', but unhappily he meant it disparagingly. Another association with the salon was the 'sentimental drawing room composer'[6] – the 'superficial genius' – and the appellation was encouraged by a self-imposed limitation of medium, by the connotations of small forms, and by the descriptive titles assigned to his music by publishers from Wessel onwards. His own comments on the trivialisation of his music by this means – Wessel included the Second Impromptu in a series of 'Drawing-room Trifles' – are a matter of record.

It is significant that the image of Chopin as salon composer was disseminated above all in Germany and England in the later nineteenth century. This is clear not only from a study of critical writing, but from the priorities of programming and from the creative praxes of a host of minor imitators in both countries. Chopin's music was a major influence on later nineteenth-century *Trivialmusik* in Germany and also on the ephemera composed for the Victorian drawing-room. A reception history would find much to investigate here. In technical terms there is the 'reduction' of Chopin's densely-woven textures into a handful of easy gestures which effectively translate 'art' into 'kitsch'. In esthetic terms there is the transformation of a cluster of original meanings (Chopin was initially viewed in both countries as a modernist[7]) by vicarious association with their progeny. And in social-historical terms there is the accommodation of a repertory to the needs of a particular status quo.

This latter point deserves to be amplified. The commodification of culture was taken further in England and Germany than elsewhere in Europe in the later nineteenth century. There is, however, a distinction to be drawn between them, albeit of a highly generalised nature. In nineteenth-century England musical life – and music – affirmed and legitimised, with no significant critical element, the bourgeois ascendancy – was indeed almost totally absorbed by it. Domestic piano music, highly responsive to the external features of Chopin's style, was part of this broader affirmative culture. This was also true of the vast repertory of music designed for the home in late nineteenth-century Germany. Yet here the domestic repertory stood in a polarised relation to an autonomous music of high ambition – an incipient avant-garde. Significantly the constituency of Chopin as 'modernist' survived in progressive German circles well into the second half of the century and beyond, and his music proved directly influential in notable cases. It is an intriguing demonstration of the permeability of the musical work that Chopin proved no less an inspiration to the German 'avant-garde' than to the music of the bourgeois home.

THE 'ROMANTIC COMPOSER'

The term 'romantic' connotes ideas and motivations more clearly than styles. Above all it is grounded in the idea that the world may be more fully known through feeling, intuition and the creative imagination than through conceptual thought or empirical observation. In music a romantic aesthetic took its stand on the primacy of the emotions and on the capacity of musical language to *express* the inner emotional world, as well as the external perceived world. In the former sense we may indeed suspect that Chopin was a 'romantic' (at least in the music of his stylistic maturity), that he allowed his music to become, in Dahlhaus's phrase, 'a fragment of autobiography'. There is in his music an intensity, a passion, at times a terrifying power, which can rather easily suggest an inner life whose turmoils were 'lived out' in music. There are even moments where an expressive imperative appears to subvert structure in a manner that contrasts sharply with the 'proper distance' achieved by the classical composer.

We should be wary of too complete a subscription to this view. In his cast of mind, and also in his attitude towards his craft, Chopin had perhaps more in common with the classical masters he so loved than with his contemporaries. His mind was dominated by a love of order and precision, by a rejection of over-exuberant or sentimental types of thought. He shared little of the romantics' enthusiasm for the descriptive, denotative powers of music, remaining committed to absolute music in an age dominated by programmes and descriptive titles. Unlike his contemporaries he had only a passing interest in literature and the other arts and he had little sympathy with the big abstract ideas that fired the imagination of the age. Italian opera apart, he was guarded in his praise of contemporary composers, reserving his unqualified admiration for the masters of an earlier age, especially Bach, Handel and Mozart.

It is when we turn from intention to reception that the term 'romantic' takes on greater meaning in relation to Chopin. The nineteenth century produced a 'romantic' listener as well as a 'romantic' composer. The inclination of such a listener was to seek out either a specific referential meaning in the musical work – and Chopin's music was granted a generous allocation of such 'meanings' in nineteenth-century criticism – or a hidden emotional content. These layers of understanding became a part of the ambience of the music for later generations, and at the same time they coloured the received wisdom about Chopin the man. For many he became quite simply the archetypal romantic composer – a figure wounded by love and exile, the 'hero of all sensitive souls'. Biographical myths followed in hot pursuit of this image, and unsurprisingly they focused on the love interest in his life.

The 'three loves' became the basis for fanciful imaginings remote from any contact with literal or psychological truth. Even Konstancja Gładkowska, to whom the youthful Chopin never declared himself, could inspire entirely fictional scenes in a Warsaw café – 'how he loathed and how unutterably he loved her'.[8] Chopin was in reality a man concerned with proprieties, conservative in social attitudes to the point of snobbishness and much preoccupied with material and financial security. Anyone further removed from the image of the reckless lover it would be difficult to imagine. The celebrated trip to Majorca was a fiasco, not an idyll, and the dominating reality of George Sand's role in their relationship was her strong maternal instinct. These facts are now well-known, and it is somehow fitting that with the destruction of one romantic legend another should have surfaced. Those inclined to colour Chopin's life will have no difficulty in deciding which side to take in the celebrated controversy of the Chopin-Potocka 'letters'.[9]

In due course the romantic aura surrounded his music too. It was especially, though by no means exclusively, in France that Chopin the 'romantic composer' – the 'poet' of the piano who expressed the depths of his inner world to all of us – was cultivated.[10] 'Chopin is *par excellence* a pianist of the emotions'; '[he] is first of all a poet, a sensitive poet who does his best to make poetry dominate'; he is 'an elegaic, profound and dreamy poet of tones'.[11] It was in France too that some of the more specific literary references were associated with his music (quite different from the fanciful titles attached to his works in England). His compositions were related in rather detailed ways to poetry by Lamartine and Jean-Paul, to stories by Charles Nodier and especially to characters from Shakespeare.

Above all it was France which promoted the view of Chopin as a composer 'de chambre de malade', a very particular dimension of the 'romantic' myth. From childhood his health was delicate and at the end of his short life consumption took a cruel toll of his creative energies. Yet the image of Chopin the consumptive, with 'the pallor of the grave', came to take on additional significance, interpreted almost as a philosophy of life and even as an explanation of his creative output. Through music he 'discloses his suffering'. Emotive descriptions by Liszt and others of his final years and particularly of his final hours (source of many an apocryphal account) fostered the image of a music imbued with a special quality of melancholy, even morbidity. Field's 'talent of the sickroom' proved an insistent image and it fused well with aspects of a romantic ideology, where illness and creative inspiration would be linked as parallel (Schopenhauerian) escapes from the commonplaces of the world. Even the fresh winds of twentieth-century change have not wholly dispersed such images.

THE 'SLAVONIC COMPOSER'

There can be no doubt of the authenticity of Chopin's commitment to Poland and of his enduring preoccupation with the 'Polish question'. Nor is it inconsistent that he should have developed such feelings in all their intensity only after he left his homeland. The 'Stuttgart diary' – a response to the collapse of the 1830 insurrection – may be extravagant in its language, but it has a ring of sincerity that is missing from some of his letters to family and friends during the preceding year in Vienna. For all his social graces, Chopin always maintained that he could relax fully only with Polish friends, and it is his letters in Polish – their tone as well as their content – which afford us the most intimate glimpses of his inner life. Nevertheless there was something of the 'professional exile' about Chopin. Life in France agreed with him and he quickly put to the back of his mind any thought of returning to his homeland (he could easily have done so when the Czar offered the first of many amnesties in 1833). He was uncomfortable too with the circle of committed nationalists centred on the Polish Literary Society in Paris (and they with him), and he refused to serve the Polish cause in the most obvious way open to a composer, through opera and tone-poem.

This is not to argue that his music was untouched by Polish nationalism. His approach to the principal national dances – the polonaise and mazurka – changed significantly following the early years in Warsaw. In a manner that strikingly anticipates later nineteenth-century developments, he transformed these dance elements from colourful exoticisms (available to all) to potent evocations of Poland, and specifically a Poland oppressed. A comparison with Liszt is instructive. Both composers cultivated images of their native lands and used musical symbols to convey those images, albeit only in selected works. At the same time they combined national material with the most advanced contemporary techniques of European music, fusing, as it were, nationalism and modernism. Their music derived energy from national material but was not confined by it nor indeed by a nationalist esthetic. Unlike Moniuszko in Poland or Erkel in Hungary, they worked in the world at large.

Chopin's Polishness was of course elaborated substantially in later reception, with the customary selection of apocryphal stories, beginning with the urn of Polish earth which he supposedly took with him on leaving Warsaw. For Europeans his nationality became a way of explaining anything unfamiliar or 'exotic' in his music. In this connection there is an amusing repertory of stories about

Warsaw, detailing camels in the streets, Varsovians in caftans and ludicrous descriptions of the city and the surrounding countryside. Poles, on the other hand, were anxious to claim Chopin for themselves, arguing that his 'national style' consisted less in folk elements than in a 'specific expressive climate permeating all his compositions; an elusive mood so characteristic of his fellow-countrymen's psyche'.[12] Such cases are difficult to make convincingly, but since 'national style' is a category determined in essence by reception, it is enough that they should be made at all. For many nineteenth-century Polish listeners Chopin came to symbolise the national struggle, helping to cement the Polish spirit at a time when the country was without political status.

For all that, his music was not immediately influential on Polish composers. In the difficult years following the insurrection musical life in Poland was conservative and insular, and the music that responded most obviously to its needs was less Chopin's, which so obviously transcended those needs, than Moniuszko's. The truth is that very few Polish composers in the late nineteenth century were able to come to terms with Chopin's legacy.[13] It was only in the early works of his great successor Karol Szymanowski in the early twentieth century that the Chopin inheritance was taken up fully in his homeland. It is indeed arguable that the most productive legacy of Chopin the 'slavonic composer' was not in Poland at all but in Russia. There his impact was considerable (and seriously under-rated) and it was inspirational in the formation of radical nationalist styles by the composers of the Balakirev circle, especially Balakirev himself. In this respect we may indeed view Chopin as a harbinger of the future, one of the forerunners of a line of development that eventually culminated in radical changes in musical language in the early years of the twentieth century.

THE COMPOSER

These perspectives on Chopin bring to the fore aspects of both the man and the music that proved appropriate, even necessary, to particular taste-publics in the nineteenth century. His music would indeed prove a useful case study in a history of taste, and maybe too a history of taste-creating institutions. Certainly the national dimension that emerges tentatively from a reception study deserves scrutiny. Russia's Chopin was not always the same as Germany's or France's. Our own century adopted yet another perspective, one which appears (on the surface) to de-contextualise the work, to let it make its own statement, to take on a monad-like character which would reveal its meaning only through analysis, itself a discipline of our age. This too is a very particular, historically 'produced' interpretative stance, one which draws a sharp boundary around the work, as though it might stand alone, unmediated by any number of social and cultural factors. It is as much a myth as any of the others.

In the end Chopin's music contains the many forms in which it has been promoted and interpreted. That it can sustain such multiple interpretation is a powerful argument for its quality – for the stability of its structures and the density and complexity of its musical materials. The 'structuralist' myth of our own age is of value precisely for its attempt to identify some of the markers of that quality – some of the structures that give the music durability. At its least thoughtful the analytical mode will tend to congeal the work into a fixed configuration. At its most enlightening it will remind us that the work is not infinitely permeable, that there are constraints embedded within it which make some interpretative codes more profitable than others. Ironically such an analysis enables us (through the offices of a validating theory) to relate the work to music as a whole and thereby to locate its specificity.

An orientation towards the music itself also has some bearing on biography, reminding us that the single most important activity of Chopin's life was the production of music. In this sense we might well argue that the truly 'eventful' years of his life were those spent with Sand in Nohant and Paris from 1839 until the tensions in their relationship broke surface in the mid 1840s. These were years of stability and routine, during which Chopin was able to compose some of his finest music. Conventional biography has, understandably, given scant justice to them, just as it has given scant justice to Chopin's composing in general – to the very activity which engaged him most completely and most passionately.

To deal adequately with composition as a dimension of biography would amount to path-breaking advances in musicology, involving an attempt to theorise the relationship that exists between the composer and the music. It would require an investigation of the mental processes involved in musical composition, as yet little understood, and it would beg the most intractable questions about the nature of truly exceptional creative talent in music, which can so often attach itself to people entirely unexceptional in other ways. A fundamental impulse underlying the mythologising of composers' lives is precisely this paradox, resulting in a need to transpose to the man something of the richness and fascination of the music. The task of explication may be beyond us as yet, but it is worth the attempt, and one is grateful to the few who have made it, even when results can appear eccentric.[14] Certainly we should not seek much help from the composers, to whom – at the deepest level – musical creativity is as much a mystery as it is to the rest of us. We are reminded of Janáček's description of the initial stages of the creative process as 'the most interesting [moments] in the history of composition – and yet the darkest ones'.[15]

PART 1

The growth of a style

1 *Piano music and the public concert* 1800–1850

JANET RITTERMAN

In the late eighteenth and early nineteenth centuries the city of Vienna, long a prominent centre of European musical life, played a leading role in the development of pianos and of piano playing.[1] Instruments from Viennese makers were sought throughout Europe, while aspiring pianists travelled there in order to study and to perform. The fact that it was with Vienna that pianists such as Mozart, Beethoven, Ries, Hummel, Moscheles and Kalkbrenner were associated gave substance to its confident claim to be *die Heimat der Klavier-Virtuosität*.[2] So when in August 1829 the nineteen-year-old Chopin gave two concerts in Vienna – the first performances of note which he gave outside his native Warsaw – the praise that Viennese critics accorded to his unusual talent was of no mean significance.[3]

It was after the second of these concerts that a critic singled out Chopin as one pursuing a path of his own.[4] This was not apparent, however, from the choice of repertoire, or from the circumstances surrounding the performances. There was nothing about the character of these concerts to differentiate them from other events of the season. Each took place in the Imperial Theatre, the Kärnthnerthortheater, using the orchestral forces available; each consisted of a mixture of vocal and instrumental items for the first half of the programme, with a ballet to complete the evening's entertainment. In each programme Chopin performed twice, playing works of his own composition. The Variations on 'Là ci darem' he performed on both occasions; for the second concert, the *Rondo à la krakowiak* replaced an improvisation on vocal themes.[5]

Items of this kind would have created little surprise: in the 1820s variations or rondos were staple concert items for pianists. As contemporary reviews make clear, it was because of the style and method of his playing and of his composition that Chopin appeared to Viennese critics of 1829 to stand apart from most piano virtuosi of his time.[6]

To a large extent, these early judgements remained true throughout his life: Chopin continued to stand apart from most pianist-composers of his time. This is evident in his approach to concert performance, as well as in his approach to

11

composition. While Chopin's early piano music conformed at least externally to the features of post-Classical concert repertoire, his later writing increasingly refined the idioms characteristic of this world and distanced itself from it. Whereas other pianist-composers treated public concerts as occasions on which to present their large-scale new works,[7] it is noticeable how small a proportion of Chopin's piano music appears to have been performed in public with any frequency during the composer's lifetime. The first half of the nineteenth century, an age of rapid development in piano performance and concert-giving, was a period in which re-putations were created and sustained largely through public performance. Chopin, although recognised as one of the leading pianists of his age, gave relatively few public concerts, preferring, in adult life, the intimacy of the salon. His connections with the world of public concert-giving were tenuous: while other leading pianist-composers who were active as teachers had pupils who were seeking careers as concert performers, the majority of Chopin's pupils did not fall into this category.[8] And unlike most of his contemporaries, whose performances, by the 1840s, re-flected the increasing importance attached to the role of the pianist as interpreter, Chopin, when performing in public, tended to perform his own music.

Chopin's documented concert performances total scarcely more than fifty. They span a thirty-year period from 1818 to 1848, from childhood appearances in Warsaw to the concerts he gave in Britain a little over a year before his death. Most were given in cities that were regarded as leading centres of piano playing and public concert life: half of Chopin's concerts took place in Paris, where he settled from 1831. Though few in number when viewed against the backcloth of general developments in public concert-giving during the early nineteenth century, Chopin's public appearances provide a perspective from which to consider some of his less familiar works, suggest ways in which the later performances he gave were subsequently to influence approaches to pianists' concert programmes, and afford insights into the reception of his music. They offer a distinctive com-mentary on the relationship of the professional pianist to the public concert during the first half of the nineteenth century.

FROM PIANIST AS COMPOSER TO PIANIST AS INTERPRETER

In the early nineteenth century, as now, it was a subtle interplay of expectations which influenced the choice of music to be performed – expectations that audiences held of pianos and pianists, as well as expectations of audiences held by performers themselves. What is distinctive about this period, however, is the extent of the change in attitude to the role of the pianist. At the beginning of the nineteenth century, most of the works that leading pianists performed in public concerts were of their own composition. It was generally assumed that an established pianist would wish to perform his own music, and that this was so devised as to demonstrate not only his facility and imagination as a composer but also the individual features of his keyboard technique.[9] The programme of Hummel in Fig. 1 is typical of such a concert.

This expectation influenced the performances of professional pianists for at least the first three decades: reviews from the 1830s reflect the extent to which critical judgements were still rooted in this belief. But during this decade the assumption that the qualities expected of the virtuoso pianist could be displayed solely through the performance of his own music began to be questioned. Many factors contributed to this change, among them the increase in the number of aspiring pianists, in the opportunities for musical education and in music publishing and journalism.

At the beginning of the century, stylistic range had not been among the qualities generally expected of the professional pianist. In piano methods dating from the early decades of the nineteenth century, such topics featured only peripherally, if at all. While it is true that the majority of these method books were directed towards the needs of beginners rather than players of some experience, until at least the mid 1820s decisions about repertoire and performance style were seen to rest essentially with the individual performer. Those early nineteenth-century pianists whose performances were most highly regarded generally played their own music and did so in ways that were accepted as properly particular to themselves. It was in these terms that the performances Chopin gave in Vienna in 1829 were praised.[10]

Between 1800 and 1850, it was the shift of emphasis from the pianist as composer to the pianist as interpreter that did most to alter attitudes of performers and audiences to the piano music presented in public concerts. Various factors – social and economic as well as musical – contributed to this change. Most were connected in some way with the rapid rise in the popularity of the piano, a phenomenon which left its imprint on many aspects of early nineteenth-century life. Public concert life of the period was transformed by the growth of interest in the piano. By the 1850s the piano recital had come into being; programming conventions that still influence judgements made by present-day performers were beginning to emerge. The extent to which this approach to stylistic range had by mid-century achieved general acceptance is confirmed by the contents of Czerny's supplement to his compendious piano method of 1838–39.[11] This supplementary volume, *Die Kunst des Vortrags des ältern und neuen Claviercompositionen* (published in English as *The Art of Playing the Ancient and Modern Pianoforte Works*), which appeared in 1847, contained chapters on the performance of music by composers of the modern Romantic school, by Beethoven, and by composers such as Bach and Handel, as well as an extensive list of suggested repertoire for study.

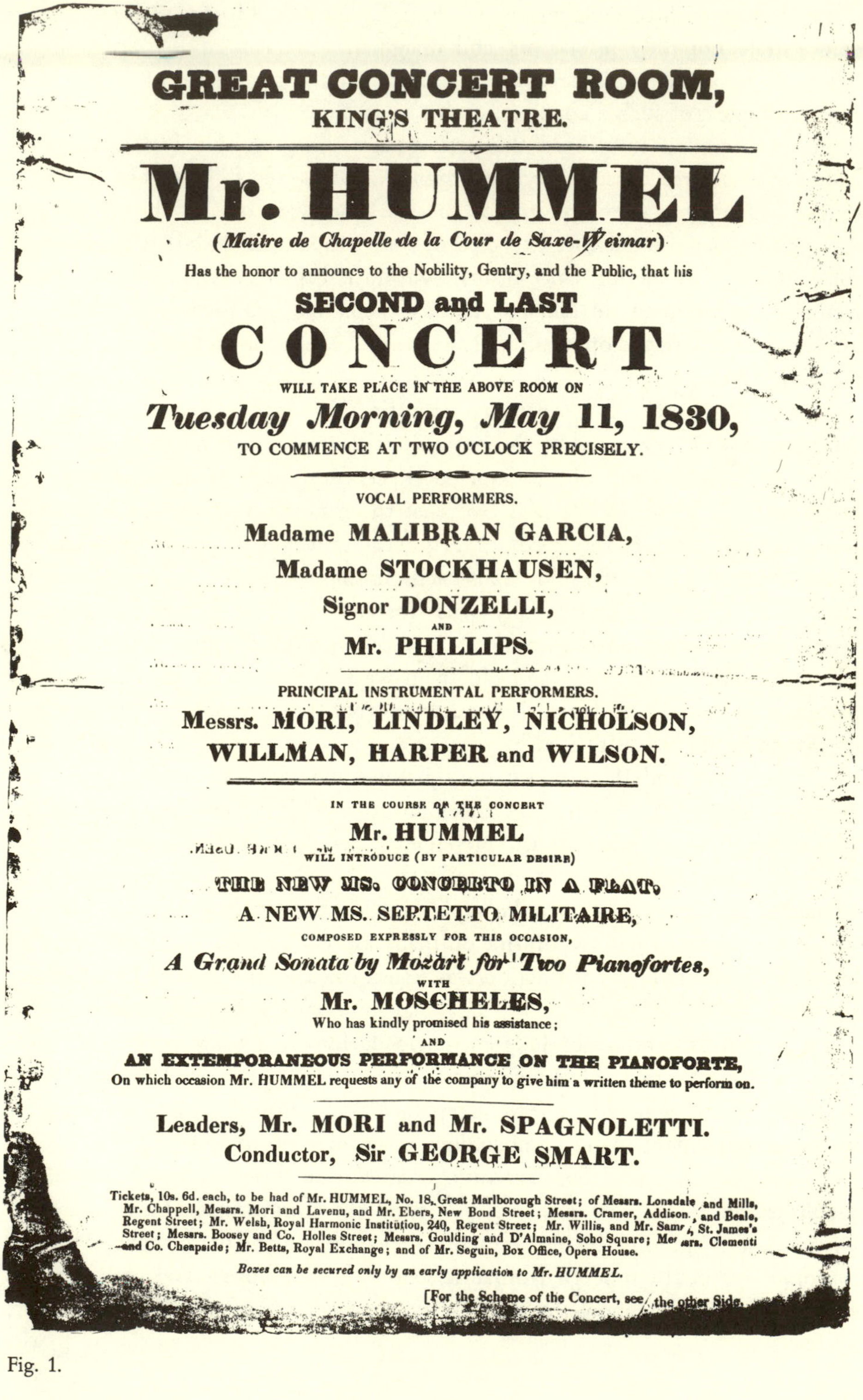

GREAT CONCERT ROOM,
KING'S THEATRE.

Mr. HUMMEL
(Maitre de Chapelle de la Cour de Saxe-Weimar)

Has the honor to announce to the Nobility, Gentry, and the Public, that his

SECOND and LAST
CONCERT

WILL TAKE PLACE IN THE ABOVE ROOM ON

Tuesday Morning, May 11, 1830,

TO COMMENCE AT TWO O'CLOCK PRECISELY.

VOCAL PERFORMERS.

Madame MALIBRAN GARCIA,

Madame STOCKHAUSEN,

Signor DONZELLI,

AND

Mr. PHILLIPS.

PRINCIPAL INSTRUMENTAL PERFORMERS.

Messrs. MORI, LINDLEY, NICHOLSON,
WILLMAN, HARPER and WILSON.

IN THE COURSE OF THE CONCERT

Mr. HUMMEL

WILL INTRODUCE (BY PARTICULAR DESIRE)

THE NEW MS. CONCERTO IN A FLAT,

A NEW MS. SEPTETTO MILITAIRE,

COMPOSED EXPRESSLY FOR THIS OCCASION,

A Grand Sonata by Mozart for Two Pianofortes,

WITH

Mr. MOSCHELES,

Who has kindly promised his assistance;

AND

AN EXTEMPORANEOUS PERFORMANCE ON THE PIANOFORTE,

On which occasion Mr. HUMMEL requests any of the company to give him a written theme to perform on.

Leaders, Mr. MORI and Mr. SPAGNOLETTI.
Conductor, Sir GEORGE SMART.

Tickets, 10s. 6d. each, to be had of Mr. HUMMEL, No. 18, Great Marlborough Street; of Messrs. Lonsdale and Mills, Mr. Chappell, Messrs. Mori and Lavenu, and Mr. Ebers, New Bond Street; Messrs. Cramer, Addison, and Beale, Regent Street; Mr. Welsh, Royal Harmonic Institution, 240, Regent Street; Mr. Willis, and Mr. Sams, St. James's Street; Messrs. Boosey and Co. Holles Street; Messrs. Goulding and D'Almaine, Soho Square; Messrs. Clementi and Co. Cheapside; Mr. Betts, Royal Exchange; and of Mr. Seguin, Box Office, Opera House.

Boxes can be secured only by an early application to Mr. HUMMEL.

[For the Scheme of the Concert, see the other Side.

Fig. 1.

SCHEME

OF

MR. HUMMEL'S

CONCERT,

TUESDAY MORNING, MAY 11, 1830.

────◆◆◆◆◆◆◆◆◆◆────

PART I.

Overture . . . . (*Don Juan*.) . . . .*Mozart*.

Aria, Signor DONZELLI . . . . (*Pirata*) . . . .*Bellini*.

(By particular desire) New Pianoforte Concerto in A flat, Mr. HUMMEL . . . ., ...*Hummel*.

Duetto, Madame STOCKHAUSEN and Signor DONZELLI . . . . (*Don Juan*.) . . . .*Mozart*.

Grand Sonata for two Pianofortes, Mr. HUMMEL and Mr. MOSCHELES. . . . .*Mozart*.

New Duettino, (MS.) Signor DONZELLI and Mr. PHILLIPS. . . . .*Hummel*.

PART II.

Swiss Air, Madame STOCKHAUSEN, accompanied on the Harp by Mr. STOCKHAUSEN.

New Grand MS. Pianoforte Septetto Militaire, Mr. HUMMEL, Messrs. MORI, LINDLEY,
     WILSON, NICHOLSON, WILLMAN, and HARPER . . . .*Hummel*.

New Duettino, (MS.) Signor DONZELLI and Mr. PHILLIPS . . . .*Hummel*.

A new MS. Tyrolean Air, with Variations, Madame MALIBRAN GARCIA . . . .*Hummel*.

Extemporaneous Performance on the Pianoforte, Mr. HUMMEL ; on which occasion
     Mr. HUMMEL requests any of the Company to give him a written Theme to perform on.

────────────────

To commence at Two o' Clock precisely.

Joseph Mallett, Printer, 59, Wardour Street, Soho.

The London concert season of 1850 concluded with a concert typical of the new programming and marks a significant development from Hummel's 1830 recital of Fig. 1. Advertised as a 'performance of classical pianoforte music', the 1850 programme consisted of Beethoven's 'Hammerklavier' Sonata and works by composers of the 'modern Romantic' school (etudes by Mendelssohn, Henselt, Chopin, Moscheles and Sterndale Bennett, and the F♯ minor Fantasie by Mendelssohn), followed in the second half by a Dussek sonata and a group of contrapuntal works (fugues by Handel and Mendelssohn, a Scarlatti sonata and a prelude and fugue by Bach).[12] The role of the pianist as interpreter was now acknowledged; and the music of those composers whose output has dominated many a piano recital since that time – among them, Chopin – had begun to appear with some regularity in concert programmes.

c. 1800 – c. 1835

Concert societies and audiences

Concert repertoire was affected by the expansion in the range of institutions involved in public concert-giving which occurred during the first half of the nineteenth century. While concerts continued to be associated with theatres,[13] the early decades of the nineteenth century saw the emergence of influential new concert-giving institutions. 1813 marked the inception of both the Philharmonic Society in London and the *Gesellschaft der Musikfreunde* in Vienna, while public concert-giving in Paris moved into a new phase with the establishment of the *Société des concerts du Conservatoire* in 1828. The example provided by societies such as these, and by the Leipzig Gewandhaus concerts, played a significant role in shaping the character of public concert life and in influencing the repertoire performed.[14]

New audiences emerged. Many eighteenth-century concerts given by professional musicians, such as the various subscription concert series in London, had catered mainly for upper-class audiences.[15] During the early nineteenth century, as many musicians became less dependent on regular patronage and more reliant on personal initiative to ensure their livelihoods, concert-giving increased considerably and concerts broadened their appeal, gathering new audiences from the emerging middle class.[16] These changes are reflected in the greater range of concert locations and types of event, in the prices of tickets and in the ways in which information about concerts was disseminated.

Pianists and concerts

Until the late eighteenth century, patterns of concert-giving were, in general, predicated on the existence of personal relationships between musicians and audience. The expanded concert life of the nineteenth century assumed a greater degree of impersonality. From about the 1820s, posters, newspaper and journal announcements and reviews became increasingly influential in disseminating information about individual performers' activities. Several commentators have discussed the development of the public concert in the late eighteenth and early nineteenth centuries in terms of the emergence of a 'mass musical culture', pointing out that one of the most significant changes in the culture was the change in the nature of the relationship between the professional performer and the concert-going public.[17] This inevitably influenced musicians' perceptions of their role, as well as their choices of music to perform. While some performers appear to have thrived in this atmosphere, the impersonality seems to have contributed to Chopin's increasing aversion to concert-giving.[18]

From the viewpoint of the performer, concerts then, as now, were of two main kinds: those mounted by bodies such as orchestral societies and those presented by artists themselves. For any one artist, opportunities of the former kind were relatively infrequent: it was in the performances arranged by individuals or small groups of musicians that piano music was most frequently heard. Many solo performers gained experience and recognition by appearing as supporting artists in the concerts of colleagues as well as by giving concerts of their own. During the period Chopin spent in Paris he was invited to appear only once in the concerts of the *Société des concerts du Conservatoire*; during the 1830s, most of his public appearances occurred in concerts presented by fellow musicians such as Liszt, Hiller and Berlioz.

Events presented by individual artists are often categorised as 'benefit concerts'. However not all such occasions would have been described as 'concerts' at the time. For an event that was presented in a small location, without a full orchestra for accompaniment, a term such as *soirée* or *matinée musicale* was often used.[19] When a performer advertised an event as a 'concert', this normally indicated a larger-scale venture. It implied that an instrumental ensemble had been assembled at least to provide an accompaniment for the main soloist (the concert beneficiary) and possibly to perform symphonic works as well.

Some pianists gave one large concert a year, for which an orchestral group was recruited and at which a concerto would usually be performed, and for the remainder of the season presented smaller, more intimate events. However, concert advertisements and reviews show that concertos performed at benefit concerts were not always given with full orchestral accompaniment; frequent references can be found to concertos being performed with quartet, quintet or double quartet accompaniment.[20] The nature of the programme for Chopin's first public appearance in Paris in 1832 suggests that the two solo works he performed – the F minor Concerto and the Variations on 'Là ci darem' – could well have been accompanied by what would be regarded today as a chamber-sized ensemble.[21]

By present-day standards many early nineteenth-century concerts were long. Benefit concerts, in particular, often featured a large number of separate items. For any musical event, large or small, variety in the range of artists heard was regarded as essential – characteristically this involved the inclusion of vocal as well as instrumental items. Although by the 1840s this practice had been repeatedly challenged,[22] throughout the first half of the nineteenth century it was among the conventions that affected the structure and content of concert programmes. This importance of vocal items can be seen not only in their prominence, but also in the nature of the billing (see Mr Ries's 1815 concert in Fig. 2).

Pianos and playing styles

The construction of the piano itself underwent fundamental change during the first half of the nineteenth century, as did the tonal ideals against which the instrument was measured.[23] This inevitably affected the character of the music written for the instrument and performed in public concerts, the playing styles which pianists developed and the criteria by which performances were judged. For Chopin, the changes in the construction of the instrument, which made possible the production of a richer, fuller tone, only served to compound the physical demands of concert performance.

By the late eighteenth century, there were two distinct types of piano, the Viennese and the English. These differed in their actions: the Viennese instrument had a light action but a thin, clear tone; the English instrument had a full, rich tone but a heavier action. Until the 1830s, it was on the light-actioned Viennese piano that most leading pianists preferred to perform. Hummel, in his method book of 1828, while acknowledging the virtues of both instruments, explained his preference for the Viennese piano on the grounds that it 'allows the performer to impart to his execution every possible light and shade, speaks clearly and promptly, has a round fluty tone, which in a large room contrasts well with the accompanying orchestra, and does not impede rapidity of execution by requiring too great an effort'.[24]

The style of playing described by Hummel as his ideal – one in which variety of nuance, clarity of articulation, sharpness of contrasts and rapidity of execution were paramount – became known as the 'brilliant style'. This style first emerged in a distinctive way in the second decade of the century and was associated with pianists such as Hummel, Kalkbrenner and Moscheles – pianists whose technique had been formed on light-actioned Viennese instruments.[25] Although his performance style was regarded by Viennese critics in 1829 as lacking in brilliance, it was with this style that Chopin's playing had most similarity, hence the comparisons with Hummel that were made by early critics.[26]

Many of the piano works intended for concert performance which appeared

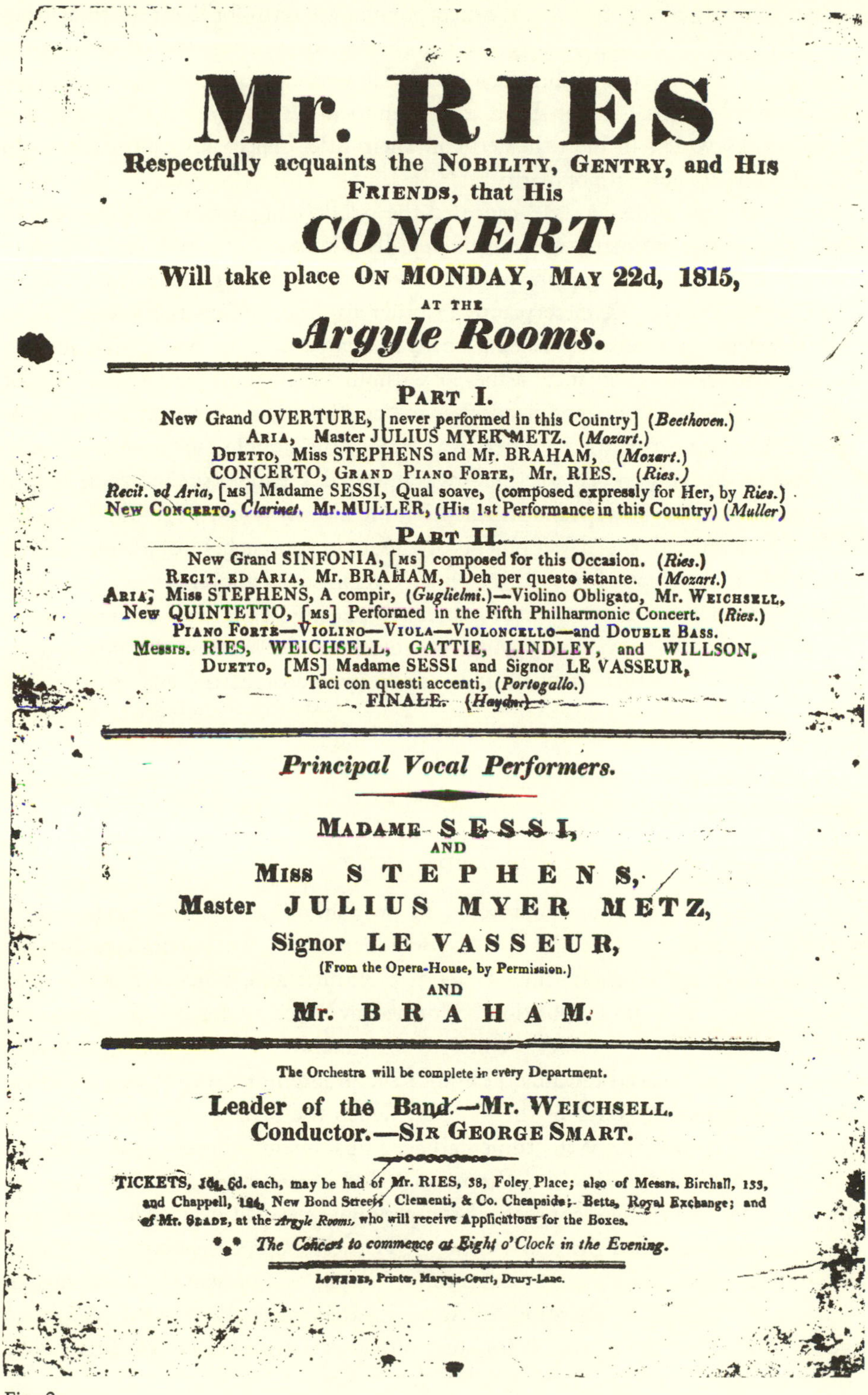

Mr. RIES

Respectfully acquaints the NOBILITY, GENTRY, and HIS
FRIENDS, that His

CONCERT

Will take place ON MONDAY, MAY 22d, 1815,

AT THE

Argyle Rooms.

PART I.

New Grand OVERTURE, [never performed in this Country] (*Beethoven.*)
ARIA, Master JULIUS MYER METZ. (*Mozart.*)
DUETTO, Miss STEPHENS and Mr. BRAHAM, (*Mozart.*)
CONCERTO, GRAND PIANO FORTE, Mr. RIES. (*Ries.*)
Recit. ed Aria, [MS] Madame SESSI, Qual soave, (composed expressly for Her, by *Ries.*)
New CONCERTO, *Clarinet,* Mr. MULLER, (His 1st Performance in this Country) (*Muller*)

PART II.

New Grand SINFONIA, [MS] composed for this Occasion. (*Ries.*)
RECIT. ED ARIA, Mr. BRAHAM, Deh per questo istante. (*Mozart.*)
ARIA, Miss STEPHENS, A compir, (*Guglielmi.*)—Violino Obligato, Mr. WEICHSELL,
New QUINTETTO, [MS] Performed in the Fifth Philharmonic Concert. (*Ries.*)
PIANO FORTE—VIOLINO—VIOLA—VIOLONCELLO—and DOUBLE BASS.
Messrs. RIES, WEICHSELL, GATTIE, LINDLEY, and WILLSON,
DUETTO, [MS] Madame SESSI and Signor LE VASSEUR,
Taci con questi accenti, (*Portogallo.*)
FINALE. (*Haydn.*)

Principal Vocal Performers.

MADAME SESSI,

AND

MISS STEPHENS,

Master JULIUS MYER METZ,

Signor LE VASSEUR,

(From the Opera-House, by Permission.)

AND

Mr. BRAHAM.

The Orchestra will be complete in every Department.

Leader of the Band.—Mr. WEICHSELL.
Conductor.—SIR GEORGE SMART.

TICKETS, 10s. 6d. each, may be had of Mr. RIES, 58, Foley Place; also of Messrs. Birchall, 133,
and Chappell, 124, New Bond Street; Clementi, & Co. Cheapside; Betts, Royal Exchange; and
of Mr. GLADE, at the *Argyle Rooms,* who will receive Applications for the Boxes.

⁎ The Concert to commence at *Eight o'Clock* in the Evening.

LOWNDES, Printer, Marquis-Court, Drury-Lane.

Fig. 2.

during the early nineteenth century incorporated the term 'brilliant' in their titles or performance markings. These contained the type of writing characteristic of the 'brilliant style' – rapid embellishments and elaborate figuration in the right hand supported by unobtrusive left-hand accompaniment. A number of Chopin's early piano works which include the term in their titles reflect his familiarity with the style and its general popularity.

But while the 'brilliant style' captured the public imagination, the thinness of tone of the Viennese piano was not universally admired.[27] Piano makers, often in collaboration with leading pianists, sought ways of combining the best features of the English and the Viennese pianos in order to produce an instrument with a full, sonorous tone, capable of being heard in a large hall and one which allowed for a greater range of nuance, achieved without sacrificing ease and rapidity of key action. To this end, modifications were continually made: iron bracing was added, the covering of the hammers was varied, the double escapement action – the basis of the modern piano action – was invented. Changes such as these helped to produce a more powerful instrument, more suited to use in public concerts, and this stimulated the development of different approaches to piano playing. Although the concept of keyboard brilliance retained its allure, during the 1830s pianists began to cultivate a more expressive playing style. By the close of the decade the favoured style of playing was one that drew from the piano tonal resources which, by their richness and variety, invited orchestral analogies.

Piano music

FANTASIES, VARIATIONS AND RONDOS

Until the late 1830s, when approaches to programming began to change, in a concert mounted by a pianist for his own benefit, it was customary for the beneficiary to appear two or three times as performer and, whenever possible, to have music of his own composition performed by other artists as well. The main item for the soloist was either a concerto or some type of ensemble work. The second, generally placed towards the end of the programme, was usually a fantasy or a set of variations. Both of the items in which the pianist appeared were performed with orchestral (or instrumental) accompaniment whenever practicable.

The concerts Chopin gave in Warsaw in 1830[28] before leaving for Paris were of this kind, as his Viennese concerts of the previous year had been. The 1830 concerts, however, included the newly-composed concertos. For the concert at which he first performed the Concerto in F minor Chopin also presented the Fantasy in A major on Polish Airs, repeating this work for the concert later in the year when the Concerto in E minor received its first public performance. For his first public appearance in Paris, in February 1832, it was with the Variations on 'Là ci darem', which he had performed for his concerts in Vienna in 1829, that Chopin concluded the programme.

Sometimes performers replaced or supplemented the fantasy or air and variations with a rondo, as in Chopin's second Viennese concert of 1829. However the formal symmetry the title implies seems to have militated against the continuing popularity of works of this kind. Although Hummel often included a rondo *brillant* in his concerts, as did other pianists of his generation, the rondo slipped from favour, perhaps with the waning of interest in the brilliant style itself. By the beginning of the 1830s the inclusion of a rondo in a pianist's concert programme was becoming far less common: the inclusion of the Mendelssohn *Rondo brillant* in Moscheles' 1834 programme (see Fig. 3) is a late example of the genre. It is noticeable that Chopin did not choose to perform the *Rondo à la krakowiak* after leaving Warsaw in 1830.

Although critics repeatedly praised Chopin's Variations on 'Là ci darem' for their inventive qualities,[29] the fantasies and sets of variations which pianists performed in concerts frequently provoked unfavourable comment: critical attacks on their banality and predictability are legion. But their place in pianists' programmes seems to have been countenanced on the basis that it was by these means that an aspiring professional's skills of musical invention were put to the test. Until about the 1830s, even pianists who chose to perform concertos by more established pianist-composers generally included in their programmes fantasies or variations which they themselves had composed.

For the most part, these pieces were based on musical material likely to be already familiar to at least some of the audience. Themes from recent or current operatic successes or folk melodies with a distinctive national character were often used,[30] as in Chopin's works of this kind. Titles of some of these items suggest that they may have served to establish bonds between performer and audience, to characterise the performer in the eyes of the audience or to signal something of the range of the his travels or reputation. Variations on Russian airs, *Souvenirs d'Irlande*, fantasias on Scottish airs and rondos with titles such as *Les charmes de Berlin* can all be found in programmes from this period.

CONCERTOS, SONATAS AND CHAMBER MUSIC

The popularity of the piano concerto as a concert item waxed and waned during the first half of the nineteenth century, as attitudes of performers and critics to its characteristic features altered. It is probably because of the waning popularity of the genre that Chopin gave so few performances of his two concertos after leaving Warsaw in 1830. Although he performed the F minor concerto at his Paris debut in February 1832, there were only two further occasions on which he played

King's Concert Rooms, Hanover Square.

MR.

MOSCHELES

Has the honor to announce to the Nobility, Gentry, and his Friends in general, that his

MORNING CONCERT

WILL TAKE PLACE AT THE ABOVE ROOMS

ON THURSDAY, MAY 8, 1834,

TO BEGIN AT TWO O'CLOCK PRECISELY.

The following eminent Performers, both Vocal and Instrumental, have kindly promised their assistance:

Madame CARADORI ALLAN and Mrs. W. KNYVETT,
Miss MASSON,   Miss CLARA NOVELLO,
AND
Madame STOCKHAUSEN
(Who will sing several new Swiss Airs).

Signor BEGREZ,   **Mr. MACHIN**
(Who will sing the *Chevalier Neukomm's* new Song, " *Our own British Oak*"),

Mons. DE VRUGT,
First Tenor Singer to His Majesty the King of Holland (his first appearance in this country), who will sing the celebrated Dutch Ballad " *Maria*," with the original words, and the *National Hymn*,
AND
Signor DE BEGNIS.

THE CONCERT TO BEGIN WITH
F. MENDELSSOHN'S NEW MS. OVERTURE
TO
Melusine, or the Knight and the Mermaid,
AS PERFORMED AT THE PHILHARMONIC.

Mons. GHYS
Will play a Fantasia on the Violin.

Mr. MOSCHELES
WILL PLAY HIS
New MS. Concerto Fantastique,
AS PERFORMED AT THE THIRD PHILHARMONIC CONCERT,

A NEW MS. RONDO BRILLANT,
WITH ORCHESTRAL ACCOMPANIMENTS, WRITTEN EXPRESSLY FOR THE OCCASION BY
F. MENDELSSOHN,

A CONCERTANTE DUET WITH MR. H. HERZ,
An Extemporaneous Performance,
And the favorite Concertante, " Les Adieux des Troubadours," for Voice, Violin, Guitar, and Pianoforte, with
Mad. STOCKHAUSEN, Mons. GHYS, and Mr. L. SCHULZ

The Band will be numerous and composed of the first-rate Performers.
Principal Violoncello, Mr. LINDLEY.
Leader, Mr. F. CRAMER.
Conductor, Sir GEORGE SMART.

Tickets, 10s. 6d. each, to be had of Mr. MOSCHELES, No. 3, Chester Place, Regent's Park ; at the principal Music-shops ; and at the Rooms.
[For the Scheme of the Concert, see the other side.

Fig. 3.

King's Concert Rooms, Hanover Square.

SCHEME

OF

MR. MOSCHELES'

Morning Concert,

THURSDAY NEXT, MAY the 8th, 1834.

PART I.

New MS. Overture to **Melusine, or the Knight and the Mermaid,**
(as performed at the Philharmonic)..............................*F. Mendelssohn Bartholdy.*

Recitative and Song, Mrs. W. KNYVETT, " From mighty kings.".. *(Judas Maccabeus.)* ...*Handel.*

New **MS. Concerto Fantastique,** Mr. MOSCHELES,
(as performed at the Philharmonic) ....*Moscheles.*

Cavatina, Madame CARADORI ALLAN, " Non v'e sguardo.".... *(Anna Bolena.)* ....*Donizetti.*

Terzetto, Miss CLARA NOVELLO, Miss MASSON, and Signor DE BEGNIS,
" Io vi dico."....................*(La Cantatrice villane.)*................

New **MS. Rondo brillant,** with Orchestral Accompaniments (written expressly
for the Occasion), Pianoforte, Mr. MOSCHELES.................*F. Mendelssohn Bartholdy.*

Dutch Ballad, " Maria," Mons. DE VRUGT, First Tenor Singer to His Majesty the King of
Holland (his first appearance in this country)................................*Van Bree.*
Followed by the Dutch National Hymn.   (Both with the original Dutch words.) .... *Wilms.*

" Les Adieux des Troubadours," Concertante Fantasia, for Voice, Pianoforte,
Violin, and Guitar; on a Romance by *Blangini,* Madame STOCKHAUSEN,
Mr. MOSCHELES, Mons. GHYS, and Mr. L. SCHULZ.. *Moscheles, Mayseder, and Giuliani.*

PART II.

Grand Concertante Duet, Pianoforte, **Messrs. HERZ and MOSCHELES,**
on a favorite Theme in *Guillaume Tell*......................................*H. Herz.*

New French Romance, Miss CLARA NOVELLO, " Tyrol m'a vue naître,"
Clarinet Obligato, Mr. WILLMAN ....*Panseron.*

New Song, Mr. MACHIN, " Our own British oak," (first time of performance)..*Chevalier Neukomm.*

Fantasia, Adagio, and original Theme with Variations, Violin, Mr. GHYS................*Ghys.*

New Swiss Airs, Madame STOCKHAUSEN.

Extemporaneous Performance on the Pianoforte, Mr. MOSCHELES.

The Concert will begin at Two o'Clock precisely.

Printed by Joseph Mallett, Wardour Street, London.

his concertos. By the second of these, the first Paris performance of the F minor concerto in 1835, the concerto itself was praised but the genre was described as 'old fashioned'.[31] These changes in thinking reflected the debate taking place about the role of the piano and of the pianist in the public concert: it is in the changing fortunes of the piano concerto that these trends can be clearly discerned.

At the beginning of the nineteenth century, the concerto was the conventional concert item for the professional pianist. When pianists such as Beethoven, Dussek, Cramer and Field appeared as soloists in public concerts, it was concertos which they usually chose to perform.[32] Occasionally the concerto was replaced by a solo or an accompanied sonata; in the late eighteenth century, sonatas were sometimes performed by pianists even when appearing in orchestral concerts. Among established performers, however, the choice of a sonata soon became unusual – when sonatas were heard, they were usually accompanied works, possibly because of the reservations sometimes expressed about the suitability of the piano as a solo instrument.[33]

But while concertos were popular with pianists themselves, in the early decades of the nineteenth century they were not always welcomed by concert societies. The reasons were both pragmatic and aesthetic. In some cases, doubts were expressed about the piano's lack of carrying power; in others, the tension that was felt to exist between the 'display' element of such works and the musical aspirations of the societies themselves made piano concertos unpopular.[34] In London the original statement of the aims of the Philharmonic Society at its foundation in 1813 specifically excluded concertos, solos and duets from the category of 'best and most approved instrumental music', which its concerts were intended to promote.[35] For the remainder of this decade pianists who performed in the Philharmonic Society concerts appeared almost exclusively in chamber works. While these were mostly quintets, quartets and works for larger combinations such as sextets and octets were also performed.[36]

From the 1820s, however, as interest in the piano grew and increasing numbers of pianists sought opportunities to perform in public, piano concertos began to appear more frequently in the programmes of orchestral societies. At the Philharmonic Society concerts concertos replaced the chamber music items in which pianists had previously been heard. But by the end of the decade there were signs that the standing of the concerto was again in question, this time because the more predictable features of the form were becoming regarded as old-fashioned. The Parisian critic Fétis, writing in 1828, urged innovation, in the hope that the status of the concerto might be 'raise[d] once again in the opinion of the public'.[37]

Established pianists continued to compose and perform concertos. Young pianists often made early appearances in concertos by their teachers or by composers such as Hummel, whose concertos were treated as standard works for the development of technical and musical skills.[38] Chopin, for example, in the concerts in which he appeared as a fifteen-year-old youth in Warsaw in 1825, performed concertos by Ries and Moscheles.

A few concerted works, such as Weber's *Konzertstück*, continued to be performed. In general, however, by the beginning of the 1830s other types of piano music – both solo and ensemble – were becoming the focus of attention. It is noticeable that when, in 1835, Chopin was given the opportunity to perform at one of the prestigious Conservatoire concerts – an opportunity which he had long sought – he chose not to play a concerto but performed instead his *Grande Polonaise brillante*, preceded by the *Andante spianato*.[39] This choice may well have represented an acknowledgement of the interest being shown in alternatives to the traditional concerto form.[40] It was only in the 1840s that concertos began to regain public interest and by then the concertos that many leading pianists chose to perform tended to be not their own compositions but those in which their interpretative skills could best be displayed.

WORKS FOR DUO PIANO

Another outcome of the improvements in the piano itself, and of the increasing public interest in the instrument which was evident from the 1820s onward, was the inclusion in many benefit concert programmes of works for more than one pianist. Some were arrangements of orchestral or chamber works, others were works specifically written for piano duet or, more frequently, piano duo. Some of the pieces written for the medium were based on popular operatic material of the time, as in the *Grand Concertante Duet* by Herz included in Moscheles' concert programme reproduced in Fig. 3.

Increasingly, however, the works that emerged were conceived independently of the operatic repertoire and of the variation forms with which this repertoire was often associated. Many of the leading pianist-composers of the 1820s and 1830s, such as Hummel, Hiller, Osborne, Onslow and Moscheles, wrote sonatas for piano duo or duet combinations and performed them in their concerts. It was in duo performances of this kind, with Liszt and Hiller in particular, that Chopin was most frequently heard in public concerts in Paris in the 1830s.[41]

IMPROVISATION

In several of his early concerts, Chopin concluded the programme with an improvisation on vocal themes. This was not unusual: until about the 1830s, those performers most confident of their skills of spontaneous musical invention frequently ended their concerts with improvisations based on tunes likely to be familiar to the audience.[42] As reviews indicate, the connection between improvisations and composed fantasies or variations was extremely close.

Contemporary comments on these improvisations also reflect changing views of the skills expected of the professional pianist. Until the late 1820s, audiences and critics alike appear to have been unstinting in their admiration of the qualities demonstrated. But as concerts became more frequent, displays of this kind more predictable, and critics more experienced, concert reviews reflect more ambivalent attitudes towards the inclusion of improvised items. By the mid 1830s it was rare for an aspiring pianist to include an improvisation in a public concert. Although Chopin's improvisations were generously praised, he appears not to have improvised in public after his arrival in Paris in 1831.[43]

Older pianists, such as Hummel, then in his fifties, did not abandon the habit.[44] Other experienced improvisers, such as Moscheles and Mendelssohn, continued to give occasional displays of improvisation in public concerts. But as respect for the role of the pianist as interpreter increased, improvisation became regarded as one of the less necessary skills for the pianist to demonstrate in concerts. This seems also to have affected the custom of 'preluding' – that is, of performing a brief passage, generally of scales, arpeggios and chords, in order to introduce the mood of the piece to follow and to establish its key. Although students were still encouraged to develop the skill, its application in public concert situations seems to have been gradually discouraged.[45]

c. 1835 – *c*. 1850

Solo and ensemble repertoire

By the late 1830s the piano had achieved a central place in public concert life. The frequency with which solo pianists were invited to appear in the concerts of the leading European orchestral societies is one indication of the extent to which the popularity of the piano as a concert instrument had increased since the early years of the century. Between 1835 and 1850 a solo pianist appeared in at least one of every two concerts of the Philharmonic Society in London and, in some years, in almost every concert.[46] Similar trends were evident in other European capitals. Rising confidence in the status of the piano as an instrument for public concerts led some pianists such as Thalberg to perform solo works even on occasions when orchestral accompaniment was readily available, such as the concerts of the major orchestral societies.[47] For most, however, works with orchestra – either concertos or works in freer form – remained the norm on these occasions.

When pianists gave their own concerts (or appeared as supporting artists in the concerts of fellow performers), repertoire choices were inevitably influenced not only by audience attitudes to particular genres of piano music but also by the resources available. From the beginning of the century, there had been a steady growth in the number of pianists touring Europe in order to establish reputations as concert artists. By the mid 1830s reports of the increase in the number of visiting artists arriving each season in order to perform in concerts appeared regularly in newspapers and journals in most of the major European musical centres. Pianists were invariably in the majority. The escalation in the demand for suitable concert locations and for supporting instrumentalists to form a band (and the effort and expense associated with concert-giving on this scale) meant that it became increasingly common for pianists organising their own concerts to present solo items or chamber works. The increasing popularity of the piano, stimulated by continued developments in the instrument's construction and the enhancement of its tonal resources, made it possible for this to be viewed as desirable rather than inevitable.

Although works designated for piano and chamber ensemble are not prominent in many pianists' concerts during the 1820s and early 1830s, some pianists had continued to produce pieces of this kind. Hummel, for example, regularly performed his two septets.[48] From the mid 1830s onwards the programming of chamber works for piano and string or mixed ensemble became more frequent in the concerts that performers mounted for themselves. By mid century a sizeable body of works of this kind had emerged: pianist-composers such as Bertini, Moscheles, Onslow, Osborne and Rosenhain composed works for large chamber ensembles including piano and performed them in their concerts.

This trend may also reflect the growing popularity of chamber music concerts. Concerts of this kind were not new – some public performances of chamber music had taken place throughout the early years of the nineteenth century[49] – but from the late 1830s such concerts became more widespread.[50] While the focus of these concerts was generally the string quartet repertoire, in many programmes a chamber work with piano was included. On these occasions piano trios and quartets by Mozart, Beethoven and their contemporaries – composers whose works had otherwise featured little in pianists' public performances – were often played. This had its impact on benefit concerts: from the 1840s, some of the more popular works also began to appear in pianists' own programmes.

Until the late 1830s most of the solo pieces included by pianists in their concert programmes were of the fantasy or variation type – works based on pre-existing material and using variation techniques. Towards the end of the decade, other types of solo piece – short character pieces, sometimes bearing descriptive titles – began to appear in the concert programmes of leading pianists. Initially many of these were described as 'etudes' – a genre for which there was well-established precedent, and where the form was created through the extension and development of the initial musical idea. Moscheles, Liszt and Thalberg were among the leading performers who produced sets of concert studies, extracts from which they included in their concert programmes. Gradually these were supplemented by short lyrical pieces and stylised dances, while Liszt's programmes expanded perceptions of piano repertoire by including his transcriptions of songs (particularly those of Schubert) and popular orchestral works.

The programmes of the concerts Chopin gave in Paris during the 1840s and during his visit to Britain in 1848 were in keeping with the spirit of these changes. The choice of a Mozart piano trio as the opening item for his last public appearance in Paris, in February 1848,[51] reflected the increasing popularity of classical chamber music. However, the solo works he performed demonstrated how far his music had moved beyond the conventional concert repertoire of the time.[52] At each of these concerts, Chopin performed at least one of his larger solo works, such as a ballade or scherzo. No parallels for these extended works existed in the contemporary concert repertoire. Each programme also included a selection of the shorter works, such as the nocturnes, etudes, preludes and mazurkas. The Berceuse appeared on several programmes, while the Barcarolle, at least two of the impromptus and several of the polonaises (including Op. 40 No. 1) received at least one public performance by the composer.

A distinctive feature of these programmes was the manner in which Chopin grouped pieces of different kinds to form items. For his 1842 concert in Paris, for example, he played three items. The first consisted of the Ballade in F major, preceded by an Andante; the second was a selection comprising a nocturne, one or more of the preludes and three of the Op. 25 Etudes. The final item, similar to the second, began with a nocturne, followed with some preludes and mazurkas and concluded with one of the impromptus.[53] Manuscript annotations on some of the later programmes confirm the impression that these items were probably grouped with key relationships in mind. For the first of Chopin's London appearances, a Largo in G minor preceded the *Andante spianato* (in G), which was followed by the Scherzo in B♭ minor;[54] for the concert he gave in Manchester in August, it seems likely that for the second item ('Nocturne, études et Berceuse') the Nocturne in E♭ (Op. 9 No. 2) was succeeded by two or three etudes from Op. 25 (chosen from Nos. 1, 2 and 7, in A♭ major, F minor and C♯ minor respectively) and then by the D♭ Berceuse.[55]

From the mid 1830s onward, when the first 'Historical Concerts' were held in Paris,[56] interest in the performance of earlier music steadily increased. As we have seen already, by the 1840s critics were beginning to maintain that professional pianists should include earlier keyboard music, as well as works by leading composers of the present time, in their concert programmes. Versatility, as demonstrated through the ability to interpret music in a range of different styles, was becoming the touchstone of a performer's standing. Although Chopin's public performances during the 1840s showed scant evidence of this trend,[57] it affected the concert-giving of most leading pianists among his contemporaries.

In these developments, Moscheles and Liszt were particularly influential: in 1837, Moscheles, then living in London, and Liszt, in Paris, each gave a series of soirées which reflected the changing climate. The series by Moscheles was described by critics as performances of 'classical music', a phrase which by the end of the decade was firmly embedded in the vocabulary of concert-giving. Each series was distinguished by the inclusion of solo piano music and by the absence of large-scale ensembles, although duo sonatas for piano and another instrument were included. The series by Moscheles included preludes and fugues by Bach, Scarlatti sonatas (including the 'Cat's Fugue') played on a harpsichord, sonatas by Weber and Beethoven, extracts from Mendelssohn's *Songs without Words* and Moscheles' own studies.[58] In the series presented by Liszt the classical orientation of the programmes was firmly signalled by the inclusion of Schubert lieder and vocal music by Beethoven and Weber. Liszt himself was heard in piano trios and duo sonatas by Beethoven and studies by Moscheles and Chopin, as well as several of his own compositions.[59]

Both series were influential in signalling a change in approach to the choice of piano music appropriate for performance in public concerts. When in the following year, 1838, Moscheles presented a further series of four concerts, described in the press as 'Historical Concerts of Piano Music', these attracted even greater attention, both in London and abroad.[60] By 1838, Liszt had embarked on his years of travel as a concert performer. The repertoire which he performed during these years reflected this new concept of the role of the virtuoso pianist.

By contrast, Thalberg, cast as Liszt's main rival, was among those who held firm to the traditional view: in public concerts he continued to perform his own music almost exclusively. Reviews of his performances indicate that by the close of the 1830s this was no longer regarded as desirable: the London critic who, writing after a concert given by Thalberg in 1842, predicted that 'executive musicians will, year by year, find it increasingly difficult to maintain a high reputation on the mere exhibition of their own wonders'[61] was alluding gently to a change of attitude already in evidence.

During the 1840s observations on the qualities expected of professional pianists appeared with increasing frequency in concert reviews. In 1844, during a visit to London, Theodor Doehler apparently reassured his critics when he demonstrated – through the inclusion of a work of Beethoven in a programme otherwise dedicated to the performance of his own works – that he had an equal command of 'the higher qualities requisite for the performance of the great composers';[62] a year earlier, Charles Hallé was praised on the grounds that he had shown that he had 'all the music of the finest masters – ancient and modern – at his fingers' ends'.[63]

It was this emerging consensus on the existence of a group of 'finest masters', whose works might be expected to feature in the professional pianist's concert repertoire, which led to the changes that were to have the most far-reaching effect on public concert giving. The inclusion of Bach and Beethoven was generally accepted. In both cases, interest in their keyboard music was fed by trends in other areas of musical life. But in order to encourage professional pianists to include works by other leading pianist-composers of the 'modern Romantic' school among those that they regularly performed in public, a new understanding of the composer-performer relationship needed to gain acceptance. As was said earlier of the concert itself, this relationship had traditionally been based on personal contact: works had generally been presented by the artist himself, or by those who had had access to his approach, such as his pupils. It was by these means that piano compositions by most of the leading pianist-composers of the period first gained a place within the body of works that was to become recognised as the 'standard repertoire'.

EARLY INTERPRETERS OF CHOPIN'S MUSIC

It is in this respect that the case of Chopin is of particular interest when tracing the emergence of the role of pianist as interpreter. Although by the late 1830s Chopin had been recognised by various critics as arguably the most outstanding representative of the 'modern Romantic' school, this was more on the evidence of publication that through public performance. As he himself rarely performed in public, Chopin was among the first of those whose reputation as a composer for the piano became largely dependent upon the performance of fellow artists. Contemporary comments, such as those in reviews of his compositions, make clear that, even for experienced pianists of the time, Chopin's music presented new and surprising challenges, the musical qualities of which the printed score alone did not always help to reveal.[64]

It was thus largely through pianists who had had direct contact with Chopin in Paris that his music first began to gain acceptance in concert programmes. Among those who helped spread knowledge of his music, Liszt was influential: as was mentioned earlier, he often included some of the shorter pieces in his concert programmes from 1837 onward.[65] Frequently these were selections from the etudes, the first set of which Chopin had dedicated to Liszt. Individual etudes from Opp. 10 and 25 became the first pieces by Chopin to appear in many pianists' concert programmes.[66]

In London it was the performances of visiting pianists such as Carl Filtsch, one of Chopin's pupils, and Charles Hallé, who lived in Paris between 1836 and 1848, which first began to arouse the interest of English audiences in Chopin's music. In London concerts in 1843 both performed some of the larger works, such as the Ballades and Scherzos.[67] The smaller character pieces, some of which Filtsch also played, he presented in mixed groups, as Chopin himself did.[68]

It is noticeable, however, that it was women pianists, such as Clara Schumann[69] and Anna de Belleville,[70] who were among the first to perform Chopin's music in public. Concert programmes and reviews suggest that it was more readily accepted, at an earlier stage, that the programmes of women pianists would not focus on their own compositions.[71] As early as 1831, Clara had learnt the Variations on 'Là ci darem'; by the mid 1830s, she had performed the E minor Concerto, the Piano Trio and the *Fantasy on Polish Airs*.[72] By 1850 her repertoire, which encompassed a wide variety of music, ranging from Bach to the leading composers of her own time, included many of the works regarded by contemporary commentators as the best of Chopin's music – etudes, nocturnes and mazurkas.[73]

It is in this concept of a canon – a body of repertoire from which the piano music heard in public concerts should be drawn – that the changes that took place in the piano music heard in public concerts in the first half of the nineteenth century are most clearly symbolised.[74] It was through his activities as a composer rather than as a performer that Chopin contributed to this change. The quality and distinctiveness of his compositions gave him an unassailable claim to a leading position among the pianist-composers who, by 1850, were recognised as representatives of the 'modern Romantic' school. The fact that, by mid-century, the role of the pianist as interpreter was generally accepted was sufficient to ensure that Chopin's music assumed an increasingly prominent place in pianists' concert repertoire.

Chopin's early critics recognised in his music qualities that reached beyond the narrow boundaries of the concert life of the time. After hearing Chopin's first public concert in Paris, the critic Fétis predicted that it would be the 'revitalisation of forms' achieved by Chopin's music for pianists that would produce a major impact on this sphere of art.[75] Time has richly borne out the accuracy of this judgement.

2   *The nocturne: development of a new style*

DAVID ROWLAND

The year 1812 was significant in the development of the early nocturne. It was the year in which John Field published his *1ᵉʳ Nocturne*, the first in a series of similar works which led directly to the mature nocturnes of Chopin. Hitherto Field's role as the inventor of the genre has been largely unquestioned, and it has been assumed that Chopin simply inherited a well-established formula; but the early history of the nocturne is more complex than it might at first appear. The keyboard style normally associated with the genre had already been established in France by the end of the eighteenth century, so that its use by Field in 1812 was nothing new. It is in any case questionable whether this style should be so closely identified with the genre, since many subsequent nocturnes fail to use it. It would also be a mistake to imagine that the term 'nocturne' was quickly accepted to mean a solo piano piece with a particular character. Jeffrey Kallberg has pointed out that the term was only defined in this way from the 1830s onwards.[1]

In the meantime, a number of works in 'nocturne style' had appeared with other titles. Perhaps most striking of all in the early history of the nocturne is how slowly the genre developed. Apart from some of Field's pupils and acquaintances it seems that very few composers had any immediate inclination to follow his example, and it was only in the 1830s that nocturnes began to appear in any number.

An investigation of the development of the early nocturne for piano solo up to and including the works of Chopin must therefore involve a discussion of the terminology, an examination of the development and use of a particular style of keyboard writing, a re-evaluation of the role of John Field and a discussion of the contribution of others to the development of the genre.

TERMINOLOGY – THE BACKGROUND

Almost every aspect of early nineteenth-century piano music, including terminology, was in a state of flux. Established forms and styles were on the decline and new ones were emerging. At the same time the sales of both pianos and sheet music were booming, so that piano music was reaching an ever wider amateur audience. Fétis bemoaned some of the new trends:

> Sonatas and other works of classical and regular form have disappeared to make way for sorts of sketches embellished on known melodies and operatic airs. All these are named *Fantasies* and *Airs variés*, though nothing could be more bizarre or less varied. The form of these pieces always seems to be divided up in the same fashion.[2]

Publishers were ready to take advantage of the situation: 'We will do far better to print all sorts of small works demanded every day, which require no great advances and on which the return is sure'.[3] Their catalogues reveal the extent of this new trend; they are full of works headed 'fantasie', 'capriccio', 'pot-pourri', 'mélange', etc. Composers produced large quantities of these works for quick profit, and in most cases Fétis's criticisms are entirely justified. It was out of this repertoire, however, that many of the forms and styles that were to become important later in the century developed.

Broadly speaking, this large body of music can be divided into two categories, one comprising works with a multi-movement or multi-section structure (the most representative type of the early nineteenth century), the other comprising single-movement or single-section works, which were usually published in sets.

The first group contains lengthy medleys of operatic airs loosely strung together as 'pot-pourris' or 'mélanges', descriptive works depicting naval battles and other national events, etc., as well as compositions in just two or three sections such as the following:

P. Caudella, *Romance (Il est trop tard) suivé d'un Rondeau pour le Pianoforte Op. 9*, advertised in the *Allgemeine musikalisches Zeitung* (hereafter referred to as the *AmZ*), October 1810

P. A. Corri, *La Carolina. . .Adagio and Rondo* (*c.* 1805)

G. F. Couperin, *Les Incroyables, Pièce musicale* (*c.* 1797): Agitato – Pastorello – Agitato

A. Eberl, *Caprice et Rondeau* Op. 21 (reviewed in the *AmZ*, August 1804)

J. Field, *Divertissement* No. 2 (*c.* 1811): Pastorale – Rondeau

L. von Esch, *Air Religieux et Pastorelle* (*c.* 1806)
Introduction, Aria and Fantasy (*c.* 1805)
Marche (– Aria –) et Valce (*c.* 1805)

H. Montgeroult, *Pièce* Op. 3 (1804): Introduzione (Adagio – Recitativo) – Agitato

This list illustrates the variety of terminology in the repertoire and contains a number of examples of one type of piece that was particularly popular in the first years of the century – the combination of a slow, expressive movement with a faster rondo. Frequently, as we shall see shortly, the slow part of these pieces is in a style very similar to Field's early nocturnes. Indeed, the slow section of Field's Second Divertissement cited in the list above was later published independently of its rondeau section as his Eighth Nocturne,[4] but not before it had appeared as both a romance and a pastorale.

There are fewer examples of the second category, those works published in sets. It contains didactic sets of small-scale compositions and longer works of three or four pages for the more competent pianist. Examples exist from the eighteenth century, but their frequency increased dramatically after *c.* 1800. The following sample illustrates the variety of titles in use:

L. van Beethoven, *Bagatelles* Op. 33 (1801–2)
J. F. Edelmann, *Airs* Op. 16 (1788)
F. J. Kirmair, *Pièces détachés* Op. 10 (advertised *AmZ* 1807)
J. Lipawsky, *Romances ou Andantes* Op. 19 (1803)
N. Séjan, *Recueil de Pièces* Op. 2 (1784)
D. Steibelt, *Préludes ou Caprices* Op. 5 (1791)
D. Steibelt, *Divertimentos* Op. 28 (1797) – a collection of single-movement pieces
    rather than the usual multi-movement divertimento
V. J. Tomásek, *Eclogues* Op. 35 (1807)

Individual movements within these sets are entitled 'Romance', 'Pastorale', etc. (and 'Nocturne' at a later date).

As well as these works, individual single-movement pieces appeared occasionally, normally in rondo or sonata form (such as Beethoven's Andante in F WoO. 57, published in 1805 and Mozart's Adagio in B minor K. 540 of 1788). Very occasionally isolated works in song forms appeared, such as the Air and the Romance by Kozeluch, both moderately substantial compositions of three pages each, dating from 1811; but such pieces were rare.

The early nineteenth century, then, saw an increasingly expanding variety of works under a similarly large number of titles. With the variety in terminology came a marked inconsistency in the way that it was used; terms such as 'Divertimento', 'Capriccio', etc., could mean single- or multi-movement pieces of almost any description, and some works, such as Field's Second Divertissement, appeared under a number of different headings. Against this background it is hardly surprising that the term 'nocturne' had a rather uncertain start.

TERMINOLOGY – THE NOCTURNE

Jousse's *Compendious Dictionary of Italian and Other Terms used in Music* (London, 1829) underlines the confusion surrounding the term 'nocturne':

Piece of music destined to be performed at night as a serenade. The vocal nocturne is written for 2, 3 or 4 voices, and is sometimes arranged in such a manner that it can be performed without accompaniment.

The name *nocturne* is also given to certain operatic pieces which have the character of a *nocturne* and are sung in a nocturnal scene. *Nocturne* is also an instrumental piece written for harp and horn, oboe and piano. These *nocturnes*, properly speaking, are only *Notturno*, a name formerly given to pieces played in the evening: now the term is applied to a *divertimento*.

(Under the heading 'divertimento' Jousse mentions 'a short and pleasing composition, generally written on a favourite air, with an introduction'.) Nowhere in the dictionary is there any mention of nocturnes for piano solo, but his identification of the 'notturno' with multi-section works is interesting; the Italian term is often (though not always) used well into the 1830s to distinguish this type of piece from the single-movement 'nocturne' for piano solo.

Jousse is not alone among dictionary writers of the early nineteenth century in omitting the nocturne for piano solo; only later do we find definitions that include it – for example, Czerny:

The *Notturno* for the Pianoforte is really an imitation of those vocal pieces which are termed *Serenades*, and the peculiar object of such works – that of being performed at night, before the dwelling of an esteemed individual – must always exercise an influence upon its character. The notturno, therefore, must be calculated to create an impression of a soft, fanciful, gracefully-romantic, or even passionate kind, but never of a harsh or strange. The construction of it is nearly that of a short Andante in a Sonata, or of an extended theme; and a slow degree of movement is most suitable to the same.[5]

Czerny here points to a connection between the nocturne for piano solo and vocal models. This connection is reinforced by a comparison of early nocturnes for piano by Field with dictionary definitions of the vocal nocturne, such as Castil-Blaze's in 1821: 'A graceful and sweet melody, tender and mysterious, simple phrases, harmony that is not elaborate, but full, mellow, and without triviality; these are the qualities that should be encountered in the *nocturne*'.[6]

Much of the discussion of Field's indebtedness to vocal music has in the past centred around his apparent use of Italian vocal models,[7] but the French vocal background has been largely overlooked. In this connection, the close relationship between the vocal nocturne and the vocal romance (a predominantly French vocal form in the eighteenth and early nineteenth centuries) is particularly striking. Several nineteenth-century writers point out their similarities:

The style of the nocturne is like that of the romance, soft and gentle.[8]
The romance resembles the notturno.[9]
The *nocturne* is a musical composition that resembles the romance.[10]

The closeness of the two terms is underlined by the fact that Field's first nocturnes, published in Russia in 1812, appeared just three years later in Germany as
'romances'. Even as late as 1835, two of his works (Nocturnes No. 8 in A major
and No. 9 in E♭ major) were published by Hofmeister in Leipzig as *Deux Nocturnes
ou Romances*. Other composers also published 'romances' similar to Field's nocturnes in the early decades of the nineteenth century, some of which will be discussed in the next section.

The apparent interchangeability of the terms 'nocturne' and 'romance' illustrates
the flexibility of terminology in the first decades of the nineteenth century, as does
the fact that several pieces of Field's that eventually became known as nocturnes
(like the Divertissement mentioned in the previous section) were originally published as serenades, pastorales or divertissements. Indeed the term 'nocturne' was
never as restricted or fixed in its meaning as some writers might like to imagine.

THE DEVELOPMENT OF THE STYLE

In view of the terminological uncertainty it is perhaps unwise to talk of the 'nocturne style' as if it were exclusive to the nocturne. It might be more appropriate
to use the term 'romance/nocturne style', or an even wider term, at least for the
first three decades of the nineteenth century. Thereafter, however, something of
a difference does seem to emerge between pieces entitled 'nocturne' and those
called 'romance', or 'romance sans paroles'. A comparison, for example, of the style
of Chopin's nocturnes and Mendelssohn's songs without words or romances by
Robert and Clara Schumann shows clear differences, though it would be inap-
propriate to categorise the genres too rigidly. 'Romance/nocturne style' is a cum-
bersome term to use, however, so for the remainder of this chapter the more usual
'nocturne style' will be retained.

The features most commonly associated with nocturne style are the characteristic left-hand accompaniment and the right-hand melody. Field's first nocturne
(see Example 1) is typical. The left-hand part (frequently in triplet rhythm, or, as

Example 1   John Field, Nocturne No. 1 (1812)

Ex. 1 (*cont.*)

here, in compound time) is made up of broken-chord figuration which spans up to two octaves later in the work. The harmony is straightforward and, perhaps most important of all, the texture is heavily reliant on the sustaining pedal for its effect. The right hand begins with a simple melody which becomes increasingly decorated as the piece progresses. The structure of most pieces in this style is simple (usually ABA or ABAB), with a single tempo throughout (although as we shall see later, the B section becomes increasingly contrasted in style and tempo from around 1830).

Before examining how this style developed it is important to point out that not all early nocturnes (or romances) use it. Field's Third Nocturne (published in 1812, see Example 2), for example, has neither of the features pointed out above

Example 2   John Field, Nocturne No. 3 (1812)

as essential to the nocturne style, with the possible exception of a few passages later in the work. The same could be said of at least three more of Field's nocturnes, while still more fail to use the nocturne style consistently throughout. Field is not alone. Other composers of his own as well as later generations also composed nocturnes without using the nocturne style. This calls into question the appropriateness of defining the genre according to its style; it might be better to define it in terms of its character (as Czerny did – see above). The majority of early nocturnes are composed in the same style as Field's first, however, so there remains a reasonable justification for using the term 'nocturne style'.

The emergence of the fully-developed nocturne style can be traced very neatly through the sonatas of Louis Adam, one of the first professors at the Paris Conservatoire. In the third sonata from his Op. 4 (Paris, 1785) there is a 'Romance amoroso' (see Example 3), similar in style to many other contemporary move-

Example 3   Louis Adam, Piano Sonata Op. 4 No. 3, 'Romance amoroso' (1785)

ments by French composers. The right hand part of this example would not be out of place in a nocturne by Field or one of his contemporaries; it shows the same mixture of simple, relatively long-note melodic writing and decorated figuration that characterises much of the nineteenth-century repertoire. The left hand, too, uses the triplet accompanying figuration found in so many later nocturnes, but its restricted range means that it does not rely on the sustaining pedal. This is not surprising, since pianists of this period either did not have them (especially in France where hand levers were the norm at this time) or did not use them to any extent.[11] The slightly later romance from the third sonata of Adam's Op. 7 (1794) follows essentially the same pattern except that the elaborate ornamentation gives the piece a more sophisticated appearance (see Example 4).

Example 4   Louis Adam, Piano Sonata Op. 7 No. 3, 'Romance' (1794)

Ex. 4 (*cont.*)

By the mid 1790s piano technique was undergoing something of a revolution. Indications for the use of various pedals begin to appear in French piano music from this time. At first, they were used for little more than to create some sort of special effect, often in imitation of another instrument. But composers soon realised that the sustaining pedal opened up the possibility of new textures unattainable on earlier keyboard instruments. One use that was particularly favoured was that which enabled left-hand accompanying textures to exceed the span of a ninth or tenth (previously the limit for Alberti-style and other accompaniments). Most French and English composers immediately took advantage of this and by the year 1800 the appearance of a large proportion of the keyboard repertoire had changed considerably. This is amply illustrated in the left hand part of the romance from Adam's Sonata Op. 8 (1800) (see Example 5) and a similar movement from the later Sonata Op. 9 (1809) (see Example 6).

Example 5   Louis Adam, Piano Sonata Op. 8, 'Romance' (1800)

Ex. 5 (*cont.*)

A lengthy note at the beginning of this movement specifies the use of the sustaining and *moderator* pedals throughout.

Example 6   Louis Adam, Piano Sonata Op. 9, 'Romance' (1809)

This new style clearly held immense appeal for composers in France and England at the beginning of the new century. Sections or movements similar in style to those by Adam are found in numerous works, both within established structures (such as the sonata) as well as in the newer types of piece that were beginning to flood the market. Examples by P. A. Corri and L. von Esch illustrate the point (see Examples 7 and 8). In Germany and Austria, however, pianists and

Example 7   P. A. Corri, 'La Carolina' from *La Carolina & Rondo* (c. 1805)

Example 8   L. von Esch, 'Aria' from *Aria & Rondo* (*c.* 1806)

composers were less adventurous, and the style took longer to establish itself. Lipawsky's three Romances Op. 19 (1803), for example, are rather disappointing. Had they appeared in England or France they might have anticipated Field's nocturnes by several years, but instead they offer little more than the technique displayed by Adam in the 1780s and early 1790s, despite the fact that they are works of substantial length (see Example 9).

Example 9   J. Lipawsky, Romance No. 1 from *Trois Romances* Op. 19 (1803)

When Field published his first three nocturnes in 1812, a number of things were already clearly established. Although the terminology of the nocturne itself was somewhat fluid, the idea of publishing small collections of pieces using song forms, including romances, was common. Individual lyrical works had also appeared occasionally, and the style normally associated with Field's nocturnes had been used for fifteen years or so, at least in France and England. Very little, it seems, was new in 1812. Yet Liszt wrote that Field's nocturnes 'opened the way for all the productions which have since appeared under the various titles of Songs without Words, Impromptus, Ballades, etc., and to him we may trace the origin of pieces designed to portray subjective and profound emotion';[12] and many more recent authors have echoed his words. Clearly, Field's position needs to be examined more closely.

JOHN FIELD AND HIS CONTEMPORARIES

John Field's achievement can perhaps best be summed up by saying that he achieved status for the 'character piece' in the formative stages of romantic piano literature. Several factors point to this conclusion. The fact that Field produced a sequence of nocturnes over a period of more than twenty years suggests that he regarded the nocturne as more than an experiment, unlike so many other early nineteenth-century composers who were apparently happy to try out a title or form once or twice before moving on to something else. The prominence of nocturnes in Field's overall output similarly illustrates his high regard for the genre – they account for about one quarter of the total number of his works. The way in which they were published is also significant. Unlike other composers, who usually chose to release relatively small works in groups of three or six, Field almost always chose to publish his nocturnes as single pieces, implying that he regarded them as works of some substance. Finally, and perhaps most important of all, the refined and sensitive performance style for which Field became renowned must have contributed to the status of his nocturnes. It is well known that Chopin considered it a compliment when Kalkbrenner likened his playing to Field's, and it is equally well documented that many pianists and critics of the nineteenth century found in Field's playing something special – an expressiveness that was rare amidst all the *bravura* of the time, but which was to become increasingly important. The nocturnes embodied this quality and were appreciated more and more as the century wore on.

With the benefit of hindsight, writers from the mid nineteenth century onwards have commented on Field's significance as a composer, but earlier writers were less forthcoming. Kallberg has pointed out the failure of the *AmZ* to highlight anything particularly significant in Field's first nocturnes when they were reviewed in that journal in 1814.[13] This apparent lack of interest is reflected in the limited enthusiasm that other composers had for the nocturne in the 1810s and 1820s. The list of nocturnes for piano solo composed before *c.* 1830 is almost entirely restricted to composers who were associated with Field in some way:

John Field published just eight nocturnes before 1830 (and only a few more after that date) as well as two romances for piano solo.
J. B. Cramer, a pupil of Clementi's in London at the same time as Field, published a single nocturne (Op. 54) for piano solo *c.* 1815.

A. A. Klengel, another Clementi pupil, spent some years in Russia, during which time he heard Field play on a number of occasions. His *6 Nocturnes* were published in 1820. (He also published *3 Romances sentimentales* Op. 34 a little later.)

C. Mayer was a pupil of Field's in Russia. He published two nocturnes in 1822 and several more some years later.

H. Herz travelled widely in Europe as a virtuoso pianist. His *Trois Nocturnes caracteristiques* Op. 45 appeared in London in 1827.

M. Glinka was a pupil of both Field and Mayer. A nocturne of his for piano or harp was composed in 1828.

M. Szymanowska was a pupil of Field who left two nocturnes ('Le Murmure', published in Paris in 1825, and a nocturne in B♭, published posthumously) and a romance.

The *AmZ* lists additional nocturnes for piano solo by O. Claudius (1829). Also of interest is Kalkbrenner, who belongs mainly in the discussion of nocturnes after 1830 but deserves mention here as the composer of three romances in the Field style *c.* 1820. Nocturnes by other composers may yet come to light, but it seems unlikely that the list will increase significantly; an investigation of all the major pianist/composers of the period as well as many minor figures has revealed very little.

The form and style of some of these nocturnes is, not surprisingly, very close to that of Field's, especially those by Mayer, Herz and Glinka and one of the two by Szymanowska. Simple forms are used (usually ABA or ABAB, with or without a coda, but occasionally a slightly more extended rondo structure) and whatever contrast occurs within the piece is achieved by a change in the texture or key (but not by changes in the tempo). The nocturne style is used, generally for a substantial part of each piece, and sometimes throughout. In common with Field's earlier nocturnes, the style is relatively simple. Left-hand parts retain straightforward broken chord or arpeggio patterns, typically not often exceeding an octave and a half or two octaves in range and usually comprising triplet or quaver figuration, while the right hand parts tend to be ornamented in relatively simple fashion.

A significant number of the nocturnes listed above do not follow this style, however. Cramer's *Notturno* is similar to those nocturnes for two or more instruments which were popular at the beginning of the nineteenth century and which were referred to in dictionaries such as that by Jousse (see above). It is in four sections, or movements, of contrasting tempo and does not use the nocturne style at all. Each of Klengel's six *Notturnos* Op. 23 is in a single tempo throughout, but the six are varied in style. The third one of the set is the only one to use the nocturne style in 12/8 almost throughout, and, while others are generally melodic in nature, they are different in texture, more in the style of some of Mendelssohn's later songs without words. The fourth one of the set is alone in being like a study, with its use of crossed-hands technique. Maria Szymanowska's Nocturne

'Le Murmure' likewise avoids the nocturne style. It retains its expressiveness but uses different keyboard figuration.

CHOPIN AND THE DEVELOPMENT OF THE NOCTURNE AFTER *c*. 1830

The list of nocturnes published in the 1830s and 1840s is extensive, compared with the earlier repertoire. It includes works by well- and lesser-known composers of the new generation (H. Bertini, C. Chaulieu, F. Chopin, C. Czerny, K. Hart-knoch, F. Kalkbrenner, I. Moscheles, C. Schumann, S. Thalberg) as well as additional works by composers mentioned already (J. Field, H. Herz, C. Mayer). Numbers vary from composer to composer: Chopin was probably the most prolific; the list of others who published several nocturnes includes Bertini, Czerny, Field, Kalkbrenner, Mayer and Thalberg. Some only managed one or two (sometimes buried in a collection of somewhat insignificant pieces such as Moscheles's *Tutti Frutti* Op. 119).

It is possible that Field's tour of western Europe was the catalyst for some of this increased output of nocturnes. He left Russia for London in 1831. In 1832 he travelled on to Paris. The following year he toured Belgium, France, Switzerland and Italy, where he stayed until 1835. Later that year he returned to Russia via Vienna, where he was a guest of Czerny for a short while. It is striking to see how nocturnes began to appear in some of these places around the same time. Czerny, for example, had previously composed a number of nocturnes for piano duet or chamber ensemble with piano in the multi-section/movement style (as had some other composers named above), but began a series of nocturnes for piano solo with his Op. 368 set, most probably written shortly after Field's visit. Impetus must have come from other quarters too, though. Both Chopin and Bertini (who was also living in Paris), for example, published nocturnes in 1832, before Field's arrival there, and Chopin is known to have begun composing nocturnes a few years previously.

Whatever the reasons, it is clear that after 1830 the circle of composers of the nocturne for piano solo widened beyond the small group of Field pupils and acquaintances. With this increase in numbers of works went a more consistent use of the nocturne style itself. The large majority of nocturnes after this date employ it, though a few exceptions remain, such as Chaulieu's nocturnes (whose full title is *Etudes Romantiques: Douze Nocturnes*), which are in a wide variety of tempos and rarely use the nocturne style.

The nocturne's growing appeal around 1830 coincided with an increasing sophistication in composers' approaches to both form and style. Nowhere are these changes seen more clearly than in Chopin's nocturnes, which are more substantial and serious than those by Field and his contemporaries (not least in their considerably greater use of minor keys).

Chopin's first nocturne, in E minor, composed in 1828–30 but published posthumously in 1855, is a transitional work. It lies clearly within the Field tradition, but more than hints at future developments. In length it matches many pre-1830s works and is relatively simple both formally and stylistically. The structure, ABAB, is that of several earlier works, and it is achieved by the simplest of means: the B section uses a pedal throughout (dominant at first, then tonic at the end of the piece) – a common feature of Field's nocturnes – and has chords in the right hand as opposed to the more melodic line of the A section. The texture is likewise conventional: both sections take place over a constant nocturne-style left-hand accompaniment. This accompaniment, however, is more adventurous than its counterparts in earlier works. Its range frequently extends to two octaves or more within the bar, but more significant is the way in which it draws attention to itself by the repetition of the falling semitone C–B (and its equivalents in later bars where the harmony is different) (see Example 10). This motif, along

Example 10   F. Chopin, Nocturne in E minor

with the increased richness of the left-hand harmony in places, gives the impression of a texture that is more complex than earlier examples, where the left-hand part tends to include only the notes of the supporting chords. Although this technique was not new with Chopin, an increased attention to the left-hand part was to become a feature of many of his later nocturnes.

John Field's performances were famous for the dream-like states that they induced in his listeners. It is not difficult to see how this was achieved in his music: numerous examples could be cited of passages in a slow tempo where the harmony is static or changes predictably to closely-related chords, the texture is constant and the melody simply follows one four-bar phrase by another. At first sight, Chopin's style is similar; but even in the early E minor Nocturne there are signs that he was not content to follow this pattern entirely. For example, the harmonic 'surprise' at the beginning of bar 6, which immediately increases the momentum, would be an unusual gesture in an earlier nocturne; but it was an idea that Chopin was to return to in somewhat similar contexts later (see, for example, bars 1–8 of the Nocturne Op. 15 No. 1). The more thorough and inventive approach to ornamentation in successive playings of the opening melody is also worthy of note: Field tends only to decorate short passages within his melodic line, without in any way altering its character, whereas Chopin's approach is altogether more comprehensive in the way that he develops and transforms his themes.

Chopin's Op. 9 and Op. 15 Nocturnes (published in 1832 and 1833 respectively) confirm the character of the nocturne in Chopin's hands as a more dynamic form. This is illustrated most obviously in his use of a different tempo for dramatic middle sections in three of them (Op. 9 No. 3 and Op. 15 Nos. 1 and 2). This idea was not unique to Chopin and perhaps originated in the form of some operatic airs of the period. Thalberg's nocturnes usually contain an agitated middle section and even composers such as Herz and Mayer, who otherwise preferred to stay within the more simple Field tradition, followed suit occasionally. Field himself indicated a different tempo for a middle section in the early Ab Nocturne (1812) and in the much later one in D minor (1835). Neither of these has anything like the intensity of Chopin's contrasting sections, however: they are interludes which barely interrupt the flow of the music.

The Op. 9 and Op. 15 pieces that do not have contrasting middle sections find other means of sustaining the listener's attention. Op. 9 No. 1 almost immediately introduces us to a style of decoration only seldom encountered in either Field's nocturnes or those of Chopin's contemporaries, and never so near the beginning of a work (see Example 11). The irregularity of the rhythmic patterns in this exam-

Example 11   F. Chopin, Nocturne Op. 9 No. 1

Ex. 11 (*cont.*)

ple is one aspect of Chopin's style of ornamentation that continues to find increasingly varied expression in later works such as the Nocturne Op. 27 No. 2. Compared with this, the decorative patterns in nocturnes by composers such as Thalberg or Bertini are thoroughly pedestrian, relying as they usually do on mathematical divisions of the beat and simple scalic or arpeggiated formulas. The slightly increased length of Chopin's Op. 9 No. 1 is also sustained by stronger contrasts in dynamics than were usual in earlier nocturnes. The passionate outbursts of bars 15–17 and 33–37, for example, contrasting with the *pianissimo* of bars 19–25, underline the generally more dramatic nature of these works.

Op. 9 No. 2 is an intriguing piece. It bears a striking resemblance to Field's Nocturne No. 9 in the same key, but the similarities are only superficial. Both pieces are in compound time, their left-hand figuration is similar (although more 'stretched-out' in the Chopin example), and both have cadenza-like passages towards the end; but in other respects they are very different. The treatment of the melody provides an interesting point of comparison. In Field's nocturne, the melody gradually unfolds in a relaxed manner, with elements of repetition and decoration. In Chopin's, there is an almost obsessive treatment of the various melodic ideas that make up the piece: the opening melody returns three times with substantially different ornamentation, as does, for example, the much shorter melodic idea of bar 25. In addition, there are harmonic 'surprises' in bars 12 and 20. All these features are much more demanding on the listener than Field's easily-flowing *cantabile*. Op. 9 No. 2 is an altogether more condensed, and intense, piece.

A different approach is found in Op. 15 No. 3. This time it is the irregularity and unpredictability of the phrasing that demands our attention. At first, the melody proceeds as if it were a conventional four-bar phrase; but it fails to reach the expected conclusion, and instead pauses on an F for three bars before descending to D. The repetition of this phrase is similarly unpredictable. Between bars 7 and 13 the melodic line descends in various intervals from D; there is nothing to indicate that its final descent to G in bar 13 is particularly significant until we realise (after the event) that it is the beginning of the opening melody again.

This unpredictable element is not confined to the melody. Harmonically, there is also a good deal of uncertainty, especially in the middle of the piece, which constantly threatens to settle in F♯ major, but consistently fails to do so.

Taken together, these early nocturnes by Chopin demonstrate that he was not content merely to follow Field into his dream world. There is more drama and a greater intensity here, moving away from the relaxed, almost improvisatory character of the early nocturne. Chopin's contemporaries never quite achieved the same degree of sophistication, with their more predictable two- or four-bar melodic patterns, and generally unadventurous texture and harmony. That is not to say, however, that they failed completely to see the need to introduce greater variety into the nocturne: Thalberg, for example, tends to introduce more virtuosic figuration for the repeats of A sections (such as the *tremolando* accompaniment to the melody at the end of the Op. 35 Nocturne) but this is more in the nature of light-hearted variation than the kind of developmental re-examination of themes that we find in Chopin's works.

Most of the stylistic elements of Chopin's early nocturnes find further development in later works. This is perhaps most clearly seen in the textures he chooses. Passages of chords, for example, play something of a role in earlier pieces (see the section from bar 89 in Op. 15 No. 3), but they become more common in later works (see the almost hymn-like interlude in bars 41–64 of Op. 37. No. 1, for example, and the more complex chordal writing of Op. 48 No. 1, beginning at bar 25). Certain textures, such as the passages in thirds and sixths from Op. 27 No. 2, are given fuller treatment (Op. 37 No. 2). As Jim Samson has pointed out, counterpoint begins to play a part in Op. 55 No. 2 and in both of the Op. 62 nocturnes, following Chopin's studies of contrapuntal treatises.[14] Generally, the role of the nocturne style diminishes in importance somewhat, though it remains strongly in evidence. The function of the middle section begins to change, too. In earlier works (Op. 9 No. 3, Op. 15 Nos 1 and 2, Op. 27 No. 1) it is faster and strongly dramatic, always forming a deliberate contrast to the slower, outer sections. In the second of the two Op. 32 nocturnes, as well as in both those of Op. 37, however, the tempo remains the same and only the figuration changes – the degree of contrast is therefore reduced. This prepares the way for the late nocturnes where, as Zofia Chechlińska has observed,[15] the central sections are much more closely related to the outer sections. Finally, in some of these later nocturnes there is a sense of development, or progression through the work, that is distinct from the early nocturne style, where straightforward and often unadventurous ABA or ABAB forms were the norm. Op. 48 No. 1 is a good example. The return of the opening melodic idea towards the end of the piece is accompanied by much richer figuration and is marked *agitato*. As a result, there is a drama in this final section which is entirely lacking at the beginning of the piece.

The sophisticated style of Chopin's late nocturnes illustrates how far the genre had come in the preceding decades. From complex and often undistinguished origins John Field established a style and gave it a status above that of most other small-scale works of the early nineteenth century. He was virtually alone among his contemporaries in so doing. Composers of the next generation were hardly less reluctant to follow Field's example: many of the major figures (for example, Liszt, Mendelssohn and Schumann) failed to compose a single nocturne, though a few others did follow his example. In the second quarter of the nineteenth century, however, one composer stands out as having made a truly significant contribution to the genre: Chopin alone produced works of real stature, which have stood the test of time.

3 *The twenty-seven etudes and their antecedents*

SIMON FINLOW

INTRODUCTION

The publication of the *Douze grandes études*, Op. 10, in 1833 provided the musical world with its first conclusive evidence of the depth of Chopin's creative talent. In many ways this was an appropriate and symbolic form of announcement. The early development of the piano etude, in which Chopin played a crucial part, was intricately associated with developments in piano technique, piano composition and the instrument itself.[1] It was to the piano that Chopin was to devote nearly all his important work. It was from the sounds and performance idioms of the piano that he drew his inspiration, this being nowhere so evident as in his etudes. Inasmuch as the Op. 10 Etudes disclosed the true quality of that inspiration for the first time, they signified a vital stage in Chopin's own development, as both composer and pianist. They mark the end of his artistic adolescence, the clear beginnings of a maturity that was resoundingly confirmed by the contents of his second collection, Op. 25, published in 1837.

'Chopin's Etudes stand alone', pronounced Tovey in 1900; '. . . [they] are the only extant great works of art that really owe their character to their being Etudes.'[2] It is true that the etudes occupy a special position in the vast repertory of didactic piano music. For one thing, they stand at the apex of a transition from early nineteenth-century prototypes (generally modest in expressive scope and technical function) to the extroverted concert etudes of Liszt, Alkan and others. Chopin's etudes are matchless in their capacity to train the fingers, while their musical quality clearly permits – or rather demands – public performance. But what most sets these works apart is the pervasive ingenuity that distinguishes Chopin's pianistic ideas and the artistry with which they are manipulated. From the magnificent striding arpeggios that introduce Op. 10 to the solemn expansive harmonies of Op. 25 No. 12, there is scarcely a single gesture that fails to evince Chopin's sensitivity to keyboard resources or his rare musicianship.[3]

In assessing the influences that may have helped Chopin achieve the degree of musicianship evident in Op. 10, it is difficult to avoid the feeling that he accomplished it mostly on his own. We shall see shortly that the composition of etudes involved special problems that severely taxed the abilities of some of his predecessors. Yet Chopin's grasp of these problems seems so intuitive, his solutions so effortless, the musical conceptions so fresh and spontaneous that one cannot adequately explain his success by invoking antecedents. There is considerable truth to Gerald Abraham's claim that 'no matter how much Chopin may have been indebted to [Hummel, Spohr and Moscheles] in his caterpillar and chrysalis stage, by the time he emerged at twenty-one as the lovely chatoyant butterfly we think of as the true Chopin, he was as free from debt to predecessors as any composer in the whole history of music'.[4] On the specific subject of the etudes, Jim Samson maintains that Chopin distinguished himself by 'conquering virtuosity on its home ground, and in doing so lifting himself clear of the surrounding lowland of mediocrity'.[5] With the etudes of Op. 10 Chopin realised not only his own musical potential but also that of the genre; and the manner in which he did both appears to have owed very little to precedent.

Nevertheless, we can recognise Chopin's independence of his predecessors without denying that there were genuine precedents for his achievements. Nor does the consistently high standard of Chopin's work invalidate the generally more variable efforts of his forerunners, even though it is this more than anything else that sets him apart from them. An interesting contemporary indication of the significance of his etudes is to be found in an article by Schumann entitled 'Some piano studies arranged according to their technical aims', which appeared on 6 February 1836 in the *Neue Zeitschrift für Musik*.[6] This article is in two sections. The first consists of a short introductory essay in which Chopin is named as one of five composers 'who are clearly the most important' writers of etudes, the others being J. S. Bach,[7] Clementi, Cramer and Moscheles. 'In Moscheles', we are told, 'and to an even higher degree in Chopin, imagination and technique share dominion side by side.' Of the lesser composers Schumann goes on to mention, some are considered original (Ludwig Berger, for example), others merely capable (J. C. Kessler). Some are distinguished by their treatment of the instrument (Kalkbrenner, Czerny, Henri Herz), or by 'romantic inspiration' (Cipriani Potter) or 'tenderness' (Maria Szymanowska), and one, Henri Bertini, is judged to be disappointing, 'though gracefully so'. After slipping in a discreet reference to his own *Etudes d'après des caprices de Paganini*, Opp. 3 and 10 (1832 and 1835, respectively), Schumann then proceeds to his main purpose, as promised in the title, which is to categorise various individual etudes according to their technical features; pieces judged as having an especially poetic character are highlighted with an asterisk. Thus under the heading 'right-hand extensions' we find Chopin's Op. 10 No. 1, asterisked of course, along with the first of Berger's *Zwölf Etüden*, Op. 12 (also highlighted), two by Clementi, one by Cramer and several others. The various categories include velocity and lightness, velocity and strength, legato, staccato, melody and accompaniment in the same hand, silent finger changes on the same note, extensions, leaps, interlocking of fingers and crossing of hands, repetitions, octaves, trills, problems of accentuation and so on. Altogether, some 350 individual pieces are classified with a high degree of accuracy – this was clearly no frivolous undertaking.

For a musician of Schumann's intelligence to go to this much trouble over what Tovey would have called 'so much inferior music'[8] implies that he detected some value even in the worst of it. And while he is predictably most generous in awarding stars to Chopin (eleven out of the twelve Op. 10 Etudes have asterisks), he is hardly less so with regard to Berger (seven pieces are highlighted out of the nine mentioned) and Moscheles (ten highlighted out of the nineteen cited from his Op. 70 collection). Clearly there is music here that warrants our attention, not only for what it can tell us about Chopin but also for its own sake. Various stylistic and functional qualities intrinsic to earlier etudes will therefore be appraised in detail during the course of what follows.

One thing that Schumann's article makes very apparent is that by 1836 the repertory of piano etudes was already large. Czerny, for instance, had by that time produced several hundred studies and exercises of his own – so many, in fact, that Schumann politely refuses to classify them individually. Other composers, such as Steibelt and Field, are not even mentioned by Schumann, while several of those he does cite have become obscure. In the interests of clarity, therefore, here is a checklist of relevant didactic works issued between 1800 and 1840 by composers who have already been or will be referred to in this chapter (these are arranged in order of publication).

SELECTED DIDACTIC PIANO WORKS, 1800 TO 1840

J. B. Cramer, *Studio per il pianoforte*, Op. 39, 1804

D. G. Steibelt, *Etude pour le pianoforte contenant 50 exercices de différents genres*, Op. 78, 1805

Cramer, *Etude pour le piano forte*, Op. 40, 1810

J. Field, *Exercice modulé dans tous les tons majeurs et mineurs*, 1816

M. Clementi, *Gradus ad Parnassum*, 1817–26

J. H. Müller, *Préludes et exercices*, c. 1817

L. Berger, *12 Etüden*, Op. 12, 1819

F. Kalkbrenner, *24 études*, Op. 20, c. 1820

M. Szymanowska, *20 exercices et préludes*, 1820

C. Potter, *24 études*, 1826

I. Moscheles, *(24) Studien zur höheren Vollendung bereits ausgebildeter Clavierspieler*, Op. 70, 1826

C. Czerny, *Schule der Geläufigkeit*, Op. 299, 1830

H. Bertini, *25 études caractéristiques*, Op. 66, 1832

R. Schumann, *6 études d'après des caprices de Paganini*, Op. 3, 1832

F. Chopin, *12 grandes études*, Op. 10, 1833

J. N. Hummel, *24 Etüden*, Op. 125, 1833

H. Herz, *24 grandes études, c.* 1835

Schumann, *6 études de concert d'après des caprices de Paganini*, Op. 10, 1835

J. C. Kessler, *24 études*, Op. 20, 1835

Schumann, *12 Etüden im Orchestercharakter*, Op. 13, 1837

Chopin, *12 neue Etüden*, Op. 25, 1837

Berger, *15 neue Etüden*, Op. 22, 1837

Chopin, *3 nouvelles études. Composée pour la méthode des méthodes de Moscheles et Fétis*, 1839

By comparing examples from these and a few non-didactic works one can trace a variety of precedents for the musical and technical features of Chopin's etudes.[9] Many such comparisons have been made by critics, mostly in order to depict thematic or motivic resemblances but occasionally also to bring into relief similarities of style or likely influences. What follows here constitutes an analysis and evaluation of resemblances that appear to signify stylistic or methodological antecedents. The discussion will be divided into two main areas. We shall look first at passagework and figuration – that is to say, at the technical raw material that generally functions as the thematic substance of etudes. The second part of the discussion will be concerned with matters of harmony, texture, structure and other large-scale processes through which this material is given musical form.

PASSAGEWORK, FIGURATION, KEYBOARD TECHNIQUE

Developments in didactic keyboard music engendered three varieties of composition which may be classified briefly as follows: (i) *exercises*, in which a didactic objective – the isolation and repetition of a specific technical formula – is assigned primary attention, any musical or characteristic interest being incidental; (ii) *etudes*, wherein musical and didactic functions properly stand in a complementary and indivisible association; and (iii) *concert studies*, in which the didactic element is mostly incidental to the primary characteristic substance (though the music will invariably involve some particular exploitation and demonstration of virtuoso technique). Many composers inclined toward one or another of these categories. Czerny and Bertini, for instance, contributed mainly exercises; Liszt and Schumann composed concert studies almost exclusively; and several, including Cramer, Berger, Moscheles and Chopin, concentrated on what was by far the most problematic of these genres in their efforts to compose etudes that would embody the quintessential idioms and performance techniques of the piano. We shall be predominantly concerned with this last group.

Exercises have a long and not very interesting history. In their keyboard incarnations they usually take the form of brief encapsulations of recurrent problems encountered in passagework playing. The emphasis is invariably on drill and repetition; expression and interpretation are seldom called for, often deliberately excluded. Composers of etudes, by contrast, endeavour to systematise and consolidate existing techniques within coherent and self-sufficient musical structures – to get to the heart of the issues of keyboard performance *and* composition. I shall try to show that this criterion is both genuine and fundamental when we appraise the stylistic features that distinguish Chopin's etudes. We shall also see that Chopin's originality derives not so much from the invention or demonstration of new techniques (a frequent preoccupation among composers of concert studies) as from his innovative conceptual insight into the basic problem: his vision, as it were, of what defines a perfect etude. First, however, we need to take a look at some of the more obvious characteristics of early piano etudes in order to establish some of the essential styles and features with which the genre came to be associated.

To illustrate the manner in which a good etude can codify and deploy a particular figuration, here are two short, almost identical passages, one taken from a concerto movement of around 1820 and the other from an etude composed about a decade later (see Example 1).[10] Hummel's figure is one among many encountered

Example 1   (a) Hummel, Piano Concerto Op. 85 third movement, bars 434–6 (right hand)

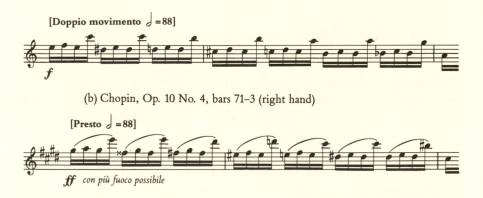

(b) Chopin, Op. 10 No. 4, bars 71–3 (right hand)

throughout the movement; its only purpose is to decorate a chromatic sequence linking a I–V progression. Chopin's figure, on the other hand, embodies a motivic structure that permeates the entire composition. After being subjected to exhaustive modifications and position changes, it here reaches a dramatic apotheosis during which it is combined with a free inversion of itself in a relentless drive towards the final cadence. Chopin's Op. 10 No. 4 realises the technical implications of Hummel's innocuous transitional passage by distilling its motivic essence and enshrining the technical ramifications of the pianistic idea within musical events of the kind just described.[11]

The motivic character of Example 1b is defined by a simple four-note structure. The strength of this pianistic idea derives from its elasticity and adaptability, features common to etude figurations, enabling not only repetition on different scale degrees, as in an exercise, but also intervallic transformation according to harmonic context, chromatic alteration, inversion and so on. Its combination with the other four-note idea developed in the work generates perpetual motion, which is also a common characteristic of etudes and of nineteenth-century virtuoso passagework in general. Example 2 illustrates the motivic structure of six similar

Example 2   (a) Beethoven, Sonata Op. 26 (1802), fourth movement, bar 1
            (b) Cramer, *84 Studies*, No. 27 (1804), bar 45
            (c) Field, Piano Concerto No. 2 in A♭ (1816), third movement, bar 561
            (d) Kalkbrenner, Op. 20 No. 7 (1820), bar 1
            (e) Beethoven, *Diabelli Variations* (1823), var. 17, bar 1
            (f) Chopin, Op. 25 No. 11, (1837) bar 5

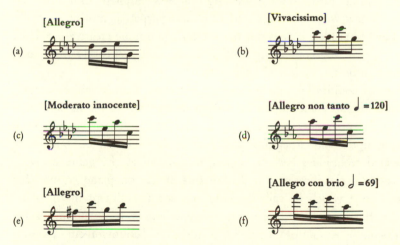

moto perpetuo figures, selected more or less at random from throughout the period under discussion. The essential pianistic similarity of these motivic cells, and indeed of the rhetorical effects of the passages from which each one is quoted, indicates the degree to which the materials of virtuoso piano music were becoming standardised in the early nineteenth century. This tendency towards what has been described as a 'cosmopolitan instrumental style' is amply reflected in the subject matter favoured by composers of etudes during the same period.[12]

The increasing prevalence of perpetual motion and other motivically-based virtuoso figurations was later remarked upon by Adolph Kullak. He saw it as the specific consequence of utilising passagework derived from ornamental fioritura, a mode of expression he calls 'sensuous representation' ('sinnlichen Darstellung'), as the thematic basis for large musical sections or entire compositions. His analysis of this development is very interesting:

> Formerly the passage had appeared as a contrast to the *cantilena*, the instrumental principle to the vocal, movement to repose. Now almost all becomes movement; contrasts appear only in the various figuration of the movement. Technique develops in everything. . . . What otherwise found room as an ornament hardly noticed betwixt the pillars of the artistic idea [see Example 1a], is now seized upon and worked up in factory-like imitation and the running figuration of the Etude form, as a problem for that mastery of difficulties now grown to be child's play [see Example 1b]. The Etude form predominates. Its principle so permeates the wide-spreading ramifications of all forms, that its law quite dominates free productivity, and almost nothing is left of the earlier ideal method of composition.[13]

A growing preoccupation with the sensuous and mechanical aspects of keyboard articulation may explain why nineteenth-century composers so often turned to etudes as an appropriate medium for expressing that new emphasis. But although Example 2 shows that 'sensuous representation' and perpetual motion were by no means confined to etudes, it does not make clear the unique creative problems that attach to constructing convincing musical statements exclusively from such material. These will be the subject of later analysis.

As the process of codification and systematisation took place in etudes, certain natural keyboard textures and formulas arising from the technical objectives recurred with sufficient frequency to become identifiable as generic clichés. Scale passages, double notes and arpeggios are some obvious examples, but other more sophisticated techniques became widely established as the genre evolved. Among the technical classifications in Schumann's article on piano studies, for example, there is one which he calls 'melody and accompaniment in the same hand'. This very effective keyboard format received perhaps its most sublime exemplification in the outer sections of Chopin's Op. 10 No. 3. Schumann cites twenty-one other examples of it, including two from Berger's Op. 12 studies and one from Moscheles's Op. 70. However, the basic technical requirements of the device – careful touch control and phrasing for the melody and precise weighting of the inner voices – had been effectively demonstrated as early as 1805 by Steibelt,[14] and their origins in non-didactic music can be traced back beyond that (to the slow movement of Beethoven's 'Pathétique' Sonata, for example). The various manifestations of this and other techniques in etudes before 1840 provide us with an interesting chronicle of the means by which composers of etudes sought to exploit developments and innovations presented in 'free' piano music. The degree to which they also responded to mechanical and structural improvements to the instrument itself should not be overlooked.[15]

In certain cases, formulas of the kind just mentioned evolved beyond mere technical clichés to become recognisable idioms that denoted specific modes of interpretation. From the mannerisms of the 'brilliant style', for example, there emerged a number of distinctive virtuoso resources. A typical device was one characterised by rapid triplet semiquavers and *leggiero* touch. Cramer was an early exponent of this idiom (see No. 31 of his *Eighty-four Studies*). Kalkbrenner was perhaps its most notorious practitioner (see his Op. 20 No. 4), and the formidable technique which he developed largely in order to convey such pianistic concepts made a strong impression on the young Chopin. Chopin's own early compositions, however, abound in pianistic brilliance of a calibre seldom approached by the older virtuoso. Moreover, in his well-known etude in this manner, Op. 10 No. 5, Chopin presents the pianist with a brilliant right-hand figure whose outlines and structure are uniquely circumscribed according to a specific topographical feature of the keyboard: by confining the figure entirely to black notes, the composer neatly encapsulates this particular pianistic idea within a rigidly defined technical format. The unique creative challenge entailed by this technical constraint is one to which he responds with an ingenuity that sparkles with every new turn taken by the figure. The restriction does not inhibit his use of chromatic harmony, for one thing. And the various melodic and linear fragments that emerge from the black-note figures in the right hand are given a captivating motivic significance by the extent to which they are imitated and absorbed by the appoggiaturas, auxiliary notes and suspensions of the left-hand chord patterns; the result is a harmonic texture rich in ninths and added sixths. The scintillating effect of this harmony combined with the glittering bravura passagework which distributes it across the keyboard is without precedent in the piano music of Kalkbrenner or any other exponent of the 'brilliant style'.

For the most part, however, the figures on which Chopin's etudes are based can adequately be described in the same traditional pianistic terms that define earlier etudes: arpeggios, broken chords, skips, extensions, thirds, sixths, octaves and so forth. He even appears to have avoided some of the established virtuoso techniques (hand-crossing, tremolos, broken octaves, etc.) that had already featured in the piano music of Beethoven, Cramer, Steibelt and Clementi.[16] The source of Chopin's originality is therefore to be found not in his selection of figures so much as in the broader schemes in which he envisioned using them. As Zofia Chechlińska puts it, 'He took over only those devices which would harmonise with his overall conception of a pianistic sound world.'[17] The pianistic sound world of the etudes is above all expressed through their large-scale harmonic structure and the manner in which this interacts with the technical effects and colourings of the surface textures. It is to this issue that we must turn in order to determine the nature of the processes at work in Chopin's etudes and the extent to which they are prefigured in earlier ones.

HARMONY, TEXTURE, INTEGRITY

The emancipation of figuration in early nineteenth-century etudes engendered an instrumental style that tended to exclude melody and produce uniform rhythmic flow within consistent, largely uncontrasted textures. This in turn precipitated a crucial reliance upon harmony as the chief means of imparting expressive character, rhythm and structure to the musical background. It was by fitting a particular figuration into a harmonic framework which would allow it to adopt diverse positions that composers endeavoured to satisfy didactic or technical criteria while simultaneously generating musical interest. The influence of the technical objectives thus extends beyond the figurations at the surface to the various harmonic and developmental operations that lie beneath. At the same time, the harmonic outlines continually dictate the range and frequency of position changes in a constant ebb and flow of mutual interaction. This distinctive feature of piano etudes constituted a severe test of a composer's basic creative methods, especially where these involved large-scale harmonic perspectives.

Perhaps because of unhappy associations with exercises there still remains a tendency among musicians to view etudes as little more than attempts to isolate technique from musical substance in the service of a purely practical end, namely the cultivation of some specific pianistic faculty. Another commonly expressed theory is that the best etudes contrive to cultivate musicianship and not just technique. The latter idea underlies a statement made by John Gillespie in connection with Chopin's etudes: 'Technique alone is but one side of piano music and piano playing, in some ways merely a means to an end.'[18] Yet the notion that music can somehow be divorced from the performance techniques that make it possible or that technique is only of incidental value to music could hardly be less appropriate to a discussion of Chopin's mature piano music. One might say of a scale, perhaps, that its only purpose is technical. But even scales occasionally sustain a musical function (as in Chopin's Op. 10 No. 2, for instance, or the endings to Op. 25 No. 11 and the G minor Ballade), albeit at a distinctly superficial level. Alternatively, whenever a pianist isolates a technical difficulty in a piece (which may even be an etude) by extracting a passage for repeated practice, we may say that he has created an exercise. But exercises cannot be said to retain any intrinsic meaning beyond or separate from the music from which they are all, in effect, extracts.[19]

To infer from their technical utility that Chopin's etudes are simply large exercises would be seriously to misinterpret their outward forms and effects. On the other hand, to see their aesthetic quality as the exclusive justification for the technical content would take insufficient account of the functional duality that defines their character. These etudes are discrete works of art in which the musical ideas constitute an embodiment of the technical material, in which the music *is* the technique. Using Gillespie's terminology, one can say that they are the technical means to their own ends. What makes them special is that their musical integrity is nowhere compromised by the very fact of their being etudes.

An excellent analysis of the creative opportunities afforded by the etude genre is supplied by Oscar Bie in his *History of the Pianoforte*. Here, for example, is his explanation of the ways in which figurations (described as the 'eternal ground-motives of all music') may suggest particular treatment:

> The one way sees in a broken chord only the means of using it in major or minor modes, or in the seventh, or in some unusual successions, first for the right hand, then for the left, then for both, and perhaps finally with sustained notes. Theory is satisfied, a practical object provided, the academic conscience laid to rest. But the other way sees in the broken chords their elementary [i.e., elemental] character. . . Thus, no less than the other, it presents all the nuances of major, minor, seventh, right, left, up and down; but it covers these technical variations so perfectly with the sense of inner meaning that they become identified, and can never be separated: the technical and characteristic content have, in the mind of a genius like this, involuntarily become a unity.[20]

In a good etude, then, the manner in which the musical ideas proliferate will be significantly influenced by the nature of the figuration; the technical substance will stand as the elemental basis of the entire structure. As to the usual character of the thematic ideas, the etude is said to favour 'fixed and limited technical models, which fit mosaic-wise into each other. It is opposed to huge, Beethoven-like emotions and their expression.' In the light of all this, Bie concludes, 'more genuine piano music than the Etude there cannot be. The essence of the piano has in it become music.'

Unfortunately, early exponents of the genre had to work without the prior benefit of these insights and in many of their etudes the essence of the piano demonstrably failed to become music. Even with later composers one can sometimes discern little more than a misguided inclination to contribute to the general 'fracas pianistique'[21] of their time. The etudes of Alexander Dreyschock, for example, drew from Schumann some of his most caustic critical notices. This was mostly on account of their failure to enliven extravagant pianistic gestures with even traces of authentic expressive substance.[22] Likewise, in a review of Edouard Wolff's Studies Op. 20, Schumann remarked that 'difficulty is their only distinguishing feature; there is more music in many a Chopin mazurka than in all of these 24 studies. Young composers cannot grasp soon enough that music does not exist for the sake of the fingers, but the precise opposite; and no-one should dare be a poor musician in order to become a fine virtuoso.'[23]

The didactic works of Czerny exist almost exclusively for the fingers, as thousands of present-day pianists can attest. And while there are undoubtedly numerous technical benefits to be gained from practising Czerny's exercises, 'exercise' (in the sense defined above) is the only term which accurately describes them. This can plainly be seen from the contents of Op. 299, the *School of Velocity*. No. 36 in C, for example, entails nothing but a series of routine figurations draped over a lengthy I–V–I tonal framework, the dominant merely providing a convenient temporary alternative to the tonic. There are no obvious structural reasons why figures of this sort should not continue indefinitely, perhaps modulating through the complete cycle of fifths with a cadential formula tacked on when the original key is reached again (Field's *Exercice modulé* of 1816 follows just such a procedure).

The failure of Op. 299 No. 36 to exhibit organic substance and integrity makes it fairly typical of Czerny's enormous didactic *œuvre*. No. 13 of Cramer's *Eighty-four Studies*, on the other hand, is a rare exception to the rule established by his other etudes in that it fails to satisfy the requirements of musical self-sufficiency. Here, we find a lively, engaging figure, but its presentation resembles that of a written-out extemporisation, a cadenza to some lost concerto: the piece assumes a natural context if one imagines a robust $^6_4$ chord before the start, a cadential shake in the penultimate bar and a lively tutti theme entering with the final chord. Lacking both the methodical rigour of an exercise and the musically finished quality of an etude it is actually neither.

Often the roots of what we may call this integrity problem can be traced to weaknesses in the 'ground-motives', the figures themselves, or to the harmonic contexts in which they are developed. This is because in etudes good music is invariably the product of versatile and idiomatic figures; the coincidence of aesthetic and pianistic quality in the best of them is more than accidental. What can often be found in the case of Bertini, Herz and one or two others is either that the presentation of the figurations generates negligible harmonic or characteristic interest or that harmonic interest is supplied in the form of an evidently gratuitous chromaticism.

These two shortcomings show up regularly in etudes both before and after Chopin. The first, for instance, features conspicuously throughout Bertini's Op. 20 (see, in particular, No. 15 in F♯ minor). Figurations of the kind favoured by Bertini often resemble those employed as accompaniments in lieder and ensemble music. The obvious difference is that they lack the melodic or lyrical component which is the only justification for such uniformly textured and harmonically attenuated passagework.[24] As an example of the second problem, we may cite No. 11 of Herz's *Twenty-four Grand Studies*, which embodies the kind of otiose chromaticism that frequently materialises in piano music of the period.

These specific problems all derived from the basic functional requirement of the piano etude: that it should present a systematic encoding of a particular keyboard technique while at the same time engendering a substantial or edifying musical process. Where the music fails to disclose organic substance and integrity (i.e. where it is purely mechanical, like an exercise), this failure is usually associated with one of the two shortcomings just outlined: weak, 'accompanimental' textures or infiltration with chromatic lines and harmonies that are functionally redundant. It remains for us to examine how the worthier composers contended with these peculiarly intractable problems in their efforts to write etudes that 'contrive a double debt to pay' to the arts of performance and composition alike.[25]

The first composer to achieve success in this respect was Cramer. His first etudes, and not those of Clementi, were the prototypes that established the etude as a distinct musical genre.[26] The *Eighty-four Studies* laid the groundwork, demonstrating through their thematic patterns, harmonic procedures and formal outlines various ways in which a satisfactory musical and technical balance could be accomplished. No. 21 (categorised by Schumann as an extension etude) is typical in that its figure is made to assume a wide variety of positions in the space of only twenty-two bars. During this brief time, non-harmonic auxiliary notes impart subtle character to the figuration and thence to the simple harmonic framework in which it is embedded. The result is an attractive, highly idiomatic, prelude-like miniature. It is pieces of this kind – incorporating clear structures, straightforward harmonies, consistent textures and regular phrase-lengths – that comprise the majority of the *Eighty-four Studies*. Most often, the structure involves a free binary form resembling the minuet sonata procedures described by Charles Rosen in *Sonata Forms*, with brief development of the figure and a shortened reprise in the B section.[27] This simple but flexible model suited the modest ends that Cramer required it to serve. As was later shown by Chopin, it could also be adapted to accommodate technical projects of a much more ambitious nature.

Cramer's major strengths can be seen in two particular aspects of his etude style that anticipate Chopin. One is the force with which his figures occasionally drive the musical ideas, generating vigorous harmonic and technical interactions with the changes in position (compare Examples 3a and 3b, the latter extracted

Example 3   (a) Cramer, *84 Studies*, No. 76, Bars 5–7

Ex. 3 (*cont.*)

(b) Chopin, Prelude Op. 28 No. 8, bars 24–5

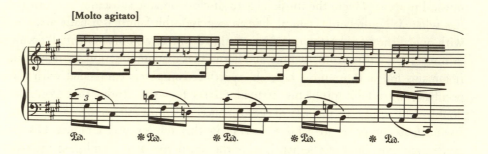

from one of Chopin's more etude-like preludes). The other relates to the musical background, the harmonic and motivic structure which remains when the figuration is removed. Czerny, in a remarkably perspicacious discussion of etudes in his *School of Practical Composition*, refers to this as 'the determinate idea' that should always form the basis of a well-written etude. He then quotes two 'harmonic skeletons' derived from Cramer's No. 31 and Chopin's Op. 10 No. 1, 'in order to illustrate the construction and the course of ideas of such pieces' (sections from both of these skeletons are quoted in Example 4). The Cramer etude, he says,

Example 4   (a) Cramer, *84 Studies*, No. 31, bars 17–21 ('ground-melody' from Czerny's *School of Practical Composition*, p. 91)

(b) Chopin, Op. 10 No. 1, bars 42–50 (ibid. p. 92)

'is built on a kind of Choral [i.e. chorale] melody, which is supported by a three or four-part harmony', while Chopin's is 'entirely built on chords, which, however, form a rhythmically disposed whole, modulate variously, and finally return again to the chords of the theme'.[28]

By means of these examples, Czerny appropriately draws attention to the large-scale harmonic structure of each work. The background shapes revealed by his reductions are in both cases cogent and audible, each retaining compatibility with the foreground figures in a way that those of, say, Kessler do not.[29] The overlay of figuration does not conceal or distort this cogency (what Czerny calls '*consequence* in the train of ideas'[30]). Instead, it simply translates it into idiomatic pianistic terms, thus allowing the music to exercise the fingers and the interpretative imagination of the performer simultaneously. The etudes work because this interaction works, successfully revealing the expressive substance by means of the natural techniques and resources of the medium.

There is an element of paradox here inasmuch as etudes that conform to these principles are intended to train the fingers by means of music, which is itself one of the principal objects of that training. This identity of ends and means has the conspicuous effect of imbuing piano etudes with a character which is uniquely dependent on the performance techniques enshrined in them: simple techniques will engender simple textures, technical difficulty will affect points of musical climax, limitations of physical endurance will restrict length, and so on. We might further speculate that the relatively uncomplicated technical substance of Cramer's etudes explains an ingenuous quality in the music itself, while the breadth, fluency and sensuousness of Chopin's extended musical paragraphs are direct products of their versatile, idiomatic and consummately manipulated figurations. Whether by design or intuition, both Cramer and Chopin tackled and resolved the etude paradox by establishing and maintaining in their etudes a delicate equilibrium between expressive style and technical content.

Of the other composers who wrestled with this problem, the most consistently successful were Berger and Moscheles. Something of the harmonic detail that distinguishes Berger's etudes (Op. 12 and Op. 22) can be sampled from the five-bar progression in Example 5a. Several features of this passage anticipate Chopin.

Example 5   (a) Berger, Op. 12 No. 1 bars 1–6 (reduced)

Ex. 5 (*cont.*)

(b) Chopin, Op. 10 No. 1, bars 1–9 (reduced)

In technical terms there is the extension of the figuration beyond the octave, as in Op. 10 No. 1 (Example 5b). Harmonically, we may compare the chromatic voice-leading (Berger, bars 1 and 3; Chopin, bars 3 to 5, 6 to 7 and 8 to 9) and the counterpointing of the accidental melody outlined by the top notes of the right hand against a powerful, quasi-melodic bass line deployed in left-hand octaves. The early introduction of chromatic harmony in both passages points to a procedure which was to become a hallmark of Chopin's mature style: the employment of chromatic chords at the structural level, with all the material consequences to tonic/dominant polarity and tonal horizons that such usage entails. The abrupt appearance of the mediant major in bar 5 of Example 5a illustrates how such chords can function as short-range harmonic goals. Three similar instances are shown in Examples 6a, b and c. The other two (Examples 6d and e) demonstrate large-scale harmonic effects derived from the same chord. In Op. 10 No. 1 the III#ʹ operates over a broad range of functions, marking off large segments of the music, enhancing the lead back to the reprise and even adopting a secondary harmonic family of its own (e.g. the $\frac{6\#}{4}$ on F in bars 22 and 64). Berger's handling of the chord is nowhere near as deft (his E major mostly connotes A minor harmony); and the overall harmonic structure of his etude lacks the inimitable finesse of Op. 10 No. 1. Nevertheless, Berger generally responded well to the special problems involved in writing etudes, particularly the need to reconcile complex

Example 6

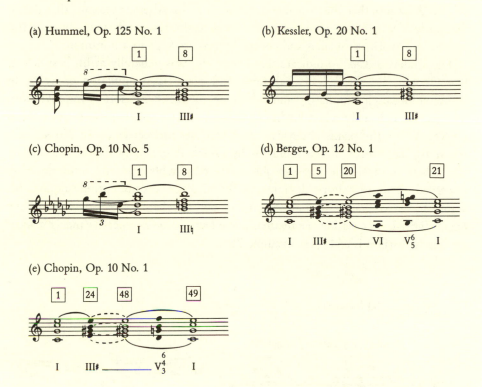

(a) Hummel, Op. 125 No. 1

(b) Kessler, Op. 20 No. 1

(c) Chopin, Op. 10 No. 5

(d) Berger, Op. 12 No. 1

(e) Chopin, Op. 10 No. 1

foreground harmony with a coherent background design. And by crafting his figures so as to be versatile he was usually able to make them – and the pianist – do useful work without vitiating the natural extension and development of his musical ideas.

A similar ability to make figurations and harmony work hand in hand distinguishes Moscheles's essays in the genre, particularly the *Studies for the Greater Perfection of Already Advanced Players*, Op. 70. These, as their title implies, encompass a more specialised and difficult technical scope than most of their precursors; Cramer's first etudes, by contrast, had ostensibly been 'calculated to facilitate the progress of *anyone* wishing to study the instrument' (as indicated on the title page to the first English edition of Op. 39; my emphasis). More ambitious techniques presuppose more intricate textures and more complex technical/harmonic interactions. Accordingly, one can see in the broad harmonic outlines of the Op. 70 Etudes how these interactions influence events on the large scale. In the very Brahmsian No. 5, for example, the chords that initiate harmonic digressions in the outer sections (see bars 5, 16 and 54) serve a dual purpose: they generate palpable foreground effects through varying degrees of dissonance (both chromatic and diatonic) while at the same time setting in motion harmonic developments at a deeper level.[31] By acting simultaneously on separate levels, these harmonics help to draw together the disparate mechanical and aesthetic functions that define the music of which they are an element. Once again, the study works because the interactions work; anomalies and contradictions are kept to a minimum.

The studies of Op. 70 indicate that Moscheles was generally at his best when, like Chopin, he allowed his harmonic and pianistic imagination to work in combination, each stimulating and enhancing the other in a sort of improvisatory interplay. It is usually when his harmonic sense falters (as in the C major section of No. 23) or the pianistic devices are themselves ineffective (as in No. 2) that the music falls short of the standards by which it generally invites assessment. But where the technical ideas are given free rein, where creative inhibitions are discarded, the results clearly demonstrate that Chopin was not entirely alone in his ability to derive poetic substance from the inert mechanism and materials of the piano. Indeed, on occasion the textures and effects of their respective pianistic ideas are barely distinguishable (see Example 7).

Example 7   (a) Moscheles, Op. 70 No. 9, bars 26–8

Ex. 7 (*cont.*)

(b) Chopin, *Nouvelles études*, No. 3, bars 49–54

Three other composers require brief consideration in the light of these issues. One is Steibelt, whose 1805 collection of fifty etudes included several techniques (such as octaves and unison passagework) that are not to be found in Cramer's Op. 39. Overall, this compilation is of an exceptional quality compared with Steibelt's other music, most of which has given him a reputation for charlatanism. Individually, the pieces exemplify how Cramer's original patterns could serve as models for clever imitation.

Maria Szymanowska's *Twenty Exercises and Preludes*[32] contain various anticipations of Chopin's figures and harmonic procedures. George Golos, in an article on 'Some Slavic predecessors of Chopin', remarks on the resemblance between the 'technical features' in Szymanowska's No. 1 and those of Chopin's Op. 10 No. 8.[33] More interesting are the respective harmonic outlines of these works (see Example 8), particularly where the harmony is in each case manœuvred back

Example 8   (a) Szymanowska, *Exercises and Preludes*, No. 1

(b) Chopin, Op. 10 No. 8

to F major by means of a chromatic twist (C♯–C♮). One should beware of exaggerating these similarities, however. Szymanowska's keyboard textures are too thin, her large-scale harmonic vision too restricted to permit the energy and intensity that we find in Chopin's etude. And nowhere does her music demonstrate the sure mastery of harmonic and technical resources that qualifies Chopin's most absorbing effects – the sensuous flush of colouristic harmony that presages the reprise, for instance, or the impeccable fioritura passagework of the coda.

A better demonstration of the expressive potential inherent in the tensions between style and technique is provided in another set of preludes and exercises, this time by J. H. Müller.[34] The near-complete obscurity which has befallen these works is not a just reflection on the originality and quality of Müller's ideas. No. 1, for instance, has an interesting harmonic basis and a figure which overlaps with the metrical units, creating incidental dissonances that characterise and enliven the foreground (see Example 9a). The latter device anticipates Chopin both

Example 9   (a) Müller, *Preludes and Exercises*, No. 1, bars 44–8

(b) Chopin, Op. 25 No. 11, bars 10–11

in tiny details (see Example 9b) and in the larger features that depend on the rhythmic layout of particular figures: in Chopin's Op. 10 No. 10, the non-alignment is repeatedly highlighted by the changes in phrasing and articulation, while in Op. 25 No. 12 it is subtly absorbed within an elastic arpeggio formula whose stretches and contractions govern phrase lengths, harmonic rhythm and even melodic germination.

Nearly all of Müller's *Preludes and Exercises* have some interesting feature. Evidence of an unusually sophisticated pianistic insight can be found in No. 6, for example, where the figuration generates powerful linear and rhythmic momentum. It can also be seen in the discreet, elegiac chromaticism of No. 12, which calls to mind Chopin's Op. 10 No. 6 in key and mood, and above all in the intricate, polyphonic blend of melody, figuration and bass that delineates the texture. One may legitimately conclude from the quality of the collection as a whole that Müller composed some of the most effective piano etudes of the first quarter of the century.

CONCLUSION: A SYNTHESIS OF STYLE AND TECHNIQUE

There remains one major influence on Chopin whom we have thus far failed to acknowledge in appropriate detail: J. S. Bach. Bach did not, of course, write piano etudes. He did compile a *Clavierübung*, though it would be folly to suggest that this monumental accumulation of Baroque keyboard forms falls into the 'exercise' category as defined above. His significance in this context is to be found not so much in his purportedly didactic works as in some of the more general features of his keyboard writing, most noticeably those represented in the preludes of the *Well-Tempered Clavier*.

Part of the explanation for the consistent quality of Chopin's etudes lay in his reluctance to let his musical thinking be trammelled by Classical precepts, particularly the kind of large-scale harmonic patterns appropriate to the sonata style. Instead he resorted to the processes that we find in many of Bach's preludes, utilising more detailed harmonic structures and more elaborate chromatic embroidery than was common in Classical forms. The result was the establishment of an essentially contrapuntal tension between the linear, horizontal aspects of the piano figures and the underlying harmonic ground-work. This largely accounts for the Bach connection, which critics have emphasised at both general and specific levels.[35] It also explains some of the obvious resemblances between Op. 10 No. 1 and the C major prelude in book one of the *Well-Tempered Clavier*.

Comparisons of these two works have yielded some interesting insights. Allen Forte and Steven Gilbert, for example, demonstrate how a 'strong resemblance' emerges from comparative analytical reduction of the kind prescribed by Czerny.

Both pieces are shown to be 'elaborated chorales', a conclusion which Czerny also anticipated in his description of the Cramer study.[36] A less sophisticated way of illustrating the resemblances is to exchange the figures and their respective harmonic skeletons. Leichtentritt has already displayed how Bach's figuration may be transcribed using Chopin's opening harmony (see Example 10a[37]); the device

Example 10   (a) Chopin, *'Praeludium* in C major for Klavier', bars 1–4
              (Chopin's harmonies with Bach's figuration)

(b) Bach, 'Etude in C major for pianoforte', bars 1–4
    (Bach's harmonies with Chopin's figuration)

also works the other way (see Example 10b). This somewhat facile illustration necessitates minor rearrangement of parts in each case; and neither figure settles entirely comfortably into its new setting. But the fact that it can be done at all makes the comparison legitimate: that two works written for different instruments and separated by a century of musical developments even suggest comparison at this level is remarkable.

Where they differ is in the relative weight assigned to the two main elements – figuration and harmony – and the incorporation by Chopin of an extra functional ingredient – technical difficulty. The performance of just one bar from each piece is sufficient to make clear their radically dissimilar technical and acoustic properties. This is not simply because they were conceived for different instruments. It is because in Bach's prelude the linear elements unfold through a figuration of secondary importance whereas in Chopin's etude, because it *is* an etude, it is the figuration (i.e. the technical element) that is realized through the harmonic structure. This is not to imply that in either case the harmony is merely an excuse for the figure or vice versa. It only indicates a difference of emphasis, and one can see this principally in the respective degrees of technical difficulty and chromaticism. The etude is more difficult and more chromatic because it needs to be so in order to make its technical points. We have already noted Chopin's exploitation of E major harmony to produce colour effects so strong that they assume large-scale implications; there is nothing in Bach's prelude to compare with chromaticism of this degree. It is by such means that Chopin stretches the tonal horizons of C major (along with the hand of the performer), thereby introducing harmonic contexts that in turn permit the necessary array of positions for his figure.

The sense in which the figuration drives the harmony can be registered particularly in the passage leading to the reprise (bars 41–48). Here, building on the forceful linear and harmonic impetus generated in bars 25–40, the figure begins to switch direction at the half-bar, simultaneously accelerating the harmonic rhythm until bar 45, where for the first time the perpetual motion is checked. Attention is thereupon focussed on the sudden chromatic shift and the blaze of E major harmony that intrudes just before the reprise. The passage is dependent on at least three interactions: modification of the figure by the addition of a kinaesthetic increment, which in turn yields intensified harmonic movement, thereby highlighting a passage of major structural import. All of this constitutes an explicit departure from the keyboard textures and harmonic perspectives of Bach's prelude; there we find nothing so precipitate, nothing so exuberantly 'romantic' as the powerful virtuoso rhetoric of Op. 10 No. 1.

A different link with Bach is suggested by Jim Samson, who relates the 'expressive semitonal part-movement' of Op. 10 No. 6 to the chromatic *Affekt* of music such as 'Betrachte meine Seel' from the St John Passion.[38] From a purely internal standpoint, however, the part-movement in Chopin's etude can be characterised as a larger reflection of semitonal movement in the figure, a decorative inner part that weaves an unbroken line from the shifting auxiliaries of bar 1 to the poignant Picardy third at the very end. This figure, or rather its integration with the various melodic and harmonic elements that interlace in the music, forms the basis of the complex technical requirements of the etude. It also functions as an effective binding agent, maintaining continuity of texture while playing a well-defined part in the expressive processes at the foreground level. But its influence seems to extend even further than this: its characteristic chromatic inflections appear, somehow, to induce the chromaticism at deeper levels, premising distant harmonic regions and continually tugging the harmony away from its diatonic base. This is not the kind of perception that admits of easy proofs and demonstrations, but there are nevertheless indications in the music that large-scale phenomena such as the E major harmony of bars 21–4 really do owe their origin to the linear contours and harmonic implications of the figure.

The chromatic element in the first bar (Example 11a) involves the semitonal

Example 11   Chopin, Op. 10 No. 6

Ex. 11 (*cont.*)

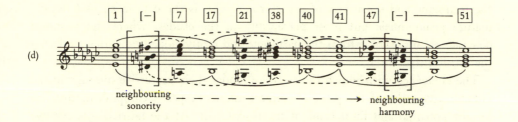

(d)

neighbouring
sonority _ _ _ _ _ _ _ _ _ _ → neighbouring
harmony

neighbours of the harmony note B♭. A melodic/harmonic reflection of this semi-tonal relationship (i.e. two notes resolving by semitone step onto one) appears in the cadences of bars 7–8, 15–16 and 47–51. In the last case, the II^{6b}–V$^{♮}$ alternations and the delayed resolution of the F♭–D♮ melodic line are repeatedly emphasised, the Neapolitan sixth even drawing in some neighbour relations of its own in bar 49. The broad harmonic structure of bars 17–40 produces a similar 'line' (see Example 11b). The figure is thus ingrained in the larger patterns of the musical fabric; it is more than just a motivic detail. And this is not all. The result of the auxiliary notes in bar 1 is a subtle harmonic iridescence that blurs the outlines of the E♭ minor tonic. What the listener hears, in fact, is the succession of sonorities shown in Example 11c: a quiet oscillation between a minor $\frac{5}{3}$ and a sort of secondary dominant $\frac{6}{5}$. The enharmonic transcription in Example 11c leads right into Example 11d, the fundamental harmonic outline: the chromatic haze surrounding the tonic in the first bar is itself drawn from the harmonic region of the flattened supertonic – it is the dominant of the Neapolitan. Now the listener can scarcely be expected to identify the middle sonority in Example 11c as V of II^{6b}. Even if that were feasible it would compromise or even contradict the superficial, colouristic function of the figure. But what the ear will definitely recognise in bar 1 is the presence of what may be termed a 'neighbouring sonority' generated by the auxiliary notes. The figure thus acts as a delicate anticipation of the kind of neighbouring harmonies (i.e. harmonies having a Neapolitan association with the tonic) which will subsequently be heard to characterise the music at all functional levels including the background.

    The various manifestations of this interaction between superficial aspects of a figuration and the kind of large-scale processes illustrated in Example 11d are fundamental to an understanding of how Chopin resolved the etude problem. They point to methods and procedures that are integral to his style. And they ultimately distinguish his etudes from those of even his worthier contemporaries. It is not that his etudes evince a deeper unity than those other works, but rather that their expressive language is so much richer, allowing both a succinctness and a breadth that were unachievable within the confines of more attenuated idioms. The refinement that characterises the creative workmanship of Op. 10 No. 6 finds its ultimate reflection in the demands such compositions make on the technique and sensitivity of a performer. This is the case in all of Chopin's mature piano music but most perceptibly in the etudes, where the technical demands are inseparable from the harmonic and motivic operations that underpin the musical structures.

The eloquence with which these etudes render their expressive message in the difficult vernacular of the piano's technical idioms bespeaks Chopin's unique feel for the potential and limitations of the instrument. At the heart of his creative method one can discern a universal principle or process, a stylistic touchstone that imparts life and vibrancy to the pianistic ideas. Gerald Abraham isolated one such principle, that of 'turning to account the inherent limitations of the human hand'. Alan Walker subsequently defined this as 'the creative principle of identity between idea and medium'.[39] I would call it the synthesis of musical style and performance technique, which we can perceive in the etudes as an exquisite coalescence of abstract creative impulses and the concrete technical apparatus whereby they are articulated. It is this principle which controls and rationalises the complex interactions that give life to Chopin's piano music. And seldom is its operation so palpable as in the musical/technical reciprocity of the F major Etude, Op. 25 No. 3.

This work presents a striking tonal paradigm which we shall endeavour to interpret shortly. First, however, one should note the extraordinary technical detail built into the figuration, its harmonic pliancy and the careful attention paid to matters of touch, phrasing, dynamics and register. The figure outlines a theme which appears in three statements linked by transition passages and ending with a coda. The first statement is immediately repeated with the figuration modified to include mordent-like demisemiquavers; these are used again six bars from the end as a means of breaking up the figure prior to its sylphine disintegration in bar 69. The chromatic transitional passages (bars 17–28 and 37–48) incorporate various permutations of the figure, using suspensions, sevenths, etc. and necessitating corresponding changes in the extension and placement of both hands. The coda (bars 56–72) begins with a retrospective chromatic flourish which descends through two octaves from a high register, adding many new positions to those already covered.

All this is to be expected in a technically beneficial, musically stimulating etude. What is unusual about this one is that the middle statement of the theme is in B major. In technical terms this can be explained as a transposition from white keys to black keys and the radically new hand positions this entails; the addition and elimination of the black notes takes place systematically in the adjacent transition passages. Musically, the effect is one of vivid contrast with the background tonality. And structurally, the B major statement forms the axis of an evident symmetrical pattern, the harmonic progress of the second half being a retrograde image of the first. This is what Leichtentritt means when he speaks of the work's 'peculiar tonal geometry'.[40]

What makes this scheme peculiar is not the foreignness of B major. Szymanowska had resorted to similarly distant 'keys' to establish new positions (as in Nos. 12 and 18 of the *Twenty Exercises and Preludes*); so had Kessler (the Eb minor etude in his Op. 20 has a short central passage in E major). Nor is it the symmetrical pattern, which unfolds naturally and convincingly. The problem lies in regarding the B major statement as a tonal event (that is to say, as resulting from a modulation in the Classical sense) and thus as a central support of the total structure. This interpretation raises an anomaly: why is music of such apparent levity and good humour presented through a structure so contrived, so obviously disingenuous? In other words, how are the form and substance of the work compatible? Where, indeed, lies the synthesis here?

A satisfactory performance of the piece is all that is required to demonstrate the basic flaw in these questions. The B major passage is not an architectural pillar supporting a massive tonal arch. It is structural embroidery, a spontaneous inter-lude, an ornamental harmonic arabesque which conjoins the surrounding chro-maticism while at the same time corroborating the characteristic playfulness of the whole. Felix Salzer, in a detailed analysis of the piece, explains it thus:

> It is not at all characteristic for Chopin to base an entire work on what one is inclined to call a clever tone game: 'how to get from F major to B major and back by means of a retrograde progression'. It would, however, be entirely within his conception of tonal organization to have the B-major passage act as a seeming or simulated goal.[41]

Salzer relies on a series of Schenkerian graphs to support this argument, but the gist of his analysis can be gleaned from his structural diagram:

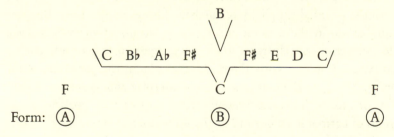

This diagram, he claims, displays the obvious symmetries of the work in their proper hierarchical order. The B major statement is to be seen as a foreground interruption of the bass progression C, Bb, Ab etc. (bars 17–48) that extends, or 'prolongs', C major harmony throughout the entire middle section of the overall ternary structure.[42]

One need not go into the fine details of this analysis to appreciate the validity of Salzer's main point. The recognition of B major as a simulated tonality is essential to any meaningful interpretation of the various musical and technical signals encoded at the musical surface. For example, the playful lingering on different dominants in bars 21–8, followed by the facetious *ritenuto* of bar 28 and the sudden *a tempo*, dynamic surge and boisterous syncopations of bar 29, make no sense as the indicators of a genuine, full-blown recapitulation. On the contrary, these surface gestures tell us that this is a false reprise, a humorously deceptive interruption of the protracted harmonic sequence that constitutes the rest of the middle section. Its very humour is what gives the true reprise its 'overpowering, jubilant logic'.[43] But if the same passage is regarded as an authentic tonal/structural goal, its spontaneity vanishes, the true reprise becomes academic, the character and details of the piano writing are made anomalous, and all of the work's 'modulations frappantes'[44] assume the function of prosaic components in Salzer's 'clever tone game'.

The point is elusive and easily laboured, but it is important enough to warrant reiteration: the formidable integration of style and technique that distinguishes these etudes is attributable above all to a dynamic fusion of separate creative impulses. For it was the discipline of writing etudes that enabled Chopin's prolific musical imagination to discover its ideal expressive outlet in a piano technique of unimpeachable opulence. Chopin's particular qualities as both composer and pianist led him, in the etudes, to a creative synthesis that had eluded most of his predecessors. The synthesis reveals itself in many forms, but its result is invariably the same: an enrichment of the expressive message and enhancement of the pianistic substance.

On the large scale we can register its most powerful effects in the final three etudes of Op. 25, wherein expansive formal conceptions and plangent technical resources combine to produce piano music of awesome cogency (though one might remark on the essential simplicity of the basic figures in all three). But it is also enlightening to see in the musical and technical details of all twenty-seven studies how the interactions are always at work, always germinating or influencing the foreground events. One can sense them, for example, in the harmonic/linear tensions of Op. 10 No. 2, or the complex motivic interplay and aggressive rhythmic articulation of No. 4. They are present in the toccata-like repetitions and sudden explosions of harmonic colour in No. 7; in the discreet traces of accidental melody in the left-hand figure of No. 9; in the immaculate spacing, voice-leading and chromatic detail of the arpeggio figures in No. 11. Interactions are also at work in the rhythmic patterns that condition the musical processes throughout Op. 10 No. 10 (with its numerous variations in touch and phrasing), in Op. 25 No. 2 (a study in combined cross-rhythm and syncopation, producing perpetual motion of an extraordinary 'fluidité'[45]), in Op. 25 No. 4 (restless, percussive syncopation, plus a minefield of secondary technical problems) and in the poly-rhythms of the *Nouvelles études* in F minor and A♭.

One might remark at length on countless other features that demonstrate this cross-fertilisation between technique and idea: the incidental harmonic sparkle and enhanced linear textures that arise from the double notes of Op. 25 Nos. 6 and 8, for example; or the use of the sustaining pedal to elicit impressionistic waves of sonority from the figuration of No. 1; or the elegiac resonance and improvisatory fioritura of the left-hand cantilena in No. 7; or the flighty skips and reversals that complicate the figuration of the 'Butterfly' etude. But perhaps nowhere is there a greater wealth of technical detail and development than in No. 5. In the contrasting middle section of this piece we encounter a typical example of Chopin's ability to transform a pianistic effect into musical substance of transcendent beauty. The expressive richness with which he manipulates the three-tiered texture featured here (figuration-melody-bass, the melody distributed between the hands) is a world apart from the shallow (though resplendent) trickery to which Thalberg reduced it in his operatic fantasies. And as if still further evidence were needed of his exceptional pianistic insight, Chopin provides it at the end: the deep E, sounded with the dampers raised in the final bar, sets all of its sympathetic overtones resonating throughout the instrument, even before they are actually picked out one by one in free time and sustained by the pedal for the duration of their natural decay. Such adroit, clear-sighted exploitation of the special acoustic qualities of the piano was absolutely without precedent. It is this uncanny pianistic intuition and the creative uses to which Chopin put it that explain his success as a composer of etudes. This is the sense in which his etudes stand alone.

Chopin's final contributions to the repertory were the three *Nouvelles études*, written for the *Méthode des méthodes*.[46] This initial context lends a somewhat ironic tinge to the epithet 'new', however. The style and technical functions of the *Nouvelles études* have virtually nothing in common with those of the other works printed in the second volume of the *Méthode*. Side by side with the concert studies contributed by Liszt, Thalberg and Henselt, these elegant, unaffected etudes seem like anachronisms, beguilingly poetic samples of a musical type that was to be transformed almost beyond recognition by the peremptory requirements of transcendental virtuosity. As the subsequent development of the piano etude makes clear, Chopin's last instructional keyboard works are also among the final examples of the genre in its pristine form.

JOHN RINK

Chopin's early music has attracted surprisingly little attention in the scholarly literature on the composer, notwithstanding its vital role in the evolution of his mature style. This comparative neglect can be attributed to certain fundamental problems surrounding the works composed in Warsaw before November 1830 (when Chopin left Poland to embark on his career as a composer-pianist) and in Vienna and Paris in 1830–2. Only a small number of autograph manuscripts from before 1830 survive, making it difficult to ensure the accuracy of modern editions, to determine the music's exact chronology,[1] and to draw firm conclusions as to how Chopin's style gradually took shape. Furthermore, an underlying critical bias in many assessments of the early works inhibits objective evaluation of their significant contribution to Chopin's stylistic development. Most commentators[2] tend to stress the early repertoire's inferior status in comparison with the composer's mature works and thus fail to view music from his 'apprenticeship' on its own terms, implicitly succumbing to notions of artistic 'progress' which are untenable from both analytical and historiological points of view.

This is not to say that the early pieces are altogether without weaknesses. Many works from the Warsaw period suffer from a somewhat rigid 'formal' conception, whereby more or less independent, closed sections were simply juxtaposed to form the whole, rather like separate beads on a string. Imperfect proportions between sections, imbalanced periodic structures, endless sequential passagework and over-abundant ornamentation in the large-scale virtuosic compositions further inhibit musical flow, while exact recapitulation in the smaller genres, most of which follow a ternary formal plan, has a similarly stultifying effect, particularly in the early solo polonaises, where section A of the typical ABA CDC ABA form is heard six times in all (taking repeat signs into account).

As Chopin matured as a composer, he gradually learnt to overcome these weaknesses and to exploit in full the many positive stylistic attributes of the Warsaw pieces (for instance, the poetic lyricism of the slow movements from the concertos and the introductions to other works with orchestra). One of the most important

78

changes in the compositions of the late 1820s and early 1830s was a much greater awareness of tonal architecture as a source of large-scale coherence in his music. Towards the end of the 1820s Chopin discovered how to transcend the formal conception characteristic of earlier repertoire by a subtle use of tonal structure, linking a work's sections through all-encompassing harmonic progressions and structural voice-leading which generate a sense of forward impulse and momentum that was largely lacking in Warsaw-period compositions.

Chopin's comments on musical 'logic' as related by Eugène Delacroix in a well-known journal entry[3] from April 1849 – about six months before the composer's death – highlight his sensitivity to tonal architecture and offer a rare glimpse into how his works were conceived. It is fascinating to observe in particular Chopin's belief in 'eternal principles' and 'higher laws' of composition, the importance he attached to counterpoint in determining the correct succession – the 'necessary course' – of a work's harmonies and his contention that musical 'logic', 'reason' and 'consistency' equally derive from counterpoint. One can also see that Chopin's music was conceived not 'by chance', but with a conscious awareness of the overall organisation: the mature works at least appear to have had as their starting-point the structural foundation of the music rather than 'picturesque externals'.

Chopin's attention to tonal architecture in his mature works, which has been noted by many analysts and which inspired the Austrian theorist Heinrich Schenker to admit Chopin to his exclusive pantheon of great 'German' composers,[4] means that his music, '. . .like Beethoven's, responds to Schenker's [analytical] methods with peculiar aptness. Not only is harmony one of the principal shaping elements in much of his music, but a distinction between structural and "contrapuntal" harmonies is central to his musical thought.'[5]

Although analysis of a piece's tonal foundation in isolation – that is, without reference to other aspects of structure – can be of limited value (particularly when, as in Chopin's mature compositions, tonal architecture works in conjunction with a number of parameters – e.g. rhythm, dynamics, register, themes, motives and phrase and periodic structures – to create the overall expressive effect), in the case of Chopin's early music focusing specifically on tonal structure poses few if any methodological problems. On the contrary, it is essential to single out this element of his style when looking at works from the Warsaw period, for it experienced more fundamental change in the late 1820s than any other feature of the early repertoire, becoming one of the central generative forces in Chopin's music precisely at this stage of his stylistic development. The discussion that follows therefore concentrates on the increasingly important role of tonal architecture in Chopin's emerging compositional style, although reference to other aspects of the music will of course be made when appropriate.[6]

THE WARSAW PERIOD: 1817–30

The music composed by Chopin during his student years in Warsaw falls into three broad categories:

a. works based on the sonata principle (C minor Sonata, Op. 4; G minor Trio, Op. 8; E minor Concerto, Op. 11; and F minor Concerto, Op. 21);
b. other large-scale 'brilliant' compositions (C minor Rondo, Op. 1; Variations on 'Là ci darem la mano', Op. 2; *Polonaise brillante*, Op. 3; *Rondo à la mazur*, Op. 5; *Fantasy on Polish Airs*, Op. 13; *Rondo à la krakowiak*, Op. 14; Eb major Rondo, Op. 16; C major Rondo, Op. 73; and Variations on 'Der Schweizerbub'); and
c. smaller genres (polonaises, mazurkas, waltzes, écossaises, nocturnes, songs, etc.).[7]

The four pieces in the first group have inspired more criticism than all the others combined, particularly the concertos (the only works from this period with an established place in modern concert repertory). Phrases such as 'weakness of key-sense', 'suicidal plan', 'eccentric' structure and 'insecure grasp of the significance and power of tonal architecture' crop up in the literature[8] in response to the highly unorthodox key relationships in all four sonata-form compositions. The first movements of Op. 4 and Op. 8 have mono-tonal expositions, while in Op. 11 the second theme is initially presented in the tonic major rather than the mediant. Recapitulation in each work stresses harmonies other than the tonic (in opposition to the role of 'recapitulation as resolution'[9] implicit in the Classical sonata): Op. 4's reprise starts in Bb minor, not C minor; the repeated second subject appears in v and III in Op. 8 and Op. 11 respectively; and similarly in Op. 21 the second group fails to return in the tonic. Jim Samson comments that

> The uneasiness one feels about all these tonal schemes is a result not of their flexibility – the Classical masters had already demonstrated this in large measure – nor even their violation of a fundamental principle of sonata thought, the tonal synthesis which results when material originally outside the tonic is brought within its fold. It comes rather from a failure to relate detail to whole. Ironically, Chopin's distance from the Austro-German tradition is never clearer than when he turns his hand to the formal archetypes most closely associated with that tradition, and this is apparent even in these early essays in extended forms. As yet, however, he had not learnt to *use* that distance to creative ends.[10]

Although the relation between detail and whole is perhaps just as strained in other large-scale compositions from the Warsaw period (i.e. those in group b above), these works have rather more successful – if equally idiosyncratic – tonal designs, indicating that Chopin felt greater confidence composing this music than he did writing works in sonata form.[11] His first Rondo, published in 1825 as

Op. 1, nevertheless lacks the 'spontaneous flow'[12] of certain contemporaneous dance pieces. Composed of several thematic blocks 'loosely strung together'[13] with transitions, the work is based on an unorthodox (but entirely logical) tonal scheme divided into two phases: first a progression by major third/diminished fourth from C minor (theme A) through E major (theme B – bars 65ff.) and Ab (theme C – 130ff.) back to C minor for the second statement of theme A (158ff.); then a motion from the tonic to its harmonic 'neighbour' Db major (themes D and B – 213ff. and 275ff. respectively) and back for theme A's final appearance (318ff.). Virtuosic passagework outlining sequential patterns connects these harmonic 'pillars'. As in the Sonata, Trio and concertos, the Rondo's main weakness lies not so much in its underlying structure *per se* (despite its deviation from Classical architectonic norms) as in the 'inorganic' nature of the material connecting the structural 'pillars': stability is greatly undermined by all the unrelated music. To make these criticisms however is not to deny the importance of the work as Chopin's first extended composition, nor the exuberance and appeal of some of the figuration; it is principally when viewed in the context of more mature music that the Rondo appears so seriously flawed.

Although based on a similar succession of themes and transitions, the *Rondo à la mazur*, Op. 5, composed in 1826–7, unfolds in an altogether more natural manner, both within and between sections. Frederick Niecks writes that in this piece '. . .the individuality of Chopin and with it his nationality begin to reveal themselves unmistakably. Who could fail to recognise him in the peculiar sweet and persuasive flows of sound, and the serpent-like winding of the melodic outline, the wide-spread chords, the chromatic progressions, the dissolving of the harmonies and the linking of their constituent parts!'[14] The Rondo has a tonal plan like that of several large-scale 'brilliant' compositions from the Warsaw period (Opp. 16 and 73, for instance), i.e. two overlapping symmetrical progressions (I–IV–I–V–I) focussed on the tonic harmony, which is stated each time the principal theme returns. Chopin highlights the second and third tonic 'pillars' in Op. 5 by placing considerably more elaborate transitions before them, and he ex-

Example 1 *Rondo à la mazur*, Op. 5, structure of cadential expansion, bars 431-49

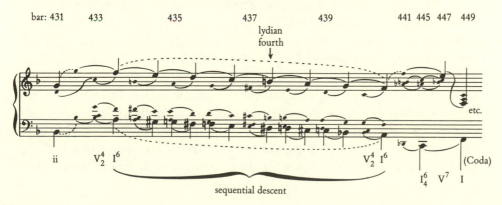

tends the final statement of theme A in bars 101ff. – thus preparing for the exciting coda that concludes the piece – by means of an ingenious sequential descent outlining an F major scale with sharpened fourth, B♮, in a subtle reference to the lydian mode characteristic of the folk mazurka. (See Example 1.) It is possible that the tonal plan typical of most of his contemporaneous mazurkas – I–IV–I – directly inspired the rather more balanced structure in this work; furthermore, the fact that Op. 5 is tighter in construction than the diffuse Op. 1 can be explained at least in part by Chopin's characteristic assimilation of folkloristic elements into the structure of his mazurkas (here, a rondo *à la mazur*), which, as we shall see, was greatly to enhance the 'organic' quality of his music in general.

In the *Rondo à la krakowiak*, Op. 14, for piano and orchestra, written in 1828, Chopin relates thematic and transitional passages even more closely than in Op. 5, stressing not only the keys of the five thematic statements (I–vi–I–ii–I) but also subsidiary harmonies in the transitions which enable the underlying structural progression to flow more smoothly.[15] Op. 14 made a very favourable impression during Chopin's 1829 visit to Vienna, and it is interesting to consider why the work has passed into virtual obscurity, at least relative to the concertos. Although 'the rondo was to the young Chopin an ever present help in time of structural trouble',[16] the imposition of rondo form – and indeed any formal paradigm – on his ideas appears in fact to have thwarted his ability to create spontaneous-sounding music, and furthermore to achieve large-scale coherence and connection. The *Rondo à la krakowiak* was certainly less rigidly conceived than Opp. 1 and 5, but a comparison of the main body of the work with its considerably freer introduction, which Chopin wrote without an inhibiting predetermined formal plan and which thus represents a more natural outpouring of his ideas (he described it himself as 'original'),[17] confirms that the composer's musical language was more effectively expressed in unique structures designed for a particular compositional purpose than in inherited formal archetypes.

Much the same impression is gained from the Variations on 'Là ci darem la mano', Op. 2 (1827–8), in which Chopin lavishes special attention on music not directly based on the theme, i.e. the introduction, the *minore* variation and the finale. The most original and attractive writing is once again in the introduction, which ends with a strikingly beautiful improvisatory passage and cadenza. The theme and six variations follow, then a bravura finale, where the soloist is put through his paces in a parade of virtuoso pyrotechnics arranged in self-contained sections – many only one or two bars in length – defined by cadences and changes in figuration. Although largely a pastiche of pianistic clichés, the finale has one extended passage – bars 51–71 – of interest for its extraordinary harmonic structure, which aptly demonstrates Chopin's command of hierarchical structures and in particular his use of sequences at this stage in his 'apprenticeship'. The upper system in Example 2 represents the relatively straightforward progression

Example 2   Variations on 'Là ci darem la mano', Op. 2, finale, bars 51–71: tonal structure and circle-of-fifths elaboration

on which the twenty-one bars are based: I–iv^6–I$^6_4$–V–I. Within this outline Chopin inserts a circle-of-fifths sequence (shown in the lower system), which is then embellished with subsidiary harmonic progressions in thirds (cf. the score). Emphasis is given to the circle-of-fifths 'pillars' by extending each one for an entire bar, thus ensuring their prominence over the interpolated ascents in thirds. Chopin's control of the structural hierarchy is remarkable: although it was not until much later that he learnt to extend hierarchical structures like this over entire works, embracing huge spans in a single compositional gesture, this twenty-one-bar passage nevertheless reveals great skill in the elaboration of a simple structural progression with complex foreground harmony, which, unlike the sequential passagework in many of his contemporary pieces, sounds coherent precisely because of this solid foundation.

It is hardly surprising that the extended virtuosic works from the Warsaw period fostered Chopin's control of structure to a lesser extent than his contemporaneous dances and nocturnes, for these pieces had far more manageable proportions than the rondos, variation sets and concertos. As noted above, Chopin generally relied on a ternary design in the three principal dance genres – polonaises, mazurkas and waltzes – he was writing at the time, whereby a trio section appears between two outer wings which usually are based on a ternary idea themselves. The three main sections – polonaise–trio–polonaise, etc. – outline a symmetrical harmonic progression (e.g. I–IV–I, I–vi–I, i–III–i, i–I–i – see Example 3) which

Example 3   Hypothetical symmetrical tonal structures

harmony: I - - IV - - I   I - - vi - - - I   i - - -III- - i   i - - -I- - - i

section: Ⓐ Ⓑ Ⓐ   Ⓐ Ⓑ Ⓐ   Ⓐ Ⓑ Ⓐ   Ⓐ Ⓑ Ⓐ

spans the entire piece and thus functions as an all-embracing tonal plan. Progressions such as these are also realised by subsidiary sections within the main ones. For instance the first extant mazurka, the G major from 1825–6 (which was improvised at a dance evening and later written down), has this tonal outline:

Tonal foundation: I-----------------------IV------------------------I
Subsidiary structure: I----III$^{\#3}$----I
Section: A   B   A   C (= trio)   A

while the G♭ major Polonaise (1829) follows a somewhat more complex plan:

Tonal foundation: I-----------------------vi------------------------I
Subsidiary structures: I---III$^{\natural3}$---I   vi---III/vi---vi   I---III$^{\natural3}$---I
                                                  (= I)
Section: A B A   C   D   C   A   B   A.

Solid tonal frameworks such as these helped Chopin relate detail and whole in the dance pieces rather more successfully than in extended compositions from the period, although some of the polonaises do strain under the weight of 'top-heavy' virtuosic ornamentation – e.g. wide leaps, arpeggios, trills and varied rhythms – which tends to distort the music, particularly the phrase structure, which is 'stretched' from the four-square patterns typical of the dance in order to accommodate the ornate figuration. Like most of the mazurkas and waltzes from before 1830, the early polonaises suffer from the literal approach to recapitulation described above: nearly all end with the ABA section repeated note for note. Exact recapitulation not only limits variety and interest, but also tends to dissipate momentum generated by closure of the symmetrical structural progression when the tonic key returns.

Despite these weaknesses, however, the early polonaises were uniquely important in Chopin's stylistic development, for they allowed him to refine a hallmark of his mature music – the art of embellishment – by requiring elaborate ornamentation while at the same time providing the structural security of tonal frameworks like those shown above. A passage from the B♭ major Polonaise, Op. 71 No. 2, reveals Chopin's reliance on simple underlying structures even when the music appears complicated on the surface. Abraham describes it as 'a sort of rudimentary development section', the 'crown' of the structural arch – ABA CDC ABA – on which the work as a whole is built.[18] Starting in the dominant of G minor (i.e. vi, the key of the trio), Chopin moves rapidly through the circle of fifths – as shown in Example 4: G[7], then C[♭7] and F[♭7], whereupon an implied

Example 4   Polonaise in B♭, Op. 71 No. 2, section D: elaboration of structural progression

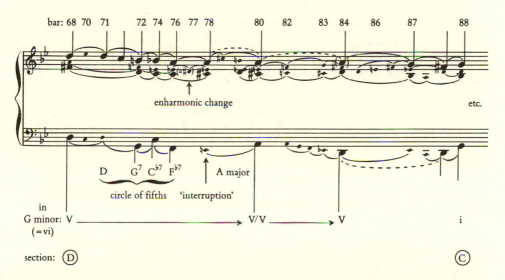

enharmonic change in bar 77 suddenly catapults the music towards A major (bars 78–81). Paul Hamburger calls the next eight bars 'a kind of bridge-passage peculiar to Chopin's polonaises, in which a bass and treble, approaching or receding from each other in regular contrary motion, form sequences that carry a modulatory process to its inevitable goal',[19] that is, V of G minor, leading into the reprise of section C. Although initially section D's harmonic structure sounds highly complex – how does the A major interruption fit in? – Chopin ensures its comprehensibility by means of the underlying progression at a remote level from D major through A major back to D major (i.e. V–V/V–V in G minor), in which A major functions not as an interruption but indeed as the pivotal harmony. All other harmonies serve to embellish this structural foundation.

Although in comparison with the polonaises and extended works from the Warsaw period the waltzes and mazurkas sound rather simplistic, their relative lack of complication greatly facilitated the development of Chopin's 'organic' compositional technique. The mazurkas were particularly important in this respect (as noted earlier), for Chopin attempted to assimilate typical features of the folk mazurka such as lydian fourths and grace-note figures into the tonal structure of these works. For instance, in the F major Mazurka, Op. 68 No. 3, the harmonic progression spanning the first three sections – A, B and A – articulates an auxiliary motion F–E–F in the treble, which Chopin restates in miniature as part of the distinctly 'modal' melody in the trio (see Example 5). The e^3 in bars 37–43 func-

Example 5   Mazurka in F, Op. 68 No. 3
        (a) tonal structure of bars 1–32

        (b) trio, bars 37–8

* Denotes lydian fourth in B♭ major

tions as the lydian fourth in B♭ major (i.e. IV); this, along with the characteristic accents, drone bass and melodic contour, gives the trio its 'authentic' flavour.

A more highly developed 'organic' technique is also evident in the E minor Nocturne, Op. 72 No. 1, which, written between 1828 and 1830, is among the most stylistically advanced pieces from the Warsaw period. Here Chopin draws the structural hierarchy together into a closely-knit whole, deriving the right-hand melody and certain bass progressions from the tonal foundation, and the left-hand accompaniment figure from the melody (see Example 6). Furthermore, as Samson comments,

Example 6   Nocturne in E minor, Op. 72 No. 1

(a) tonal structure

(b) right-hand melody, bars 2–4, and left-hand accompaniment figure, bar 1 *et seq*.

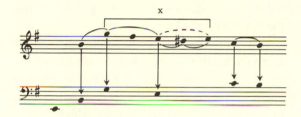

(c) bass line, bars 1–4

. . . there are indications here of a new approach to melody and ornamentation. The successive ornamental variations of the opening idea are less concerned to dress it with fancy frills than to enhance and intensify its expressive qualities and to reveal it in constantly changing lights. The ornamentation becomes in short integral to the melody.[20]

THE VIENNA AND EARLY PARIS PERIOD: 1830–32

Chopin's departure from Warsaw in November 1830 had a profound effect on his stylistic development: works from late 1830 onwards tend to be considerably more sophisticated than earlier pieces and much closer to the style of his mature music. Prolonged separation from Poland and his family at a time of great political upheaval no doubt caused some of the changes in the compositions of this period:

in Samson's words, ' ... it seems possible that the added depth and richness of the works whose inception dates from his year in Vienna, together with their tragic, passionate tone, reflect at least in part a new commitment to express Poland's tragedy in his music'.[21] Other factors included Chopin's exposure to more cosmopolitan musical influences in Vienna, his frustrating lack of success as a performer there (which hastened his disillusionment with the career of virtuoso pianist and therefore with music in the 'brilliant' style) and the greater amount of time devoted to composing, given his virtual inactivity as a performer.

While in Vienna Chopin wrote all but two of the mazurkas published as Opp. 6 and 7, many of the Op. 10 Etudes, the *Grande Polonaise brillante* (published with the *Andante spianato* in 1836 as Op. 22) and possibly the E♭ major Waltz, Op. 18. The Op. 9 Nocturnes and Op. 15 Nos. 1 and 2 were also composed, at least in part, during his stay in Vienna, although it was only after reaching Paris in September 1831 that he completed them, along with the Rondo Op. 16 (which had been started in Warsaw) and the remaining etudes of Op. 10.

Perhaps the most significant development brought about by Chopin's eight months in Vienna was a new sensitivity to the 'structural momentum' of his music, which he learnt to maximise by using more 'dynamic' harmonic progressions as remote tonal structures. Whereas earlier compositions tend to have closed, symmetrical harmonic foundations (such as I–IV–I and i–III–i) which lack a strong sense of goal-directed motion and therefore endow the music with only limited forward impulse, most of the repertoire from the later period is based on large-scale cadential progressions in the background, among them i→III→V→i (also, I→III$^{\sharp3}$→V→I and I→iii→V→I); I→IV→V→I (i→iv→V→i and i→IV$^{\sharp3}$→V→i) and i→$^{\flat}$II^6→V→i (i→ii^7→V→i). (See Example 7.) In each of

Example 7   Hypothetical 'dynamic' tonal structures

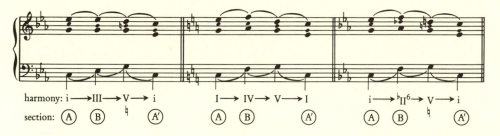

these, the tonic is followed by a subsidiary harmony – mediant, subdominant or supertonic – which resolves, usually after extensive elaboration and prolongation, to the first of two harmonic goals, V. The tonic is restored thereafter, in most cases at the start of the recapitulation. These more comprehensive progressions unite all the sections of a work into a single gesture directed towards long-range resolution of V to I, creating an underlying momentum that is largely absent from earlier music. It is fascinating to observe the gradual appearance of these progressions and Chopin's increasing exploitation of structural momentum in repertoire written after 1830: for instance in Op. 7 Nos. 3 and 4, the middle section of Op. 22, Op. 9 Nos. 2 and 3, Op. 15 No. 2 and, above all, the Op. 10 Etudes, where the arrival on V after the subsidiary harmony often results in a monumental climax. By the end of the Vienna and early Paris period, 'dynamic' progressions like these had become a well-established feature of Chopin's style: fully mature works such as the C♯ minor Scherzo, Op. 39, the Barcarolle, Op. 60, and the *Polonaise-fantaisie*, Op. 61, have tonal foundations based on such progressions.

Greater structural momentum in the music of the early 1830s also results from a new approach to recapitulation and closure that was foreshadowed in five 'brilliant' works from the earlier period – Op. 3, Op. 5, Op. 13, Op. 73 and the E minor Waltz – in which Chopin transcends the structural weaknesses inherent in other early compositions with literal recapitulations. By expanding and elaborating the 'final' cadence (that is, the cadence just before the start of the coda) in each of these five works, Chopin emphasises completion of the tonal structure spanning the main body of the piece (to which the coda functions literally as a 'tail'), differentiating the last statement of the recurrent A section from earlier ones and, more importantly, generating momentum towards closure.[22]

Assimilation of this feature from the 'brilliant' style into Chopin's mature music can be observed in the nocturnes and etudes of the Vienna and early Paris period and to a lesser extent in Op. 18 and several mazurkas from Op. 6 and Op. 7. By avoiding exact recapitulation in these works, Chopin achieves greater variety and interest than in earlier pieces based on a strict da capo principle. His subtle use of phrase structure to highlight the underlying tonal foundation of a work is particularly noteworthy. In these more sophisticated compositions (especially the nocturnes and etudes), he deviates from four- and eight-bar phrase patterns at precisely the most important point in the tonal plan: the approach to the final tonic harmony in the overall structure, i.e. at the close of the main body of the work. Such agogic deviations in phrase units, which usually involve an extension of the four- or eight-bar 'hypermeasure',[23] come to have tremendous expressive power in the music of this period, as they temporarily withhold closure in the recapitulated material and therefore undermine expectations formed during the first section of the work, where closure is normally achieved within a 'regular' phrase structure. The stress given to these extensions is made all the more prominent when Chopin also abbreviates the recapitulated material, as in most of the Op. 10 Etudes and some of the nocturnes, in which the third section of the ABA' form typical of these works is considerably shorter than its counterpart earlier in the piece, even with the extension of the concluding phrase.

Several mazurkas from the Vienna/early Paris period show signs of Chopin's new approach to recapitulation and closure, among them Op. 7 No. 4, which exists in two versions. The earlier of the two (dated 1824 by Wilhelm Kolberg, but undoubtedly from much later)[24] has the form |: A :|BA CCD A, whereas in the second, published, version the reprise is rather more complex: the repetition of A (bars 37–40) is followed by a varied statement with rests and a fermata added after the first-inversion subdominant in bar 43 to enhance the sense of closure.[25] Even more remarkable is the Mazurka's tonal structure (see Example 8

Example 8   Mazurka in A♭, Op. 7 No. 4: 'dynamic' tonal foundation with subsidiary progressions

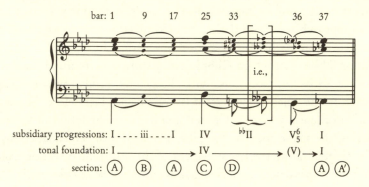

and the diagram below), which is based on an innovative 'dynamic' progression whereby the trio flows directly into the reprise.

Tonal foundation:	I		IV	(V)	I
Subsidiary progressions:	I----iii--I		IV	♭♭II vii♭⁷ (=V⁶₅)	I
Section:	A B A		C	D	A A'.

From the subdominant harmony of bars 25–32, Chopin moves not to the tonic (as he would have in earlier mazurkas, thus completing a symmetrical I–IV–I structure at once) but to A major – i.e. the enharmonically altered Neapolitan – after which a diminished chord on g (vii♭⁷ acting as V⁶₅) leads to I at the start of the recapitulation. Marked *molto rallentando*, *pp* and *sotto voce*, this four-bar link has an important expressive function in the work, gently propelling the music away from the trio towards the varied recapitulation.[26]

Another innovation in the mazurkas of the early 1830s occurs in Op. 7 No. 3 in F minor, which was Chopin's most ambitious to date, rather like Op. 6 No. 3 in form and scope but structurally more comprehensive. Hamburger describes it as a 'symphonic type of mazurka',[27] although in the same breath he dismisses the work as a 'loose assembly A B C D', neglecting to observe the 'dynamic' tonal structure – i→III→V→i – and the linear descent through an octave joining the four main sections (see Example 9a). For the first time in the genre (as in most

Example 9   Mazurka in F minor, Op. 7 No. 3

(a) tonal structure

(b) phrase extensions, bars 99–105

contemporaneous nocturnes and etudes, from which the procedure could have derived), variation within the recapitulation involves phrase extension, which Chopin skilfully manipulates to withhold closure and to emphasise completion of the tonal structure when it does occur. Bars 93–6 are answered not with another four-bar passage (as in previous statements of the same material) but with a longer phrase comprising three separate cadential motions after the repeat of the melody in bars 97–8: 99–100, 101–2 and 103–5, of which only the last effects definitive closure (see Example 9b). The insistent bass pedal on F keeps resolution at bay until the i–iv$^6_4$–i progression in 104–5, which aptly summarises the many plagal relationships in the piece (e.g. bars 9–12 *et seq.*, and section C's I–IV I motion in Ab major).

Varied recapitulation by means of phrase extension also characterises the *Grande Polonaise*, Op. 22, one of only two 'brilliant' works from the period (the other is the introduction to Op. 16, completed in Paris in 1832). Chopin inserts a dramatic six-bar passage near the end of each A′ section in the two ABA′ outer wings, expanding register, intensifying harmonic activity and driving the rhythm ahead to propel the music towards the cadence closing the section. Between the outer wings lies a through-composed middle section significantly different from the standard CDC trio found in earlier polonaises. Chopin enhances unity by recycling material from the outer sections in this central one, exploiting two motives in particular at a structural level. The sequential progressions on which the section is built derive from harmonic patterns articulated at the start of A, B and A′, while the linear arch traced by these sequences in the treble comes from a similar melodic shape in the A and A′ sections (see Example 10). The significant structural role

Example 10   *Grande Polonaise*, Op. 22, bars 77–161: sequential structures

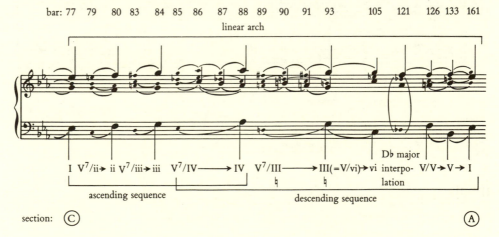

given to the pair of sequences is one of the most striking features of the *Grande Polonaise*. Whereas in earlier 'brilliant' works Chopin tends to confine sequences such as these to the foreground and particularly to the more virtuosic passages within a piece (where they often appear in endless concatenations), here they form the structure of an entire section, generating momentum by their contrasting harmonic rhythm and resultant asymmetry. By establishing the expectation of symmetry and therefore of closure in the first part of the section, and then denying it by greatly distorting – i.e. expanding – the harmonic proportions of the second sequence (note especially the Db interpolation in 121ff.), Chopin invests the underlying structure of the middle section with great energy.

In the E♭ major Waltz, Op. 18, Chopin again uses a sequence as the foundation of an extended structure: the circle-of-fifths progression on which bars 1–180 are based links the successive sections in this 'suite of waltzes'[28] into a structural entity, overcoming the impression of disunity alluded to by Hamburger when he writes, 'the Waltz on the whole is not closely organized'.[29] Op. 18 starts with a harmonically open ABAB group ending in A♭ major (i.e. IV), followed by closed CDC, EFE and G units, of which the first two are centred on D♭ major (♭VII) while section G is in G♭ (♭III).[30] (See Example 11.) This comprehensive circle-of-fifths

Example 11   Waltz in E♭, Op. 18: tonal outline (showing principal keys only)

structure ends with an eight-bar retransition in V following section G, which leads to section A's reprise in bar 189. Chopin heightens the structural coherence effected by this large-scale sequential progression by means of 'rhythmic, motivic and textural links'[31] which help relate detail to whole.

Chopin's enhanced ability to base extended passages on solid tonal frameworks such as the circle-of-fifths motion in Op. 18 and the paired sequences in Op. 22 was matched in the Vienna/early Paris repertoire by an increased command of smaller-scale hierarchical structures, as in bars 4–9 of the F major Nocturne, Op. 15 No. 1 (see Example 12). Here Chopin embellishes the basic I→iii→V skeleton found at a remote structural level (shown in the top system) with an implied circle-of-fifths sequence in the middleground (i.e. the middle system), which is then prolonged by a bass descent through an octave (see the bottom level). That each structural layer can be understood only in terms of the other two – and of course the music itself – points to the tightness of Chopin's 'organic' conception in this highly expressive passage, which reveals an original approach to ornamentation whereby the melody itself is kept simple but harmonic shadings in the accompaniment are continually altered, in contrast to the 'ornamental melody' of other nocturnes such as Op. 9 No. 2.

Although stylistically distinct, the nocturnes and etudes of the late 1820s and early 1830s share many structural features. All but one are based on ABA' forms

Example 12   Nocturne in F, Op. 15 No. 1, bars 4–9

(a) 'dynamic' tonal structure

(b) implied circle-of-fifths sequence

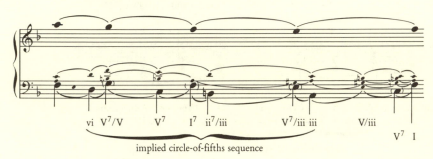

implied circle-of-fifths sequence

(c) octave descent in bass

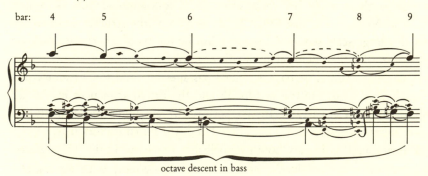

octave descent in bass

in which the reprise is abbreviated despite the use of phrase extensions to high-light closure of the underlying tonal foundation; the shift in structural weight towards the end of these pieces compensates for concentration of the most complex music in their middle sections, some of which are extremely chromatic (as in Op. 10 No. 3). There are of course profound differences between the two genres. Samson writes that 'the Op. 10 Studies have a special importance in Chopin's output. More than any other works at the time they act as a bridge between the *stile brillante* of the apprentice years and the unmistakable voice of maturity.'[32] The sophistication of Chopin's style at this stage of development can easily be seen in Op. 10 No. 1, in which subtle opposition between two principal melodic motives – a turning figure around E (bars 1–9, 9–16, 15–24, 49–57 and 57–69 – see Example 13) and either chromatic or diatonic linear descents (bars 25–36,

Example 13   Etude in C, Op. 10 No. 1: melodic patterns outlined by uppermost pitches in right-hand arpeggio figures

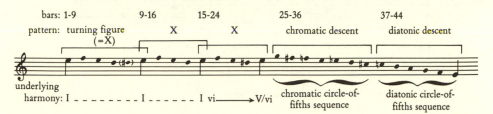

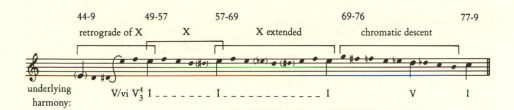

37–44 and 69–76) – generates tremendous momentum over and above the waves of arpeggios that provide the Etude's technical *raison d'être*. The insistent focus on E in the treble is broken only in the middle section, where two circle-of-fifths progressions accompany a twenty-bar linear descent (demonstrating yet again Chopin's use of sequential structures in extended passages), and in bars 69ff., where the chromatic descent from G to B in the top voice overcomes the turning figure's reiteration of E once and for all, reaching the tonic pitch in the melody and thereby achieving definitive closure for the first time in the piece. Although seemingly complex, the harmonies accompanying the final descent arise from a straightforward I–V–I progression in the bass: as in so many works by Chopin, a simple structural foundation gives rise to highly chromatic writing in the piece itself.

Foreground harmonic complexity is even greater in parts of the Ab major Etude, Op. 10 No. 10, especially the middle section, where Chopin moves through five keys in rapid succession – E, Db, A, Gb and Eb – of which the second and last clearly stand out by virtue of the emphatic cadential progressions in bars 25–6 and 40–2 respectively.[33] A 'dynamic' tonal structure can thus be inferred at a remote level, whereby the tonic harmony of section A leads in the middle section to the subdominant (Db) and subsequently to the dominant (Eb). (See Example 14.)

Example 14   Etude in A♭, Op. 10 No. 10

(a) 'dynamic' tonal structure

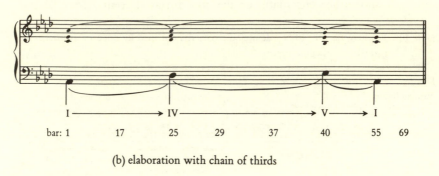

(b) elaboration with chain of thirds

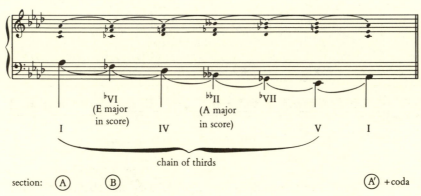

Within this I → IV → V outline, two of the intermediate keys function enharmonically as ♭VI (F♭ major) and ♭♭II (B♭♭ major) to form a chain of thirds in combination with the other harmonies:

'Dynamic' tonal foundation: I ⟶ IV ⟶ V → I
Subsidiary chain of thirds: I   ♭VI   IV   ♭♭II   ♭VII   V
Section: A   B   A'   +coda.

Chopin prolongs the goal of the 'dynamic' structure – i.e. the dominant in bars 40ff. – in a climactic twelve-bar passage before resolving to I at the start of the recapitulation, which strictly speaking lasts only six bars (55–60): in 61 the music takes a new direction leading eventually to bar 68's perfect cadence, which completes the underlying tonal structure and launches a nine-bar coda. Before that, however, tension is wound up in a dramatic phrase extension (61–7) which delays resolution to the tonic and thus heightens its effect when closure is achieved, and which also counterbalances the twelve-bar dominant prolongation at the end of section B, thereby ensuring overall stability.

Generation of structural momentum through phrase extension, varied recapitulation and use of a 'dynamic' tonal structure embellished with the subsidiary chain of thirds means that the Etude flows with virtually seamless connection between its principal sections: Chopin masterfully unites the constituent parts into a whole, further enhancing coherence by subtle correspondences between motives.[34] The 'organic' synthesis that results reveals the extent to which his style had changed from the formally rigid compositions of the Warsaw period, which, as we have seen, were created by juxtaposing independent sections in somewhat arbitrary successions. In several respects, the Ab major Etude summarises Chopin's approach to structure in Op. 10 (and for that matter in much of his mature music), for all twelve etudes[35] rely with a remarkable degree of consistency on 'dynamic' progressions and techniques of prolongation such as those apparent here.

It is striking that at a structural level the Ab Etude and indeed Op. 10 in general should so closely resemble the nocturnes, mazurkas and waltzes that Chopin was writing in the early 1830s. Virtually all the pieces dating from his arrival in Vienna are marked by the emergence of an increasingly well-defined, highly personal musical style in which principles of tonal architecture occupied a position of central importance, shaping works from different genres in similar ways. Perhaps it would not be too presumptuous to suppose that these were among the principles Chopin had in mind during his 1849 conversation with Eugène Delacroix when he referred to 'higher laws' and 'eternal principles' of composition: surely the fact that tonal structures like the ones shown here lay at the very foundation of his music from 1830 onwards provides at least some evidence to support such a conjecture.

PART 2

Profiles of the music

5 *Extended forms: the ballades, scherzos and fantasies*

JIM SAMSON

INTRODUCTION

It is widely recognised that Chopin's music took on new dimensions following his departure from Poland in 1830. It is recognised not least by pianists and concert promoters, who have conspicuously avoided most of the music from the Warsaw years. In some ways this is a pity since, as John Rink argues,[1] there are works of great value from the early period and they should be assessed on their merits – as some of the highest pinnacles of post-classical popular concert music – rather than measured against the inimitable products of his full maturity. What is not in doubt, however, is the qualitative change that took place in the early 1830s. It was nothing less than a major transformation of his musical style.

That transformation, however slowly prepared, was in the end rather quickly effected and the full range of impulses underlying it are as yet only partially understood. Certainly there were biographical factors beyond the usual growth to maturity – a radical change in Chopin's self-image as Warsaw's admiration gave way to Vienna's indifference; an increasing disenchantment with the proposed career of a composer-pianist; a nostalgia for, and commitment to, his native country, sharply focussed by the Polish insurrection of 1830. Whatever the underlying causality, the result was a change not only in Chopin's musical style but in his whole approach to composition, amounting in effect to an investment in the work rather than the performance. There is too a wider context for this change in nineteenth-century concert life, as Janet Ritterman's essay in the present volume demonstrates.

It is not especially difficult to pinpoint the nature of the stylistic change, at least in general terms. An essential starting-point is the recognition that Chopin's musical style was grounded less in Viennese classicism than in a post-classical repertory of concert music, sometimes described as the 'brilliant style',[2] whose basic conventions and materials he retained but at the same time refashioned and transcended. In the Op. 10 Etudes the conventional figuration of the brilliant style took on fresh meaning above all through an unprecedented density of contrapuntal information. In the early nocturnes the ornamental devices of the brilliant style were refined and ultimately fused with melodic substance to create the ornamental melody characteristic of the mature music. Most important of all, Chopin gradually developed a long-range harmonic vision which enabled him to gain structural control over the materials of the brilliant style, habitually presented in highly sectionalised formal designs which alternate lyrical and figurative paragraphs.[3]

These stylistic transformations were the essential prerequisites for Chopin's new-found mastery of extended forms in the early 1830s. His extended works from the Warsaw period were either rondos, variations (or pot-pourris) and concertos in the brilliant manner or multi-movement cyclic structures (Op. 4, Op. 8) modelled closely on classical archetypes. Following the new textural, melodic and harmonic developments of the early 1830s he effected a kind of synthesis of these two originally separate worlds, drawing together the formal methods of a post-classical concert music – above all the alternation of melodic and figurative material[4] – and the sonata-based designs and 'organic' tonal structures of the Austro-German tradition. The First Scherzo and the First Ballade were the first fruits of that synthesis, with the Scherzo (predictably) leaning towards the brilliant style and the Ballade towards the sonata principle. There are, however, additional ingredients in the mix of Chopin's extended formal designs. Among the most important are elements drawn from popular genres which took on a much more substantive and integral role in Chopin than in an earlier classical repertory, notably, but by no means exclusively, in the two mature fantasies.

Sonatas apart, the major genres for Chopin's mature extended structures were the scherzo, ballade and fantasy, and these genres – as Chopin conceived them – made their own demands on form and structure. The stylistic changes of the early 1830s were accompanied by changes in Chopin's view of genres and genre titles. His approach might be described as renovative, creating something like a self-consistent order within the permissive world of early nineteenth-century piano genres. Chopin did not select genre titles arbitrarily or use them loosely. They had specific, though not necessarily conventional, generic meanings. He did not, however, ignore the connotative values of genre titles. Rather he absorbed and built upon those values, and ultimately he transcended them.

Dates are difficult to determine accurately, but it seems likely that the First Scherzo and the First Ballade were composed around 1834–5.[5] By then both titles were already conventional, but they were newly defined by Chopin in these works, even to the point of changing the medium – at least for the Ballade. The Fantasy Op. 49 was composed rather later, in 1841, and here Chopin retained the conventional associations of the title, but added to them much more specific genre markers.[6] One piece does not of course define a genre. It is the remaining pieces in each case which enable us to describe the genre as a class with exemplars, where normative features are confirmed rather than undermined by deviational elements.[7] The dates of these remaining pieces are outlined below and it may be helpful to place them briefly in relation to the conventional periodisation of Chopin's evolving musical style. The First Scherzo and the First Ballade were the first extended major works of his stylistic maturity, composed in the early stages of his second major creative period; the Fourth Scherzo and the Fourth Ballade stand at the beginning of a widely-acknowledged third creative period dating from around 1842; the *Polonaise-fantaisie* arguably belongs to a so-called 'last style'.[8]

Scherzos	Ballades	Fantasies
No. 1, 1834–5*	No. 1, 1834–5*	
No. 2, 1835–7		
No. 3, 1839	No. 2, 1839	
	No. 3, 1841	Op. 49, 1841
No. 4, 1842	No. 4, 1842	
		Op. 61, 1846

* precise date uncertain

SCHERZOS

Before Chopin used it the term 'scherzo' customarily designated a movement of a cyclic or multi-movement work, part of a historical development associated above all with Beethoven, who created the tradition of the scherzo, but not only with him. Chopin himself used it in this sense (and in a manner more closely resembling the Beethoven model) in his mature sonatas. There were, it is true, little-known independent scherzos before Chopin,[9] but it is unlikely that he would have been familiar with these. Contemporary lexicographers describe the scherzo mostly in terms of the word's literal meaning (loosely translated, 'joke'), its characteristic metre (triple) and its tempo (lively, but not too quick). Some also refer to more specific features, such as sharply differentiated articulations and alternating ascending and descending melodic patterns. In these latter respects the contrast which is essential to the larger form is built into the detailed substance – a feature to be taken further by Chopin. Musical praxis before Chopin – especially late Beethoven – broadened the affective range of the scherzo and added specific details, such as syncopated *sforzato* stresses, which became part of the scherzo tradition.

Chopin's transformation of the genre was indeed so radical that his four scherzos confused not only his contemporaries, but also late nineteenth- and early twentieth-century critics. The basic tripartite design of the scherzo (with contrasting 'trio') is preserved, albeit often expanded by more complex repetition structures. So too is the triple metre, and some of the more specific markers of the

Beethoven scherzo – notably the contrasts in articulation and the *sforzato* markings. But Chopin changed the tempo to *presto* (with *con fuoco* in the B minor and C♯ minor Scherzos) and expanded immeasurably both the scale of the genre and its expressive range. Little is left of the 'joke' in these works. Indeed the first three are characterised rather by an almost demonic power and energy.

But the essential aspect of Chopin's view of the scherzo as a genre lies in his reinterpretation of the element of contrast at its heart. As Zofia Chechlińska has pointed out,[10] Chopin built the central formal contrast of the genre right into its detailed substance, notably through the characterisation of the opening gestures of each of the four pieces, where fragmentary motives are presented with calculated discontinuity. Since it is far from common for Chopin to begin a work with discontinuous gestures, the internal contrasts found at the opening of all four scherzos is striking. It will help to review the openings of the works (see Example 1).

In the B minor Scherzo opening there are contrasts of texture, register and dynamics, and the gesture is repeated at several points in the work. At the opening of the D♭ major the initial contrast is part of the main theme of the work, such that the dramatic tension it generates provides a key to the character of the work as a whole. In the C♯ minor the contrast is less extreme, but the gesture (unison/

Ex. 1

No. 1

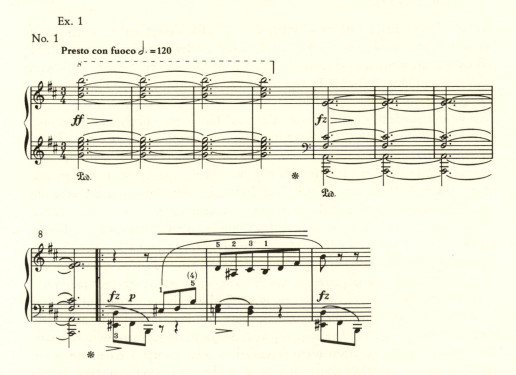

Ex. 1 (*cont.*)

No. 2

No. 3

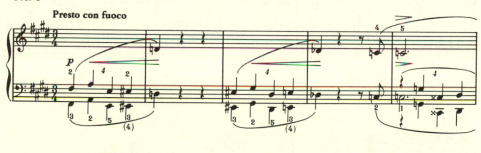

Ex. 1 (*cont.*)

No. 4

chordal, soft/loud) is identical to that of the Second Scherzo. The E major work opens with a succession of fragments contrasted in texture and harmony and separated either by silence or by sustained chords. It seems, then, that Chopin regarded the independent scherzo as a separate genre, clearly differentiated from the scherzos in his sonatas, and marked by its own kind of musical material, above all by the gestural contrasts embodied in short, separated ideas presented at the outset of each work.

Scherzos 1 and 4

In considering overall design, as well as specific aspects of construction, it may be helpful to examine the First and Fourth Scherzos together, enabling us to show both normative generic features and aspects of stylistic change. True to the historical archetype (and reflecting dance-piece origins) both take their starting-point in an extended ternary design with a contrasting trio, similar in outline to the more extended polonaises. The larger components of the form tend to optimise closure, the formal divisions are clear-cut and there is a high degree of internal repetition.

The First has the more straightforward design, really just an expansion of a simple ternary form, whose still centre or 'trio' is traditionally associated with the opening phrase of a Polish carol. The even rhythm and unchanging texture of this trio offer a marked contrast to the outer flanks of the scherzo, where the dynamic energy and power of the material already establishes the ambition and pretension of the genre in Chopin's hands. As in late Beethoven, the traditional ternary design of the opening flank is expanded into an ABABA scheme, while the closing flank leads into a bravura coda, as in ABAB'. The overall concept is still close to the formal precepts of the brilliant style, not only in its alternation of figurative and lyrical paragraphs, but also in the *nature* of the enclosed lyrical material – a familiar traditional melody.

The Fourth Scherzo expands this scheme into a lengthy, spacious design – more than twice the dimensions of the earlier work. More important, it strains beyond the closed components associated with the brilliant style by admitting in a limited way some of the characteristics of the sonata principle. The outer flanks, for example, each incorporate an extended central section which has something of the chromatic, tension-building character of a development. The point should not be overstated. Even in these central sections thematic statements remain relatively self-contained and stable, and the reprise, when it comes, is virtually literal. Yet the potential for opening the closed form is present, and it is realised briefly just before the trio. Here (bar 338) Chopin increases the intensity curve and allows the music to take on a goal-directed character, stretching beyond the closed symmetries of the work towards a climactic transformation of the opening motive (bar 377). Only a hint of new developmental possibilities is offered before the tension is released and the extended tripartite trio in the relative minor begins. Yet in relation to the First Scherzo this is enough to indicate an essential change in Chopin's approach to the formal organisation of a single genre.

Two further compositional issues are highlighted by the two scherzos, though they have wider applications in Chopin's music. The first concerns the role of texture. The outer flanks of the B minor Scherzo illustrate well the kind of 'shading' of function between texture, motive and harmony that is often found in Chopin's mature music. In the first section texture (determined by values independent of precise pitch content – register, density, articulation, dynamics) plays the dominant role. The powerful energy of these opening paragraphs is generated largely by rhythmically driven figuration in a context where melodic and harmonic information is minimal. As that energy is dissipated, however, motivic definition begins to take precedence over figuration, and the subtle transition between the two is entirely characteristic of Chopin. Then, in the second section (bar 69), the opening material is transformed in such a way that texture and motive make room for voice-leading and harmony as the chief means of achieving the goal-directed momentum of the music. As so often in Chopin, the borderlines between figuration, melody and harmony have been purposefully blurred.

The primary significance of texture as a compositional determinant – a means of shaping and directing the musical phrase – is already apparent in the First Scherzo. In later works it becomes a basic feature of style, even to the point of foreshadowing at times the so-called 'impressionist' composers of the early twentieth century. It is enough to point out that in the Fourth Scherzo the main thematic substance is determined by a chain of contrasting elements, where the contrasts – in a context of uniform dynamics – are largely textural in character, determined as much by voicing, register, contour and articulation as by harmony and theme.

The second compositional issue that may be raised briefly here is phrase structure. In Chopin's music generally the eight-bar sentence is a norm of construction, and especially so in dance pieces and the larger ternary designs. Yet within that constraint there are usually many ambiguities and subtleties which enliven the music and ensure a flexible, pliable rhythmic profile. Again the opening of the B minor Scherzo will make the point. Here the introductory chords establish the eight-bar structure against which subsequent figuration will be measured. Right from the outset of the figuration, however, there are disruptive features. The elision of openings and closures at bars 9 and 11, together with the contraction of groupings (hemiola fashion) at bars 13–15, generates a surplus of energy in relation to the metric norm which requires a restorative silence at bar 16. And similarly the transition to the second group (bars 25–46) employs a calculated 'interruption' of an expected sixteen-bar double sentence (after twelve bars) to raise the intensity curve as the second theme approaches.

The Fourth Scherzo, on the other hand, is significant precisely because there is much less deviation from the eight-bar norm. In the outer sections of the work we are presented with a balanced set of eight-bar statements, each distinct and contrasted, yet at the same time related. In the trio the same sentence structure provides rather a background symmetry for more flexible foreground shapes, but the invariance of the eight-bar sentence remains, even during the long monophonic line that leads back to the reprise of the trio melody. At this late stage of Chopin's output we might well argue that such regularity has a (confirming) generic purpose. Certainly it is a major element in defining the cheerful, benign and essentially untroubled character of this work. It is almost as though in this, his last scherzo, Chopin finally allowed himself to recover something of the original connotations of the genre title following the tempests of its three predecessors.

Scherzos 2 and 3

In relation to the model established in the First Scherzo and confirmed in the Fourth, several new elements are added or existing elements extended in the second and third. One new feature is the tonally inductive opening, where the true tonic is not revealed at the outset. There is, however, a difference between the two scherzos in this respect. The introduction to the C# minor is harmonically opaque even by the standards of Chopin's many other evasive openings, but its ambiguities (in which tonal hierarchies gradually take precedence over symmetrical patterns) function really as an harmonic curtain which is gradually raised to reveal the clearly-defined C# minor of the main theme. The Second Scherzo, on the other hand, opens in an unambiguous B♭ minor which is identified only in retrospect as an anacrusis to the D♭ major tonic defined at bar 49. The 'tandem' of B♭ minor and D♭ major (in an upbeat-downbeat relation) remains fundamental to the later course of the work – built into its harmonic structure rather than confined to an introductory gesture.

This brings us to a second issue which comes into focus with these two scherzos. Much more than in the First and Fourth, Chopin adopts an organicist approach to the basic materials of the Second and Third, taking them yet further from their origins in a 'scherzo and trio' and closer to the sonata principle. In the C# minor this is largely a matter of thematic integration – a single 'parent cell' (A–G#) which is already implicit in the introduction, is spelled out clearly in the main scherzo theme and is used to effect a subtle link to the trio, a 'hymn' in the tonic major which recalls in some ways the trio of the B minor Scherzo.[11] Much of the material in the work may be derived from this parent cell.

In the D♭ major Scherzo the organicist concerns extend beyond motivic substance to influence the larger tonal organisation of the work. It is worth noting in this connection that the trio acts as a structural *parallel* to the main scherzo material, not only echoing its sequence of ideas (a resolution of unstable material to stable) but also its third-related tonal relationship (see Example 2). The scherzo

Ex. 2

as a whole derives much of its coherence from this third relationship. Indeed, as Example 3 illustrates, the integration of part and whole is particularly close in this work, compensating for the explosive surface contrasts which are its most immediately striking and memorable feature.

Ex. 3

A final, and related, observation about these two works concerns their formal organisation. It was noted that at one point in the Fourth Scherzo Chopin opened the closed form of the ternary design, albeit fleetingly, to admit an unexpected goal-directed development of its material. This 'opening' of the form is taken much further in the Second and Third Scherzos. We will consider first the C♯ minor. Following the second trio in E major/minor, where we expect a heightening of tension in preparation for the scherzo reprise, Chopin unexpectedly interpolates a quite new sequence. He slows the harmonic rhythm to a near standstill in preparation for a sustained, expansive melody which grows in passion and intensity until the powerful octaves at bar 567 signal a non-thematic bravura coda, a gesture with origins in the brilliant style, but here transformed into an essential formal component. In context the entire sequence is remarkable, utterly changing our perspective on the enclosed material of the 'scherzo' and 'trio'.

The D♭ major Scherzo moves yet further in this direction. Indeed in this work Chopin allowed his preoccupation with developmental processes and the integration of extreme contrasts to take the scherzo and trio, its undoubted formal starting-point, very close to the sonata-form movement. Here, much more than in the other three works, he is alive to the possibilities his materials may offer for unexpected openings in the structure, where previously self-contained ideas might suddenly take exciting new directions. The expected reprise of the scherzo material is replaced by just such an opening of the form at bar 476, resulting in what can only be described as a powerful development section. And when the reprise finally creeps in on the ebb of a single extended rhythmic impulse, it has all the structural weight of a sonata-form recapitulation.

Within the reprise Chopin opens the form on a further two occasions – at bar 692, where earlier material (bar 109) is extended and at bar 716, where the cadential figure is unexpectedly interrupted by the return of the B section of the scherzo. In sonata-form terms we have then a developmental coda as well as a development section. Formally the second is indeed the most ambitious of the four scherzos, embodying all the drives and conflicts of a sonata movement and synthesising them through development. If we view the four works as a single generic class, this is the scherzo which (paradoxically) *confirms* the norm established in the other three by deviating most obviously from that norm, clarifying its terms through their temporary falsification.[12]

BALLADES

When Chopin first used the title 'ballade' for a piano piece he effectively created a new genre, at least for his own purposes. It was, however, a genre which drew sustenance from the existing associations of the title in both literary and musical contexts. In the remarkable flowering of early romantic poetry the ballad (essentially a revival of the medieval form) came into sharp focus in contrast to the lyric, and that contrast was in turn reflected in the development of the nineteenth-century art song. It should be noted too that settings of ballads (notably by Schubert and Loewe) often couch their narrative in the same 6/8 or 6/4 metre associated with Chopin's ballades. A further association is with opera, especially French, where the title 'ballade' was used at times to describe a simple narrative song. The ballade in Act I of Meyerbeer's *Robert le diable* is a case in point, and its similarity to Chopin's Second Ballade has been pointed out by Anselm Gerhard.[13]

Through their response to literature and also to vocal music Chopin's ballades aligned themselves to a central – almost a defining – preoccupation of an early romantic esthetic in music, a preoccupation with the expressive and narrative capacities of musical language. The ballades were Chopin's closest point of contact with the programmatic interests of his contemporaries, given expression in works of the quality of Liszt's *Harmonies poétiques et religieuses* as well as in the many trivial descriptive works (especially battle pieces) that emerged in the early years of the century. In a piece such as Challoner's *The Battle of Waterloo*, for instance, formal and expressive events are dictated in entirely specific ways by the unfolding narrative.

Chopin of course eschewed any such programmatic associations, allowing his title to signify only the most generalised aspects of literary inspiration, in particular a narrative quality. In recreating that quality in musical terms he turned first and foremost to the sonata-form archetype, though he drew upon it in a very different spirit here than in his three mature sonatas. The ballades are in effect reinterpretations of sonata-form. In general their structures are end-weighted, very often structural 'crescendos' with an accelerating rate of change in their formal activity and of growth in their intensity curve. In the First, Third and Fourth Ballades the reprise is in the nature of an apotheosis[14] and in the First and Fourth it culminates in a bravura coda.

This formal conception is in turn part of a more fundamental change of emphasis within the sonata-form archetype, aimed at channelling its dramatic, goal-directed qualities towards narrative ends. The ballades are still of course anchored by a tonal argument, but much more than the classical sonata they highlight *thematic* process, using variation and transformation techniques to describe the adventures of two contrasting themes. This thematic 'narrative' is further enhanced through explicit association (chiefly of rhythm and metre) with vocal music and also with popular genres, whose origin in specific social functions gives them unique referential value. The ballades, in short, have their own very particular kind of musical material, utterly different in kind from that of the sonatas, despite obvious formal parallels.

Ballades 1 and 4

We will attempt to locate the genre through comparative examination of the First and Fourth Ballades, composed more or less at the same time as the First and Fourth Scherzos. It may be worth reiterating that the First Scherzo and First Ballade were Chopin's earliest mature essays in extended forms and that they established two contrasting independent genres based on the same stylistic background – the figuration and melody of the brilliant style. The Scherzo couches these materials in a simple design, where the larger divisions are clear, sections are contrasted and closure is optimised. In contrast the Ballade presents them in a through-composed, directional structure, where variation and transformation are seminal functions, integration and synthesis essential goals.

Formally the parallels between the First and Fourth Ballades are obvious enough. Each has an anacrustic introduction which leads directly into the first subject of a sonata-form exposition. In the G minor this introduction has something of the character of a recitative, skilfully dovetailed to the first subject's 'aria'. In the F minor, on the other hand, the introduction is integrated motivically with the main theme (through its repeated-note pattern) and this integration in turn makes possible an ingeniously unobtrusive, yet wholly unexpected, return of the introduction just before the reprise.[15]

Following these introductions, both ballades present contrasting first and second subjects in formal and tonal contexts which have clear points of contact with sonata form. No less significant than these formal parallels, however, are parallels in the nature of the thematic material itself. The first themes of the two ballades are linked by their metre (6/4 and 6/8 respectively) and by their waltz-like accompaniment pattern (see Example 4). The suggestion of a waltz rhythm here

Ex. 4

remains just that – a suggestion – since there is clearly a difference between triple and compound duple metre. But later in the G minor Ballade there is an unambiguous waltz episode (similar to that in the Third Ballade at bar 124), complete with the *moto perpetuo* arabesques so characteristic of Chopin's independent waltzes, and this renders explicit a link with popular genres which remained implicit in the main theme. The second themes of the two ballades also share a similar rhythmic character (see Example 5), and this time it is a different popular genre – the

Ex. 5

Ex. 5 (*cont.*)

barcarolle – that lurks behind the surface of the music. As we shall see later bar-carolle (or siciliano) characteristics are important markers of the Chopin ballade. The parallels not only in formal design but in the nature of the thematic material in the two exposition sections of these works are already enough to suggest a common generic basis.

The subsequent formal organisation of the two ballades clearly makes its point against a sonata-form background, but in each case there is a calculated ambiguity – a blend of different formal perspectives – which enriches and enhances the structure. In the G minor the central ambiguity is between a sonata-based structure, allied to an accelerating intensity curve, and the more formal symmetry of an arch design. Both the thematic pattern and the tonal scheme may be read as non-congruent arch structures (see Example 6), where 'C' is the pivotal waltz

Ex. 6

Tonality								
Themes	A	B	A	B	C	B	A	coda

theme. In this interpretation the reversed order of the two themes in the reprise is clearly significant.

Counterpointed against this 'formal' reading, however, is a goal-directed sonata form in which the initial repetitions of the two themes are tension-building and developmental, sweeping powerfully towards the waltz episode, which defuses the intensity only to build it again for the reprise of the second theme. It is charac-teristic of the intensity curves of Chopin's extended single-movement works that they rise sharply at the end. The reprise of the first theme, far from representing a completion, is itself tension-building, presented over a dominant pedal and reach-ing towards the work's highest peak of intensity – a bravura, non-thematic coda.

In the Fourth Ballade the formal ambiguity results in part from a blend of different formal functions, where the first theme of a sonata-like design (with second subject transposed in the reprise) is subjected to cumulative variation treatment, involving a counter-melody (bar 58), a canonic presentation (bar 135) and a nocturne-like fioritura statement (bar 152). The rapid succession of canonic treatment and ornamental variation in the reprise is on the one hand a bold synthesis of different stylistic characters (or 'topics', to use Leonard Ratner's term[16]) and on the other a refinement and stylisation of the normal practices of contemporary improvisation. There are other reminders of Chopin's origins in the 'pianist's music'[17] of the early nineteenth century – the non-thematic figurations which act as buffers between different thematic elements, for example, and also the final bravura coda. As in the G minor Ballade this emerges as the outcome of a rapidly accelerating intensity curve in which the reprise functions more as a glorious apotheosis than a synthesis.

It was in 1842 that Chopin began to review comprehensively all the elements of his craft, resulting in a dramatic drop in his rate of production and also in a perceptible change in his musical style. There are several features which mark out the fourth ballade as a product of this later creative period. The renewed interest in counterpoint is one, and the controlled, and essentially structural, role of ornamentation another. But it is above all the formal richness of the work – a richness that can only be hinted at in this essay – which establishes the work not only as one of Chopin's mightiest achievements but as one of the unchallenged masterpieces of nineteenth-century music.

Ballades 2 and 3

As with the scherzos we may use the First and Fourth Ballades as reference points for a discussion of compositional issues in the other two. One such issue concerns thematic treatments. All four ballades are built around a 'narrative' based on the interaction of two contrasting themes. In the first and fourth the initial relation between them is that of a tension-release pattern, where the second theme is a resolution of the tension generated by the first. In the G minor there is a further point of dramatic contact when the first theme leads without break or transition into the second as part of a single tension-building paragraph (bar 106). And in both works the reprise functions as an apotheosis of the two themes.

The Second and Third Ballades extend these treatments, but in very different directions. The Second (in F major/A minor) markedly sharpens the differentiation between its two themes, affording a highly charged contrast between the innocent siciliano of the First in F major and the brutal figuration of the Second in A minor, barely a theme in any conventional sense. The alternation of theme and figuration here is in part a residue of the brilliant style. Much of the dynamic of the piece flows from this initial opposition which needs to be mediated and eventually synthesised. In the middle section the mediation takes place in two stages. Initially the second theme is allowed to subside gradually and imperceptibly on to the first. Then the first theme is built to such a peak of intensity that it can lead naturally into the second. In the closing bars of the work there is a gesture of synthesis in the whispered reference to the first theme again, now accommo-dated to the tonal region of A minor.

The Third Ballade is concerned less with thematic opposition and contrast than with processes of thematic transformation. These processes include the trans-formation of the rather stilted second theme into a powerfully expansive, impas-sioned peroration (bars 157ff.) in the development section, and they culminate in a remarkable fusion of the two initially separate themes into a single melody. Here Chopin 'opens' the initially closed shape of the first theme to create an extended melodic arc encompassing a transposed version of the second theme, and in ensuing bars the two themes are woven ever more tightly together. As in the First and Fourth Ballades, the reprise of both themes is in the nature of an apothe-osis, the culmination of an accelerating rate of formal change and a rapidly rising intensity curve.

A second area of contrast between these two ballades concerns their tonal organisation. In the Third the tonal scheme remains deliberately inert for much of the work, underlining the fact that this ballade gives especially pronounced expression to a general tendency of Chopin's music (already noted in this chapter) towards end-weighted structures. It should be noted that – in sonata-form terms – the 'exposition' here takes up a full 156 bars, which amounts to rather more than half the total length of the Ballade. The 'development section' lasts for 56 bars and the reprise a mere 29 bars. Now throughout the lengthy exposition – incorporat-ing the first and second themes, a new semiquaver theme, a 'waltz' episode and the return of the second theme – the tonality remains stable, encompassing only the tonal relatives within a single key signature of Ab major.

In context this tonal inertia is powerfully anticipative, generating an expectancy of, and need for, change. And the two stages of the development section – the impassioned peroration based on the second theme and the fusion of both themes – answer that need. The first stage is characterised by its tonal distance from the home key (C# minor) and the second by its ambiguous and unstable tonal setting. Given the compression of events following the exposition, the tonal adventures of this (relatively) short development section play a critical role in redressing the balance of the structure.

The Second Ballade is unusual as one of the only extended works of Chopin to employ a two-key scheme (F major–A minor), as distinct from an 'emergent' tonality, such as that noted in the second scherzo.[18] For music theorists the two-key scheme has presented teasing questions, though it seldom troubles the listener. Some analysts have viewed the work against a background of monotonal theory, employing the methods of Heinrich Schenker to explain the tonal scheme as a deviation from, or alternative to, monotonality.[19] Others have attempted to explain the two-key scheme in its own terms, taking as their starting-point the theories of Robert Bailey concerning the 'double-tonic complex' found in some later nineteenth-century music.[20] Others again have examined unifying elements in the pitch structure which remain independent of tonal harmonic functions.[21]

A style-historical (rather than analytical) approach to the Ballade would find the two-key scheme less problematical. Such an approach might well relate the work to the numerous pieces within post-classical concert music that offer alternatives to monotonality, not only pot-pourris and operatic fantasies but single-movement independent pieces such as the Kalkbrenner *Grand Fantasy* Op. 68 and the Hummel Op. 18 Fantasy, the latter offering the same tonal progression as the Second Ballade. Equally it might seek to view the two-key scheme in relation to Chopin's response to aspects of a Romantic esthetic, referring to the role of popular genres in his music and also to the possible influence of extra-musical designates.

Both these latter issues have already been touched upon, but they deserve fuller treatment at this point. It has become a commonplace of criticism that 'popular' and 'significant' musics became increasingly incompatible in the nineteenth century, establishing an opposition between conventional language and an incipient avant-garde. It has been less often remarked that in some nineteenth-century music this opposition was actually embodied within the individual work, as popular genres increasingly took on a parenthetical, as distinct from a supportive or enabling, role in art music. Chopin played a part in this development, establishing in his major works a counterpoint of genres which at times seems to foreshadow Mahler.

It has been noted that in the First and Fourth Ballades waltz and barcarolle elements characterise some of the main thematic material. As Example 7 indicates,

Ex. 7

Ex. 7 (*cont.*)

the Third Ballade also counterpoints these two popular genres, and here the counterpoint is more abrasive. It is enough to note that the rather 'lumpy' effect of the
second theme's insistent iambic rhythm (barcarolle/siciliano) is in the sharpest
possible contrast to the ensuing waltz episode. That iambic rhythm does indeed
merit special attention in any consideration of the ballades. It is so characteristic of
all four works (as Examples 5, 7 and 8 suggest) that it might well be regarded as
a genre marker.

It is prominent again in the opening theme of the Second Ballade (see Example 8). Here the associations with a siciliano, as traditionally representing the

Ex. 8

naive or pastoral, are explicit and the tonal setting of F major strengthens them.[22]
The figurative material of the second theme also suggests a generic basis. It is not
just etude-like in a general way, but is remarkably close in phraseology and texture
to the so-called 'Winter Wind' etude, Op. 25 No. 11, remarkable for what Camille
Bourniquel called its 'irresistible unleashing of power'. The opening theme's tonal
differentiation from the figurative material might be viewed then as part of a more
comprehensive differentiation with an underlying generic basis, and the loss of
the initial tonic would take on a symbolic meaning.

This brings us finally to the question of extra-musical designates. By choosing the title 'ballade' for these works Chopin was indeed inviting associations with literature. But we should note that he *only* uses the title 'ballade'. Speculation about Mickiewicz – specifically the ballad *Switeż* in relation to the second ballade – is of limited value, since no specific designate is part of the subject or content of the work, in the way that Lamartine's poetry is part of the subject (because it is part of the title) of Liszt's *Harmonies poétiques et religieuses*. Chopin's title is indeed a signifier, but one that points only to the narrative quality of the music and the referential code created by a network of generic allusions.

It was partly through this referential code that nineteenth- and early twentieth-century critics arrived at the descriptive and even programmatic interpretations of Chopin's music which we tend to dismiss today. The difficulty with such interpretations is that they allow connotative values to congeal into fixed meanings. And that is also the difficulty with references to Mickiewicz. Given the music's referential code, we scarcely need a Mickiewicz poem to read the second ballade's narrative of innocence under threat, a narrative that presents in turn confrontation, mediation and transformation. The two-key scheme is a part of that narrative.

FANTASIES

In early nineteenth-century concert life the borderline between improvisation and composition was by no means as clear-cut as it is today. Much of Chopin's early music – in particular dance pieces and variation sets such as the 'Là ci darem' Variations and the *Fantasy on Polish Airs* – is closely related in idiom to the practices of contemporary improvisation. And even in the mature music this relationship can still be traced – between the Preludes and improvisatory 'preluding', between the ornamental melody of the nocturnes and impromptu melodic embellishment and between the two mature fantasies and the extempore performances that were an important ingredient of concert programmes at the time.

It is clear from contemporary accounts that such extempore performances permitted greater and more frequent changes of mood, tempo and tonal region than was usual in composed music, though it should be stressed that formal coherence was considered a prerequisite of the successful improvisation. It was above all in pieces described as 'fantasies' that something of the spirit of improvisation – apparent freedom and irregularity couched within a coherent structure – was captured for composed music. The fantasy, stretching the conventions of more orthodox genres, was in a sense a composed-out improvisation.

Like many other early nineteenth-century fantasies, Chopin's two mature works shared with common-practice improvisation a multi-sectional structure, a wide range of contrasting materials and a reference to some of the characteristic gestures beloved of the improviser – in particular preluding figurations (arpeggiations, recitatives) and themes suggestive of the opera house or the folk dance. The parallels between the two works leave us in no doubt at all that for Chopin they had a common and rather specific generic basis. Both begin with a slow, improvisatory introduction involving preluding arpeggiations and, in the case of the Op. 49 Fantasy, a slow march clearly related in idiom to the choruses of French grand opera.[23] But Chopin makes the association still closer by establishing unmistakable thematic links between the two introductions, as Example 9 illustrates. It is surely

Ex. 9

no coincidence that the only other genres in which there are motivic as well as generic links are the impromptu and (at least arguably) the prelude,[24] as though Chopin were spelling out his transcendence of the obvious associations with improvisation.

Both fantasies also have an extended 'slow movement' at their heart – a feature shared by many other early nineteenth-century fantasies. But it might be noted that the tonal setting for these slow movements is identical (B major), as is also their tonal *context*: in each case the B major melody is embedded within a prevailing Ab major. Our knowledge of the genesis of the *Polonaise-fantaisie* strengthens this tonal association yet further. The 'slow movement' of that work was originally drafted in C major, and it seems possible that generic association was a telling factor in the decision to change the tonal setting to B major. It is also intriguing that the introduction to Op. 61 was at one point planned in F minor, the opening key of Op. 49.

The slow introduction and slow movement are accommodated in each case within structures which have elements of large-scale ternary design and at the same time elements of sonata form. The difference between them in this respect might be clarified in relation to our earlier discussion of the ballades and scherzos. Where the Fantasy Op. 49 leans towards the ballades, allowing the influence of improvisation to loosen and stretch a sonata-form archetype, the *Polonaise-fantaisie* is closer to the large-scale ternary design characteristic of the scherzos, once more obscured (and enriched) by a response to the generic association with improvisation.

On the face of it the Fantasy Op. 49 brings together a range of contrasting characterisations of a kind common in contemporary improvisation – slow march, prelude or recitative, *motivische Arbeit* and chorale. The binding agents are on the one hand a sonata-form framework and on the other a firmly grounded, albeit directional, tonal structure. Chopin undoubtedly composed the work against a sonata-form background, though its dialogue with that background is rather free. Following the extended introduction (comprising the march and the prelude) the exposition presents a first subject in F minor/Ab major, a second subject in C minor/Eb major and a new march-like codetta theme affirming the Eb major. The introduction of this new and lengthy march theme following the brief presentation of the main tonal and thematic contrast of the exposition is also a gesture reminiscent of improvisational practice. The reprise (bar 235) is in the subdominant, allowing Chopin (like many before him) to bring the second subject into the tonic while preserving the tonal relationships of the exposition, thus:

Exposition	Reprise
f – Ab – c – Eb	bb – Db – f – Ab

Since the development section highlights Gb major, it will be clear that the surface tonal organisation is a chain of ascending thirds, to which the 'slow movement' in B major forms an inspired parenthesis, thus:

$$f – Ab – c – Eb – Gb – [B] – bb – Db – f – Ab$$

It has indeed been plausibly suggested[25] that this tonal scheme is already present in microcosm in the introduction to the fantasy, not just in the F minor/Ab major of the march but even more in the cycle of thirds underlying the subsequent prelude (bar 43).

The logical, even schematic, organisation of surface tonal events outlined here is complemented by a much more compelling background progression to Ab major which has been charted by Carl Schachter in an exciting Schenkerian analysis of the work.[26] Here the underlying tonal structure is identified as a progression from F minor (the opening march and prelude) through Eb major (the goal of the exposition, or 'first cycle', as Schachter calls it, and also the controlling tonality for the development section or 'second cycle', including the 'slow movement') to Ab major (the goal of the reprise or 'third cycle', affirmed by the coda). This interpretation goes far beyond an identification of these regions as primary. It demonstrates through voice-leading not only that a wealth of surface harmonic detail has been accommodated to the larger progression, but also that the final Ab major is not simply the resolution of a single section (the reprise) but of the entire fantasy.

The *Polonaise-fantaisie*, Op. 61, was Chopin's last extended work for solo piano. It occupied him longer, and gave him greater trouble, than any other single work apart from the coeval Cello Sonata, suggesting that right at the end of his creative life he approached his art in a spirit of renewed exploration, resulting – in the view of one of the most perceptive of Chopin commentators – in a 'last style'.[27] The *Polonaise-fantaisie* acquired its title rather late in the day. It seems that Chopin originally thought of it simply as a fantasy, adding the 'polonaise' much later, just as he apparently added the characteristic polonaise rhythm to the main theme (its only significant presentation in the work) at a late stage of the creative process.

Sonata-form models have some relevance to the *Polonaise-fantaisie*, not least in the tonal synthesis of the reprise where the 'slow movement' theme returns in the tonic. But the composition-draft of the work suggests that it took its starting-point in a large-scale ternary design and this remains the most helpful inroad to its seemingly obfuscatory formal organisation. In this reading the outer flanks (following the introduction) are the main polonaise theme and its transformations (bars 1–115) and a reprise of both the polonaise theme and the slow-movement theme, all in the key of Ab major. The heart of the middle section is the 'slow movement' in B major (originally C major).

As Jeffrey Kallberg has suggested,[28] this ternary design is then purposefully 'blurred' by the introduction of unexpected elements at each of the two main divisions of the form, recreating in the process something of the apparent irregularity and discontinuity of an improvisation. Between the first section and the middle section Chopin introduces a new nocturne-like theme in Bb major (originally B major in the composition draft), whose self-contained character (tonally stable and melodically 'complete') makes it an unlikely candidate for any transitional function. Only in retrospect do we recognise that it is an interpolation into the larger ternary design. Between the middle section and the closing section, Chopin similarly blurs the outlines of the form by recalling in rapid succession two moments from the earlier stages of the work, allowing them to interrupt the expected course of events within a ternary design. The first such interpolation is the introduction to the work, which interrupts the slow movement, only to be itself interrupted by the recall of the middle section of the slow movement. The tonal strategies involved here, as to both compositional process and final structure, are of remarkable subtlety.

Like the Fantasy Op. 49, the *Polonaise-fantaisie* has something of the formal variety and irregularity of an inspired improvisation. It embraces a wide range of characters – slow introduction, dance theme, sonata-like motivic development, nocturne-like ornamental melody and 'slow movement' – within a tonal and formal setting whose sequence is unpredictable yet entirely satisfying and cohesive. While a large ternary design was clearly the starting-point and remains a perceptible background, the foreground highlights processes of interruption, discontinuity and asymmetry. On one level this fits well with the associations of the genre title. But on another it is testament to the exploratory spirit in which Chopin approached his art right at the end of his creative life. It is symptomatic of this spirit that he should have followed the *Polonaise-fantaisie*, arguably his most challenging work for solo piano, with a cello sonata – a bold enterprise indeed for a composer whose creative output had been until then synonymous with a single medium.

Over a period of about fifteen years Chopin produced a handful of extended single-movement works which created such an innovatory synthesis of existing methods that they stand alone in the pianist's repertory – even to the point of establishing their own genres. Yet so powerful were the associations of the salon in Chopin reception that these works were habitually undervalued in critical commentaries of the late nineteenth and early twentieth centuries. Chopin was widely regarded as a miniaturist with an undeveloped, even primitive, sense of form, and his self-imposed limitation of medium appeared only to confirm this assessment.

Later twentieth-century writing about Chopin has changed all that. Yet in registering something of the whole complex of ideas associated with a structuralist poetic, much of this writing carries its own prejudice. We may recognise today that the scherzos, ballades and fantasies are triumphs of architecture, but we perhaps need to recover something of the associative and allusive qualities which earlier commentators identified in these works, something of their combinative as well as their integrative features. There may indeed be a further price to pay for the insights of our own age. Perhaps the central irony in Chopin reception is that the extended forms have been habilitated only at the expense of a true understanding of the role and significance of the miniatures.

6 *Small 'forms': in defence of the prelude*

JEFFREY KALLBERG

Chopin was a master of small forms. Few beliefs more centrally govern modern perceptions of Chopin than this one. It supports not only the myriad manifestations of his high stature in our culture (performances and critical analyses alike can be read as endorsements of the composer's extraordinary skill at miniatures), but also the occasional barbs that are thrown his way (some writers profess a complementary axiom that mastery of large forms eluded him).

But while the centrality of this belief may lend it the appearance of a timeless truth, it seems instead that the meaning of its fundamental term, *form*, has altered substantially over the past century and a half. When we unreflectively discuss form in Chopin's music as if its intent were self-evident, we therefore at least to some degree misrepresent its significance to his culture. All of us – pianists and amateur enthusiasts as well as musicologists – need to be aware of this disjunction between past and present: before we can probe aspects of form in Chopin's miniatures, we need to explore some of the ways in which the ideas of form and (to a lesser extent) smallness were construed in the first half of the nineteenth century. That these explorations can have very practical applications I hope to show in the second portion of my essay, which will focus on Chopin's smallest forms, the preludes.

What then was meant by musical form in Chopin's day, and for whom was it an issue? While other interpretations are sometimes aired (these will be noted below), form in modern parlance most often refers to the structure, morphology, or plan of a musical work ('sonata form' and 'binary form' are two commonly invoked examples in this sense). It is generally the concern of composers, performers and listeners alike (the study of it has become, in the words of one authority, 'a basic tool of musical analysis'[1]). But this definition and this function only partially circumscribe the possibilities of what was a richly nuanced concept in the 1830s and 1840s. Two other senses of form prevailed during Chopin's lifetime, the first deriving from aesthetics and generally embracing all of the constructive means by which beauty might be expressed in music, and the second serving more particularly as a synonym for *genre* or *kind*. I will discuss these three meanings separately, beginning with the most general.

AESTHETIC FORM

One of the legacies of late eighteenth- and early nineteenth-century aesthetic debates about form was a profusion of definitions of the concept. While the general terms of the debate – ideas of order, proportion, coherence, pattern and unity that dated at least as far back as the Pythagoreans and Plato – remained roughly the same, successive writers tended to characterise form somewhat differently. Most of them, however, did not react directly to Platonic or Aristotelian ideas about the concept, but rather to the notion, expounded by the eighteenth-century philosophers who founded the discipline of aesthetics (among them Baumgarten, Shaftesbury and Hutcheson) that form was the means by which beauty was expressed in the arts.

In what consisted this form? Consider the following array of representative citations from philosophers, theorists and critics:

> Beauty should surely be a question only of form. . . . Any form of an empirically perceived object (whether external or internal) is either a *pattern* or an *interplay*. In the latter case the interplay is either of shapes (in space: mime and dance) or simply of emotions (in time). The *charm of* colours or the pleasurable sounds of instruments may also be involved; but in the first case the *design* constitutes the actual object of any pure judgement of taste and in the second, the composition. (Immanuel Kant, *Kritik der Urteilskraft*, 1790)

> . . .musical form is a process whereby the infinite is embodied in the finite; hence the forms of music are inevitably forms of things in themselves. In other words, they are forms of ideas exclusively under a phenomenal guise.
>
> Since this has now been demonstrated in the general sense, it must also be true of rhythm and harmony, which are the [platonic] forms peculiar to music. In other words, rhythm and harmony can express the forms of eternal things to the extent that those forms are thought of entirely as discrete entities. (Friedrich Schelling, *Philosophie der Kunst*, 1802–3)

> But what delights and enchants us is how the composer uses sound to create melody and harmony, thereby evoking a specific reaction: in other words, it is the *form* of the music. . .no piece of music should be loosely constructed from sections that effectively cancel each other out and neutralise the overall impression. Everything should possess unity in diversity. (Christian Friedrich Michaelis, *Allgemeine musikalische Zeitung* 9 [1806])

Form. In music, as well as in the other fine arts, there is often talk of the form of the art work, and by the form of a musical composition, one understands the way it is brought before the soul of the listener.

Daily experience indeed teaches that the different genres of musical compositions are distinguished merely by their forms; the symphony has a different form from the concerto, the aria a different one from the song; even so, if the aestheticians maintain that that which one calls the beauty of a musical composition is contained in the selfsame form, then there must certainly also exist an incidental [*zufällige*] form in which the beauty is contained, and that not only exists, but is wanting, otherwise, e.g., any rondo, if it conforms to its usual form, would maintain the character of beauty without further conditions.

If accordingly the discussion is of the form of art products in such a way that it is dedicated to the content of beauty, then one does not thereby understand that external [*äußerliche*] form of art works whereby the genres themselves may be distinguished, rather on the contrary the particular way in which variety is consolidated in unity, or the particular way in which the composer transmitted to the art work the moments of pleasure that were contained in his ideal. (Heinrich Christoph Koch, *Kurzgefaßtes Handwörterbuch der Musik für praktische Tonkünstler und für Dilettanten*, 1807)

[Music's] essence is play, through and through; nothing else. It has no content of any kind that men have tried to adduce from and give to it. It simply comprises forms, regulated combinations of sounds and sequences of sounds. (Hans-Georg Nägeli, *Vorlesungen über Musik*, 1826)

The idea of beauty. . . .is expressed either completely, or at any rate in large measure, in form, and it awakens a pleasure that is in the highest degree disinterested. . . . Now form is not merely a matter of the shape of a thing, nor can the uninterrupted contemplation of individual words, notes or ideas make them more or less beautiful, or more or less displeasing. Beauty of form really results from the ways in which variety is moulded into a unity according to the rules of taste. (Gustav Schilling, 'Beauty and the beautiful', *Encyclopädie der gesammten musikalischen Wissenschaften* [Stuttgart, 1834–8; 2nd edn, 1840–2])

Beethoven mastered these rich resources and exploited them as he strove so astonishingly to break the bonds of the traditional forms that his predecessors had established. What is musical form but the natural body that a piece of music must assume in order to establish itself as a living organism? The laws of nature apply just as much to what is heard as to what is seen. . . . Mendelssohn showed a constant concern for organic construction, for form as it is called in short . . . (August Kahlert, 'Über den Begriff der klassischen und romantischen Musik', *Allgemeine musikalische Zeitung* 50 [1848])[2]

To search in the above accounts for a general meaning of form is to risk smoothing over disagreements among significantly distinct philosophical traditions.[3]

Nevertheless, three ideas recur often enough to be worthy of note. First, most aestheticians included notions of pattern or design in their definitions. Kant stated this belief expressly (at the same time broaching the complementary idea of 'interplay'), whereas Schilling admitted it while claiming that form should not be limited to design or morphology ('form is not merely a matter of the shape of a thing').

Schilling's last assertion alerts us to the second important trend in aesthetic discussions of the period: the constructive features that constitute form usually remained rather loosely defined. Hence Michaelis vaguely located form in melody and harmony, while Nägeli more ambiguously thought that forms were 'regulated combinations of sounds and sequences of sounds'. And Michaelis, Koch and Schilling all took refuge in the hackneyed aesthetic dictum of form as unity in diversity (more on this formula below). Kahlert's conception of form as 'the natural body that a piece of music must assume in order to establish itself as a living organism', as 'organic construction', lies somewhere between the view of form as pattern ('the natural body') and form as a broader constructive entity that gives the work life ('a living organism'). Kahlert's theories bear the strong imprint of Hegel (compare the latter's statement in his *Aesthetik* that 'the inner consciousness itself thus becomes the form in which music contrives to embody its content'[4]).

We find the third significant idea broached in Koch's distinction between form as a schematic 'incidental' or 'external' concept, and form as the manifestation of the content of beauty, represented by the consolidation of variety in unity. Koch's opposition draws on the previous two notions about form, and assesses their respective worth. Composers and dilettantes help distinguish genres through a form both 'incidental' and 'wanting'. The form revealed in 'particular' mixtures of diversity in unity or feelings of the composer helps elucidate the 'content of beauty', a positive goal.[5] This distinction between 'outer' and 'inner' form recurs, expressly or implicitly, in later aesthetic discussions. Thus when Schelling identified 'rhythm' as one of the 'forms peculiar to music', he understood 'rhythm' (by which he meant 'the periodic division of something uniform') to express some of the 'inner' meaning of the work (rhythm 'constitutes the concept of unity expanding into diversity'; its 'beauty is not material').[6] Likewise Schilling's remark, cited above in a different context, that 'form is not merely a matter of the shape of a thing' hinges on this opposition between 'outer' and 'inner'.

In practical forums (such as composition manuals or newspaper criticism) from Chopin's time, the precise philosophical lineage of citations of aesthetic form cannot usually be determined. Most often, writers who invoked the concept referred generally to the entire organisation of the composition, and the ways all of its parts related to one another.[7] These references nonetheless demonstrate that at least a general, sometimes casual, cognisance of the positions of the aestheticians reached the populace at large. At the same time, the very broadness with which form in the aesthetic sense was cited suggests that the idea did not occupy a particularly prominent niche in the minds of this populace.

GENERIC FORM

Far more significant in musical circles was the second pervasive sense of form, meaning genre or kind.[8] The quotation from Koch already introduced us to this usage, which is still with us today: when we hear talk of, say, nineteenth-century Polish dance forms, we understand this to refer to such genres as the mazurka and polonaise. But we have repressed and even reversed the understanding held in musical cultures of Chopin's time of the relationship of this meaning of form and form meaning *structure* or *plan*. For form as a synonym of genre was by far the more common of the two; indeed, for most composers, critics and listeners, structural form was widely considered but one of many constructive and affective features that might enter into the composition and perception of genres.

When the word form appeared in journalistic criticism from Chopin's day, it usually meant genre or kind. The following excerpts show this clearly:

> The true Polish mazurka, such as M. Chopin reproduces for us here, carries so particular a character, and at the same time adapts with such advantage to the expression of a sombre melancholy as well as to that of an eccentric joy – it is suitable as much to love songs as to war songs – that it seems to us preferable to many other musical forms. (a review of the Mazurkas Op. 17)[9]

> The form of the sonata maintains its authority amidst the countless small forms of salon pieces occasioned by the taste of fashion. Because it traverses in its three or four movements a whole scale of sentiments, it offers the composer not merely occasion to verify his richer and persistent ingenuity, rather it also demands great mastery in the accomplishment of extended forms. (a review of the Sonata in B minor, Op. 58)[10]

Here too, as in its aesthetic guise, form as genre admitted a much wider variety of musical experience than did the simpler notion of schematic form. For the concept of genre (when properly understood to extend beyond a simple classificatory notion derived from a list of shared characteristics) involves the conceptions and perceptions of composers, performers and listeners.[11] Social constructions lie at the heart of genre: the composer employs some of the conventions and gestures of a genre in writing a piece, and the listener (or the performer) interprets certain aspects of the piece in a way conditioned by this genre. The genre is not situated solely in either the composer's deeds or the listener's responses; rather the interaction of the two yields this significant framework for the communication of musical meaning. The interpretation of a genre, as Laurence Dreyfus observes, depends largely on the people who use it, which helps explain the emphasis given to affect and values in early nineteenth-century descriptions of genres.[12] And the way in which a genre was used also reveals much about contemporary attitudes toward the past and the present: the genre embodied tradition and experience, and sometimes the rejection of the same. Hence references to form in the sense of genre often reveal much about the ideological functions that a particular kind served in its societies.

STRUCTURAL FORM

In considering the meanings of structural or morphological form in Chopin's day, we need to distinguish among the groups who used the concept. For something quite akin to our modern structural sense of form (and in many cases – e.g. the sonata and the concerto – serving as the basis of it) was in common employ during the eighteenth and the first part of the nineteenth centuries. But it has been insufficiently stressed in the modern literature that form in this sense appeared almost exclusively in contexts intended primarily for composers, which is to say in composition manuals.[13] Throughout the eighteenth and early nineteenth centuries, in other words, structural form was primarily considered part of the technical arsenal that a composer presumably mastered, along with such skills as counterpoint and harmony. Like all facets of technique, and in particular like the precepts of rhetoric from which it was derived, composers deployed it in order to produce expressive reactions; it was not necessarily understood as an expressive feature in itself. And like other technical features, listeners tended to consider it secondary to such aspects as genre and expression.

Yet the matter is not quite so simple. For we can date precisely to Chopin's lifetime the tentative beginnings of the modern attitude that grants to structural form a leading role in the musical understanding of both composer and listener. The *Berliner allgemeine musikalische Zeitung*, a new and liberal music periodical, ran in the mid and late 1820s several articles and reviews that touted the benefits for listeners of grasping structural form. (Many of them were by the editor, A. B. Marx, who would later become the central figure in the establishment of the doctrine of structural forms.) Robert Schumann's famous 1835 review of Berlioz's *Symphonie fantastique* apologetically demonstrates the comprehensibility and symmetry of the first movement by comparing it to the 'traditional model' for symphonic first movements.[14] In the following excerpt, from an 1842 review by the French critic Maurice Bourges, we can see an example of such early formal analysis applied to Chopin's Nocturnes Op. 48 (I cite only the discussion of the first of the set, in C minor):

> Here in a few words is the outline [*coupe*] of the thirteenth nocturne. A first period, in C minor, is distinguished by the character of predominant melody [*mélodie dominante*]. The second, in C major, begins pianissimo; it belongs to the complex

form that has been very nicely dubbed melodic harmony [*harmonie-mélodique*]. Then it is ended by the reproduction of the first theme, accompanied this time by throbbing chords [*d'accords battus*] that give a new warmth to the general rhythm. . . .

I might have feared your reproach, madame, about this exactitude in analysing the outline of these pieces, if I had not known that you are among those who attach a great interest in the intelligence of the plan. It is the sole means of giving the performance a character of indispensable unity. Without this, how would one render sensible the distinction of essential and accessory ideas? To make one's playing a kind of painting, to give it perspective, profundity, one absolutely must master the material plan of the work, even if it is a question of a simple prelude where the arrangement hides beneath an apparent disorder.[15]

The last, rationalising paragraph as well as the general tone of Bourges's review suggests that structural form – *plan* or *coupe* in his vocabulary borrowed from the theorist Antoine Reicha – had in 1842 something of the quality of a new-found toy that one might place at the disposal of an amateur pianist or listener.[16] And Bourges's simplistic attempt at the description or analysis of structural form remained very much the exception in criticism – French criticism, at least – for the remainder of Chopin's life. Far more common, as remarked upon above, were references to 'form' in its aesthetic or generic aspects.

The structural sense of form really began to catch hold firmly in Germany in the 1840s. To a large degree, this resulted from the widespread influence of Hegel's ideas on aesthetics, particularly as promulgated by such musical apologists and followers as Eduard Krüger and A.B. Marx.[17] In the pages of the *Neue Zeitschrift für Musik*, Krüger in 1842 undertook an extensive critique of Hegel's aesthetics as they applied to music. The new attitude toward the concept of form emerges clearly when we compare the earlier accounts of aesthetic form with Krüger's discussion of Hegelian 'musical form' in terms of 'fundamental binary and ternary structure[s]'.[18] Form was no longer identified amorphously with all that constructively contributes to the perception of beauty in a musical work. Rather, for Hegel (as interpreted by Krüger), it was something more structural, more architectonic. And Marx carried this sense of architectonic form even further when he codified a doctrine of structural forms (his *Formenlehre*) in a variety of theoretical works (including the *Allgemeine Musiklehre* of 1839 and the famous *Lehre von der musikalischen Composition* of 1842). While Marx's theories were intended primarily to inform the activities of composers, their influence spread generally in the musical culture of the time, in part because of the primacy Marx gave to form in the remarkably lucid pedagogical layout of his volumes (Marx taught at the University of Berlin). As Dreyfus has noted, Marx's *Formenlehre* began to reverse the perceptual hierarchy of previous generations in its grossly anachronistic assertion that structural form determines musical genre. The comparatively incidental quality of genre in Marx's scheme, as well as the power-

ful influence of his *Formenlehre* for nearly a century after its inscription together
dealt the concept of musical genre a blow from which it has only recently begun
to recover.

The relative novelty of structural form for listeners (as opposed to composers),
and its greater prominence in German circles than in French or Polish suggest
that it would not have figured very centrally in contemporary perceptions of
Chopin's works. For a few progressive amateurs and for his professional cohorts,
it may have been another story, but for the majority of his audience, form
remained primarily a generic concept, and to some degree an aesthetic one.

SMALLNESS: THE STATUS OF THE MINIATURE

Unlike the concept of form, more richly inflected in the 1830s and 1840s than
today, the resonances of the adjective *small* – especially the negative ones – were,
when applied to artworks, not so much different from those we encounter today.
It is nonetheless useful to remind ourselves that our own often covert evaluations
of small forms have rather more overt historical roots.

In particular, the notion that smaller types rank lower hierarchically than larger
kinds has remained ingrained since Chopin's time. An extended controversy developed in France over the perceived assault on the hierarchy of genres by Romantic
artists such as Géricault.[19] Something similar followed in musical circles, according
to an article by August Kahlert from an 1835 issue of the *Neue Zeitschrift für
Musik*.[20] Its title, 'Die Genrebilder in der modernen Musik' ('Genre painting in
modern music'), reveals its goal: to articulate an explicit link between French
genre painting and the recent glut of short instrumental compositions. Kahlert
drew what he saw as alarming parallels between the situation in contemporary art,
where genre painting seemed to profit at the expense of historical subjects, and
that in music, where small instrumental genres gained at the loss of larger kinds:

> Genre painting has also become visible in music. It is characteristic that enthusiasm
> for the great, the far-reaching, the deep must make way for a multitude of small
> designs, accomplished forms for the graceful, charming, coquettish. The lowest
> and most popular music genre, dance music even, must have recourse to the
> most expensive finery in order to corrupt the meaning. Dramatic music is with
> the greatest of pleasure composed of nothing but small forms (Romances, Couplets,
> Lieder, etc.). The catalogues swarm with Sketches, Eclogues, Impromptus,
> Bagatelles, Rhapsodies, Etudes, etc. One wants as much variety as is possible,
> however nothing but the small. Because however the newer art works are too weak
> to represent themselves, a content is therefore *pressed upon* them, and thus arise
> instrumental pieces with *literary titles* [*Ueberschriften*].[21]

Kahlert laid bare a typical complaint against small forms, namely that the various
eclogues and etudes, with their inscriptions that attempted weakly to compensate

for their lack of genuine musical content, had displaced attention away from the more deserving and accomplished monumental kinds (in which category he presumably included symphonies and sonatas). And in what would also prove to be an influential strategy for the reception of Chopin (the tale of which I must leave for another essay), Kahlert's descriptive language reveals the role of gender in the formulation of his evaluative stance. The notion that 'finery' might 'corrupt the meaning' of a genre-piece already deflects judgement onto a gendered criterion. Still more telling in this regard are his polar oppositions that pit 'far-reaching' and 'accomplished forms' against 'coquettish' and 'small designs'. Kahlert (and many others) devalued small forms in part because they were perceived as being 'feminine' music.

Even among progressives, smaller kinds could seem suspect when they were pursued to the exclusion of larger genres. Critics most often raised this concern in connection with Chopin when considering the limited instrumental sphere within which the composer worked. Hence while Schumann, one of Chopin's earliest and most staunch advocates, generally praised his achievements, he nonetheless found himself wondering if the Pole would ever take the next step in his artistic development:

> Ever new and inventive in the external qualities [*im Äußerlichen*], in the construction [*Gestaltung*] of his compositions, in special instrumental effects, in the internal qualities [*im Innerlichen*] however he remains the same, so that we would fear that he will not rise any higher than he has already risen. And although this is high enough to render his name immortal in the history of modern art, his effectiveness is limited to the narrow sphere of piano music, whereas with his powers he might climb to far greater heights, and gain an influence on the general development of our art.[22]

Schumann went on to urge contentment with Chopin's output as it stood; nonetheless, the familiar comparison with the 'greater heights' to be achieved in what we can safely interpret to be the larger genres remains a significant feature of Schumann's view of Chopin.[23] As we shall see, the same comparison still lurks silently – and invidiously, I would say – even among the most well meaning of contemporary performers and critics.

SMALL FORMS: THE PRELUDES OP. 28

How can the preceding analysis of both halves of the term *small form* affect our practices as pianists and listeners? I would hope it might expand our awareness of its historical possibilities, and in turn suggest some alternative (and perhaps more historically appropriate) modes of understanding than those delimited by our customary notion of structural form. As just one instance of the fascinating and productive ways in which this historical orientation might affect our interpretation of Chopin, I would like to consider his smallest forms, the Preludes Op. 28. I am particulary concerned with their supposed status as a cycle to be performed integrally by pianists (one seldom hears it any other way these days) and analysed as a unified or organic set by critics.

The assertion that the twenty-four pieces of Op. 28 constitute an integral set grew in large part from lingering insecurity over the meaning of Chopin's title, 'Preludes'. The issue troubled commentators from the very start, as witness these famous reactions by Schumann (in a curt review of the entire set) and Liszt (in an account of Chopin's 1841 Parisian recital):

> I would term the Preludes remarkable [*merkwürdig*, which also carries the connotation 'strange']. I confess I imagined them differently, and designed in the grandest style, like his Etudes. Almost the opposite: they are sketches, beginnings of Etudes, or, so to speak, ruins, individual eagle pinions, all disorder and wild confusion.[24]

> Chopin's Preludes are compositions of an order entirely apart. They are not only, as the title might make one think, pieces destined to be played in the guise of introductions to other pieces; they are poetic preludes, analogous to those of a great contemporary poet, who cradles the soul in golden dreams, and elevates it to the regions of the ideal.[25]

Neither Schumann nor Liszt found what he expected in the Preludes. Schumann was trumped and mildly disturbed by their brevity and apparent disorder; Liszt was impressively struck by the disparity between the function suggested by their title and what he perceived as their more exalted artistic purpose.[26] A century later, André Gide concisely summed up this last line of thought when he wrote 'I admit that I do not understand well the title that Chopin liked to give to these short pieces: *Preludes*. Preludes to what?'[27] At stake for these observers is precisely the status of Chopin's preludes when viewed against the tradition of the genre – or form, as Chopin's cohorts would likely have said – to which they evidently belong.

The preludes known to Chopin's contemporaries (and Gide too) functioned in just the way their title would suggest: as brief, often improvisatory introductions to other, larger works. At the most utilitarian level, these pieces allowed the performer to test the feel of the keyboard before launching into a longer work, and gave the listener a chance gradually to settle into the musical experience. Czerny stated this directly in 1836:

> It is akin to a crown of distinction for a keyboardist, particularly in private circles at the performance of solo works, if he does not begin directly with the composi-

tion itself but is capable by means of a suitable prelude of preparing the listeners, setting the mood, and also thereby ascertaining the qualities of the pianoforte, perhaps unfamiliar to him, in an appropriate fashion.[28]

More engagingly, preludes tested either the pianist's improvisational mettle (when actually conceived in performance) or the composer's skill at conveying the impression of impromptu display (when notated). Composers frequently deployed block chords, rapid scalar or arpeggiated figuration and sudden deflections toward other keys (though ordinarily without tonicising them) to produce this sensation. They normally avoided lending much prominence to themes (preludes were ordinarily monothematic or, better, 'monomotivic'), nor did they typically develop their themes or motives. Since the practice of the day demanded that the prelude conclude (though not necessarily begin) in the same key as the work that it preceded, composers published examples of preludes in all the major and minor keys: the amateur pianist who could not manage to improvise a prelude could thereby find published examples suitable to any tonal circumstance. Czerny mentioned one other interesting harmonic permutation: longer and more elaborate preludes attached to works for which the composer provided no introduction should end on the dominant seventh chord, so as to lead directly into the theme.[29] (The possibility of open-ended conclusions has provocative ramifications for our understanding of Chopin's essays in the genre.) The preludes by Chaulieu and Czerny shown in Example 1 typify the genre as it was understood in the first half of the nineteenth century.

Example 1   (a) Charles Chaulieu, Prelude in D♭ major (from *Vingt-quatre petits préludes* Op. 9, c. 1820–25)

(b) Carl Czerny, Prelude in E♭ major (from *Systematische Anleitung zum Fantasieren auf dem Pianoforte*, 1836)

Ex. 1 (*cont.*)

'Utilitarian' is a word that rarely escapes the lips of a Chopin critic. It would hardly do for the 'Raphael' or 'Ariel' of pianists (as he was often styled in his day) to be allied with the functional or even the more aesthetically appealing aspects of the prelude described above; instead critics sought more poetic or analytically ambitious explanations for Chopin's efforts in the genre. Hence Schumann's stunning and romantically charged metaphors, hence Liszt's veiled analogy with the poet Lamartine, hence Gide's musings over the title, and hence – I believe – the tendency to conceive of Op. 28 as an integral, organic set.

Proponents of the grand unity of the Preludes often quite explicitly reject the 'prosaic' tradition of the genre. Indeed, such rejection would seem to be a necessary step for arguments in favor of the artistic wholeness of Op. 28. Jean-Jacques Eigeldinger, for example, prefaces his otherwise subtly conceived comments on the motivic unity of the set as a whole with this remark:

> Clearly the collection no longer fulfils any of the functions to which its title had laid claim hitherto. To take out some of the Preludes and couple them with other Chopin pieces in the same key might be an interesting experiment at best, but could hardly be termed necessary.[30]

Having found the tradition of the prelude wanting in explanatory power, Eigeldinger goes on to construct a case for the unity of the entire set. He argues that this unity derives from the apparent omnipresence of a motivic cell characterised by a rising sixth falling back to the fifth, a cell that he contends is generated by the dictates of the temperament of Chopin's piano. Apart from this ingenious claim about the correspondence between the motivic cell and the tuning process, Eigeldinger's stance typifies those who would assert a larger meaning for Op. 28.[31] In essence, critics locate the highest artistic achievement not so much in the individual preludes themselves (though they seldom deny the quality of these works) as in the nuanced motivic relationships that may be teased out of all twenty-four of the preludes working together. And concert pianists would seem to echo this position by seldom performing them as anything but a complete set of twenty-four.[32]

Two intertwined problems weaken the force of these arguments. First, they confuse levels of form, privileging a type of extended structural form (and more precisely, a later nineteenth- and twentieth-century type of structural form), and devaluing or ignoring what Chopin and his contemporaries would have understood to be the generic – formal – resonances of the prelude. Said another way, they take a willfully anachronistic viewpoint of the formal organisation of the Preludes. Second, these arguments endorse – unwittingly, perhaps – the view that smallness of form works to the aesthetic detriment of a musical work. In contending that Op. 28 represents a unified whole, they essentially claim that 'large forms' (as an integral Op. 28 must surely be considered) were a desiderata for Chopin and all his audiences. While this was certainly true of the conservative wing (represented above by August Kahlert) of the 1830s and 1840s, and occasionally even of more progressive types like Schumann, it cannot be maintained as a generally accepted attitude of the time. More worrisome still, to argue for the worth of Op. 28 on the basis of its supposed function as a sublime 'large form' rather than on the basis of its individual small numbers would seem at once to perpetuate some of the gender-based aesthetic justifications of the nineteenth century and to accept the premises of the old canard that Chopin was not a master of large forms even as it attempts to refute them. The attitude betrays a continuing distrust of the small, a refusal to accept Chopin's Preludes at face value.

André Gide to the contrary, then, we have no reason to worry the title to Op. 28. Chopin and his contemporaries understood perfectly the genre of the prelude; what is more, they valued it on its own terms. Even in the remarks of Schumann and Liszt, we can detect their awareness of the traditional generic functions served by Chopin's Preludes. Schumann's reference to 'individual eagle pinions' [*einzelne Adlerfittige*] shows that Schumann entertained no thought that Op. 28 might constitute a unified set; indeed, the solitary pinions were 'all disorder and wild confusion'.[33] And when Liszt wrote 'they are not only. . .pieces destined to be played in the guise of introductions to other pieces', the key word is 'only': Liszt at once admitted the traditional function of the genre while he praised the poetic ways in which Chopin's contributions exceeded this tradition.[34]

In Chopin's own practice as both a performer and a composer we find further confirmation that the Preludes drew on the tradition of the genre for at least some of their comprehensibility. First, in Léon Escudier's critique of Chopin's 1841 Parisian recital (which Liszt also reviewed), we read testimony of his skills at preluding:

> One may say that Chopin is the creator of a school of piano and a school of composition. In truth, nothing equals the lightness, the sweetness with which the composer preludes on the piano; moreover nothing may be compared to his works, full of originality, distinction and grace.[35]

Escudier may well have referred to preludes that the composer improvised (the verb *préluder* generally signified the improvisatory practice) as opposed to those that he composed and published (later in the review, he commented separately on the four published preludes performed at the recital). Nonetheless, by underscoring Chopin's skills in this area, he identified one of the traditional formal models against which Chopin's Op. 28 would have been judged.[36]

Second, we have a hint that Chopin in performance coupled a prelude 'in the guise of an introduction' (as Liszt would say) to another of his works. A surviving printed programme from his recital in Glasgow on 27 September 1848 lists as the first item to be performed an 'Andante et Impromptu'. Beneath the printed line, someone entered in ink (presumably contemporaneously) 'No. 8 & 36'.[37] The last penned number conclusively places the impromptu as the F♯ major, Op. 36. The identity of the first work is more problematic. While sometimes taken to allude to the *Andante spianato* in G major that precedes the *Grand Polonaise* Op. 22 (a work that Chopin liked to detach from the *Polonaise*), I would suggest instead that the 'No. 8' refers to the Eighth Prelude of Op. 28, in F♯ minor. Of course, Chopin left a tempo marking for this Prelude of 'Molto agitato', not 'Andante'. But the parallel tonalities of the Prelude and the Impromptu (Example 2 re-

Example 2   (a) Chopin, Prelude in F♯ minor, Op. 28 No. 8, bars 1–2

(b) Impromptu in F♯ major, Op. 36, bars 1–13

Ex. 2 (*cont.*)

produces the first bars of each piece) make a more logical join (one further facilitated by the turn to F♯ major toward the end of the Prelude, bars 29–31; see
Example 3 below) than would follow from a linking of the *Andante spianato* and
the Impromptu.[38]

More commonly, Chopin performed the preludes as separate pieces, or in groups
with other preludes. (A typical programme listing, this from his 1842 Parisian recital, was 'Suite de Nocturnes, Préludes, et Etudes'.) In this routine we can detect an
expansion in the functional possibilities of the genre, such that preludes might also
serve as separate concert pieces. Chopin appears to have been largely responsible
for this functional expansion. In promoting these 'concert' preludes, he essentially
followed his practice in the etude, where his contributions to the genre served
equally as didactic and as concert works. Chopin's last published prelude, the
C♯ minor Op. 45, an extended work that plainly was meant to stand alone in
performance, clarifies that he was moving in the direction of the 'concert prelude'
in Op. 28. In any event, this sort of expansion of the possibilities of the genre
occurs throughout Chopin's *œuvre* (indeed, it counts among the chief reasons we
celebrate him as a composer). It would be a mistake to presume that 'expansion'
of the genre meant 'negation' of its tradition. Far from it: the expansion in meaning could not have taken place without a deep understanding of and complicity
in the tradition from which it partially departs.

As to evidence of the force of formal tradition in the musical construction of
the Preludes, adequately to discuss it would overwhelm the boundaries of this
essay. In any event, a number of studies have chronicled quite nicely (if not always

explicitly in terms of the tradition of the genre) many of the ways in which the formal qualities of brevity, monothematicism, openness, fractured syntax and stylised improvisation reveal themselves in various individual preludes.[39] For the purposes of this essay, I wish to draw attention to only one compositional aspect of the Preludes, closure.[40] The endings are one of the most striking features of the preludes, and have much to reveal once we expand our sense of form beyond the structural into the generic.

The endings to the Preludes seldom give comfort. By this I mean that the endings often seem to stand somewhat apart from the body of the prelude; their gestures at closure sound unrelated to what has passed before. In some instances, this difference can be understood as a consequence of the monothematic tendency of the genre: when the musical figure unfolded throughout the body of the

Example 3   (a) Prelude in A minor, bars 18–23

(b) Prelude in D major, bars 32–9

(c) Prelude in F♯ minor, bars 31–4

prelude seemed unsuitable as a closing idea, Chopin evidently imported some other kind of notion to serve as the ending. The stark final cadences of the A minor, D major and F♯ minor Preludes (Example 3) produce an arresting textural contrast to the disjointed (in the case of the A minor work) and exuberant (in the other two instances) figuration that precedes them. Other times, though, the dissimilar close arrives despite the capability of the principal motive to support a similar cadence. The endings to the E minor, C minor and G minor Preludes fall into this category (see Example 4). On still other occasions, Chopin separated

Example 4   (a) Prelude in E minor, bars 20–5

(b) Prelude in C minor, bars 9–13

(c) Prelude in G minor, bars 36–41

perceptually a cadence that otherwise continued to reproduce the principal motive of the piece. The blurring caused by the open pedal in the B minor Prelude and the *ritenuto* in the last two measures of the D♭ major Prelude effectively isolate the cadential gestures from what precedes them (see Example 5). And finally, there are

Example 5   (a) Prelude in B minor, bars 22–6

(b) Prelude in Db major, bars 83–9

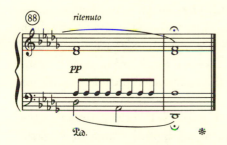

those cadences that flow smoothly from the body of the prelude but nonetheless simply undermine full closure in one way or another. The imperfect cadence of the B major Prelude provides a mild example, and the famous eb^2 that colours the end of the F major Prelude a more radical one (see Example 6).

Example 6   (a) Prelude in B major, bars 21–7

Ex. 6 (*cont.*)

(b) Prelude in F major, bars 20–2

Now plainly the structural qualities of these 'irregular' endings contributed to the 'poetic' ethos of the Preludes as constructed by the likes of Liszt and Schumann. It is not difficult, for example, to perceive a connection between the nature of closure in Op. 28 and Schumann's characterisation of the individual pieces as 'ruins'. But the generic resonances of these endings cast even more fascinating light on Chopin's strategy. For the frequent deflections of closure in Op. 28 at once evoke and transform a particular strand of the generic tradition: the conclusions of improvised, longer preludes, which Czerny described (we saw above) as ending on dominant seventh chords. The evocation is nowhere more charged than in the F major Prelude (Example 6), the E♭-tinged ending of which has been the subject of many elaborate, and not entirely adequate, 'structural' explanations. But the final measures make most sense when heard in generic terms as an ironic commentary on this tradition of the open-ended prelude. The eb^2 of bar 21 recalls the similar gesture of bar 12, where the added seventh helped push the harmony to the subdominant in the following bar. While the harmony of the ending of the prelude cannot really be heard as an applied dominant (Agawu observes that 'the identity of the F^{b7} is. . .transferrable [from bar 12], but not its syntactical property'[41]), the memory of its earlier function is enough to call to mind the tradition of dominant-seventh cadences. And this tradition leads us, if ever so fleetingly, to consider whether the F major Prelude should quirkily serve as an introduction to a larger work in B♭ major.

Chopin evoked this quality of open-endedness in order to transform the nature of closure in the short, notated prelude, where previously (and indeed still, in several of Chopin's Op. 28) full closure had prevailed. As we have seen, Chopin ordinarily transformed the closural tendencies of the genre less radically than in the F major Prelude: rather than challenge the very idea of closure, Chopin normally preferred simply to leave matters somewhat undone at the ends of preludes. And curiously enough, one reason that he may have been prompted to transform the genre in this way was to facilitate one of its traditional generic functions. For when a prelude lacks full closure, it more effortlessly serves 'in the guise of an introduction' to another work. In other words, by ending preludes abruptly and incompletely, Chopin allowed for an ensuing longer work to fulfil the closural promise left hanging in the introductory prelude. The memory of this possibility for fuller closure would have animated the 'concert' prelude too, with closure deferred from prelude to prelude (if they were performed in groups together) or even into the next gathering of pieces. Perhaps actual full closure might arrive; perhaps it might not: the ambiguity or insecurity thus embodied in the unfolding recital would have had a strong appeal to the aesthetic sensibilities in Chopin's time.[42] The most common kind of accolade that befell Chopin after his recitals in the 1840s – he was constantly dubbed the 'poet', 'Ariel' or 'sylph' of the piano – probably had something to do with the play of ambiguity created by his 'concert' preludes. Indeed, this ambiguity might well have influenced Liszt's roundabout description of the genre as acting in the *guise* of an introduction.

Chopin issued a kind of challenge to his audiences in publishing the Preludes, a challenge we have by and large not met. By asking listeners and performers to accept a transformed genre whereby individual preludes might serve both as introductions to other works and as self-standing concert pieces, he challenged the conservative notion that small forms were artistically suspect or negligible. But in considering just the endings of preludes, we have seen how the modern practice of interpreting form primarily as a structural attribute has led on the one hand to a blinkered view of the possibilities of the genre, and on the other, to a problematic conception of the Preludes as a unified set. An examination of other attributes of Op. 28 would only magnify these conclusions.

Perhaps it is time to accept Chopin's challenge. Rather than continue to schedule performances of the complete Op. 28 and to construct analytical monuments to its 'unity', we need to perform and study the preludes individually. We need to stop reading the title 'Prelude' as an obfuscating irritant, and instead to see it as a highly significant clue that can lead to powerful interpretative insights. Understood in this way, Chopin's historical challenge proves to be a good deal more provocative than the anachronistic performing and analytical practices of today, for it would ask audiences to accept the possibility of a work like the A major Prelude (Example 7) standing alone in performance. In short, it would demand that we finally remove the veil of aesthetic suspicion from smallness.

Example 7   Prelude in A major

Ex. 7 (*cont.*)

7   *Beyond the dance*

ADRIAN THOMAS

When the exiled Polish poet Adam Mickiewicz (1798–1855) closed his epic poem *Pan Tadeusz* ('Master Thaddeus', 1834) with a vivid description of a polonaise, he was not only evoking the romantic image of Poland and Lithuania in 1811 but also investing the dance with Polish history, with its continuing patterns of partition and insurrection. In Book 12 of *Pan Tadeusz*, the inn-keeper Jankiel – renowned for the power and brilliance of his dulcimer playing – sparks off the wedding celebrations for Tadeusz and Zosia with the *Polonez Trzeciego Maja* (Polonaise of the Third of May), written to celebrate the enlightened but short-lived Constitution of 1791. Mickiewicz – through his description of Jankiel's performance – darkens the mood with reference to the renegade Confederation of Targowica in 1792 and to the horrific slaughter by the Russians of the citizens of the Warsaw district of Praga during the Polish insurrection of 1794. Jankiel then pays homage to General Dąbrowski, who commanded the exiled Polish Legions in Italy in 1797, by strumming the famous *Mazurka Dąbrowskiego* (since 1926, the Polish national anthem), and a second polonaise concludes the festivities.[1]

Mickiewicz wrote *Pan Tadeusz* in Paris, where he and many other Poles, including Chopin, had settled in the aftermath of the Polish uprising of November 1830. By then, polonaises, mazurkas and other indigenous folk dances were very much part of Polish art culture. But they had not always been so: their history lay principally outside Poland, and, in finding exotic colour in their rhythms and melodies, Mickiewicz was following a well-trodden European path (the tapping of overtly patriotic sentiments, however, was a relatively recent phenomenon).

In the Europe of the mid-sixteenth to the mid-eighteenth century the 'Polish Dance' was a generic concept and, as a title, it is found only in non-Polish sources of the period. The first surviving printed example, 'Der Polnisch Tantz', is to be found in a Nuremberg lute tablature of 1544.[2] In the ensuing decades, other titles emerged, such as the 'Chorea polonica' or 'Saltus polonicus'. These covered an intermingled range of metric, melodic and rhythmic types, and the assumption must be that these anonymous 'Polish' pieces were by ex-patriot Poles, or were based on melodies and rhythms thought to originate in Poland. Often the melody might be authentic, with the metre and rhythm drawn from elsewhere in Europe ('Volta polonica').[3]

The principal Polish source of the late Renaissance, Jan of Lublin's tablature (1537–48), contains many dances, each with a specific Polish title, such as 'Chodzony' (Walking Dance) or 'Wyrwany' (Snatching Dance).[4] Some are arrangements of songs, a feature that is deeply rooted in folk dance traditions. The dances are bi-partite, the first part in slow duple time, the second in a lively triple metre, the latter governed sometimes by the principle of *proportio* and usually possessing the strong Polish rhythmic character of the later mazurka. But neither *mazur* nor *polonez* occurs in titles at this stage, either in Poland or abroad.

By the end of the seventeenth century, the predominant *mazur* rhythms of the European 'Polish Dance' were being infiltrated by salient characteristics of the *polonez*, which then began to establish itself as an independent compositional form.[5] And, by the mid-eighteenth century, the *polonez* had acquired the French *polonaise* or *polonoise* as its enduring title. By this time, a considerable body of European compositions contained polonaises, including works by Telemann (who spent several years in Poland) and J. S. Bach, whose polonaise from the Suite in B minor appropriates and stylises the melody of the Polish folk song 'Wezmę ja kontusz' (I'll take my nobleman's robe). In the meantime, the art polonaise in seventeenth- and eighteenth-century Poland shows a consistent progression paralleling that of other European dances. The earliest known polonaise melody, 'W żłobie leży' (the mid-seventeenth century carol Lying in a Manger), has a simple repeated binary structure (4+6) in which the second half shifts directly into the relative minor. Already it exhibits several characteristic features: the rhythm of the opening bar, the cadential flourish, two-bar phrasing and the transparent use of sequence (see Example 1).

Example 1   'W żłobie leży' (melody line)[6]

A century later, the daughter of King Augustus III of Poland, Princess Anna Maria of Saxony (1728–97), had amassed over 350 polonaises (composers unknown),[7] whose features are symptomatic of how enriched the genre had become by the 1770s: instrumentally conceived melodic lines, with rococo figuration and often 'ragged' syncopations (Book 3 no. 1); the use of the folk-derived lydian fourth (notably in Book 8 no. 5, where it colours both polonaise sections and the start of the trio; see Example 2a); and a harmonic language that also reflects folk practice in its use of VII[7] and V[9], where the submediant is stressed in the melodic line (a striking, but by no means isolated, instance occurs in Book 11 no. 41; see Examples 2b and 2c).[8]

Example 2   (a) Polonaise, Hławiczka, book 8 No. 5, opening

(b) Polonaise, Hławiczka, book 11 No. 41, trio, opening

(c) 'Czarna chmureczka' (Tiny little black cloud)[9]
      folk dance from Wilanów, near Warsaw

Structurally there has been considerable expansion. There is now a fully-fledged binary or da capo trio section (sometimes in the same major key as the polonaise). The proportions overall and within the polonaise and trio sections vary quite significantly, although the trios are more regularly compounded of multiples of two than are the polonaises, where single-bar extensions can distort the established patterns. The sixth polonaise from Book 5 is not untypical:[10]

Polonaise |:A 13 bs: 4 (2+2)+3 (2+1) + 4 (sequence: 2+1+1)+2 :|
             |:B 6 bs: (2+2+2):|
                  A
Trio (Duma)[11] |:C 6 bs: (2+2+2):|
             |:D 4 bs: (2+2) plus
                  C 4 bs: (2+2):|
Polonaise   da capo

In the latter years of the eighteenth century, Polish composers responded to turbulent times by elevating the polonaise to the status of national symbol, noble, majestic, but also melancholic, much as recalled by Mickiewicz. Jan Stefani (1746–1829), Józef Kozłowski (1757–1831), Michał Kleofas Ogiński (1765–1833) and Karol Kurpiński (1785–1857) were seminal figures, not only composing keyboard polonaises, but also extending Polish dance influence to other genres.[12] Stefani's stirring folk opera *Krakowiacy i Górale* (Cracovians and Highlanders, 1794) includes many dances, ranging from the polonaise and mazurka to the *oberek* and *krakowiak*, most of them choral or solo numbers.[13] Ogiński, on the other hand, came to personify the melancholic aspect of the polonaise, anticipating Chopin's later developments. His 'Pożegnanie Ojczyzny' (Farewell to the Fatherland, 1794),[14] one of the most famous programmatic keyboard polonaises of the period, is relatively straightforward structurally, although its minor mode and melodic demeanour, along with an improvised flourish in the B section and the martial quality of the trio's opening bars, are characteristic of the emotional depth with which this dance had newly become associated (see Example 3).

Example 3   Ogiński, Polonaise in A minor, bars 1-12

But the type of polonaise being composed twenty years later was a much reduced force. It had become what one might call a *polonez domowy* (family polonaise), mirroring the political and social weaknesses brought about by the country's partition in 1795 by Austria, Prussia and Russia: ' "Poland", as an abstraction, could be remembered from the past, or aspired to for the future, but only imagined in the present. It had not merely been broken into three parts; it had been vaporised, transposed into thin air, fragmented into millions of invisible particles.'[15] Cultural demoralisation, a condition we tend to associate with our own times, was an inevitable result.

And yet the polonaises, mazurkas and other dance-influenced works of Chopin's youth (which we may date from his first pieces in 1817 to the time of his departure from Poland in the autumn of 1830) are far from pale imitations of the middle-of-the-road salon pieces which had been the norm when he was born in 1810. And it is clear, from the earliest stage, that the folk dimension of Polish dances provided the primary focus for the reassertion of cultural, and therefore national, pride.

As a young boy and teenager, Chopin turned naturally to existing music in developing his own response to his musical and social environment.[16] The prime inspiration, however, was Polish music. Ogiński exerted a certain influence, and loose thematic correlations may be made between a number of his polonaises and those of the young Chopin. There is a distinct (if arguably folk-generic) resemblance between the melodic line of Example 3 and the opening bars of the trio of Chopin's B♭ Polonaise (1817), while improvisatory flourishes and similar chordal fanfares occur in 'Pożegnanie Ojczyzny' and Chopin's G minor Polonaise (also 1817).

More blatant and deliberate borrowings occur in the two show pieces for piano and orchestra, the *Fantasy on Polish Airs*, Op. 13, and the *Rondo à la krakowiak*, Op. 14.[17] The *Fantasy* is a chain of embellished melodies appropriated from a number of sources: a popular tune, 'Już miesiąc zaszedł psy się uśpiły' (The moon had set, the dogs were asleep);[18] a theme by Kurpiński, probably based on an original Ukrainian *kołomyjka* (a duple-time round dance); and a *kujawiak* (like the Ukrainian *kołomyjka*, a round dance).[19] The similarity of the principal theme of the Op. 14 *Rondo* to a well-known krakowiak of the time may have been subliminal or the result of Chopin's assimilation of common folk features such as initial rising triads, short motivic repetitions and (in subsequent ornamentations of Chopin's theme) the lydian fourth (see Example 4).[20]

Example 4 'Albośmy to jacy jacy', folk dance from Proszowic near Kraków

Krakowiak kopieniacki, od Proszowic

Albośmy   to   jacy   jacy,   jacy   jacy,   chłopcy kra - ko - wiacy

The theme of the introduction of Op. 14, on the other hand, 'is original; more so than I myself in a beige suit', as Chopin whimsically put it.[21] Here the melodic and rhythmic contour draws closely on pentatonic folk models from the central Polish regions of Mazowsze and Kujawy, not least in the concluding phrase, where the rise through the triad to the minor seventh above is characteristic of a wide geographical spread of Polish folk melodies. The notion of a sequence of dances in both Op. 13 and Op. 14 may seem casual, but, in the case of the latter, Chopin appears to be following in part the practice observed by the folklorist Łukasz Gołębiowski in Kraków in 1830: '[the dancing] starts with a *Polski*, and next they call a *Mazur*: as the gaiety increases, only at that moment does the *Krakowiak* take over'.[22]

What is clear in the few works so far cited is that Chopin saw whatever primary material he chose as precisely that, and that his structures are designed to display ideas and their elaboration to best advantage. Op. 14 is not the only rondo with folk material, as the finales of the two piano concertos amply demonstrate. In the F minor Concerto, Op. 21, the mazurka provides the main impetus, particularly in the episodes, although the principal ideas actually hover between the mazurka and the waltz. In the E minor Concerto, Op. 11, however, Chopin adds a further dimension to his chosen genre of the krakowiak. Although notated in the standard 2/4, the soloist's opening four-bar phrase is evidently conceived in a teasing sub-metre of $3+3+2$ beats, the syncopations of the krakowiak transformed through harmonic manipulation and idiomatic melodic ornamentation into something more robust and integral.

When we return to the music for solo piano, the dance impulse is found in many works whose titles are other than mazurka or polonaise.[23] The Rondo in C minor, Op. 1, draws on krakowiak rhythms, while the minuetto and trio from the First Piano Sonata, Op. 4, show signs of the mazurka rhythm heard elsewhere in the finale of Op. 21. The *Rondo à la mazur*, Op. 5, speaks for itself, but the Bolero, Op. 19, is a rum mix of Spanish intentions and Polish actuality. The remaining youthful piano pieces are predominantly polonaises. In Chopin's hands, the genre remains the independent composition that it had become in the eighteenth century and its rhythms, unlike those of the mazurka, rarely stray into other areas of his œuvre. The seven keyboard polonaises of 1821–30[24] move away from the simplicity of the one in B♭ (1817) with its invitatory fanfare and folk-related triadic theme, to the temporarily prevailing sophistication of the 'brilliant style' in the G♯ minor polonaise, where the folk basis of the dance is overwhelmed by a welter of trills and decorative cascades.

But a reappraisal of the expressive potential of the polonaise has clearly taken place with ensuing works, starting with Op. 71 No. 1 in D minor and particularly Op. 71 No. 3 in F minor. For the first time, the melancholic *Affekt* informs the dance, and showy elements are more sparingly in evidence (the later Op. 71 No. 2

is a good example of the new subtlety of melodic inflection). In both Nos. 1 and 3 of Op. 71 the fanfare is more weighty, even sombre, and both display an increasing formal mastery. This manifests itself in the expanded structural concept (still based on the model ABA:CDC:ABA) and in the improvisatory passages, which distort the sections' relative proportions. No. 1, for example, has an extraordinarily developmental B section, while the weird strumming of the trio (see also the trio of No. 2) initiates ideas which seem to unfurl extempore rather than fulfil any expectation of neat melodic ideas and phrases. In the larger-proportioned No. 3 the initial A section is expanded to A¹A² and the 'vamp till ready' at the end of B (a regular feature of later polonaises and of some of the mazurkas) not only balances this expansion but has a precise function based on dance practice. The last polonaise of this period, that in G♭ (1830[?]), is a true bridge to the later polonaises, not least in the vigorous return, as a key element, of the dance's fundamental martial rhythm. Its dark hues are offset by rising sequences (bs 13–15) of a kind to be met elsewhere in the mature polonaises and by registral antiphonies (bs 21–4), which are not only characteristic of this early group but also have firm folk origins. In the trio the initial melodic contour (a rising octave followed by an essentially scalic descent) is typical of the folk genre, while the expanded D section contains prophetic pianistic fireworks.

In the final seven essays in the form, from the two polonaises of Op. 26 (1831–6) through to the *Polonaise-fantaisie*, Op. 61 (1846), Chopin takes something of a quantum leap in his concept (his approach to the mazurka proved to be quite different). For, whereas it is still possible in the earlier polonaises to sense their ties with dance reality, almost as if 'translations from the original', from Op. 26 onwards there is an irreversible process of abstraction, of a distancing from folk impulses. Indeed, these are superseded by concerns for structural experiment in the pursuit of thoroughly 'Romantic' fantasy. That Chopin had difficulty in deciding on the nature of Op. 44 ('a kind of polonaise, but it's more a fantasia')[25] and the title of Op. 61 is indicative of his changing perceptions.

This is not to say that there are not passages that show their ethnic roots. In the E♭ minor Polonaise, Op. 26 No. 2, for example, both the B section and the trio to which it is related have short-breathed phrases and simple melodic and rhythmic ideas, with the trio particularly limited in its developmental aspects. In contrast, after the initial eight bars of the B section, Chopin raises its profile dynamically and tonally away from any folk model. The very opening of Op. 26 No. 2 shows how Chopin is now beginning to isolate, for expressive and functional purposes, the characteristic features of the traditional polonaise. It is actually initiated by the familiar cadential figure, relocated as if to suggest we are coming in on an existing activity. In the companion Polonaise in C♯ minor, Op. 26 No. 1, the folk and dance emphasis is primarily melodic: in bs 34–40 the melodic profile is close to primary folk sources yet is treated as a transition; the simple melodic line of the trio is barely perceptible in the context of fast-changing harmonic and tonal shifts, which in later stages also incur metrical cross-rhythms.

What is particularly noticeable in the Op. 26 polonaises is their emotional range. Both begin with rousing introductory passages, yet within a few bars power has given way to lyricism. One might be forgiven, when considering Chopin's situation at this time, for thinking that there was no other way his feelings of anger, frustration and sentiment could be expressed (let alone reconciled) except, as in the opening twelve bars of Op. 26 No. 1, by the stark juxtaposition of extremes. The two polonaises of Op. 40 in a sense sidestep this dichotomy by concentrating more intently on a single *Affekt* (the same is true of the Ab Polonaise, Op. 53). In the case of the C minor Polonaise, Op. 40 No. 2, the sinister bass phrase informs the entire work. Jachimecki sees this as no coincidental reference to Kurpiński's 'Coronation' polonaise, 'Witaj, Królu polskiej ziemi' (Hail, King of Polish Land, 1825), sung in Warsaw at a ball in honour of the newly-crowned Tsar Nicholas I.[26] Whether or not Chopin was sending a symbol of solidarity with his compatriots back home, the implied derivation from Kurpiński's folk-related theme gives some indication of the variational process that may lie behind many of Chopin's seemingly folk-free melodic ideas. Certainly the texture of a predominant theme with secondary accompaniment, seen to particular advantage here and later in the famous trio with basso ostinato of Op. 53, reminds us of the essentially linear nature of Polish dance in which non-melody instruments come lower in the ranking.

Arguably the best-known polonaise, Op. 40 No. 1, presents the alternative, determinedly optimistic side of Chopin's patriotic sentiments.[27] It is the most compact of the mature polonaises, is in a major key and might be regarded as representing a European view of heroic Poland. In that sense, it is the closest Chopin came to European examples from previous centuries. And yet, for all its straightforward qualities, it represents the ultimate stage in the integration of one aspect of the earlier polonaises, the fanfare. In those polonaises (the majority) where there is a prefatory flourish, Chopin incorporates it into the body of the work through the repeats. But incorporation is not integration: in Op. 26 No. 1 the 'fanfare' ostensibly has more presence than the gentle response. Likewise in Op. 26 No. 2, although here the insistence on the polonaise's hallmark first-beat rhythm ties the fanfare tightly in with what follows. Op. 44 utilises motivic connections to integrate, while the repeated semiquaver patterns at the start of Op. 53 look forward to the basso ostinato of its trio. And the strikingly discursive opening of Op. 61 (despite its motivic link with the start of Op. 26 No. 1) is totally in keeping with the new directions of this last 'polonaise'. In these contexts, it is evident that Op. 40 No. 1 had no need for fanfare or introduction. They are superfluous: the whole composition is a singleminded call to arms.

The *Polonaise-fantaisie*, Op. 61, has been extensively analysed elsewhere, and its improvisatory quality, although in keeping with folk traditions, belongs to a different order. The polonaise framework at this point had burst its seams, so the rhythmic impulses and formal designs of the genre, while integral parts of the new concept, are not the primary focus. That lies in the abstraction of key elements and their reinterpretation, at a remove, within a developing 'symphonic' context. This cannot yet be said of the earlier Polonaise in F♯ minor, Op. 44, although it shares with Op. 61 a grander scale than other polonaises. Yet, in its own way it, too, breaks significant new boundaries. Its structure is greatly expanded.

> Intro A B A¹ B¹ A²
> C B² C¹
> D D¹ 'Tempo di Mazurka'
> A B A¹ B¹ A² Coda

The variation techniques in the flanking polonaise sections are highly characteristic of folk practice, but the addition of a coda indicates the implications of extending the genre's basic design. This is brought even more to the fore in what normally would be regarded as the trio section. Were it not for the reappearance of B material instead of new D ideas between the C sections, we would recognise by the end of C¹ a familiar trio pattern. Despite the inclusion of B², there are persuasive arguments on tonal, textural and thematic grounds to mark the division between polonaise and trio at the first appearance of C.[28] What seems to off-balance the structure is the subsequent appearance of a self-contained second central section (D D¹), an unmistakable mazurka. In fact, the combination of two disparate sections as a trio also occurs in Op. 53, and this might on the face of it prove a satisfactory explanation for the enlarged dimensions of this trio. But its very disparateness provides an enigma. On the one hand, the C passages show the composer moving out of the sphere of the folk dance (despite lydian fourths) into the objectivity of disembodied flurries against an insistent pedal-point, a move foreshadowed in the strange other-worldly trio of Op. 26 No. 2. In contradiction of this, the appearance of a fairly traditional mazurka (unique in a polonaise, but not in the light of *Pan Tadeusz*'s dance sequence) seems to indicate a return to overtly patriotic sentiments which sits oddly if fascinatingly within the overall abstract direction in which Chopin was taking the polonaise.

If the polonaise in Chopin's hands ventured willingly and patriotically into the public domain, the paths of the other dances remained much more private. In letters from Vienna in 1831, Chopin wrote: 'Here, waltzes are called works!. . .I don't pick up anything that is essentially Viennese. I don't even know how to dance a waltz properly. . . . My piano has heard only mazury'.[29] On the evidence of the fifty-five surviving authenticated mazurkas, there can be no doubt that Chopin invested the genre with his personal sense of being Polish, at the same time developing in particular the harmonic and chromatic language in which his deeply-held patriotism could be couched. On a number of occasions he expressed his regional roots in words, acknowledging 'a little Kujaw blood'[30] and to being 'a real blind Mazur'.[31] While other genres, including the waltzes, nocturnes and songs, show these roots from time to time,[32] it is with the mazurkas that most musicians begin their search for this aspect of Chopin's personality, fascinated by the richness of his vision.

Yet those looking for clear-cut and frequent instances of borrowings are in for a disappointment. Chopin preferred the subtler approach of inference, of general allusion and the fragmentary incorporation of 'fingerprints'. He was dismissive of the early folkloristic efforts of Poland's greatest collector, Oskar Kolberg ('good intentions, but too narrow shoulders'[33]), and yet it is through the painstaking work of Kolberg (1814–90) and his successors that we can at least attempt to ascertain the referential nature of Chopin's approach. Certain features are more or less self-evident: instrumental textures, dance-derived elements, rhythmic patterns, modality and melodic designs.

The traditional folk ensemble of central Poland consisted of a melody instrument (the violin played in first position on the upper strings, or the *fujarka*, a high-pitched shepherds' pipe) plus an instrument or two to provide a drone (lower open strings on the violin, or the *dudy* or *gajdy*, a Polish bagpipe) and/or a rhythmic pulse (the *basetla* or *basy*, a string bass played unstopped). There can be little doubt whence came the inspiration for the trio of the Mazurka in F major, Op. 68 No. 3, from 1830 (see Example 5).

Example 5   Trio from the Mazurka in F major, Op. 68, No. 3, bars 1-11

A fujarka melody over an open fifth drone, it betrays its unadorned oberek origins with an insouciant ease.[34] A similar texture, at a lower register, occurs in the downward-leaning *sotto voce* interlude of the Mazurka in B♭, Op. 7 No. 1 (see also the duda introduction to the first version of the Mazurka in A minor, Op. 7 No. 2), while a more sophisticated rendering in the context of a trio may be observed in the Mazurka in B♭, Op. 17 No. 1, where both solo line and drone are enhanced by metrical, registral and chromatic subtleties. Fleshing out the interior of such a texture occurs across the genre, from the trio of the A minor Mazurka, Op. 17 No. 4, and the short central section of the Mazurka in A♭, Op. 7 No. 4, to the introduction of the first C♯ minor Mazurka, Op. 6 No. 2, where the melodic line is embedded within the drone. In the C major Mazurka, Op. 56 No. 2, the drone is maintained throughout the opening section, its rooted quality relieved later by the running tenor line of the subsequent episode and by the canonic section preceding its ultimate return. In the B major Mazurka, Op. 41 No. 3, the initial drone figure recurs to punctuate wild tonal excursions which, in the final section, are recapitulated together without its calming presence: it appears only at the very end, as a quiet reminder that it has been there all the time.

The use of an introductory drone, or fanfare-like pedal-point, is common to many of the mazurkas. At its simplest, as in the C major Mazurka, Op. 7 No. 5, it is a four-bar dominant introduction (the equivalent of a caller's 1–2–3–4) that then underpins the opening texture of the ensuing kujawiak (see a developed tonic version of this technique in the Mazurka in E major, Op. 6 No. 3). In the D♭ Mazurka, Op. 30 No. 3, the dominant fanfare develops melodically as it reaches for its goal, as also, in their different ways, do the more sombre two-voice introductions to the mazurkas in F minor, Op. 7 No. 3, and B♭ minor, Op. 24 No. 4. Chordal variations on the idea are particularly masterful. The three alternating chords of the opening bars of Op. 17 No. 4, above an A♮ pedal, presage with uncanny accuracy the ambiguous tonality of the mazurka proper. And, echoing the open fifths of the string bass, the perfect cadence oscillations at the start of the C major Mazurka, Op. 24 No. 2, return substantively as its coda, reinforcing our initial doubts – were they perfect or plagal? But perhaps the most striking example of a drone whose stabilising function is under question comes in the Mazurka in B minor, Op. 56 No. 1. Without any establishment of key, the opening six-bar phrase sinks downwards through a disguised cycle of fifths until it lands on an open fifth drone based on G♮. The dance attempts to rise against this unsubstantiated foundation, which, six bars later, turns out to be the root of an augmented sixth on its way to the dominant note, F♯, and the section finally reaches some sense of stability with an arrival in the tonic. It is an extreme, though significant, example of Chopin locating a familiar device in a new context and with a new function.

From the time of his exile, Chopin regarded the mazurkas as not for dancing.[35] Yet they do themselves dance, and part of their fascination lies in their compositional appropriation of dance gestures. The one- and two-bar motifs, with their unaltered restatements or subtle variations, their grouping into four- and six-bar phrases and into larger multiples, themselves alternating with contrasting sections to create a whole piece, all these have their basis in dance movement.[36] Extrovert melodic lines, striding arpeggic themes, registral plunges and leaps, as well as quieter, smoother passages, have their dance counterparts, as do the 'call and response' patterns which manifest themselves in a number of ways (see the trio of the Mazurka in A minor, Op. 68 No. 2, and the B sections of Op. 6 No. 3 and Op. 67 No. 2 in G minor).

Accents and dynamic contrasts play a fundamental role, often emphasising the foot-stamp or heel-clicking leap (*hołubiec*), on the second or third beat of a bar as well as the first[37] (see Example 6).

Example 6　Windakiewiczowa, selected examples

(a) Kolberg, Lud. IV. Nr. 904 – Chopin, Op. 17 No.1

(b) Kolberg, Mazowsze. I. 95 – Chopin, Op. 67 No. 1

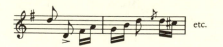

(c) Kolberg, Lud. IV. Nr. 18 – Chopin, Op. 7 No.2

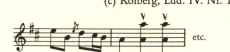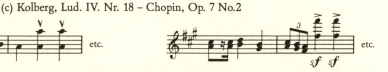

First-beat emphases may be long-breathed, initiating four-bar phrases (Op. 6 No. 3, B section; Op. 56 No. 3 in C minor and Op. 59 No. 2 in A♭, A section). Alternatively they may be short-breathed, initiating two-bar phrases (though with occasional second-beat ricochets). This latter is especially common at the beginning of the B section (Opp. 68 No. 3 and 6 No. 1 in F♯ minor; Opp. 17 No. 1 and 50 No. 3 in C♯ minor, etc.). Second-beat accents pervade the genre and often characterise the opening A section, combining accents with expressive harmonic or melodic stresses (Op. 33 No. 3 in C) or utilising an accompanimental rest on the first beat in order to emphasise the second (Op. 7 No. 3). Longer-breathed accent phrases also occur (Op. 67 No. 3 in C major is a fine, undemonstrative example). Third-beat kicks abound, ranging from the quiet understatement of the trio sections of Op. 63 No. 1 in B major and Op. 50 No. 2 in A♭ to the vivacity of the opening of Op. 33 No. 2 in D major and the bravado of the B section of Op. 68 No. 1 in C. The mazurkas come closest h3 reflecting the multiple accents of the dance when successive bars emphasise different beats (see the A sections of Opp. 50 No. 1 and 67 No. 1, both in G major, and Op. 6 No. 4 in E♭ minor).

None of these accentual models, nor the variety of rhythms of which they are a part, corresponds with the base, unimaginative pattern of a couple of mazurkas once sent to Chopin, who thought them merely 'respectable: – "ram didiridi, ram didiridi, ram didiridi, rajda"'.[38] Their wooden, repetitious limitations bear no relation to the myriad interlockings of duplet, triplet and dotted rhythms that enliven the pulse of a Chopin mazurka. In his extensive study of the folk influence on Chopin, Wiaczesław Paschałow has included a table outlining which sections of each mazurka come from the three rhythmic traditions of mazur, kujawiak and oberek.[39] According to his categorisations, less than half of the mazurkas belong to one tradition alone, and most of these are mazurs (he classifies Opp. 7 No. 5 and 33 No. 2, however, as kujawiaks, Opp. 6 No. 4 and 68 No. 4 in F minor as obereks). As a general rule, the gentler the melodic and rhythmic outline, the more likely it is to be a kujawiak or an oberek (despite the kujawiak being regarded as slower than the mazur, and the oberek as faster, there is also some blurring of tempo boundaries between the three). Among the several mazurkas that draw on all three traditions, Op. 7 No. 3 has a clear sequence of oberek, followed by two kujawiaks flanking a mazur, while Op. 56 No. 1 is constructed from an alternation of kujawiak and waltz-like oberek, with a mazur bringing up the rear.

The strength of references to these dances varies from the high-density repetitions and accented whirling of Op. 33 No. 2 (*pace* Paschałow, this is more an oberek than a kujawiak) and the bucolic Op. 56 No. 2, with its lack of upbeat, its repeated two-bar mazur phrases, low-register triadic outline and persistent drone, to the more abstract 'symphonic' mazurkas at the opposite end of the spectrum. Many of these come as the concluding dance of a set, such as Op. 24 No. 4, Op. 41 No. 1 in C♯ minor (in Ekier's chronology, renumbered as the last of the Op. 41 set)[40], Op. 50 No. 3 and Op. 56 No. 3. Op. 41 No. 1 is one of five mazurkas in this key, which seems to embody in its melancholy that elusive but tangible quality of Polish *żal*, fed as it is here with fleeting reference to the waltz, to mazurs and to the kujawiak. Op. 50 No. 3 has a more powerful, developmental persona, although one that still teases the ear with its expressive fluctuations. All these elements combine in Op. 56 No. 3 to create a rich stream of loosely associated ideas, by turn gentle and assertive, underpinned by the four-bar phrase and, in overall concept, by the distant folk practice of dance sequences.

Aside from the frontal folk energy of dance rhythms and textures, the binding agent in the mazurkas is the melodic and modal influence. The modal element, while by no means as pervasive as diatonic and chromatic idioms, includes the aeolian/dorian inflections of Op. 17 No. 4 and the more pungent phrygian modality of the main themes of Op. 41 Nos. 1 in C♯ minor and 2 in E minor. More central is the lydian mode, with its sharpened fourth. This informs the mazurkas to a striking degree, ranging from the straightforward trio of Op. 68 No. 3 (Example 5) and the F-based theme from Op. 24 No. 2 to the Op. 7 No. 1 B♭ minor melody with lydian fourth (set against a G♭–D♭ drone). This latter device (the lydian fourth set against a fifth drone) is an exoticism that colours more subtly the opening of Op. 59 No. 3 in F♯ minor. A number of mazurkas make play with the sequence of sharp fourth/natural fourth, including Op. 50 No. 3 and Op. 67 No. 4 in A minor. The direct quality of the theme of Op. 56 No. 2, described by Jachimecki as being as vivid as the colourful stripes of Łowicz cloth,[41] draws its strength from folk melodies such as those in Example 7.[42]

Example 7   (a) '*Czyja ja tero(z) da teraz*' ('Whose am I now?') — from Sadlno, Kujawy

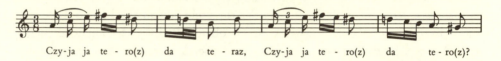

Czy-ja ja te - ro(z)   da   te - raz,   Czy-ja ja te - ro(z)   da   te - ro(z)?

(b) '*Oj wziął mi Janek wianek*' ('Oh, Janek stole my garland') – from Błonie, Warsaw

Oj   wziął mi Ja - nek wia - nek   da   już mi   go nie wró - ci

In her detailed study of Polish folk models in Chopin's mazurkas, Helena Windakiewiczowa draws attention, with examples from Kolberg, to a number of common features. These include the many combinations of one- and two-bar structures and registral 'call and response' patterns. In the nature of the exercise, we may observe similarities of type, but the occasional eye-catching correlation is doubtless accidental.[43] Her discussion of chromatic models is closely argued, as is her revealing survey of the different types of oberek figures. These include not only the hołubiec discussed above but also *wahadłowy* 'pendulum' patterns (where a melodic-choreographic swing in one direction is answered by one in the other, a familiar two-bar figure alternation in the mazurkas – see, for example, the *con anima* section of Op. 24 No. 4) and the intermittent 'whirling' *wirowy* figure, which in Chopin's hands tends to chromaticise the folk model (see Op. 41 No. 1, bs 17–32, and one of a number of more substantive derivations in the mazurkas, the opening theme from Op. 67 No. 3).

The contours of the wahadłowy and wirowy types are the wide-ranging and compressed extremes of one of the most significant aspects of Polish folk melodies and the dance movements which they accompany: the *falujacy* 'wave' figure.[44] Like the accentual patterns already outlined, these figures may span one, two, four or more bars. Two-bar arch shapes and their inversions are particularly frequent: Op. 6 No. 2 (with lydian fourth), Op. 24 No. 2 (arpeggic examples) and Op. 33 No. 2 (diatonic), Op. 50 No. 3 trio (pentatonic) and Op. 56 No. 1 (sequential). Four-bar patterns range from the exuberant mazur of Op. 30 No. 3 (bs 17–20, in thirds) and the running quavers of the first episode of Op. 56 No. 1 to the inverted contour of the opening of Op. 59 No. 1 in A minor and the combined shapes in contrary motion that open Op. 50 No. 3. Where Chopin moulds his arches into eight-bar phrases, such as in the thrusting main theme of Op. 6 No. 3 or the quieter, mordent-based rise and fall of the opening of Op. 63 No. 3 in C♯ minor, the structural implications of the technique are brought to the fore. Because wave-forms are almost a *sine qua non* for repetitious folk patterns, and because their song structures and dance sequences are the result of an ebb and flow of all their expressive components, so the finely controlled balance in the mazurkas between statement and variation is the result of Chopin building on these embodiments of a long-lived folk tradition and investing them with the individual imagination of an exile.

8 The sonatas

ANATOLE LEIKIN

If this were a book on Mozart or Beethoven, one would have needed more than a single chapter to analyse all of the sonatas. Seventy sonatas of Mozart and fifty-five of Beethoven make up substantial chunks of their output. In fact, almost everything they composed for one or two instruments, except for variation sets and a few trifles, were sonatas.

With the next generation of composers the sonata lost its overpowering dominance. Mendelssohn limited himself to thirteen sonatas; Schumann settled on eight (including the C major Fantasy); Chopin tried one at the age of eighteen, subsequently contributed two great sonatas to the piano literature and later added to them a cello sonata; among Liszt's dozens of instrumental compositions, there are only two sonatas.

One cannot say that Romantic composers lost interest in the sonata. It still remained the most prestigious instrumental genre, an obsession for many composers striving to prove their ability to handle complex structures. In this respect it might be compared with the fugue in the Classical era.

Composers' uneasy relationships with the sonata were not at all alleviated by the readiness of nineteenth-century music criticism to disparage their attempts at the genre. Traces of this criticism persisted well into the twentieth century. Some writers still consider that sonata forms in Romantic music suffer from a lack of structural continuity, and from composers' inexperience with large forms or their inability to develop material and to conceive large organic wholes.[1]

The basis for these and many other harsh judgements on nineteenth-century sonata forms is apparent. Romantic sonatas have been measured against the Olympian feats of Haydn, Mozart and Beethoven. The later sonatas do, indeed, differ in many respects from the Classical ones, and it has been automatically assumed that any changes could only be for the worse. As we shall see in Chopin's sonatas, however, these changes were impelled by a strong urge to renovate a form that had been around for many decades, to make it more spontaneous and less predictable.

Chopin's first mature piano sonata, Op. 35 in B♭ minor, was composed in 1839.

Almost instantly, it both won popularity with the audience and provoked misunderstanding in most music critics. Only in recent commentaries has the air of structural inferiority about the Sonata begun to dissipate. Schumann's description of it as 'four of Chopin's maddest children under the same roof' is remembered now as a historic curiosity; the conviction that Chopin could not quite handle sonata form is fortunately fading away.

The Sonata is literally written around a funeral march which had been finished two years before and became the third movement in a four-movement cycle. The choice of a funeral march as the centre of gravity is no accident. Chopin was attracted to this genre perhaps more than any other composer. Even though he wrote only one piece designated as such (*Marche funèbre* in C minor), he injected elements of the funeral march into his other compositions. Both the C minor Prelude from Op. 28 and the slow introduction to the F minor Fantasy, Op. 49, are straightforward funeral marches. The nocturnes Op. 37 No. 1, Op. 48 No. 1 and Op. 55 No. 1 are clearly marked by the attributes of the funeral march.

Various reasons may be put forward to explain why the funeral march – the slow movement – follows the scherzo in the B♭ minor Sonata; the usual order of movements in a sonata cycle is just the opposite. The simplest and most compelling reason is that the plan of Op. 35 follows that of Beethoven's Piano Sonata Op. 26. This sonata, with a *Marcia funèbre* as one of its movements, was Chopin's favourite. He played it, taught it and analysed its structure for his students more often than he did any other of Beethoven's sonatas.[2] Since the first movement in Beethoven's Op. 26 is relatively slow, it was only logical for the composer to insert the scherzo before the funeral march in order to introduce tempo contrasts between the movements. The opening movement in Chopin's sonata, on the other hand, is fast and, unlike the set of variations in Beethoven's Op. 26, is a sonata (more or less). But the difference in tempo between Beethoven's and Chopin's movements did not prevent Chopin from following Beethoven's plan, and the difference in form is not so substantial after all.

The thematic unity in the first movement of the B♭ minor Sonata has been frequently discussed, in the classic writings of Hugo Leichtentritt[3] and in more recent publication.[4] While these analysts have addressed questions of thematic unity exhaustively, they have ignored one crucial point: the mixing of forms by Romantic composers striving to renovate the Classical formal patterns and to depart from the predetermination of the traditional sonata mould. As a result, the principles of different forms coexist in a single composition, overlapping, intertwining and even at times suppressing each other.[5] In Op. 35, Chopin blends together the sonata and variation principles. At times, the idea of variations all but supersedes the traditional sonata structure. The difficulty is that the variational interrelationships are so subtle (unlike, for example, Liszt's thematic transformations) that they are not immediately audible. It takes painstaking analysis to uncover the full spectrum of these connections, but the reward is a better under-standing of the piece.

The basis for virtually all subsequent events of the first movement of Op. 35 is contained within two thematic kernels. In the opening two bars of the slow introduction, Chopin contrives to map out not only one of the leading thematic components, but also the terms of its further development. This component is the falling trochaic (i.e. stressed-unstressed) interval in bar 1, Db–E. Since no key has yet been established, the notated diminished seventh is heard as a major sixth. Indeed, the identical ascending interval in bar 2 *is* a major sixth (see Example 1).

Example 1　Op. 35, I, bars 1–4

What happens here, however, is more than a mere enharmonic reiteration of the opening interval. Bar 2 presents a variation of bar 1 in which the downward skip Db–E is inverted, both melodically and metrically. The accent and the thick-ening of the second note in bar 2 (with the added G♯) transform the metrical foot of this little motive from trochaic (stressed-unstressed) to iambic (unstressed-stressed). The startling – for the performer, of course, rather than for the listener – C♯ minor notation in the midst of Bb minor places an additional, if psychological, emphasis on the chord at the end of bar 2.

The second crucial thematic element of the slow introduction (and, con-sequently, of the whole movement) is the rising iambic semitone E–F in the bass. Like the sixth, this is immediately inverted, both melodically and metrically. The appoggiatura concluding the slow introduction in the uppermost voice imitates the bass semitone through its descending trochaic variant, Db–C.

The melodic and metric inversions in the introduction are only the opening salvo. The subsequent accompanimental preamble (bars 5–8, see Example 2) in-troduces new developments. To begin with, Chopin converts the sixth, initially major, to minor: interpreting the descending interval Db–E as a diminished seventh, he resolves it into a minor sixth, F–Db, in the first bar of the Doppio movimento[6] (Db serves as the common note for the two sixths). Another obvious modification is the rhythmic diminution of the original sixth. Finally, in bars 5–8 the ascending sixth, F–D♭, and its intervallic inversion, the descending third (also F–D♭) are juxtaposed.

Example 2   Op. 35, I, bar 5

The entrance of the principal theme in bar 9 continues the variational techniques used in the slow introduction and the accompanimental figure of bar 5. The rhythmic diminution and intervallic inversion of an ascending sixth into a descending third (D♭–B♭) stem from the accompanimental preamble; the major sixth D♭–B♭ (bar 11) and its trochaic metrical structure grow out of the introduction. The rising iambic semitone (the second thematic element in the introduction) links the repeated minor thirds with each other and with the rising major sixth (bars 9–11, see Example 3).

Bars 12–16 extend the preceding phrase sequentially. The first G♭ in bar 13, redirecting the course of the sequence, serves as the second note in a rhythmic augmentation of the trochaic minor third (augmented second), shown by a bracket in bars 12–13 of Example 3. On the one hand this augmentation recalls the slower-moving sixths from the introduction, while on the other it anticipates the leisurely beginning of the secondary group in bars 41–2. The phrase concludes with a suspension (bar 16) that rhymes with the end of the introduction (see Example 1); in a sense it is also the true melodic and harmonic resolution of the appoggiatura from bars 3 and 4.

The continuation of the principal group, from bar 17 on, presents further relationships of this sort. Bar 17 seems to derive from four separate sources. It begins as a sequence, in diminution, of the preceding appoggiatura from bar 16. At the same time, the first two descending notes in bar 17, D♭–C, are the same as those of the original appoggiatura in bars 3–4; as there, the falling semitone is conjoined with the upward semitone E–F in the bass. It is interesting to note how Chopin manages to present the motive D♭–C at two speeds within the same melody (see D♭–C as two quavers and, in octaves, as two minims in the right hand in bar 17).

The last three quavers in bar 17 (B♭–A–C in the treble) are an exact inversion of the last three from the opening bar of the principal theme (C–D♭–B♭ in bar 9). In this movement, inversion typically involves more than just melodic line. Unexpected crescendos towards the final quavers in each bar of 17–20 seem to defy

Example 3   Op. 35, I, bars 9–11

bass: (E) ⟶ (F)

conventional notions about normally unstressed offbeats and, indeed, not many pianists are willing to indulge in these inexplicable dynamics. These crescendos, however, indicate a metric inversion that reinforces the melodic one. Resonant octaves on every final quaver in the right-hand part of bars 17–20 (and, in bar 20, an even more resonant chord) show a deliberate shift of metric pattern, with the stress on the last treble note of the bar. Also, the last two quavers in the right hand in each of these bars resemble texturally the iambic sixths/thirds in the accompanimental preamble (Example 2) and represent a melodic inversion of the right-hand figures from Example 2: the thirds now move up and the sixths down.

The remainder of the movement is built almost entirely from these two thematic components, producing a work of almost Webernian structural rigor. The subordinate section forms a new variation. The two opening intervals – the familiar descending trochaic minor third and the rising semitone – lead directly into the concluding appoggiatura (see Example 4). As in the slow introduction, this appoggiatura is a 6–5 suspension over a dominant chord; at the same time the sonority of a major seventh between G♭ and F makes this appoggiatura the same as that in bar 16 of the principal group.

Example 4   Op. 35, I, bars 41–4

The presence of variation form in this movement is not the only reason for the thematic similarity of the primary and secondary groups. In addition to combining different forms, the Romantics were also fond of blending different sections within the same form.

What are the functions of Classical exposition, development and recapitulation? The exposition presents a conflict between two tonal levels, usually (but not always) reinforced by a thematic contrast. The development drastically increases tension and instability. Incessant modulation introduces a mercurial flow of tonalities; there are no long stays in a single key (the tonic is especially avoided) and no expansive thematic statements. The recapitulation, according to customary definitions, releases harmonic tension and resolves the conflict through the restatement of both the principal and secondary groups in the tonic.

The tonal unity of the recapitulation is only one facet of the final integration of the primary and subsidiary groups. Since the expositional confrontation usually includes a thematic contrast in addition to the tonal one, it is logical to assume that this thematic opposition should also be somehow settled at the end, that the secondary group should be drawn closer to the principal group thematically as well as tonally. This aspect of reprise has been strangely neglected in writings about sonata form, but analysis confirms it beyond doubt.[7] In sonatas with little or no thematic contrast within the exposition (Haydn's, for example), the secondary theme in the recapitulation, after being transposed to the home key, assumes the pitch level of the principal theme. When the secondary theme contrasts with the principal one, there is still at least one thematic link between them, and often more than one. In the reprise of the secondary group, the identical motive or motives inevitably appear at the same pitch level they occupied in the primary theme (compare Examples 5, 6 and 7). Composers usually project these motives, placing them conspicuously either at the very beginning or at the very end of phrases, or at climaxes. Often these motives are repeated to emphasise their importance and to draw the listener's attention to them.

Example 5   Beethoven, Sonata Op. 31 No. 3, I, principal theme

Example 6   Beethoven, Sonata Op. 31 No. 3, I, secondary theme, exposition

Example 7   Beethoven, Sonata Op. 31 No. 3, I, secondary theme, recapitulation

Romantic composers, trying to move away from the predetermination of the Classical sonata structure, began blurring sections of the sonata and their functions. They injected developmental techniques into the exposition and recapitulation, thus undermining the contrast between the more and the less stable sonata sections and inciting criticism that their development is at a disadvantage because the exposition has already 'digressed into developments of its own'.[8] As if in defiance, nineteenth-century composers conversely infused expositional/recapitulatory stability into the development, devoting extensive portions of this section to tonally stable presentations of thematic material (and, of course, their development sections were promptly reproached for having insufficient intensity).

One finds a similar diffusion in exposition and recapitulation. While the tonal and thematic opposition is diluted in many nineteenth-century expositions, it is common for recapitulations to end in a conflict between the primary and secondary groups. A traditional, if questionable, analogy likens the relationship in the Classical sonata between a more forceful principal group and a more lyrical (feminine) secondary group to that between literary or dramatic hero and heroine: being apart at first, they are happily united at last. The Romantic aesthetic favoured a different sort of love relationship. For one reason or another, the hero and the heroine could not be together and thus suffer a painful separation, just as, in nineteenth-century sonata forms, the primary and subsidiary themes are frequently closer to each other in the exposition than in the recapitulation.

In some sonatas the tonal relationships in the exposition and recapitulation are openly reversed. Chopin's Sonata Op. 4, his Trio Op. 8 and the E minor Concerto are famous examples of this reversal of Classical procedure. The later C♯ minor Scherzo, Op. 39, even though hardly ever mentioned in this respect, is another such example. Its secondary section is placed in the tonic major in the exposition and then transposed to the mediant (E major) in the reprise. Referring to Chopin's earlier works in which the exposition-recapitulation tonal relationships are reversed, Charles Rosen remarked that, not only did Chopin make a mistake Mozart would not have made even as a child, but they 'evidently did not have very clear ideas about sonatas out there in Warsaw'.[9] In answer to this admittedly facetious comment, I should like to point out that Joseph Xavier Elsner, who taught Chopin theory, harmony, counterpoint and composition, and who received his musical education in Breslau and Vienna, was the author of more than a dozen operas, fifty-five cantatas, thirty-three masses, eight symphonies, six string quartets and so on. His instrumental music adheres faithfully to the Classical models of Haydn and Mozart and reveals a perfectly sound mastery of sonata form. Moreover, his illustrious student, on his first visit to Vienna in 1829, astonished this musical city with the depth and extent of his musical training, which was to be later confirmed by Liszt in his biography of Chopin. (The Vienna visit was the occasion of Chopin's famous retort to one such compliment that 'with Messrs Żywny and

Elsner even the greatest jackass would have learned'.[10]) With a remarkable display of wisdom and open-mindedness, Elsner did not fetter Chopin's experimentations. When Elsner's friends wondered why he did not object to Chopin's frivolous use of theoretical rules, he answered, 'Leave him in peace. His is an extraordinary path, for he has an extraordinary gift. He does not follow the old rules, because he seeks those of his own.'[11] Chopin continued to juggle expositions and recapitulations long after he had left Warsaw. Moreover, he shared this 'vice' with other Romantic composers, Schubert and Schumann among them. Either the poor devils never learned the difference between exposition and recapitulation, or – and I certainly subscribe to this alternative – they were persistently and purposefully experimenting with sonata structure.

Tonally, the exposition of the first movement in Chopin's B♭ minor Sonata follows the Classical procedure (B♭ minor–D♭ major). Thematically, however, this exposition includes the recapitulation principle, because two extensive closely related motives use identical pitch-classes in both the primary and subsidiary sections. One of these motives is particularly important, not only for an understanding of the recapitulatory ties between the principal and secondary groups in the exposition, but also for the performance of the transitional section (bars 25–40).

The accents buttressed by three-part chords on the off-beat quavers in bars 25–32 appear so bizarre that pianists frequently ignore them, while some pedagogues and editors (e.g. Attilio Brugnoli) have chosen to transform the accents into small *diminuendo* signs. Indeed, in the principal theme (bars 9–16) the same melodic thirds and sixths are unquestionably trochaic, like the prototypical sixth from the slow introduction (bar 1). But in bars 2 of the *Grave* and 5–8 of the accompanimental preamble Chopin shifts the stress from the first to the second note of the sixths and thirds. After disappearing from bars 9–16, it is this iambic pattern which returns in bars 17–20, to be even further strengthened in bars 25–36.

Besides contributing to metrical interplay, these accents fulfil a very important role in the thematic structure of the exposition. They echo the first of the two identical motives mentioned above: the bass ascent from B♭ to F in bars 25–33 (the circled notes in Example 8). This portion of the transition, in turn, is a restatement – reinforced by the three-note chords – of the same ascending line from the principal section (bars 9–17).[12]

Example 8   Op. 35, I, bars 25–33

Ex. 8 (*cont.*)

This motive is then transplanted to the subsidiary section. The secondary theme opens with the downward minor third A♭–F in bars 41–2. After the repetition of the opening phrase in bars 45–8, this falling third is transformed by intervallic inversion – as was the similar third in the principal theme – into an ascending sixth. Unlike the open sixths in the earlier theme, however, this one is filled in with the familiar ascent from B♭ to F – the change of key notwithstanding (see Example 9). Moreover, the pitch identity of this motive even affects the secondary key area at one point. The reiteration of the ascending motive, in bars 51–3, arrives at the dominant of B♭ minor, as in bars 17 of the principal section and 33 of the transition.

Example 9   Op. 35, I, bars 49–53

The second of these identical-motives-at-identical-pitches is a long stepwise fall from the topmost F down to E♭. This scale figure, which grows out of the descending appoggiatura at the conclusion of the slow introduction (bars 3–4), first emerges in the last four bars of the principal group (bars 21–4, Example 10a); later it concludes the first half of the secondary group (in bars 53–6, Example 10b). In both cases it leads to a half cadence. Thus the principal and secondary themes are like two variations of the same introductory material.

Example 10   (a) Op. 35, I, bars 21–4

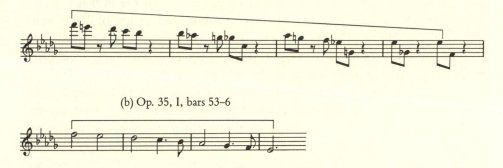

(b) Op. 35, I, bars 53–6

The closing section (bars 81–106) forms the next variation. All thematic ingredients are easily recognisable. The section begins with the falling trochaic minor
third; despite being in a different key, the melodic third is the same as in the
primary theme, Db–Bb (bar 81). It is followed, as at the beginning of the principal
theme, by a three-note figure with the stress on the second note. The crotchet
triplets – the dominating rhythm in the closing section – can be traced back to
the secondary group (from bar 57 on).

The development and recapitulation of this sonata are still clouded by a popular
myth that the principal theme is not recapitulated because it forms the basis of the
development. This is simply not true. To begin with, all the themes find their way
into the development. The first three bars (106–8) come from the principal group;
the next bar (109) from the secondary theme (see bar 56); the following bar from
the slow introduction, and so on. Since all the melodies in the exposition are
actually variations on the same material, the development becomes yet another
variation. A seemingly new tune in bars 122–5 (Example 11) is made up of appoggiaturas filling in the descending sixth Eb–G and is therefore a free inversion of
the filled-in rising sixth that figured earlier in the secondary section. This phrase
anticipates the dotted rhythm of the funeral march. The rhythm of crotchet
triplets in the left-hand part from bar 126 onwards recurs from the secondary
and closing section. In bars 138–53, Chopin combines three different elements at
once: the slow introduction in the bass, the crotchet triplets in the middle and
the gasping motives of the principal theme in the treble.

Example 11   Op. 35, I, bars 122–5

Secondly, even if the primary group *were* the sole basis of the development, many classical developments built entirely on material from the principal theme are followed by a full recapitulation (e.g. the first movements of Beethoven's Sonatas Op. 2 No. 3, Op. 13 and Op. 31 No. 1). Heavy exploitation in the development does not make the recapitulation of the principal theme redundant; on the contrary, after the material of the primary group has been atomised and its fragments thrown around to various, often quite remote, keys, hearing it again in one piece and in the home key brings a colossal relief. This is what Chopin obviously did not want. In some of his other recapitulations he drove the principal and secondary sections apart, separating, rather than uniting, them at the end. In the Bb minor Sonata, the tonal conflict of the exposition is left unresolved for a different reason: the principal group disappears along with the principal key. To continue the literary analogy, the hero and the heroine cannot be united because the hero dies – and a funeral march follows.[13]

There is, however, a second reason for omitting the principal section in the reprise. Such a compression of the recapitulation is not really 'one of Chopin's chief contributions to the history of sonata form', as Alan Walker suggests.[14] It is rather a restoration of the older binary sonata form, typical, for instance, of Domenico Scarlatti's sonatas. Jim Samson devoted an entire chapter in *The Music of Chopin* to the composer's affinities with Baroque procedures.[15] The partial recapitulation in the Bb minor Sonata (as well, for that matter, as in the two following Sonatas, Opp. 58 and 65) is obviously inspired by the pre-Classical pattern and illustrates Chopin's Baroque leanings.

The furious insistence of the repeated octaves and chords in the scherzo, its explosive rhythmic and dynamic power place it, as many observers have noted, right in the midst of the Beethoven tradition. But while Beethoven's scherzo is a transformed minuet, Chopin's is a transformed mazurka, with all the characteristic jumps, stamps and heel clickings on the third or the second beat.

Thematically, this scherzo is an integral part of the cycle. Alan Walker points out the role of the minor third, 'a unitive force throughout the sonata'.[16] A pianist should be aware of other links between the movements as well. The scherzo begins as a natural extension of the first movement – or, more precisely, of its closing section. The triple-metre crotchet motion in the scherzo (Example 12b) is similar to the triplets there (Example 12a). The predominance of reiterated octaves and chords in both movements reinforces the similarity, and the repeated cadential phrases are, simply, identical. The scherzo's growth out of the closing section can somehow explain the puzzling (for some) absence of a tempo indication. Most probably, there is no tempo indication merely because there is no new tempo – just a change in notation, from triplets to triple metre. Other thematic elements common to both movements include a melodic line rising from the first to the fifth scale degree (cf. Example 13 and Examples 8 and 9) and the turning

Example 12   (a) Op. 35, I, bars 213–15

(b) Op. 35, II, bars 12–14

figure that occurs at the beginnings of bars 13, 14 and 15 of the first movement and, slightly altered intervallically, at the beginning and at the centre of the opening melody of the trio (see Example 14). In the middle part of the trio, the

Example 13   Op. 35, II, bars 1–6

Example 14   Op. 35, II, bars 87–8

Example 15   Op. 35, II, bars 144–6

bass descent through a ninth (see Example 15) is reminiscent of similar melodic falls in the primary and secondary groups of the Doppio movimento (shown in Example 10a and b). This bass line is divided into two parts by the repeated F; the stepwise motion from this F – the third scale degree – down to the fifth degree is a modified version of a melody from the development of the first movement (see Example 11) which, in turn, is a modification of the rising hexachord between fifth and third degrees in the secondary theme (bars 1–3 in Example 9).

The form of the second movement seems conventional enough: scherzo–trio–scherzo. The first disturbing sign is the ending in the relative major. This is not unique in Chopin's œuvre: the Mazurka in B minor, Op. 30 No. 2, the Waltz in F minor, Op. 70 No. 2, and the Scherzo in B♭ minor, Op. 31, all end in the dominant or mediant key. Already in the comparatively early G minor Ballade, Op. 23, the composer eliminates the tonal distinction between exposition and recapitulation. The secondary group in the mirror reprise (the principal and secondary sections return in reverse order) is in the same key as in the exposition, E♭ major.[17] Once the distinction between exposition and recapitulation has been eliminated, the next logical step is to blend their functions. The reprise of the B♭ minor Scherzo (from bar 584) does not differ tonally from the exposition. Both sections are completely levelled, which accounts for the ending in D♭ major. The second half of the Mazurka Op. 30 No. 2 is written in the minor dominant, causing it to assume the role of the secondary group in a sonata exposition/recapitulation; when the entire mazurka is repeated, both halves retain their original keys. Likewise, the second section of the Waltz Op. 70 No. 2 functions as the subordinate group. It is in the mediant, the key in which the composition ends.

In the sonata movement, the scherzo presents the principal group, as it were, in E♭ minor and the trio the subordinate group, in G♭ major. Following this both the principal section (the scherzo) and the subordinate section are recapitulated, but in their original keys.

When we consider the cadences at the centre and end of the scherzo the form of this piece becomes even more multi-dimensional. The first section ends in bars 34–6 in the minor mediant, F♯. At the end of the scherzo, in bars 78–80, the same cadence occurs in the tonic. Such 'rhyming cadences' are common in the binary dance movements of the Baroque.

The overall form of the scherzo consists, then, of at least three layers: a compound ternary, a sonata and an old-style binary. Interestingly, in the very last statement of the scherzo theme, Chopin does not use the expected cadential pattern, replacing it instead with a condensed reprise of the secondary section (in sonata terms) – the trio theme, bars 174–83 – and, therefore, with the relative major key, G♭. In Table 1, P indicates the primary section, S the subordinate section and a downward arrow the repeated cadence figure.

Table 1. *Sonata Op. 35, scherzo*

EXPOSITION

sonata:	P					S		
compound ternary:	scherzo					trio		
	a		b	a		c	d	c
Baroque binary:	I →			II →				
keys:	eb	f♯		eb	eb	Gb	Db	Gb
bars:	1–34	34–6	37–64	65–77	78–80	81–144	144–60	161–84

RECAPITULATION/EXPOSITION

sonata:		P				S ⇢ (c) ⇢ Gb
compound ternary:		scherzo				a (c)
		a		b	a	
Baroque binary:		I →			II	
keys:		eb	f♯	eb	eb	Gb
bars:	185–9	190–223	223–5	226–53	254–73	274–88

Op 35, II

The 'Marche funèbre' opens with a funereal bell ringing in the left hand while the melody consists of a mere reiterated note for almost three bars. These prolonged repetitions of a single note were the backbone of both the closing section of the first movement and the main theme of the scherzo (of course, the process of creation was the opposite for Chopin, since the funeral march was the first movement to be completed). Alan Walker has noticed that the melody following the repeated B♭ is a strict retrograde of the first movement's principal theme (see Examples 16a, b). Then comes a motive of a descending hexachord (with one

Example 16   (a) Op. 35, III
             (b) Op. 35, I

note omitted), B♭–A♭–G♭–F–D♭, in bars 7–8, reminiscent of the middle part of the scherzo's trio (Example 15). All of this is set against the ostinato bass figure B♭–D♭, the interval that weaves through the entire cycle, starting with the first theme of the Doppio movimento. Descending scalar motion from the third down to the fifth degree is also discernible in the opening of the trio of the march movement (see Example 17), in spite of the register change.

Example 17   Op. 35, III, bars 31–2

The finale is probably the most enigmatic piece Chopin ever wrote. Playing with both hands in parallel octaves is not such a rarity by itself; his Op. 28 Prelude in E♭ minor attests to that. But the prelude's monophonic line actually forms a melody with a broken-chord accompaniment underneath, while the sonata finale consists of a winding, Baroque-style single line. The texture is not idiomatic for keyboard. It sounds more like a piece for an unaccompanied cello.

Chopin was well acquainted with the cello repertoire. In Warsaw he was capti-
vated by the playing of Joseph Merk, to whom he dedicated his *Introduction and
Polonaise brillante* for cello and piano, Op. 3. In Paris he admired the art of his close
friend, the cellist Auguste Franchomme. The similarity of timbre to that of an
unaccompanied cello and the Baroque-like structure of the melodic line point to
Bach's suites for solo cello as one possible source of inspiration. More specifically,
the prelude from Bach's Suite in D major for solo cello is a similar *perpetuum mobile*
of four quaver triplets per bar, and one of its most frequently repeated motives
bears a striking resemblance to the principal theme from the first movement of
Chopin's sonata (cf. Example 18 with bar 11 of Example 3).

Example 18   Bach, Suite in D, Prelude

A descending hexachord between the third and fifth scale degrees is also a very
important figure in the Bach prelude. The role of descending and ascending hexachords in the first three movements of the sonata has already been mentioned.
It should be noted that a hexachord, in either quavers or augmentation, is one of
the leading motives of the finale as well. Such parallels make one wonder if this
finale did not come about as a result of a bet with Franchomme that it was quite
possible to write a piano piece in the manner of a cello solo, with no differentiation
between tune and accompaniment – just an improvisatory monodic line.

These parallels also raise doubts about the wisdom of playing this movement
too fast, as one indistinct, amorphous sound stream. Not much remains of the
Bach connection in such a performance, and the listener does not stand a chance
of grasping the finale's form. In a very fast rendition, the movement appears
athematic, whereas in reality it has a system of tonal and melodic repeats that
creates a tangible trace of sonata form. After the first four introductory bars, the
principal section begins in Bb minor. It drifts away into the partially atonal transition, which leads to the secondary section in Db major. A short development
follows (bars 31–8), and the recapitulation opens with the return of the introductory passage in bar 39. The reprise is very compressed; the hexachords of the
subordinate section encroach already in the upbeat to bar 47. A lengthy coda
crowns this masterpiece of nineteenth-century sonata cycle.

Chopin's next piano sonata, in B minor, Op. 58, was completed five years later.
The first movement of this sonata is in many respects the antipode to the Bb minor
Sonata. Next to the tightly organised, utterly economical use of thematic material
in Op. 35, the Allegro maestoso of Op. 58 sounds like a sprawling motivic mosaic.
Yet from the viewpoint of sonata pattern these two movements are virtually twins.

Chopin's efforts in this sonata were not directed towards new experiments with the form. He was apparently satisfied with the sonata design he had created in Op. 35; the first movements of both Op. 58 and Op. 65 are cast in the same mould. The area of experimentation this time lay elsewhere.

Chopin had become increasingly interested in polyphony prior to his working on the B minor Sonata. His veneration for Bach reached an apogee; he immersed himself in studying counterpoint treatises by Cherubini and Kastner. The result is incontestable. The first movement of Op. 58 contains more imitative passages than any other of Chopin's works. Most of its texture is a colligation of contrapuntal lines rather than a melody with accompaniment.

More than that, the way of musical thinking here is polyphonic. The Allegro maestoso has been often criticised for being too dry – with the exception of its melodious second theme. The supposed dryness is caused by a different approach to composition, by a musical philosophy, typical rather for older masters of counterpoint. One aspect of that approach is the conviction that what is done with a theme is much more important than what the theme is *per se*. That is why so many old polyphonic compositions are based on borrowed melodies. Another difference between the old counterpoint and Romantic custom is that a polyphonic subject tends to be melodically neutral, because if a distinctive and 'beautiful' tune undergoes the procedures of inversion, retrograde, etc., it becomes distorted and loses everything. An abstract, 'impersonal' line is far more suitable for polyphonic treatment.

Such is the melodic subject of the B minor Sonata. Its first statement even opens in a typically polyphonic manner, with an unaccompanied voice. The leading component is a semitone G–F♯, echoed in augmentation an octave lower (see the arrows at the beginning of Example 19). An arpeggio connects the first and the last notes of the opening motive. This short motive spawns the entire piece, and here is the composer's tremendous challenge: to build a profusion of melodic ideas from a mere half-step, gradually enriching it with neighbouring notes and appoggiaturas, inverting it, transforming it into an occasional whole step, mingling it with the arpeggio or its parts, and linking all of these elements together, as presented in Example 19.

The transition section, which is practically absorbed into the primary section, offers new variants of the basic motive. The first one is the B♭ major march fragment in bars 17–18. An imitation within the two-bar march unfolds into a more elaborate canon in bars 23–8, followed by a simultaneous combination of three thematic layers in bars 31–7.

The thematic affinity between the principal and subordinate sections has been noted in several recent writings.[18] The pitch identities within the principal and subordinate themes reveal, in addition to their variational kinship, an influx of the recapitulatory traits into the exposition (demonstrated in Examples 20a, b, c, d, e, f).

Example 19   Op. 58, I, bars 1–8

Example 20   Op. 58, I
(a) principal section, bars 2–4
(b) secondary section, bars 56–9
(c) principal section, bars 6–7
(d) secondary section, bars 53–4
(e) principal section, bars 5–12
(f) secondary section, bars 61–3

Ex. 20 (*cont.*)

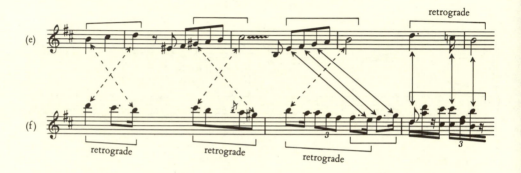

The richness of the tonal picture in the exposition matches the melodic abundance. The circle of tonalities here is neither whimsical nor erratic. A special place in the exposition belongs to the monotertial tonal relationship. This is a more complicated version of parallel keys, where instead of a common tonic and fifth degree – as, for instance, C–G for C major and C minor – two tonalities are related by a common third (e.g., E in the case of C major and C♯ minor). Beethoven rarely used monotertial keys. The first movement of his E♭ major 'Emperor' Piano Concerto provides one of very few examples, with the secondary theme played first by the piano in B minor and then repeated by the orchestra in B♭ major. Starting with Schubert, nineteenth-century composers employed monotertial keys systematically, but in theory the realisation of this phenomenon did not occur until Leo Mazel published his seminal article in 1957.[19] The principal/transitional key area of the Allegro maestoso revolves almost exclusively around the primary harmonic functions of B minor. It consists of: (1) the tonic and its monotertial major, B♭; (2) the subdominant and its monotertial major, E♭; (3) the major and minor dominants (F♯, f♯) and their monotertial minor and major (g, F); and (4) D minor, the relative major's parallel minor. The secondary group contains *no new keys* – only D major and the principal key of B minor with its subdominant and dominant. Instead of an expositional contrast, the primary and the secondary key areas converge in a recapitulatory manner (see Table 2).

Table 2. *Sonata Op. 58, first movement exposition*

P/T	b	Bb	e	Eb	f#/F#	F	g	d
bars	1–6	17–18	8–12	20–1 29–30	6–8 14	13 32	18 27–8	23–6 31 32–40

S	b		e		f#			D
bars	49 70 73		65–6 69 75		53–6			41–8 50–2 57–64 68–9 73–5 76

P = principal group
S = secondary group
T = transition

The first two-thirds of the development section are devoted to a contrapuntal working of the previous material. The development then congeals into prolonged statements of the secondary theme, first in Db major and then in Eb. This break-through of the expositional/recapitulatory stability into the development is further evidence of the Romantic fusion of formal sections rather than of Chopin's inept-ness in matters of sonata form.

The Allegro maestoso offers additional proof that Chopin's abbreviation of the reprise has little to do with what material is used in the development. Although the last portion of the development dwells on the subordinate theme, the recapitulation still opens with a preparation of the same theme in D major. The omission of the principal group in this recapitulation does not have the tragic overtones of the previous sonata. The disappearance of the principal subject here is more a resignation, a self-withdrawal of the hero.

As in the Bb minor Sonata, the scherzo of Op. 58 comes as the second move-ment in the cycle, but instead of the subdominant key Chopin now uses Eb major, the subdominant's monotertial major. Example 21 shows the basic thematic material at the beginning of the second movement. This movement has none of the formal adventures of the Op. 35 scherzo. As in the first movement, polyphony is the main point of interest here, and the trio puts forward a rare display of contrapuntal richness (Examples 22a, b).

Example 21   Op. 58, II, bars 1–2

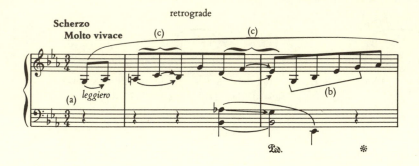

Example 22   Op. 58, II

(a) bars 61–9

(b) bars 73–6

The third movement is often likened to a nocturne. However, its slow stride in duple metre, assisted by dotted rhythms and melodic restraint, has all the characteristics of a funeral march – all but the mode. This makes the Largo sound more like the aloof trio of a funeral march than of a nocturne. It is comparatively easy to hear the melodic connections between the Largo and the first movement's secondary group, especially when the latter appears in the recapitulation in the key of B major. What is less noticeable is how the basic thematic elements are woven organically into the texture of the slow movement (see Examples 23a, b, c, d).

Example 23   Op. 58, III

(a) bars 4–8

(b) bars 20–21

Ex. 23 (cont.)

(c) bars 29–30

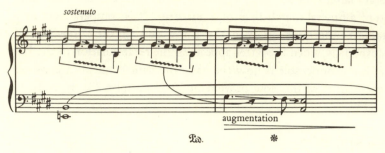

(d) bar 39

The form of the slow movement is ternary, with nothing out of the ordinary except for its proportions. In the trio Chopin lapses into a nirvana that lasts almost three times as long as the first part and more than four times as long as the reprise. The tranquillity of the trio is broken only in bars 71–6, after a sudden switch from E major to its monotertial minor (f); then the hypnotically serene current of triplets resumes. The trio softens the initial mood of the solemn procession in the Largo, and when the opening theme of the slow movement returns in the reprise, the triplets are retained in the accompaniment. There is, however, one small but important change. The steady flow of triplets is broken with a quaver rest in alternate rhythmic groups. This subtle detail alters the genre character of the main theme, making the new rhythmic ostinato in the accompaniment reminiscent of Chopin's Berceuse, which had been finished just a few months before the sonata. As a result, the solemn procession of the first part turns, in the Largo's reprise, into a lullaby.

The finale steps out of the B♭ minor Sonata pattern – indeed, it is difficult to imagine another finale written in the same vein as the last movement of Op. 35. The form of the Presto, non tanto is a clear-cut sonata-rondo – a rarity in Chopin's music. Perhaps this explains why Chopin, for the first time in this sonata, experiments with form, shifting the focus of interest away from polyphony.

The first deviation from expectations comes in the secondary section in the exposition. After the transition (bars 52–75), the subordinate theme enters in bar 76 in the customary dominant key of F♯ major. In its second half, however, the melody is transposed to B major; of all keys, the parallel major of the principal tonality! This incursion of recapitulation into the exposition presents an immediate dilemma: what to do in the exposition of a sonata-rondo, if the secondary section ends in the main key? One answer is to strengthen the recapitulatory mood and to reiterate the principal theme in the tonic. Another is to move the primary theme to a different key. Normally, a retransition would lead back to the tonic, up a fourth. The retransition here modulates up a fourth as customary, but since the secondary section concluded in the tonic, the modulation is to E minor, and the principal theme is restated in that key.

This statement of the main theme in E minor entails yet another problem when the reprise is reached. If the subordinate theme were to return in the home key of B, there would be no recapitulatory rapprochement at all. Chopin's solution is paradoxical: E♭ major for the reprise of the secondary section. As remote from the tonic as this tonality is, it nonetheless performs a recapitulatory function: E♭ is the monotertial major to the E minor used in the first restatement of the principal section. Only in the last iteration of the principal theme is the home key of B minor restored.

Thematically the finale stems entirely from the basic motives of the sonata. In the eight-bar introduction rising semitones in the bass are echoed in the last bar by a descending semitone in the treble. Example 24 highlights the same bass

Example 24   Op. 58, IV, bars 9–12

semitone in the main theme, followed by an inversion of the very beginning of the sonata (cf. Example 19). The transition opens with a figure reminiscent of the beginning of the opening movement's subordinate theme (see Example 25). The

Example 25   Op. 58, IV, bars 52–3

upper voice of the secondary theme (Example 26) moves in tones and semitones, while the middle voice utilises a motive that figured in both first- and second-movement themes (see the motive labelled c in Examples 19 and 21). These are only a few instances of the close-knit thematic structure of the finale. The listener can easily add dozens of other examples, such as the chain of semitones dominating the ending of the main theme, or the obsessively repeated descending semitones in retransitions to the refrain.

Example 26   Op. 58, IV, bars 76–7

Apart from the Flute Variations and the G minor Trio, both works written before the age of twenty, Chopin composed for only one instrument other than piano: the cello. It is difficult to explain this preference; one might think that the violin, for example, would have been a more suitable instrument for the subtle melodic turns and fioriture of Chopin's music. Perhaps personal influences of Josef Merk and Auguste Franchomme played a decisive role in his choice.

Fifteen years separate the early *Introduction and Polonaise* for piano and cello from Chopin's last major work for the combination, the Sonata in G minor, Op. 65. Jim Samson describes the painstaking process of revising and rewriting this sonata, a task that took Chopin two years and that produced a record number of sketches and drafts.[20] His difficulties apparently had to do with the less familiar medium and not with formal design. By the time he began work on the cello sonata, Chopin had created a sonata pattern with which he felt comfortable, and he followed this pattern again in Op. 65. The primary group is omitted in the first-movement recapitulation, which begins with a preparation of the secondary group. The second movement is once again a scherzo with a strong mazurka flavour; and the fast fourth movement is dominated by quaver triplets and, like the finale of Op. 58, is in sonata-rondo form.

One can even say that Chopin introduced his own type, not only of sonata form, but of the sonata genre as well. His sonatas, like his mazurkas or nocturnes, are marked by a special musical idiom. This accounts for a certain thematic affinity between them, particularly the last two. One of the basic thematic elements in the B♭ minor Sonata is a semitone appoggiatura; the entire structure of the B minor

Sonata is built upon a falling semitone, and in the cello sonata, as Jim Samson has pointed out, the motive of an ascending and a descending semitone achieves a special prominence.[21] Indeed, in the principal theme of the latter, it is hard to imagine greater emphasis given a single motive, short of blatant repetition. Even the tonal scheme of the principal section reflects this motive: g–Ab–g in bars 1–9 and c–Db–c in bars 12–15. The motive is most clearly accentuated at phrase endings, including the end of the opening piano statement, where the cello enters before the beginning of the actual cello melody. The motive undergoes inversion, fragmentation and diminution along the way.

What sets this sonata apart from the others is that it seems to refer to, or take its inspiration from, an earlier work. The motive just described is identical to a leading motive from Schubert's *Winterreise*. It appears in the opening song, 'Gute Nacht', and runs all through the cycle. Example 27 shows a few selected excerpts.

Example 27   (a) Schubert, 'Gute Nacht'

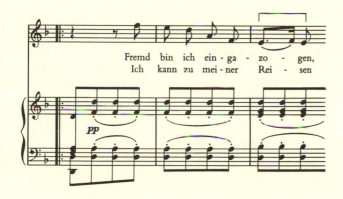

(b) Schubert, 'Gute Nacht'

Ex. 27 (*cont.*)

(c) Schubert, 'Erstarrung'

Ziemlich schnell.

(d) Schubert, 'Der Leiermann'

To these the reader can easily add songs like 'Rast', 'Frühlingstraum', 'Einsamkeit', 'Die Krähe' and 'Das Wirtshaus', in all of which the vocal part begins with this motive. Another motive used frequently in *Winterreise* is the ascent from the fifth to the first scale degree. Sometimes the two motives come together, as in 'Mut' (Example 28); this is exactly what happens in bars 2–3 of the principal theme of

Example 28   Schubert, 'Mut'

the cello sonata. There is even an outward resemblance between 'Gute Nacht' and the opening of the sonata's Allegro moderato. This seems hardly a coincidence, if one considers the subject matter of *Winterreise* – the disappointed lover leaving his beloved in despair – and the circumstances of Chopin's life at this time. A few years earlier Schumann had invoked Beethoven's *An die ferne Geliebte* in his Fantasy Op. 17 to express his desire for a blissful reunion with Clara. Chopin turned to *Winterreise* at the time of his highly painful separation from George Sand.

The basic motive also stands out in all the remaining movements: the dance-like scherzo, the remarkably contrapuntal Largo and the final Allegro. The finale, as in Op. 58, is in sonata-rondo form without a development or central episode, and it continues Chopin's tonal experimentations with the sonata. In the exposition the secondary section is in the subdominant key, C minor, rather than in the customary minor dominant. In the recapitulation, on the other hand, the secondary theme appears in the minor dominant (D minor) instead of in the expected home key.

Chopin played the sonata with Franchomme for the first and last time in 1848, a year and a half before his death. On this occasion the first movement was left out. Was it omitted because of its personal, autobiographical nature, in other words because the composer feared the ruthless witticism of the Parisian audience, who might have noticed the parallels with *Winterreise*?

The three mature sonatas of Chopin are among the most precious examples of that rare musical species, the Romantic sonata. It is gratifying to see the traditional underestimation and misconstruction of these works gradually giving way to an understanding of their true structural and aesthetic power.

PART 3

Reception

9 *Chopin in performance*

James Methuen-Campbell

It was just over a hundred and fifty years ago that Parisian audiences were hearing Chopin play his newly-composed piano works for the first time. His music was accepted very rapidly into the repertoire of the piano and by the end of the nineteenth century he was widely regarded as *the* piano composer *par excellence*. Since that time virtually every pianist has at some stage of his career included Chopin's pieces in recital programmes. This chapter considers the playing of a selection of noted Chopin exponents and examines various influences that have affected the style in which his music has been interpreted.

Of the century and a half of Chopin playing, we are fortunate in having sound recordings of pianists whose careers have covered over three-quarters of this period. Thus a relatively comprehensive study of changes in the style of Chopin playing is possible. However, sadly we do not possess discs of any Chopin pupils, the last of whom died as late as 1922; the earliest-born pianist to record his music, the Frenchman Francis Planté, was a mere ten-year-old when the composer died in 1849.

There are only two sources that can be consulted in investigating performances by pianists of the period closest to Chopin: firstly, the written accounts of those who heard them play and, secondly, critical editions prepared by performers, such as von Bülow, which reflect their ideas on how the music should be interpreted. This data, however, leaves a number of questions unanswered. Perhaps the most controversial aspect of all is that of tempo.

Although Maelzel's metronome was in existence in Beethoven's day – and he made use of it – no-one in the nineteenth century would have considered taking the noisy instrument to a concert to check if an artist was playing the music at the designated speed. Chopin's own metronome markings, for the most part to be found only for those pieces composed before 1837, have to be viewed within the context of the lighter-actioned pianos he had in mind when writing; many of the tempos prescribed are on the fast side. It is often said that today's pianists play faster than did those at the beginning of the century; however, this is not really substantiated by discographic evidence. Pianists of our own time frequently hold articulation and clarity of texture as a priority, and this gives an effective impression of greater velocity.

Whether or not the early nineteenth-century pianists played the text of the music as printed, we know from various extant copies of Chopin's works used in teaching that he himself was in the habit of altering the ornamentation, adding fiorituras and the like, even after the music had been published.[1] Accounts relate that pianists contemporary to Chopin who took up his works, such as Liszt and Thalberg, would also change details, for instance by playing a particular episode in octaves, adding cadenza-like material or concluding with a different flourish; once the music was published the composer relinquished any control over the way in which it was performed. During the first half of the nineteenth century the printed text was seen by many as the reference-point on which to build an 'interpretation'. It was not perhaps until the inter-war years of this century that the published text of music became sacrosanct, and even then this applied only to selected composers.

One is on much firmer ground, however, in determining the dynamic range of early Chopin performances. We can gain a very accurate idea of how loudly or softly artists played by examining the pianos of the day and testing their capabilities. On this point it is relevant that the current fashion for using authentic instruments has as yet made few inroads into the performance of Chopin. Whereas the keyboard instruments of the eras of Bach and Beethoven were of a sonority and construction sufficiently different from our own for one to be able to demonstrate the cause for using an original instrument, by Chopin's time the piano was on the borderline of evolving into the instrument of today. During the decade of the 1820s alone – shortly before Chopin arrived in Paris – three inventions had considerably advanced its capabilities: the use of metal in the frame to support greater string tension, hammers covered with impacted felt that gave a more rounded and sonorous tone and the double-escapement action that facilitated a greater control in fast passages and made possible the rapid repetition of notes. Within twenty years of Chopin's death in 1849 Theodore Steinway was producing instruments in New York that were the prototype of the modern grand.

Regarding Chopin's own preference in pianos, one notes that he chose to play on an instrument capable of refined nuance, rather than on one constructed to maximise volume (despite the fact that there are frequent *fortissimo* markings in his works and *fff* in the two polonaises Op. 26 and Op. 40 No. 1). Chopin's pupil Emilie von Gretsch wrote that

> things that come out perfectly on my solid and robust Erard became abrupt and ugly on Chopin's piano [almost certainly a Pleyel – ed.]. He found it dangerous to work on an instrument with a beautiful, ready-made sound like the Erard. He said these instruments spoil one's touch: 'You can thump and bash it, it makes no differ-

ence: the sound is always beautiful and the ear doesn't ask for anything more, since it hears a full, resonant tone.'[2]

This view of the requisite tone for a good instrument is entirely complemented by what we know of Chopin's playing. Another pupil, Karol Mikuli, in the preface to his complete edition of Chopin's works (published by F. Kistner in Leipzig, 1879) described his master's approach to the piano thus:

> the tone he could draw from the instrument, especially in *cantabiles*, was always immense; in this regard Field alone could be compared with him. He gave a noble manly energy to appropriate passages with overpowering effect – energy without roughness – just as, on the other hand, he could captivate the listener through the delicacy of his soulful rendering – delicacy without affectation. For all the warmth of Chopin's temperament, his playing was always measured, chaste, distinguished and at times even severely reserved.[3]

This description is typical. Four of the most celebrated pianists of the day – Hiller, Mendelssohn, Moscheles and Hallé – all stressed one point, that Chopin's playing was quite unlike anything that had gone before, although the virtuoso Kalkbrenner thought, too, that it derived from the style of the Irishman John Field.

Mikuli also tells us that Chopin had a complete grasp of the technique necessary to play his own compositions, which were then considered to be of an almost unprecedented difficulty. His hand was small, but extremely flexible. He had mastered the art of legato playing to such an extent that he could make the piano sing as vividly as any vocalist.

The definition of the true Chopin rubato is a thorny subject that has elicited a good deal of poetic simile over the years and there is less concurrence here amongst those who heard the composer himself play. Mikuli's description would appear to be precise: 'the hand responsible for the accompaniment would keep strict time, while the other hand, singing the melody, would free the essence of the musical thought from all rhythmic fetters, either by lingering hesitantly or in eagerly anticipating the movement with a certain impatient vehemence, akin to passionate speech.'[4] A critic in *The Athenaeum*, writing of Chopin's recital at the home of Mrs Adelaide Sartoris on 23 June 1848 agrees with this concept for the main part: 'He [Chopin] makes frequent use of *tempo rubato*; leaning about within his bars more than any other player we recollect, but still subject to a presiding sentiment of measure such as presently habituates the ear to the liberties taken.'[5] However, no less a musician than Berlioz offered a contradictory and more negative view when he wrote that 'Chopin chafed under the restraints of time, and to my mind pushed rhythmic freedom much too far. . .Chopin simply could not play in strict time.'[6]

One might suggest that a likely explanation for this discrepancy of perception was that Berlioz and Mikuli were approaching Chopin's music from different levels of familiarity and understanding. For instance, Mikuli would have known where Chopin had marked (or had intended) a stretto, an accelerando or ritardando in the score of the music, and would have taken a change in rhythm as an integral part of the piece, whereas Berlioz, more concerned with what he was actually hearing – the finished result – would make no such allowance. Despite Mikuli's definition, there appears to be another application of rubato that has some claim of authenticity: this is when the whole tempo shifts into a faster or slower speed for a particular episode, such as in various bars of the Berceuse. These fluctuations, which can be heard in the discs of this work by Koczalski, Rosenthal and Pugno, each of whom studied with pupils of Chopin, can be used to hurry on the progress of the music towards material of special significance.

It is certainly the case that Chopin's mazurkas cannot be played successfully if the pianist adheres strictly to exact note values, and it is in these works that pianists who studied with pupils of Chopin demonstrate some of their most convincing and idiomatic playing on disc. But leaving the complexities of this dance rhythm aside, it is accepted without question that no music of the classical or romantic era can effectively be conveyed unless it is underpinned by a fundamental metre, such as is prescribed in the time signature, and it is hard to believe that Chopin, with his admiration of Bach and Mozart, would have transgressed this.

Chopin spent a large portion of his time in teaching the piano. The majority of his students were from the aristocratic and moneyed classes, although there were also a few who were intending to become professional musicians. The extraordinary dedication with which he approached the instruction of so many semitalented people is remarkable. The reminiscences and writings of these students are of primary importance in defining an authentic Chopin style, since many recorded aspects of his artistry. However, in terms of actually passing on his precepts of interpretation to future generations, there were only two of these pupils who can be regarded as having had any long-term impact: Karol Mikuli and Georges Mathias, whose professional lives were spent in far distant parts of Europe. From 1862 to 1893 Mathias was a piano professor at the Paris Conservatoire; Mikuli taught piano and harmony in Lwów (Lemberg) for thirty-five years or so from 1858.

If one examines a list of the pupils of Mathias and Mikuli one can see how their teaching, which incorporated what they had learnt from Chopin, had the potential to be passed on to pianists and pedagogues active in the late nineteenth and twentieth centuries. Amongst Mathias's pupils were Isidor Philipp, Raoul Pugno, Ernest Schelling, Teresa Carreño, the composers Paul Dukas and Camille Chevillard and the American critic James Huneker. Philipp, in turn, was the teacher of Guiomar Novaes and Nikita Magaloff; Carreño was the teacher of Egon Petri as a child. Mikuli's students included Aleksander Michałowski, Moriz Rosenthal and Raoul Koczalksi. Michałowski taught Mischa Levitzki, Wanda Landowska and for a time the Russian pianists Heinrich Neuhaus and Vladimir Sofronitsky; Moriz Rosenthal taught Charles Rosen and Robert Goldsand. However, since a number of those mentioned above were also in contact with other equally potent musical forces during their formative years, it is impossible for one to be able to establish an unbroken link in more than about two cases. Aspects of the authentic Chopin tradition were also said to have been passed on by other pupils of the composer, such as the Princess Marcelina Czartoryska (whose playing was described as being the most faithful of all to Chopin's precepts), Mme Dubois and Emile Decombes.

In discussing the Mathias/Mikuli legacy one should caution that as a teacher at the Paris Conservatoire Mathias most probably was pressured into conforming his advice on technique to that of the well-established tradition of the institution as developed by the successive teachers Louis Adam, Pierre Zimmermann and Antoine-Francois Marmontel. Mathias had been a pupil of Kalkbrenner before he came to Chopin, and piano studies composed by him reflect this training rather than Chopin's. Also, we know that when Mikuli came to publish his Chopin edition he did not adhere strictly to his teacher's fingerings – he admitted as much to Michałowski.[7] Nor is it likely that far away in Lwów Mikuli would have taught his pupils on the type of piano to which Chopin was devoted, the Pleyel, so that some of the effects that his master had demonstrated on his own instrument could well have been severely altered on one with a heavier action. It is therefore necessary to question what aspects of the Chopin tradition *might* have been transmitted through the composer's pupils.

It would appear that Mikuli insisted on a refined and poetic approach to Chopin, on the plasticity in phrasing that was so much a characteristic of his master's playing and especially on a firm adherence to the text. Of the three pianists listed above as his pupils, only Raoul Koczalski has left a full account of Mikuli's priorities:

> his teaching was so revolutionary that even today [1936] it commands all my admiration. His analyses opened my eyes and trained me not to dissociate technique from mental work. Nothing was neglected: posture at the piano, fingertips, use of the pedal, *legato* playing, *staccato*, *portato*, octave passages, *fiorituras*, phrase structure, the singing tone of a musical line, dynamic contrasts, rhythm, and above all the care for authenticity with which Chopin's works must be approached. Here there is no camouflage, no cheap *rubato* and no languishing or useless contortions.[8]

Fortunately, the legacy of Koczalski's recordings of Chopin is very extensive. He left discs of the four ballades, the twenty-seven etudes, the Preludes Op. 28, the Concerto in F minor, six of the nocturnes, ten of the waltzes and several other pieces (see Appendix), though none of the sonatas. These discs are of the greatest significance, not only because they are so comprehensive, but because Koczalski's tuition by Mikuli was unique in that he specifically passed on to the young man all that he could recollect of Chopin's teaching.

If a comparison is made of Koczalski's performances and those of the French pianist Raoul Pugno, who was Mathias's pupil only seventeen years after Chopin's death, one finds a great divergence in style between the two, perhaps reflecting that it was never Chopin's intention to found a 'school' of playing. After all, Adolph Gutmann, one of Chopin's favourite pupils, had a heavily physical style which from all accounts was antithetical to the tenets of Chopin's teaching.

Both Koczalski and Pugno recorded the F♯ major Nocturne, Op. 15 No. 2, and in listening to the performances it is evident that their conceptions of the piece were quite different. Pugno takes an excessively slow tempo (M.M. ♪ = 52), which was reputedly passed on to him by Mathias.[9] Koczalski's is conventional. However, Pugno's discs of the Berceuse, the A♭ major Waltz, Op. 34 No. 1, and the A♭ major Impromptu, Op. 29, reveal him as a much more energetic and mercurial player than Koczalski. The Pole, a rather passive pianist, employs his highly developed finger technique to inflect the music with subtle nuances; in the fioritura passages of the Berceuse and a version of the E♭ major Nocturne, Op. 9 No. 2, with extra ornamentation added by Chopin one admires a singing fluidity of tone that belongs to a distinct pianistic style. In Koczalski's performance of the waltzes, where there are some small divergences from recognised texts, he pays special attention to the sophisticated rhythmic patterns of the music, as in the A♭ major Waltz, Op. 64 No. 3. His readings of the more rapid etudes feature frequent ritardandos at phrase endings.

Aspects of the same style can also be found in the Chopin discs of Moriz Rosenthal, who was Mikuli's pupil before he went on to Liszt. Rosenthal's approach in the mazurkas is highly effective in capturing a mood of poetic reverie. Like Koczalski, he phrased with the utmost plasticity, whilst wholly avoiding the rhythmic excesses of Leschetizky's pupil, Ignaz Friedman, who was also a famed interpreter of the mazurkas. Rosenthal saw the mazurkas not as dances rooted in a rustic folk tradition, but more as nostalgic and idealised reflections of a vanished past.

Aside from Chopin's pupils, a number of other pianists took up the composer's works during his lifetime and performed them in public; these included Henri Herz, Friedrich Kalkbrenner and his pupil George Osborne, Mme de Belleville-Oury, Marie Pleyel and Julius Knorr. Unquestionably, however, the two most notable champions of his music during this early period were Clara Schumann and Franz Liszt.

It was whilst the composer Robert Schumann was living in the household of the piano pedagogue Friedrich Wieck in 1831 that he wrote his celebrated 'Hats off, gentlemen, a genius!' article for the *Allgemeine musikalische Zeitung* some time after hearing Chopin's 'Là ci darem la mano' Variations, Op. 2. Clara Wieck, then a girl of twelve, was in the process of being launched as a child prodigy and she soon included the Variations in her concerts. As early as 13 January 1833, when the composer himself was only twenty-two, she played a programme containing mazurkas from Opp. 6 and 7 and an unspecified nocturne. The following September she gave the finale of the E minor Concerto at the Leipzig Gewandhaus and throughout a career of more than fifty years she regularly presented Chopin's works, making one of her final appearances in the F minor Concerto.

From contemporary descriptions one learns that Clara Schumann made as much of an impact through her musicianship as through the brilliance of her virtuosity. The critic Eduard Hanslick wrote of her in 1856, 'To give a clear impression to each work in its characteristic musical style and, within this style, to its purely musical proportions and distinctions, is ever her main task.'[10] He then went on to praise her 'strict conformity of measure' in matters of rhythm and describes how she spurned a sloppy application of rubato in Chopin. Her entire training at the piano had been with her father, who believed in 'a yielding, flexible wrist' and the importance of a developed legato,[11] ideas of technique that were much better adapted to Chopin's music than were those of most other pedagogues of the day. The pianist Alice Mangold Diehl in praising Clara Schumann's playing echoes a characteristic that Mikuli had attributed to Chopin himself: 'to hear a melody played by Clara Schumann was to hear it as its utterance could hardly be equalled, certainly not surpassed, by the greatest among vocalists.'[12]

Although one should not underestimate her influence in familiarising the public, especially German audiences, with Chopin's works, Clara Schumann was more intent on preserving the correct performance of her late husband's music than she was that of any other composer. Thus, amongst her pupils one does not find the names of pianists especially noted for their Chopin.

The situation regarding Liszt's relationship with Chopin and his music is more complex. He was already living in Paris when the Pole, a year his senior, arrived in September 1831. Liszt attended Chopin's Parisian début at the Salle Pleyel on 26 February 1832. The two were on friendly terms and played several times together in public. Chopin envied Liszt his supreme gifts of communication with an audience and he recognised that his friend had the more dynamic personality. In a letter to Ferdinand Hiller of 20 June 1833 Chopin wrote: 'at this moment Liszt is playing my Studies, and putting honest thoughts out of my head: I should like to rob him of the way to play my own Studies.'[13] Wilhelm von Lenz, himself a pupil of Chopin, remembered how Liszt (with whom he also had lessons) would alter harmonies and ornamentation when playing Chopin's mazurkas and that he took the matter very seriously, making sure not to distort the original character.[14] Liszt left Paris in 1835 and from this date until 1847 he toured widely as a virtuoso, often including Chopin's works, especially a selection of etudes or mazurkas, in his programmes. Rather than using Chopin's favourite piano, the Pleyel, in concerts, he played on the seven-octave Erard grand with its heavier action and enhanced brilliance.

In the late 1830s Liszt broke new ground in giving concerts for the piano alone.

The first time the term 'recital' appears is in the advertising for an appearance he made at the Hanover Rooms in London on 9 June 1840. Until this time it was the accepted practice for a pianist to share a concert with other instrumentalists; there were usually vocal items included as well. This format survived in London concerts until the time of the First World War. Chopin himself gave only one solo recital – at the Hopetoun Rooms in Edinburgh on 4 October 1848 – when he was already mortally ill and in no condition to organise the participation of other artists. The solo recital, once established, was to have a profound effect on the role of the pianist in the world of music. Not only had the artist gained complete control over the content of the programme, but the occasion also offered an unlimited scope to develop the cult of personality and hence to earn considerable amounts of money.

After Liszt's break with the concert platform in 1847 his energies were directed towards composition and, especially later, teaching. Occasionally, however, he did continue to appear as a pianist, usually in order to raise money for various causes he had espoused. During the Weimar years (the period in which he assimilated aspects of Chopin's compositional style into his own works) his interpretations are said to have gained in spiritual insight. As an old man it was generally to the works of Beethoven and Chopin that he would turn when asked to play.

Two of Liszt's pupils of the early years at Weimar in the 1850s became famous virtuosos: Hans von Bülow and Carl Tausig. Both programmed Chopin's works regularly, although von Bülow was regarded as an intellectual player and Tausig as the archetypal technician. It was the latter who was considered to be the more sympathetic in Chopin. Von Lenz was deeply impressed by Tausig's understanding of the structure of Chopin's music and of his command of the piano's resources; he wrote, 'Tausig's playing was flawlessly moulded. How he would have charmed Chopin, whose perfect ease and grace in overcoming the greatest difficulties he possessed, together with far superior strength and power.'[15]

In 1867 Tausig gave a series of four recitals in Berlin devoted entirely to Chopin; he was most probably the first artist in Europe to devise such a series (the American pianist Carl Wolfsohn is said to have given a cycle of Chopin's complete solo works in Philadelphia a few years previously). Tausig made a complete revision of the E minor Piano Concerto, both reorchestrating the work and adding to the density of notes in the piano part. A fragment from this version can be heard in the recording by Moriz Rosenthal, who interlaces right-hand octaves with left-hand single notes in the semiquaver triplet runs at the end of the finale. Bernard Shaw was scathing about these 'improvements', commenting, 'I am now more than ever convinced that Tausig's early death was, like that of Ananias, the result of supernatural interposition for the extermination of a sacrilegious meddler.'[16]

But of all the virtuosos active in the nineteenth century, other than the composer himself, it was Anton Rubinstein who was the most influential interpreter of Chopin, and the most imitated. Born in Russia in 1829, he came to Paris a decade later and began touring as a *Wunderkind*. He visited Chopin and heard him play the F♯ major Impromptu, Op. 36. It made an everlasting impression. Rubinstein's teacher, Alexander Villoing, was of Field's school and hence the young pianist and his equally talented brother Nikolai were trained in the art of legato playing – the smooth transition from one note to another that can make the piano sing in imitation of the voice.

Anton Rubinstein's temperament was one of violent contrasts and he used this to great effect in his playing. At one moment there would be a climax of elemental force, at another a gentle, limpidly vocal approach to the instrument. These conflicting moods were applied to works such as the polonaises, ballades, scherzos and sonatas with devastating results – audiences were stunned. This was a new Chopin they were hearing and one that was now wholly dissociated from the salon; it was a Chopin fitted for the concert hall. The full grandeur and dramatic range had at last been revealed and any undertones of effeminacy cast aside.

The view of Anton Rubinstein as a Chopin player of monumental stature is confirmed by the content of his recitals, which would often be inordinately long, as were those of von Bülow on occasion. Rubinstein would construct programmes devoted entirely to Chopin and during one of his celebrated Historical Concerts of 1885 he played in Vienna a recital containing the F minor Fantasy; six preludes from Op. 28; the Barcarolle; three waltzes; two impromptus; the B minor Scherzo; three nocturnes; four mazurkas; all four ballades; the 'Funeral March' Sonata, Op. 35; the Berceuse and three polonaises, ending with the A♭ major, Op. 53. After one of his concerts the previous year the critic Hanslick had written: 'Yes, he plays like a god, and we do not take it amiss if, from time to time, he changes, like Jupiter, into a bull.'[17]

Understandably, Rubinstein's treatment did not meet with the approval of Chopin's pupils. It was largely antithetical to what they understood to be the authentic Chopin style with its emotional restraint. Sir Charles Hallé, who had been a friend of Chopin, branded it as 'clever, but not Chopinesque'.[18] The general public of the 1850s and 1860s were very unlikely to have heard either Chopin or any of his pupils play, so that they would not have had any such affiliations to 'correct' style. But if the playing in recital of Rubinstein's pupil Josef Hofmann was a realistic indication of his master's approach to Chopin, then the validity of the qualms of Chopin's friends and pupils was wholly justified.

In 1862 Rubinstein had founded the St Petersburg Conservatory, and one of the first pianists he engaged to teach there was the Pole Theodor Leschetizky. Like Liszt, Leschetizky had been a pupil of Czerny in Vienna, where he had formed a childhood friendship with Rubinstein (also with Carl Filtsch, Chopin's most talented pupil, who died at fifteen). Leschetizky's links with the Viennese keyboard tradition were strong through his association with Czerny. He had studied

Chopin's music from an early age, although it was not especially to his master's taste. Leschetizky developed into an exemplary technician and thoughtful interpreter and by the date the Conservatory opened he was already a teacher of experience. One of his first great successes was Annette Essipoff, who had lessons with him from 1866.

Since Liszt and Leschetizky have been widely acclaimed as the most celebrated piano teachers of all time, it is inevitable that one should compare the Chopin playing of their pupils. Nevertheless, their roles as instructors were rather different because Liszt's pupils were, for the main part, already finished artists when they came to him. It is demonstrable that Leschetizky's disciples had a more consistent approach to style in Chopin than did those of Liszt. From the most famous of the later Liszt pupils at Weimar D'Albert, Ansorge and Lamond all eventually concentrated their energies on Beethoven; Friedheim (who had previously worked with Rubinstein) became a highly erratic artist better suited to the music of Liszt; de Greef, with a background at the Brussels Conservatory, developed into a sobre pianist with a special affinity for Grieg; Sauer lent towards a Viennese style, despite having had lessons from Nikolai Rubinstein for over two years before he came to Liszt and Rosenthal owed much of his Chopin style to Mikuli's tutelage. All these pianists recorded Chopin's music, and from this discographic evidence it is seemingly Rosenthal and Sauer who present the most stylish interpretations.

Sauer had a naturally communicative and full tone. His suave elegance was well-adapted to the smaller-scale pieces, and yet he had an equal ability to master the larger forms – all factors that contributed to readings that did justice to the range of Chopin's genius. His recitals would include a number of pieces that were infrequently programmed during this period, such as the *Allegro de concert*, Op. 46; the F♯ minor Polonaise, Op. 44; and the *Polonaise-fantaisie*, Op. 61. Sauer's disc of the E major Etude, Op. 10 No. 3, demonstrates some aspects of a Chopin style that are often lost in modern-day performances: specifically, the utmost care in shaping phrase-endings and a considerable range in layering dynamics. The phrasing of the opening melody, reminiscent of a singer in its success in communicating meaning with every note, has a freedom that is contrasted starkly with a tautly metronomic treatment of the middle section of the etude.

Of Leschetizky's pupils one can include a far greater number who achieved fame as Chopin pianists: the Poles Ignacy Paderewski, Ignaz Friedman and Józef Śliwiński (regarded by many of his fellow countrymen to have been their finest pianist in the earlier years of this century), the Russians Ossip Gabrilowitsch, Mark Hambourg, Benno Moiseiwitsch and Alexander Brailowsky and the American Fannie Bloomfield-Zeisler.

As was the case with the Liszt pupils, many of the Leschetizky students were great individualists, and as such one should not look for a consistency of artistic vision in their playing. However, a highly developed appreciation of and attention to the polyphonic life of Chopin's music does establish some common ground, as does a profoundly mellow and soulful use of tone. The former characteristic is more regularly noticeable here than in the Liszt pupils. All these artists were of East European-Slavonic ancestry and they appear to have possessed a natural affinity with the metre of Chopin's music that derived from a shared cultural heritage.

Paderewski, along with Vladimir de Pachmann (see below), is so inseparably associated with Chopin's music that he deserves special attention. In recent years it has become fashionable to denigrate his artistry because of the poor discs he made at the close of an illustrious career. In these the lack of synchronization between the hands is admittedly somewhat excessive, especially in slow music. However, it should be noted that this style of playing was common during that era (with pianists born before the 1880s) and it was only the post-1900 generations who regularly have played with their hands together. The now abhorred practice was developed so as to highlight the division between melody and accompaniment or to separate the various voices in contrapuntal writing, such as is found in the Nocturnes in C♯ minor, Op. 27 No. 1, and E♭ major, Op. 55 No. 2.

There is enough in the way of evidence from Paderewski's earlier recordings to justify his reputation. He had a rare ability, possessed today perhaps only by Horszowski, Arturo-Benedetti Michelangeli and Radu Lupu, to create an almost hypnotic aura through sound alone. This was accomplished by the combination of a highly developed legato with a harmonically imaginative use of the sustaining pedal.

During the time of the First World War and the years just following, Paderewski's advocacy of a free Poland and his role as a great Chopin player became inextricably linked and he was responsible for establishing Chopin as a great Polish patriotic figure. The quiet dignity of the old man seated at the piano, channelling his deeply felt cares about Poland's future into a performance of the A♭ major Polonaise, Op. 53, was a potent symbol of liberty.

Throughout his career, which extended effectively from 1887 to 1939, Paderewski had a rival who could also lay claim as the greatest Chopin interpreter – Vladimir de Pachmann. He was born just a year before Chopin's death and studied in Vienna with Czerny's pupil Joseph Dachs. He thus came from a musical background similar to that of the Leschetizky school, but without the influence of Anton Rubinstein. Pachmann left several recordings of Chopin, but very few of the larger-scale pieces.

Pachmann, whilst having the Slavonic insight into Chopin's rhythms and melodies, was essentially a miniaturist, whose technique was best suited to the nocturnes, waltzes, mazurkas and impromptus. His rather rarified style was rooted in the salons of the mid-nineteenth century, for which, it should be noted, Chopin wrote much of his music.

Pachmann did not favour the full dynamic range of Chopin – *pianissimo* playing was his speciality – and the more masculine elements were often diluted in his readings. For instance, the D minor Prelude, which concludes the Op. 28 set, should, according to the text, end on three D¹s (in the lowest octave of the instrument), an effect which makes a haunting impact. Pachmann, having played these three notes (incidentally, in an entirely different tempo from the preceding music), then adds a tonic chord. This strongly suggests that he was unable to appreciate the full scope of Chopin's genius for dramatic effect. In the mazurkas, however, Pachmann's humour, pathos, charm and moments of rustic gaiety were inimitable and highly idiomatic.

A personality of eccentricity almost equal to Pachmann's (whose recitals would customarily veer between séance and circus), though nine years his senior, was the Frenchman Francis Planté. He recorded seven of Chopin's etudes in 1928. Given his age, these are a valuable document, for Planté not only had contacts with several of Chopin's pupils, but was active as a mature concert artist from the 1860s. These readings, despite being a good deal slower than the authentic metronome markings, have incomparable rhythmic buoyancy and one hears a considerable amount of unexpected detail highlighted in the left-hand parts, most notably in the C major Etude, Op. 10 No. 7. The effect of much of this detail would be lost at a faster tempo. These are studies that to perfection marry technique with poetic inspiration.

Around the turn of the twentieth century the American critic James Gibbons Huneker, who had studied with Chopin's pupil Mathias, wrote a damning indictment of the way in which French pianists usually approached Chopin: 'If the Germans treat him in a dull, clumsy and bruted manner, the Frenchman irritates you by his flippancy, his nimble, colourless fingers and the utter absence of poetic divination.'[19] Apart from Planté and one or two others this was a fair assessment of a school that had put the display of shallow virtuosity above all else; however, around the time of the First World War the situation began to change and France produced a number of serious Chopin interpreters, the most notable of whom was Alfred Cortot.

Cortot was born in 1877 and he came into contact with various ancient pupils of Chopin, including Mathias and Mme Dubois. His first teacher at the Paris Conservatoire was Emile Decombes, accredited as having studied with Chopin. This legacy gave Cortot a strong sense of tradition. His model, however, was the Alsatian-born pianist Edouard Risler, who was a few years older. They had both worked in the advanced class of Louis Diémer at the Conservatoire and, having completed his studies there, Cortot followed in Risler's footsteps and spent some time with the Cosima Wagner circle at Bayreuth. He returned with a much broader view of the repertoire than was current in France at that time. Cortot's playing signified that the French school was finally coming of age, and this impression is confirmed by the interpretations on disc of his contemporaries Marguerite Long, Robert Lortat, and, a little later on, Yves Nat and Robert Casadesus.

As with Pachmann before him, Cortot immersed himself in every facet of Chopin. Aside from devoting entire recitals to the composer, some of which were of monumental proportions, he collected Chopin manuscripts and even wrote a book, *Aspects de Chopin*,[20] which is sadly flawed. Cortot's playing reveals not so much a modern view, but one that was eclectic. He had the ability to inflect every note of the music with nuance and hence achieve a focussed and highly concentrated level of interpretation. Rather than being attracted to the brilliancy of the Erard or the light tone of the Gaveau, he favoured a Pleyel grand piano. The rich and well-defined tone of this instrument bore little similarity, however, to that of Chopin's day. It was on such a piano that Cortot made his legendary Chopin recordings of the 1930s.

Cortot retained an idiomatic and extremely graceful rubato that belonged to the nineteenth century. Better suited to the 'French' works of Chopin (i.e. the etudes, impromptus and waltzes) than to the Polish ones (mazurkas and polonaises), it was often heavily stylised and predictable. But what was really striking was Cortot's convincing understanding of the complete spectrum of Chopin's mind, a mind that he perceived as both innovative and serious. Nowhere is his authority more evident than in his recordings of the elusive Preludes Op. 28. Cortot's interpretations are as much admired by today's musicians as they ever were, and one might say that his advocacy of Chopin was comparable to Schnabel's of Beethoven.

Although there were several successful Chopin players of various nationalities in the early years of the twentieth century, it is to the Russians that one must look to find another definite tradition. Anton Rubinstein's pupils Ossip Gabrilowitsch and Arthur Friedheim, together with the Pole Josef Hofmann, all eventually crossed the Atlantic and taught numerous pianists in the United States and Canada. Hofmann, who had very small hands in contrast to his master's giant ones, was one of the truly outstanding pianists of the century and he embodied many aspects of his teacher's style in his own performances: explosive *fortissimos*, the utmost clarity in shaping voices in polyphonic episodes and a perfect legato. In various discs taken from concerts of the late 1930s one hears playing that is wilfully original in its obsession with balancing right- and left-hand parts. Carefully selected notes of the accompaniment are brought out to grotesque, though tantalizing, effect (e.g. in the Berceuse and the E♭ minor Polonaise, Op. 26 No. 2). Active from 1887 to 1946, Hofmann was the last great representative of Rubinstein's style of playing.

There were other teachers in Russia who towards the end of the nineteenth century produced Chopin players of note. For instance, Vassily Safonov taught both Josef and Rosina Lhévinne, who emigrated to the United States and became mainstays of the Juilliard School in New York; Alexander Siloti taught Sergei

Rachmaninov, and Felix Blumenfeld taught Horowitz. There were also four highly influential teachers who remained in Russia after the Revolution of 1917 – Alexander Goldenweiser, Leonid Nikolayev, Heinrich Neuhaus and Konstantin Igumnov – and it is on their respective schools that latter twentieth-century Russian pianism, which has always given Chopin's music an especially high place in its repertoire, has been founded.

Rachmaninov and Horowitz have played the most interesting Chopin of all the twentieth-century Russians, each retaining the traditional strengths of a poetic tone and a complete awareness of the potentialities of the sustaining pedal, which Anton Rubinstein had labelled 'the soul of the piano'. With Horowitz one hears a Chopin that is an unusual fusion of styles. The rhythmic bite of his rapid passagework, such as in the B minor Scherzo, Op. 20, demonstrates a post-Prokofiev technique in which angularity makes its first inroads into Chopin. On the other hand, a whiplash treatment of rhythm in the mazurkas sounds wholly convincing – until, that is, one hears the gentler playing of Mikuli's pupils Rosenthal and Koczalski. Horowitz has, more than most, taken Chopin's music as a medium with which to express his own neuroticism.

Running alongside Horowitz's career was that of Artur Rubinstein from Poland, who, although seventeen years the Russian's senior, did not come to prominence until the late 1920s. Rubinstein's training in Berlin had brought him into contact with mainstream European music life and he, too, constructed his pianism not from one source, but from taking the most attractive aspects from different traditions. In many respects Paderewski's successor in conveying Chopin as 'a noble son of Poland', Rubinstein was also a Francophile. For over forty years he produced a great number of Chopin discs that display both an adherence to textual accuracy unusual in a pianist of his generation and an overall discipline in seeking out the thought behind the notes was again uncharacteristic. Not only did he have extraordinary authority as an interpreter, but also a thoroughness of musicality very much in keeping with our own time.

The problems involved in putting some perspective on current trends in Chopin interpretation are compounded by the fact that the music world has become internationalised to such an extent that it is virtually impossible for an artist trained in Western Europe or the United States to have his development restricted to a specific school of playing; such influences no longer exert much power. The approach of the majority of today's Chopin players is therefore, of necessity, an eclectic one and this has acted against a 'styled' treatment.

One does note, however, a uniformity of interpretation that perhaps results from the influence of the recording industry. With the ever-improving technology of sound reproduction there is a consequent demand for playing of the highest technical finish. In attaining this, the pianist generally sacrifices spontaneity, which is a very important factor in conveying the concentrated poetry of the mazurkas and the improvisatory mood found in many of the late works.

Nor does the preoccupation with programming complete sets of Chopin's works, whether these be the four ballades, the four scherzos or either book of etudes, act in sympathy with the composer's mind. There can be little musical rationale for grouping together works that have nothing in common excepting genre title and general formal structure. The trend is symptomatic of our time in which everything has to carry intellectual weight: thus the move towards favouring large-scale forms. One seldom hears Chopin's smaller pieces played by the better-known pianists, except as encores. In giving Chopin his due as a great composer we appear to have divested him of a definite stylistic ethos.

ZOFIA CHECHLIŃSKA

Every age views musical works in its own way. The study of reception documents the changing functions and meanings attributed to a given corpus of music in particular milieus and at particular times, and in doing so it can enable generalisations about the role that music plays within society. This chapter assesses the part played by Chopin's music in nineteenth-century Polish culture, describing prevailing attitudes to his works and identifying the specific distinguishing features of Polish reception.

Literature on Chopin reception in Poland is exiguous,[1] addressing only small corners of the field and concentrating for the most part on the views of composers and critics. The present study broadens this to consider 'social' reception (a historical-aesthetic interpretation of the ways in which the music was received by listeners) as well as 'artistic' reception (the influence of the music on the artistic world). Even so the study has certain constraints. From the artistic viewpoint, it will consider only Chopin's influence on other music. And from the social viewpoint, it is hampered by the restricted nature of source materials and by limited opportunities for research.

A study of present-day reception is of course facilitated by modern sociological methods such as questionnaires. These enable us to establish differences among various social circles and to determine the extent to which the reception of a composer's work is uniform at a given time and in a given milieu. Thus one can study fairly systematically the socio-functional aspect of reception in today's world.[2] For earlier periods, however, the possibility of such study is very limited. In this case social reception must rely upon indirect sources such as critical literature and the repertoire performed. A very limited circle of people wrote about Chopin's music – books, articles and reviews were written mainly by professional musicians, and these transmit primarily the views of their authors, rarely passing on more general opinions or describing audience reactions. The picture painted on this basis must naturally be incomplete. We can give a definite appraisal of how contemporary music criticism received and interpreted Chopin. We may even hazard a guess that the opinions of music critics also dominated professional musical circles. But on the basis of extant sources, it is difficult to determine with any certainty the extent to which critical literature influenced Chopin reception, the extent of agreement between the views of critics and those of audiences, or the size and nature of those audiences. Nor can we establish how wide a social range was familiar with Chopin's music or how the reception differed in different milieus. The sole documentation here would be memoirs and correspondence, but these are relatively few in number and were mostly written by members of the country's cultural élite. In a few memoirs and letters there are references to Chopin's music, but these are usually of a very general character and add relatively little to the picture emerging from an analysis of contemporary criticism. They will play only a minor part in the present study, which will be based mainly on nineteenth-century Polish criticism (including newspaper reports).

REPERTOIRE

The first task is to determine what Chopin repertoire was played in Poland. The frequency with which specific pieces were performed at public concerts, salons (where both professional and amateur pianists played) and private houses is at least an initial indicator of audience preferences. The main sources of information here are music journals, non-musical periodicals and the daily press, all of which advertised concerts and published reviews. A comprehensive survey of non-musical journals has not yet been undertaken, but a significant proportion has been examined, and some useful generalisations about repertoire can be made on the basis of these. Periodicals and newspapers did not of course announce every concert, and there are significant variations in the practice of different towns and different periods. Even the Warsaw-based musical press, which was more systematic about announcing and reviewing concerts, gave nothing like a complete documentation of concert life: there were periods in the century when music journals failed to appear at all.

In other Polish towns the situation was worse, though in general it improved later in the century. Press notices rarely included full details of programmes, confining themselves to giving the names of the performers or at best an abbreviated reference to the composers represented (e.g. 'pieces by Chopin'). Just occasionally – especially with large forms – works would be described in more detail. Given this situation, only an approximation of the representation of Chopin genres in the repertoire is possible.

The earliest performances of Chopin in Warsaw were given by the composer himself. Following his initial public appearance in 1818, when he was described as 'a musical genius',[3] Chopin played frequently in the salons of the aristocracy and also in public concerts. In addition to concertos by other composers (Ries,

Moscheles) he played his own shorter compositions and, above all, he improvised. His reputation in Warsaw increased steadily and during his final years there he took a very active part in the artistic life of the city. He frequently played and improvised in the salons and appeared in public on several occasions (1829, 1830) performing his works with orchestra: the Variations Op. 2, Fantasy Op. 13, Rondo Op. 14 and the two concertos. These pieces were warmly received. Following a performance of the E minor Concerto in the Chopin's salon, one reviewer wrote: 'This is the work of a genius. The originality and charm of his thought [. . .] Chopin's genius will assure him uncommon and enduring fame'.[4] His concerts played to packed halls, with audience figures reaching 900, a colossal number for Warsaw in those days. Often he had to play encores.[5]

Thus the works for piano and orchestra were well known and highly regarded in Warsaw before Chopin left Poland. Admittedly Chopin's other music (the early mazurkas, polonaises, waltzes, variations and the March in C minor) were not appreciated by contemporary critics, but clearly they were known to and appreciated by the Warsaw musical milieu in which Chopin frequently played. His music had not yet been performed in public by other pianists, however, and it is by no means certain that the published compositions were widely played in private homes. In general published editions in Warsaw were small at the time and even if Chopin's pieces were played in private homes the audience would have been a very restricted one.[6]

Already before 1830 Polish writers had defined those characteristics of Chopin's playing and music that would later be valued by the emergent Romantic era and highlighted in nineteenth-century European criticism: its national character, its poetic and emotional qualities ('the expression of the heart', 'the voice of the soul'), its originality and its melancholy and delicacy.[7] Unsurprisingly, it was the national dimension which played a very special role in Polish reception.

The concept of nationalism in art, typical of the Romantic era, fell upon particularly fertile ground in Poland. As a result of the loss of national independence in 1795, art was one of the few areas in which a sense of Polish national identity could be displayed and preserved. The postulate of music's national character dominated the whole of Polish musical culture of the day, and the saturation of compositions with a national element became an essential criterion in their appraisal. Thus even prior to 1830 the Polish features of Chopin's compositions were strongly emphasised: the Polish melodies in the Fantasy Op. 13 and the dance elements in the Rondo Op. 14, the Variations Op. 2 and the finales of the Concertos were most enthusiastically received. Polish elements, and in particular Polish dances, were commonly exploited at the time, but Chopin was the first and only great composer to use them. Right from the start his works came to be perceived as the essence of 'the Polish soul', and he was treated as the property and symbol of the nation.[8] In 1830 Wojciech Grzymała, subsequently a friend of Chopin in the Paris years, wrote:

The land which gave him life with its song, affected his musical disposition. . . many a note of his music sounds like a happy reflection of our native harmony. In his hands the simple mazur willingly yields to alterations and modulations yet preserves its own accent and expression. In order, as Chopin did, to include the beautiful simplicity of native song in his refined compositions of genius he had to feel and to recognize the echoes of our fields and forests, to hear the song of our Polish villages.[9]

Elsewhere we read:

The national song that breaks through his compositions does not make them monotonous, it simply serves as a backdrop for thoughts of genius. . .[Nationalism] is the path for real talents, taking part of their inspiration from the nation. . .in their compositions they give back inspiration to the nation.[10]

It was not only in Poland that Chopin was considered a nationalist composer. Liszt wrote that the Polish composer was 'annointed' by everything that Poland held sacred,[11] while Schumann stressed the Polish character of not only the mazurkas and polonaises. The distinctive style of his music, which western Europe attempted to explain as 'exotic' nationalism, was almost certainly a factor contributing to the widespread nineteenth-century perception of Chopin as a nationalist composer.[12]

Also particularly valued was 'feeling' – as it was known at the time – or 'the voice of the heart'. It is characteristic that in the cyclic works, as well as in those extended works containing stylisations of Polish dances, the slow lyrical passages produced the most pleasure and applause. Critics and public alike especially praised the second and third movements of the concertos, while the first movements were not singled out for special comment. A reviewer from the *Kurier Warszawski* (The Warsaw Courier) described the Concerto in E minor as 'one of music's sublime works. . .particularly the Adagio and Rondo. . .which enjoyed great public success',[13] and in a review of the Concerto in F minor we read that 'even Hummel would have been proud of the Adagio and Rondo'.[14] (One must remember that comparison with Hummel was at that time an expression of the highest regard, particularly in Poland, where he was considered the foremost composer of piano music.) Mochnacki, the distinguished historian and music critic, in describing the Concerto, singled out its central movement: 'The Adagio of this concerto drew the attention of the connoisseurs for its outstanding beauties.'[15]

The nineteenth century viewed Chopin primarily as a lyricist. This despite the widely held view (particularly in German criticism) of him as a 'morbidly unhealthy' composer prey to life-long suffering and homesickness. That he was received in Poland primarily as a melodist is partly shown by the prevailing attitude to transcription, through which – to nineteenth-century ears – Chopin's works lost none of their worth, despite being deprived of their pianistic qualities. Moreover, it was the works or fragments of works with a cantilena melody which received most performances and praise. This applies not only to the lyric subjects and slow movements of the cyclic pieces but also to the etudes, preludes and waltzes. Of the etudes, for example, Op. 10 No. 3 and Op. 25 Nos. 1 and 7 are specially mentioned as being 'particularly lovely' on account of their melodious qualities.

Chopin was also valued as an utterly original pianist and composer. On this matter, however, the opinions of the critics are not always consistent. Although he was described as being so original that there was no trace of influence on his music, at the same time relationships between his work and Hummel's were detected.[16] The predominant view, however, was that Chopin's music was of such a far-reaching originality that it showed no connections with the work of anyone else, and this view was to characterise Chopin's reception in Poland throughout nearly all of the nineteenth century.

Although Chopin's music was treated in Polish writing up to 1830 from an aesthetic rather than a technical perspective – which was after all typical of the contemporary reception and criticism of music throughout the whole of Europe – two things must be noted: first, that before 1830 Chopin's works were never given programmatic interpretations in Poland, and, secondly, that even at that time certain aspects of his compositional technique that were later to be regarded as typical stylistic features were observed.

The absence of picturesque interpretations may have resulted from Chopin's own attitude: he was – as we know – definitely opposed to this way of reading his works. However, it seems also to be the case that programme music was virtually nonexistent in the Polish tradition in which he grew up. The lack of such interpretations applied therefore not only to his work but to musical composition generally. It was not until the 1840s that programmatic readings of Chopin's music began to appear in Polish writing. The technical features observed at that time were described in a very general way. Emphasis was placed on the subordination of virtuoso elements to expressive demands,[17] the wide spans in the accompaniments[18] and the harmonic innovations,[19] though there were no suggestions at that time of the precise origins of these innovations or of Chopin's individuality.

The number of public performances of Chopin's works was small during his lifetime. The first following his departure from Poland – Edward Wolff playing the second and third movements of the Concerto in E minor[20] – was reported in the Warsaw press in 1835, and just thirteen concerts with performances of Chopin's music were listed there between 1830 and 1849. Public performances of his works did not begin to occur in other Polish towns until the end of the 1830s. Although Warsaw was at that time the main centre of Polish musical activity, Russian repression following the collapse of the November uprising in 1831 meant that Polish cultural life was curtailed for several years, and the number and frequency of concerts fell significantly. It was only in the second half of the 1850s, as a result of the relaxation of the partitioning powers' regime, that a revitalisation occurred.

Even during Chopin's lifetime the proportion of his music in the overall repertoire of public concerts in Poland was high. The problem is that there were relatively few concerts. Table 1 records the number of public performances – of works by Chopin and of works by the other most frequently performed composers – in Warsaw in the lean years from 1831 to his death in 1849, and in the entire period up to the second uprising against Russia, 1831 to 1862.

Table 1 *Number of Warsaw concerts at which a work by the given composer was performed*

Composer	1831–49	1831–62
Chopin	13	61
Beethoven	3	41
Thalberg	8	19
Mozart	7	19
Rossini	21	35
Weber	7	21
Mendelssohn	2	32
Liszt	5	18
Donizetti	16	25
Bériot	19	22
Bellini	18	26
Dobrzyński	8	22

(Liszt performed in Warsaw in 1843 and played his own compositions.)

The figures in the table are based on press information and are incomplete; the numbers given here are only an approximation. However, if they are taken to be representative, it appears that in the period up to Chopin's death he was the fifth most frequently performed composer, while in the following period he ranked first. This position remained unchanged until the end of the nineteenth century.

The repertoire of Chopin's works that were performed publicly in Poland during his exile cannot be precisely determined. It is known that it included the concertos, the *Rondo* Op. 14, the *Andante spianato and Grande Polonaise* Op. 22, the Grand Duo for cello and piano, the Fantasy Op. 13, the etudes, a ballade and a series of mazurkas, polonaises, nocturnes and songs. During the composer's lifetime it appears to have been predominantly his earlier pieces that were performed. This domination of the repertoire by the early music continued long after his death. In Poznań in 1842, M. A. Szulc, subsequently author of the first Polish monograph on Chopin, wrote 'there is hardly a mention of [Chopin's works] anywhere to be found',[21] which suggests that even press information about Chopin – at least in Poznań – was scarce. In Wilno the first press report about Chopin appeared as late as 1839. The Warsaw press, on the other hand, systematically published information about Chopin: his recent and published works, his circumstances and life-style, his illnesses, public appearances, successes and standing in the European musical world – in short, everything connected with the composer. This information fixed in the Polish mind the image of Chopin as a national artist, a representative of the Polish nation in Europe, a composer whose name a Pole should, at the very least, know and admire. Those compositions that were published in Leipzig were systematically brought to Poland and, judging from press reports and the correspondence of Chopin's family, very quickly sold out:

> Your Nocturnes and Mazurkas have been republished in Leipzig, and they sold out here in the course of a few days.[22]

> Look how they'll buy you up when we get the Leipzig editions.[23]

> Your concerto has reached us already. Ernemann [a Warsaw pianist] told me he's got it and other people have bought it as well.[24]

One does not know, however, in what quantities these editions were imported and sold. Nor is it known whether the people who bought them actually played them. In 1833 Mikołaj Chopin wrote to his son, 'There are people here who want your compositions; I don't know if they'll play them.'[25] But there is evidence that they were played in musicians' homes.[26] It is likely that the minor works, especially the mazurkas and nocturnes, were performed in salons and were quite widely known, at least by the élite,[27] and that some of these pieces were used as dance music.[28] In the second half of the century the domestic performance of Chopin's pieces by amateurs must have been widespread and far from accurate, since the press is full of complaints about the 'popular mania for showing off with Chopin'[29] and the widespread 'torture of Chopin' in the salons. A view of Chopin perceived in national sentimental terms became fashionable; it was the duty of every well-bred young lady to play Chopin's pieces. The Chopin repertoire performed in the salons was restricted to the minor, technically less intricate pieces. Even by the mid-nineteenth century, the knowledge of the larger forms must have been limited, because in 1850 Józef Sikorski, the famous music critic, asked performers to play the larger pieces more frequently in order to make them familiar to the public.

The Chopin repertoire performed in Poland increased significantly in the latter half of the century, especially in the last three decades. This was bound up with the fact that the number of concerts increased considerably, both in Warsaw and in other Polish towns. Concerts in Poland at this time adhered to a specific structure. Because there were no permanent symphony orchestras or philharmonic societies, the majority of concerts in Poland were solo performances, primarily by pianists, but also by singers and violinists. The piano repertoire therefore constituted a significant part of the total musical repertoire, within which Chopin's works occupied a substantial place. According to the critics of the day, no pianist could expect a concert in Poland to be a success unless he included at least one composition by Chopin.

The choice of Chopin repertoire performed in Poland during this time did not depart significantly from that in other European countries. This was partly because many of the pianists were either foreign, or were Poles who performed widely throughout Europe. Even in this period the paucity of sources prevents one from determining the exact nature of the repertoire. It is possible, however, to identify the most frequently performed pieces, as well as those that were programmed only rarely. As in the first half of the century, all the pieces for piano and orchestra were performed, though in the later period the concertos predominated increasingly. They were performed more frequently in their entirety now than they had been earlier, although the performance of individual movements continued until the end of the century, with the second and third movements of the Concerto in F minor enjoying undiminished popularity. Besides the concertos, works most frequently performed in public included the polonaises, immediately followed by the mazurkas, nocturnes and etudes. Of the polonaises, those in E♭, Op. 22,[30] A♭, Op. 53, and A, Op. 40, were especially popular. The *Polonaise-fantaisie*, Op. 61, did not appear regularly in programmes until the last quarter of the century. It is impossible to establish which were the favourite mazurkas, nocturnes and etudes, since the necessary information was seldom provided. In cases where a work was named unequivocally, the nocturnes of Op. 27, Op. 15 No. 2 and Op. 9 No. 2 appear most often. Again one is struck by the fact that the late pieces seldom appear. Performances of the large forms such as the ballades and scherzos, the Fantasy in F minor and the impromptus were also rare. The Ballade in G minor was the most popular, the Ballade in F minor the least often performed; the first three scherzos were performed with more or less equal frequency, though the C♯ minor gained popularity more slowly than the first two. The E major Scherzo, on the other hand, was hardly ever performed. Of the impromptus, the C♯ minor enjoyed the greatest popularity – again an early work. The Rondo in C major for two pianos was also frequently performed, as were the early songs, which were often heard on Polish concert platforms already in the first half of the century. The Tarantelle, Berceuse, Barcarolle and, particularly, the *Allegro de concert* made sporadic appearances in programmes. The situation remained unaltered until the last decade of the century, when later works (particularly the F minor Ballade) began to appear more frequently.

The sonatas were also performed extremely rarely, both in Poland and throughout Europe. The first report of a complete performance of the Sonata in B minor dates from as late as 1866.[31] Even after this date, the sonatas – in their entirety or as individual movements – were performed only sporadically until the turn of the century. The Sonata in G minor, the final work to be published during the composer's lifetime, was the most underrated of the three mature sonatas, and was hardly ever performed. Only the funeral march from the Sonata in B♭ minor enjoyed popularity; this was performed separately, both for piano and in transcriptions. Indeed, Chopin's works were often performed in transcription. The most common were for solo voice with accompaniment (the main themes of the Second Ballade, for instance, became the songs 'A barcarolle at dawn' to words by H. Bellamy and 'La fille d'onde' to words by E. Richebourg), or for violin and piano, but arrangements were also made for other instruments and, especially at the end of the century when there was a lively choral tradition, for orchestra and choir. Patriotic texts, or texts connected with Poland, her landscape and customs were often set to Chopin's music. Transcriptions of Chopin were common all over Europe in the nineteenth century, as we know from the plethora of editions. In Poland an additional factor in the rise of the transcription was the knowledge that Chopin's name on a programme helped to sell a concert to the Polish public. For example, B. Bilse's German orchestra, which played several seasons of concerts in Warsaw, included in its repertoire the Scherzo in B♭ minor transcribed for orchestra by a Warsaw composer.[32]

In summary, the repertoire described above was dominated by works with a distinct national flavour (polonaises, mazurkas), early works whose structure and harmony departed little from the musical norms of the first half of the nineteenth century and works in which a cantilena melody was particularly prominent. Published reviews of Chopin's composition show that the repertoire reflected not only the tastes of the wider public but also those of the critics.

RECEPTION BY CRITICS

Polish writing of the nineteenth century contains only sporadic criticism of Chopin's works. However, the prominence given to certain works and the acknowledgement of their particular value, together with the total neglect of others, enables us to recreate a contemporary scale of values.

The polonaises received particular attention, while the mazurkas were regarded as the crowning glory of Chopin's music. Of the polonaises the critics particularly admired those most often played: those in E♭ major Op. 22, A major Op. 40 and A♭ major. Op. 53, the last being described as 'a high point even in Chopin's work'.[33] At the same time the following was written about the *Polonaise-fantaisie*: 'the main ideas are unclear and their statement is lost in convolutions and fails to impress. . .the work is one of Chopin's least fortunate creations.'[34]

Of the larger forms – the ballades, scherzos and impromptus – the earlier works were again appreciated more than the later ones. Even leading critics regarded the Ballade in G minor as 'the most magnificent'. 'None of the other ballades equals this masterpiece',[35] wrote Szulc, while the Ballade in F minor was described as 'less happily conceived'.[36] Similarly the first two scherzos were regarded as the zenith of Chopin's achievement in the genre, while of the impromptus, that in C♯ minor is particularly praised, with attention drawn to its melodious character.

The lukewarm reception of the later works is also apparent in other genres. The nocturnes of Op. 55 were not greeted by the superlatives that the earlier nocturnes attracted, while Op. 62 was described by Kleczyński as evidence of an enfeebled creative power.[37] One should stress that Kleczyński's appraisal of the nocturnes is typical not only of Polish criticism. In common with Kleczyński, Niecks considers the nocturnes of Op. 27 to be the best, while he writes that those of Op. 62 are not worth dwelling upon.[38] Even in the twentieth century Leichtentritt described Op. 62 No. 2 as 'lacking the features of great artistry'.[39] Against this background Szulc's opinion is striking, for – like Barbedette[40] – he praises the artistic value of these later works highly and asserts that precisely they are proof that Chopin's creative powers remained unimpaired to the end of his life. Nevertheless, both the predominant critical views and the repertoire performed lead one to conclude that the later works were not fully accepted until the twentieth century.

The sonatas were clearly undervalued in Poland, just as in Europe, where Schumann's opinion as to the lack of organic qualities in the B♭ minor Sonata carried great weight. Press notices devoted to the sonatas were sporadic. According to Szulc, who was an ardent admirer of Chopin, the sonatas were among the composer's less successful works, since their 'wealth of thoughts' made it difficult for the composer to maintain proportion, to develop thematic balance and to adhere to the obligatory rules of the genre. Yet, at the same time, Szulc stressed the value of portions of the sonatas (particularly their lyric themes), the slow movement of the Sonata in B minor and the scherzos. In common with Schumann, he appreciated the beauty of fragments of the sonatas but failed to see their value as complete works. Conceiving the sonata as a classical form, Szulc was not in a position to appreciate Chopin's innovations and the changes that were underway in the genre.

The general favour with which Chopin was viewed in contemporary Polish criticism from the outset of his career should be stressed, since his music by no means met with universal approval. The Vienna concerts in 1829 were well received and Schumann's famous review of the Op. 2 Variations did much to launch Chopin's career, but for many years Rellstab's influential reviews were a source of adverse publicity in Germany.[41] The early Parisian reviews, although positive, were by no means as enthusiastic as those from the Polish critics. In due course, nevertheless, Chopin established himself well and truly in France.[42] Not so in England, where as late as 1835, after Wessel's publication of the E minor Concerto, a reviewer wrote:

> This concerto (we would fain say, this heterogeneous mass, and compound of filthy sounds) commences in E minor. . .and consists of the most ludicrous and extravagant passages – modulations we cannot call them, for they 'Out Herod' everything of the kind we ever before heard. . . It is altogether beneath criticism, and we shall be much surprised if even John Bull's silly predilection for foreign trash will induce him to purchase such a farrago of nonsense and caterwauling.[43]

In Stockholm after a performance of the F minor Concerto in 1842 a critic described Chopin as 'a somewhat uncouth, careless and half-savage Pole'.[44] It is clear that even the concertos, firmly rooted in the 'brilliant style', did not everywhere meet with instant understanding.

In the critical writings of the day Chopin was received primarily in aesthetic-subjective terms. Simplicity, refinement, elegance, poetry, fantasy, angelic sweetness, tenderness, originality and suffering were the main epithets used to describe his music. His technical achievements were mentioned far less often. They were discussed only in very broad terms and in a manner not dissimilar to that of reviews published prior to 1830. Indeed it seems that Chopin's later works had little effect upon the tenor of his reception. The following qualities were highlighted: boldness and innovation in harmony (chromaticism, frequent and distant modulations, tonal instability), innovation in texture (new figures and combinations of figures, widely spaced chords, a change in the function of the accompaniment), variety of ornamentation, originality of melody, perfection of form. Only occasional mention was made of specific techniques, such as the combination of metric groups, irregular rhythmic divisions and the bourdons, triplets and repetition structures that result from the stylisation of folk practice.[45] Innovative features were attributed very generally to Chopin's work, and if they were identified with specific works, it was with those that were most often performed. It was, above all, the novel features that were noted in Chopin's music, the very features that from the outset placed him apart from his colleagues, and that were already present in his earliest mature works. Chopin's later achievements – developments in formal process, harmony, melodic transformation and ornamentation – were regarded as obscure and eccentric or were simply not recognised at all, while the stylistic changes in his last works were perceived as indicating a decline in his creative powers caused by the ravages of a serious illness.[46] The truth is that Chopin had strayed too far from the norms of his epoch to be understood, not merely by his contemporaries but also by the next generation.

Polish writing fostered a Chopin cult, and as a cult figure the composer was, as a rule, beyond criticism. The non-appreciation of certain of his compositions was expressed either by their being passed over in silence or by the claim that they were not up to the composer's usual standard; there was never the harsh criticism that was found in English and German writings.

One might question whether this esteem and even worship of Chopin was the expression of a profound understanding of his work. Even before Chopin left Poland he had become a national property and symbol. His world standing and his distance from his native land strengthened this image. The collapse of successive national uprisings (1830–31, 1863–4) and the growth of anti-Polish politics in the partitioning powers further increased the Poles' need to affirm their national identity. In these circumstances Chopin and his music helped to unify the nation by

symbolising Poland's strength and spiritual individuality. The nation was convinced that only a Pole could fully understand and appreciate Chopin, since he
'succeeded in. . .transforming the personality of his people into the realm of art'.[47]
Emphasis was placed upon the purely Polish hallmark of his pieces, and this determined their success. Those fragments of his works that were associated with his
native land – as for example the middle section of the Scherzo in B minor, which
is a Polish carol – were highlighted and interpreted in nationalist sentimental
terms. 'What is this wonderful, melancholic, pastoral melody if not. . .an echo of
his native song, a memory of his native pastures, a yearning for a paradise lost?'
Szulc wrote in his monograph on Chopin.[48] Chopin was regarded as a creator of
national music because he expressed to the full 'the spirit of the nation'.

> In his music the national character is revealed in its finest splendour: the very same
> air that we breathe, the same sky to which we raise our eyes, the same longing
> and sorrow that permeates the songs of our people. He has sung most movingly of
> our unhappiness, he recounts better than anyone the greatness of our past and of
> our hopes, he alone has sapped the sweetest nectar from the flowers that bloom
> in abundance on our native soil. . . . He is one of the worthiest representatives of
> our nation.[49]

This quotation gives some idea of the manner in which Chopin was perceived –
almost unchanged – throughout the whole of the nineteenth century; it conveys,
too, the atmosphere that grew up around the composer's works and explains the
particular praise accorded the polonaises and mazurkas. With increasing frequency
semantic interpretations of these dances appeared in which scenes from Poland's
chivalrous past (in the polonaises) and pastoral vignettes from Polish village life
(in the mazurkas) were perceived.[50] Other pieces were seen as reflections of the
Polish countryside, of the type of emotion and personality that was supposed to
characterise the Polish race.[51] The national character was detected in all of Chopin's
works, even the etudes. The picture of Chopin ennobled as a national hero dominated the reception of his music, and it is this, more than anything else, that distinguishes the way it was received in nineteenth-century Poland from its reception
elsewhere in Europe. Chopin's compositions probably affected his wider audience
more because of his name than because of their artistic value. This is confirmed
by the exceptional popularity in the mid-nineteenth century of the mazurkas of
Szopowicz, an amateur composer of fashionable salon pieces whose music seized
upon some of Chopin's melodic phrases and was regarded as Chopinesque in style.
The leading music critic Józef Kenig accurately diagnosed the situation, 'To us
Chopin is still more a musician of the future than a musician of the present. . . .
Much time must elapse before he is understood and appreciated as widely as he is
adored. These praises contain much good-will but little good sense.'[52] The truth is
that the level of musical culture in nineteenth-century Poland was low, and the
circle of musical cognoscenti narrow.

RECEPTION BY COMPOSERS

Because of the difficulty and complexity of his music, Chopin was not a composer with a wide constituency. Even among the cultural élite of the day his art was not fully understood. In reviewing some typical salon *mazurs* the Polish popular writer and music critic, Józef Kraszewski, rated them above Chopin's late mazurkas, intending this as high praise of the former. This appraisal in turn drew a harsh rebuke from Moniuszko. Józef Sikorski, a leading music critic in mid-nineteenth-century Poland – and the author of a scholarly work on Chopin, begged composers of pieces based on folklore to 'smooth over the irregularities' that characterised the folk original, and by means of the rules of major/minor harmony to 'level out' the folk characteristics.[53] In 1877 W. Żeleński and G. Roguski, quoting a fragment of the Mazurka in C♯ minor, Op. 30 No. 4 in *Nauka harmonia* (The Study of Harmony), cautioned in their commentary: 'All the above licences are to be employed with great care . . . over-zealous pursuit of originality distances us from robust and clear harmony.' At that time no one had yet grasped the deeper relationships between Chopin's music and its folk models. The issue had instead been reduced to a superficial phenomenon: the imitation of rhythmic features and melodic phrases. Nor had anyone foreseen the potential consequences of Chopin's harmonic achievements.

The type of reception given Chopin's works by nineteenth-century Polish composers was further evidence of this superficial perception. It may be assessed in relation to 1) genres, 2) isolated compositional devices, 3) a collection of compositional devices, 4) the concept of a musical work and its relation to musical devices, 5) complete pieces or fragments.

In nineteenth-century Polish music there was a mania for imitating the genres cultivated by Chopin. Besides polonaises and mazurkas, which had been written before Chopin's day, composers started turning out countless nocturnes and waltzes, and – less frequently – impromptus, scherzos and ballades. These pieces, sometimes described by their composers as 'in the style of Chopin' generally had, in fact, nothing in common with the Chopin genres apart from their titles. Even during Chopin's lifetime his admirers attempted to imitate him. Chopin's pronouncements show what he thought of these efforts. Nowakowski's etudes were supposedly written in the style of Chopin and were dedicated to him. Chopin dismissed them thus: '[Nowakowski is] glad to be published. He's too old to learn anything new. . .what he bites he eats. . .there are still so many Poles around who live without knowing how, why and for what'.[54] Of Sowiński's pieces he wrote:

> Just look how pleased I am when he gets hold of something of mine (first here then there) whose beauty often depends on its accompaniment. Then he plays it in his vulgar, parochial style and one can't say anything because he hasn't the first idea about the stuff he's stolen.[55]

The ideas that were most frequently imitated included Chopin's extended orna-
ments deployed as a variational device, irregular rhythmic divisions, extended
mordent phrases, melody steeped in chromatic changing and passing notes, and
even certain concrete melodic phrases – for example, the staccato phrase under a
slur that was copied from the Nocturne in E♭, Op. 9.[56] As a rule these imitations
were modelled on Chopinesque phrases taken out of context – chiefly melodic
phrases but sometimes instrumental figurations. One should add that the imitation
was usually of devices drawn from the arsenal of the 'brilliant style' which was
prevalent in Warsaw before Chopin's day and which later composers acquired
via Chopin's early compositions. These devices were not used universally by later
composers but only in the particular genres that Chopin had employed. There was
nothing unusual in this general wave of unsuccessful imitation. In the latter half
of the century the *manière à la Chopin* was a phenomenon common in many
countries, in France, for example, and even in Sweden.[57] But the fact remains
that at least a portion of these pieces met with a favourable reception from the
critics, who saw them as a continuation of the Chopin style,[58] thus confirming
the thesis that, despite an intuitive feeling for Chopin's greatness, the style of his
pieces was perceived very superficially, with no understanding of its true nature.

Chopin's compositional devices were rarely imitated in a more complex manner.
One example is the work of K. Mikuli, a Chopin pupil, who took not only
Chopin's melody as a model but – particularly in the mazurkas and waltzes – his
harmony as well. The tonal ambiguity, the linking of functionally distant chords
by means of chromatic shifts and the suspension of common notes, the expansion
of the sphere of subdominant relations, the vacillation between major and minor,
the separation of the texture into voices accompanied by harmonic filling-out are
just some of the devices Mikuli took from Chopin. However, even in this instance
there was no development of Chopin's compositional devices, only a simplified
imitation. Although some of Mikuli's miniatures do indeed recall the character of
Chopin, they fall far short of his artistic stature.

About the only nineteenth-century Polish composer upon whom Chopin's
music exerted a creative influence was Juliusz Zarębski (1854–85), an extremely
talented pupil of Liszt. Like Chopin, Zarębski wrote mainly piano music, and this
showed influences of both Chopin and Liszt. Of the genres cultivated by Chopin,
Zarębski composed mazurkas, polonaises, etudes, waltzes, an impromptu, a ballade, a berceuse, a tarantella and a barcarolle, along with suites and pieces with
programmatic titles. Zarębski's approach to folk music also links him with
Chopin. Zarębski did not 'smooth over the irregularities' of folk music as J. Sikorski had recommended; on the contrary he exposed typical tonal features by
expanding traditional relationships, particularly in the sphere of the subdominant,
and by linking chords related by thirds. Chopin was for Zarębski – as he was for
Grieg and the Russian composers – a model for a creative approach to folklore.

In particular Zarębski adopted Chopin's conception of the polonaise as a kind of extended piano poem. In Zarębski's polonaises there are clear references to the texture of Chopin's, despite influences from Liszt. Octave chords reinforcing the underlying harmony contain a melodic line realised in the top, middle or lowest voice. Brief imitative passages are also common, occasionally in the form of a two-part counterpoint accompanied by chords. More specifically, the middle section of Zarębski's Polonaise in F♯ minor is a distant echo of the middle section of Chopin's Polonaise in A♭, Op. 53. Instead of the Chopin ostinato, there is a repeated note in the bass which functions as the main reference point. Chromaticism, numerous modulations, widely extended lines of figuration and changing rhythmic divisions (triplets, quintuplets, etc.), together with an 'advanced' harmonic language, all helped Zarębski's polonaises to develop and extend the world of Chopin's. Despite the clear influences of Liszt in the piano texture, Chopin's influence is also visible in Zarębski's other compositions, notably in his preference for the upper register, his avoidance of massive sonorities and, above all, his use of texture as the source of colouristic effects. Devices leading in the direction of Impressionism, which occurred in embryonic form in Chopin's music,[59] were significantly developed by Zarębski, so that some of his music is considerably closer to Debussy than to Chopin. Zarębski's reception of Chopin, like that of Grieg, the Russian composers and Debussy, amounts in short to a creative reinterpretation of the musical material.

SUMMARY

From the moment Chopin came onto the scene he was recognised and accepted in Poland. In the second half of the nineteenth century his music occupied pride of place in the concert repertoire, while in the final quarter of the century it became extremely popular and was performed at all types of public concert as well as by amateurs in the salon.

The public, however, was not made aware of Chopin's complete œuvre; it knew only a selection comprising primarily works for piano with orchestra and compositions from the 'second' period (the 1830s). The later works, the sonatas and those of the earlier works whose musical technique deviated markedly from the norms of the time (e.g. the Prelude in A minor, Op. 28 No. 2) were not readily understood, and it was not until the end of the century that they became a part of the standard repertoire. The pieces with a nationalist character, and those displaying a lyrical, cantilena character were the most appreciated. Chopin was therefore perceived primarily as a nationalist and a romantic, and thus was interpreted in an emotional/sentimental manner.

Chopin reception in Poland was dominated by the image of the composer as national symbol and hero. The artistic value of his works was only superficially understood and was reduced to purely surface properties. The nature of his attitude to folklore was not understood, nor was his original approach to sonority, his innovations in genre and form or his harmonic and textural explorations. This lack of understanding applied both to Chopin's wider audiences and to the musical milieu, and it was reflected in the flood of salon miniatures composed in a superficial Chopinesque manner by other composers. Zarębski's music apart, most of these compositions were unsuccessful imitations.

A paradoxical situation had arisen. In the country where the cult of Chopin was undoubtedly strongest, the influence of his work on the future development of music was negligible, not at all comparable to the effect that it had on the music of the Russian composers or upon Grieg and Debussy. An explanation for this must be sought in the decidedly backward and provincial character of Polish music when compared with European music in the second half of the nineteenth century.

Prior to 1830 – and the immediate recognition of Chopin's talent – there were indeed no great composers in Poland, but the musical idiom of Polish composers differed little from contemporary European norms. The 'brilliant style' out of which Chopin's music grew was a widespread and firmly accepted style of the day. The concert repertoire (except for the works of Beethoven) did not depart from the repertoire played in the main musical centres of Europe. The distance, therefore, between the musical language of Chopin's Warsaw compositions and the expectations of his audience was not great. This enabled the unconditional acceptance of Chopin, no doubt helped by the composer's skill as a performer.

Throughout the entire nineteenth century Chopin was as a rule received in much the same manner. This is because Polish music in the second half of the century rarely ventured beyond the musical idiom established in the first half; the concert repertoire in the latter half of the century included practically no new works. The late compositions of Liszt and Wagner went unrecognised, while performances of the music of these composers were so sporadic as to have no bearing on the listening habits of even professional musicians.

Chopin was so far ahead of his time that continuation of his achievements was not possible immediately. Such a continuation was enabled only by subsequent developments in European music, when – as Debussy described it – the richness and complexity of Chopin's music were finally recognised.[60] A parallel further development did not occur in Polish musical culture, and this explains why Chopin was persistently seen from the perspective of the first half of the nineteenth century there. Only in the twentieth century did a Polish composer – in the person of Karol Szymanowski – make genuine contact with Chopin's music, penetrating to the essence of his achievement and recreating that essence in twentieth-century terms.

11 *Victorian attitudes to Chopin*

DEREK CAREW

But you must not think I don't like good music. I adore it, but I am afraid of it. It makes me too romantic. I have simply worshipped pianists – two at a time, sometimes, Harry tells me. I don't know what it is about them. Perhaps it is that they are foreigners. They all are, ain't they? Even those that are born in England become foreigners after a time, don't they? It is so clever of them, and such a compliment to art. Makes it quite cosmopolitan, doesn't it?

Lady Henry ('Harry') Wotton in *The Picture of Dorian Gray*, published 1891

It was Oscar Wilde's patrimony as an Anglo-Irish writer which allowed him to combine the detachment of a foreigner with the first-hand experience of a native. This, together with his sharp social observation, unfailing ear for dialogue and biting wit, resulted in characters who were often only just larger than life, and, far from being caricature, the above quotation encapsulates a view of music and musicians in Britain which hardly changed between 1850 and 1930.

The Victorian attitude to music exhibited the compartmentalisation with which we now characterise the era in general. Musical entertainment for the aristocratic and upper-middle classes was largely opera (invariably Italian), together with orchestral and benefit concerts, at which the centre-middle classes were also to be seen. These concerts would include symphonies and other orchestral works as well as concertos and that staple of the British concert, solo vocal items, usually featuring a soprano. The Victorian penchant for public displays of piety was satisfied by frequent oratorio performances in the choral concerts that became fixtures in many parts of the country; the best-known of these, the Three Choirs Festival, still thrives. For the lower-middle and working classes there were the various spa and seaside orchestral concerts and, later, the Music Hall.

There was also the sphere of private music-making, whether in the salons of the rich, some of which were semi-public in terms of size of audience and quality or fame of performers, or in the drawing-rooms of the less socially exalted, from the prosperous centre-middle class to working-class artisans. It is the field of private music-making, particularly in its latter manifestation, and centred around the piano with its substantial repertoire, which is my main concern here.

Domestic music-making took much of its character from the special properties and appeal of the instrument itself. The piano was self-sufficient for solo performance as well as being the prime accompanying instrument for other soloists (singers vastly predominating, but also including violinists, flautists and cornet-players). Similarly, as its soubriquet the 'Household Orchestra' implies, it was the main agent for the acquisition of familiarity with the orchestral and choral classics in an age before radio and mechanical reproduction of music and before the widespread publication of full scores, an age in which concerts were nothing like as frequent or tickets as comparatively inexpensive as nowadays.

There were other advantages: the piano was easy to play and had a large and accessible literature and a sizeable band of perambulating virtuosos to titillate and thrill the many emulators, domestic and otherwise. Also, the mere possession of a piano had become a mark of respectability, culture and gentility, and a commentator in 1875 considered that the instrument had 'done more in the cause of civilisation (*musically* speaking) than all others put together'.[1] It has been estimated[2] that the number of pianos increased from 400 (representing a million players) to between one and two million in the period from 1871 to 1911; this was helped by a fall in the instrument's price during the 1880s.

The practice of drawing-room music-making underlined several Victorian preoccupations. Home ownership was, and remains, very dear to the British, and the happy, comfortable, inward-looking family projected as typical by the Queen and her beloved Albert was the condition to which all except the very highest classes aspired. Like all desirable social conditions, it had to be reinforced and displayed, and the drawing-room 'concert' with the family gathered around the piano, with or without visitors, was a powerful communal affirmation of this particular set of values.

Another factor, not confined to Britain, but existing in a particularly prominent form there, was that of taboos involving the fitness of certain instruments for the respective sexes. It was not done for ladies to play the violin or flute, and the cello was unthinkable. Singing and the harp were for them, and above all the piano. Yet the peculiar situation arose in which the professional pianists were almost all men, whereas the amateurs, as we shall see, were almost all women.

The notion of improvement – social and individual – as a facet of the more general belief in progress, was another preoccupation in this period. Music, as one of the examples of 'rational recreation', was viewed as a means to this end in certain restricted circumstances, in particular for women, whose whole existence was directed towards the twin goals of marriage and child-bearing. All their fathers' expenditure on matters such as clothes and education (usually confined to reading, writing, simple accounts, dressmaking and embroidery, with a smattering of

French if they were really serious about moving up the social scale) was viewed as investment for nuptial speculation: so much the better if they could also charm by playing the piano or singing. Music, in this limited sense of drawing-room performance, became a valued accomplishment for middle- and many working-class females and a mark of respectability and social advancement. The increase in prosperity and leisure time in general, and the swelling, in particular, of the ranks of clerks, schoolmasters and foremen – white-collar workers and what we might call lower middle management – made many more aware of the accessibility for their daughters of this relatively cheap mark of gentility.[3]

In spite of all this, typical Victorian double standards could still prevail: the music profession in general was disparaged, in varying degrees and for a variety of reasons. In a letter to his Chancellor, an Oxford don in the early years of this century bewailed the disrespect in which the musician was held and that even if he be 'ever so talented and exemplary in moral conduct, [he] ranks scarcely above an ordinary artisan'.[4] It is possible, too, that the death of the Prince Consort may have affected the status of musicians, since, unlike Albert, Queen Victoria showed little interest in music for its own sake. Nor, in spite of the odd knighthood, did things appear to change much under her successors, according to our don, who went on to express concern about 'the belief still held by many educated persons in this country. . .that the pursuit of the musical career necessarily exerts an emasculating and unhinging effect on those who embrace it.'[5]

This attitude has much to do with xenophobia, in that most solo and chamber (as opposed to 'career' orchestral) musicians living and appearing in Britain were foreigners, a fact which was at least partly due, according to one writer, to native performers being 'caught in a vicious circle of inexperience and neglect'.[6] Native imitation of foreign types was also a problem. The world would, we are told, be the poorer 'if all British composers play[ed] the sedulous ape to the calculated eccentricities of foreigners'.[7] An illuminating *résumé* of this attitude is given in the following passage about one of the British 'stars' who 'made it' during the time, the singer Charles (afterwards Sir Charles) Santley:

> you could never have told from his bearing that he was a musician at all. He was simply contented to look like an ordinary, unaffected, burly Englishman, with a certain *noli me tangere* air about him, as of one who would stand no nonsense and would be a good man in a tight place. Mr. Santley, in short, never experienced the temptation, which has assailed so many of his colleagues, 'to belong to other nations' either in name or deportment. He just remained an Englishman all through, and we have no doubt that his good sense and sincerity in this regard have contributed not a little to his popularity.[8]

As late as 1926, Sir Henry Hadow was still able to assert that 'our bluff, sturdy manhood has little in common with the keenness and mobility which marks one side of the artistic temperament' and that the British were not good at understanding 'alien characters or alien nationalities', and although there had been an advance beyond 'unreasoning hostility, . . . for the most part we have only substituted a half-contemptuous compassion which is equally galling and almost equally unintelligent'.[9] In spite of this, many native musicians used either foreign names, or foreign forms of their own names, and the attitude of Lady Wotton, as quoted at the beginning, represents only the slightest exaggeration in its view of the professional solo performer.

For the Victorian woman, however, the importance of music transcended that of a mere social accomplishment in a large number of cases: it became an important profession. For those otherwise 'respectable' ladies who, perhaps because of widowhood, impoverishment or through some other circumstances, were forced to seek employment, music-teaching offered a welcome and less restrictive alternative to being a governess, while for many, knowledge of music and a basic instrumental skill could obviate the drudgery of domestic service. The value of this musical outlet was clearly recognised in the period and was widely sought after. Mrs. Gaskell shows this in one of her typically objective letters, in which she writes candidly about one of her daughters, Marianne (or 'MA', as she often referred to her).

> I wish you could hear MA sing. It is something *really* fine, only at present she sings little but Italian and Latin Mass Music. It is so difficult to meet with *good* English songs. . .MA looks at nothing from an intellectual point of view, and will never care for reading, – teaching music, and domestic activity, especially about children will be her forte.[10]

The status of the music-teacher was rising slowly but surely even as this letter was being written (1853), and this was paralleled by a swelling of the ranks of women teachers, whose numbers increased by a factor of three during the years 1851–81. Indeed, the trend continued after that, particularly as this already improved status was felt to have been given a significant boost by the introduction of paper qualifications. The numbers examined by the Associated Board of the Royal Schools of Music (founded 1890) in the decade from 1903 increased from ten thousand to twenty-five thousand, of whom eighty per cent were elementary pianists. More than ninety per cent of the candidates were girls and they were prepared by teachers of whom some ninety per cent were themselves women.[11]

The market created by the ever-increasing popularity of the piano is reflected in the quality and kind of the musical product with which it was supplied. The domestic venue and the type of performer ensured that the music would be firmly in keeping with the dictates of Victorian preoccupations and mores. This was especially evident in the rash of sentimental and patriotic ballads which are so characteristic of the period and milieu, but the Victorian ethos can also be detected, in a different way, in the various comic songs that ultimately formed the backbone of the burgeoning Music Hall. Instrumental music, most of it for solo piano, also reflected the tendencies of the age in title as well as in spirit. Many of the pieces were dances, though not always for dancing, and included, in an unsympathetic characterisation of 1926, 'hoydenish polkas' and 'ill-bred slangy waltzes',[12] as well as the interminable galops and quadrilles. There would also be variations and rondos on well-loved themes and even fantasias and medleys. While most of the composers were foreign, this field of musical effusion was practically the only one in which native composers could gain a toe-hold, and many recognised subsequently for output of a more musically substantial kind began their careers by dabbling in – and in some cases periodically revisiting – this market.[13]

A significant proportion were mood-pieces such as songs without words, nocturnes and romances, with surface prettiness and 'undue reliance on a rather hot-house type of emotionalism'.[14] As we shall see, they were often dignified with French titles, usually descriptive, and revelled in sentiment of all kinds. This music placed little strain, emotional or intellectual, on its consumers; digestion was instantaneous and effortless and there was a placatory and self-satisfying blandness which stimulated no ripple of curiosity and invited passive assent rather than participation, a world of lyrical transience in which all musical expectations are gently articulated and gratified without stress. Nostalgia and past times were endemic in these pieces which provided a retreat from emotional and mental questing into a world of certainties, paralleling the ethos and function of the (with)drawing-room itself. Unity and uniform flow of one diluted mood was of the essence, a single *Affekt* with minimal contrast and unsullied by dialectic.

This was, of course, a flower gone to seed. One of the artistic manifestations dearest to the Romantic heart was the evocation and enshrining of mood in short, often small-scale units, and the corresponding vehicle in music, the piano pieces of Schubert, Schumann, Mendelssohn and Chopin, have all enriched the literature. It should come as no surprise that their simpler essays in this vein were used as models; in fact, they were tailor-made for the emulator and especially for the imitator. Brevity encouraged not concentration but curtailment of matter and of substance, and the most meagre inventiveness sufficed in terms of melody and harmony. Texture in this music is dictated by a basic homophonic approach adapted according to the stereotype implied in the titles. Foursquare phrasing and regular harmonic rhythm are contained in short-breathed units,[15] usually strung together with additive rather than cumulative intent. In outward shape, these works are episodic with recurring material, or, as often in the case of dances, simply open-ended. Conventional and undemanding, melody and harmony rarely give any hint of individuality or innovation.

The fixing of drawing-room music of this kind in a stylistic time-lock is symptomatic of the period's attitudes towards art and creativity. Like the contemporaneous mania for pressed flowers, stuffed animals and mounted butterflies, this cultural embalming resulted in lacklustre reflections of the living, breathing art of their early-Romantic progenitors, the oldest of whom had ceased production by the middle of the nineteenth century. As late as 1922 an influential book on 'Modern Music' published in Germany – a book considered not unfair in its criticisms – castigated a general attitude to music in England, 'where 'pretty pretty' artistic devices attain a green old age, and the new idea has no chance of acceptance unless securely linked with the old'.[16]

The assimilation of Chopin into this milieu is as fascinating an example of the transformation of early Romantic art into Victorian kitsch as it is paradoxical in its choice of this particular figure. Chopin certainly stuck in the craw of British commentators – and of many others as well. There are large islands of agreement in a sea of unease. His virtual confinement to keyboard composition and the technical difficulty of his music are always remarked on, as is its fitness for the instrument. Melodic beauty is usually singled out as the prime feature – the 'lyric gift, indeed, has always been allowed a special immunity from criticism'[17] – though not always without qualification:

> his melody is never sublime, never at the highest level. Its more serious mood stands to the great tunes of Beethoven as Leopardi stands to Dante, rising for a moment on a few perfect lines to follow the master's flight, and then sinking back to earth under some load of weariness or impatience.[18]

Similarly, the notion of Chopin as a 'poet' or as 'poetic' runs like a leitmotiv through almost all criticism; 'a typical poet of the introspective order', 'almost wholly a lyric artist',[19] and Hadow expands: 'In his lightest moment he is a poet: graceful in fancy, felicitous with expression, and instinct with the living spirit of romance.'[20] He is often characterised as elegant, refined and aristocratic, with 'dreaminess and voluptuousness',[21] a 'dreamy, mystic power of inspiration',[22] 'preoccupied with the fairyland of his own creations. . .ethereal, unearthly, enchanted, an echo from the melodies of Kubla Khan'.[23] These are seen as 'feminine' qualities, which, in terms of the period, however, are viewed negatively. 'Feminine' easily becomes 'weak' and 'unmanly': Chopin is credited with a 'hermaphrodite nature',[24] accused of 'want of virility',[25] lacking 'vigour of purpose and loftiness of aim'.[26] The Op. 37 Nocturne 'bewitches and unmans' if we 'tarry too long' in its 'treacherous atmosphere',[27] and the accusation of morbidity lurking just below the surface in such statements is articulated on a number of occasions.[28] Chopin manages to hide his 'mental sickness' while striking 'sorrowful chords, which do not occur frequently to healthy normal persons' and it has become a 'very bad habit to place this poet in the hands of our youth' although the 'grown man who understands how to play [him]' need not fear – all this from an astute, sensitive, and much-admired commentator.[29] Much of the melancholy and some of the morbidity has been laid at the door of Chopin's Polish ancestry, reinforced in the association of these qualities with the political tribulations of the country during the nineteenth century. His refinement and grace, however, are imputed to his chosen French domicile and aristocratic connections.

A picture emerges of a musician who embodies a number of apparently conflicting characteristics. One of the most perennial manifestations of these dipoles – passages of harmonic audacity which are, in period terms, completely 'wrong' but 'work' – is tackled by Sir Henry Hadow, noting how, against a normative harmonic background

> we come across passages, the sight of which is enough to make orthodox professors of music 'stare and gasp;' – passages which seem to break with resolute and unflinching defiance the elementary rules that stand at the beginning of our text-books. . . . These are not obvious slips. . .[or] importations from some alien musical language, like the occasional extravagances of Grieg or Dvorak. . . . we can find harmonic schemes which it is probable no other musician would have dared to devise, schemes which set at naught our established distinctions of concord and discord. . .which, nevertheless, are as undoubtedly intentional as they are undeniably successful in their aim.
>
> There is no shirking the difficulty. Here is a composer who is brought up on Bach, and whose general sense of harmony is as pure and sincere as that of his great master. Here are passages, written by him with obvious care and deliberation, the acceptance of which would seem impossible without throwing discredit on the harmonic code. And, as climax of bewilderment, the code is right and the passages are beautiful.

Hadow concludes that such passages are 'not really harmonic at all, they lie in the same plane as the melody, and, for their support, imply a separate and distinct scheme of chords, which the ear can always understand for itself'.[30] Most commentators feared to tread on such ground, and the more common rigidity of critical approach would not admit of any reconciliation of such apparent opposites, thus engendering uneasy paradoxes, a lack of comprehension and mistrust of the composer and his music.

We have seen some of the more conventional ways in which misunderstandings of Chopin surfaced in commentaries, but the criticism became more damaging when explanations were sought at more fundamental levels in the music itself, giving rise to a critical solecism which persists even today: Chopin is simply a miniaturist. In cleaving to one instrument he shows artistic timidity and an inability to handle the larger instrumental forms. In so narrowing his scope, he eschews universality and forfeits the right to be considered with the 'Greats'. In an age innocent of Webernian compression, the correlation between size and potential for quality was simpler and more direct than we would nowadays be prepared to countenance. Even critical 'fans' of the composer are content with the generalities of this position. One instance is a generally sympathetic article in the *Monthly Musical Record* of January 1875 by a Eustace J. Breakspear entitled 'The works of Chopin and their relation to art'. Here the author rather shoots himself in the foot, not only by parading the arguments against his position and neglecting to refute them, but also by stating baldly early on in the article that the composer's 'best works are cast in simple moulds' without further qualification. This produced a flurry of correspondence. J. S. Shedlock pointed out: 'The real fact is this – that Chopin confined himself to writing for one instrument and (with few exceptions) in the minor and less important forms of art. His works, therefore, cannot have the same general interest and attraction as those of Haydn, Mozart and Beethoven'.[31] Another correspondent leaps to the defence of his hero on the grounds that the piano wasn't just any old instrument but 'the one universally called the "household orchestra"'.[32]

We are told that the composer was 'at his ease' in 'the lesser rhythm of dance and song forms', that there was 'an essentially mundane quality in his work' and a lack of stomach for 'the majestic logic of the great [forms]'.[33] 'True' thematic development was not his *métier*; 'in structure he is a child, playing with a few simple types, and almost helpless as soon as he advances beyond them',[34] and he had 'but small power in the architectonic handling of complex tonal processes'.[35] The appearance of Chopin's piano sonatas in 1840 and 1845 respectively was a godsend to pedlars of these critical wares, confirming their worst fears. In his book on the piano sonata, Shedlock (quoted above) finds the B♭ minor 'lacking organic development, unity', while the B minor was 'an inferior work',[36] and both are seen as 'failures of a genius that has altogether overstepped its bounds'.[37] Hadow blames Polish folk music for much of this:

> it may perhaps account for Chopin's indifference to the requirements of key-relationships. Not only in his efforts at Sonata form does he show himself usually unable to hold together a complex scheme of keys, but in works of a more loose structure his choice seems to be regulated rather by hazard than by any preconceived plan. Sometimes, as in the end of the F major Ballade, he deliberately strays away from a logical conclusion; sometimes, as in the sixth Nocturne, he forces himself back with a sudden and inartistic violence; more often he allows his modulations to carry him where they will, and is so intent on perfecting each phrase and each melody that he has no regard left to bestow on the general principles of construction.[38]

Hadow's final summing-up echoes more than a few other commentators in the condescension with which this subtle master of structure and unparalleled harmonist was viewed: 'Icarus has flown too near the sun, and the borrowed wings have no longer the strength to support him.'[39]

So it was in the 'simple' pieces that the 'real' Chopin was sought and found. In spite of the morbidity, decadence and eroticism that were discerned in some of the music, a 'certain drawing-room atmosphere' was noted with hindsight. Indeed, it was 'ideal' for such a venue,[40] and the fact that an aura of refinement or 'classi-ness' seems to have attached itself to the playing of Chopin's music would be no disadvantage at all in that status-conscious atmosphere of sibling and peer-group rivalry.[41] Given such a simple prescription, little effort is needed to arrive at a representative Chopin repertory for domestic use. One would expect it to be made up mostly of the shorter works, those least, or at any rate less, demanding techni-cally, which also do not flaunt their intellectual laurels. The vast bulk would be of the more avowedly 'salon' kind, and miniature forms were preferred: some of the waltzes, polonaises and mazurkas, but above all the nocturnes and preludes, as well as sections of larger works such as the etudes, sonatas and perhaps the concertos. And, indeed, the evidence of publishers' advertisements and catalogues, as well as of the sizes and numbers of editions, does bear this out. Also informative are publications such as a three-booklet series of *Well-Known Piano Solos, How To Play Them With Understanding, Expression And Effect.* Among such figures as Schütt (parts of whose *Carnaval* Leschetizky is reported to have found more beautiful than Schumann's[42]), represented by two *Valses* ('Bluette' and 'Mignonne'), Rubin-stein (*Trot der Cavalrie*), Bendel (*Spinnradchen*), Gutmann (*La Sympathie*), Jensen (*The Mill*) and Schumann (*Vogel als Prophet, In der Nacht* and *Aufschung* [sic]), Chopin is given pride of place with the 'Minute' Waltz, the G major Nocturne, the Polonaise in C♯ minor, the Berceuse, and the D♭ major Prelude. Each piece is allotted something between 300 and 700 words of generally pianistic-technical advice, and from this it is possible to form some sort of impression of the typical buyer at whom this series is aimed. Whereas the technical standard of the music itself (variable though it is) would require a fairly advanced pianist of perhaps 18–20 years of age, the content of the text, with its 'firm-but-gentle' tone, genteel language, modest educational presumptions and very naïve pictorial glossing, is clearly aimed at a middle-class female, but one with an emotional age and general outlook of a 12–15 year-old. The whole *raison d'être* seems to be to impart a veneer of 'expression' and technical proficiency but without soul-searching. Blandness rules.

The Chopin prelude included is, of course, the 'Raindrop', and the opportunity for note-painting in this 'noble composition, full of humanity' is not missed, although the article is one of the less cloying examples. The monastery is men-tioned, and so are the raindrops, falling

> perhaps from the eaves above his open window. It is not difficult to conjure up in the memory the impressions of such a wet day, and we may well feel surprise that under depressing circumstances Chopin's music should sing into his ear sweet melody. In the middle section. . .the deep voices of the brethren are heard chanting in two parts in the cloisters. As they approach the composer's window, their breath might almost be felt, and as they retire behind the pillars their voices become

subdued. . . . Make your two parts sing like a double file of monks. At the *ff* where they are close on the composer one can almost see one peep curiously from his book toward the open window. Then they go round again, to return once more.[43]

The author is a great believer in such programmes, and encourages his anonymous and distanced pupils to 'cultivate their imaginations'. The same impulse prompted the contemporary habit of publishers adding descriptive titles to Chopin's pieces. Each of the sets of nocturnes Opp. 9, 17 and 24 was subtitled 'Souvenir de Pologne', the Op. 15 'Les Zephirs' and the Op. 32 'Il lamento e la consolazione'. The Op. 1 Rondo was subtitled 'Adieu à la Varsovie' and the Bolero 'Souvenir d'Andalousie'; the *Introduction and Polonaise brillante*, Op. 3, was graced with the title 'La Gaite' [*sic*].

This addition of gratuitous 'meaning' is simply part of a process of normalisation by which the pieces were made to conform to the drawing-room canon, stripping them of their abstraction and stifling at birth any attempt at purely musical appraisal. For the more mawkish salon pieces which so desperately needed such emotional crutches, the range of titles was surprisingly narrow and almost invariably in French. Paris was the hub of the *bel monde*, symbol of all that was *chic* and sophisticated in dress and in music, and of the foreign names possessed or affected by the great majority of salon composers, a large proportion were also French. *Metzler and Co's Circular of New and Popular Music For Pianoforte* included Gaston De Lille, Charles Fontaine, Ignace Gibsone, Lucien Lambert and Georges Pfeiffer. Pieces, or, rather, '*morceaux*', rejoiced in a large representation of *rêves* and *rêveries*, of *légendes*, *chansons* or *chants*, *mélodies* and *romances*. Many of them were *sans paroles, charmant*[e] and seasonal – *du printemps, de l'automne* – and rural settings were common: *près du lac, au bois*, etc. Even generic titles were qualified, occasionally by the addition of *caractéristique*, but more often by full subtitles. Waltzes were usually *grande* and/or *brillante*, though not invariably so, as A. C. Mackenzie's *Valse sérieuse* shows, and there are a number of examples of *élégant*[e] and *de grâce*. The second nocturne of Leÿbach is entitled '*Fleur du salon*', another by Ascher, '*Esperance*', and Henri Ravina's *Grande valse*, Op. 61, '*L'enchanteresse*'. Even when titles were in English (or, more rarely, German), they were very much in the same vein. The numbers of such pieces produced in this socio-musical mycelium was vast. In spite of the great British fondness for Mendelssohn (especially, within the drawing-room context, the *Lieder ohne Worte*) and the popularity of the shorter piano works of Schumann, and, to a lesser extent, of Schubert and Liszt, it is the ghost of Chopin which hovers over much of this music.

Many of the generic titles and the types of pieces these titles stimulate stem from Chopin, primarily the nocturne, mazurka, polonaise and characteristic etude, and, occasionally, a Barcarolle or Berceuse. One also finds the prelude, waltz and ballade (or ballad), though these tend to be less obviously based on their Chopin counterparts.

Studiously avoided in these drawing-room pieces were Chopin's originality and his pioneering qualities. These were always acknowledged, although there was disagreement as to wherein they lay and whether they were matter for praise or blame. Most of their manifestations were still considered *outré* and suspect, even in the 1920s. But there were externals, the more obviously foreground features of his musical style which found their way into the music of the drawing-room composers, serving very well to season their plainer fare, and perhaps even add a peck of mild exoticism, often in contexts that did not otherwise suggest the Polish composer.

The direct influence of Chopin's melody – as opposed to echoes of his manipulation of melody by development and decoration – is difficult to demonstrate. For one thing, his familiarity with early nineteenth-century Italian opera would have been shared by the drawing-room composers and players. In addition, the latter were nurtured on composers who had perpetuated that operatic tradition in their own works, and there were also the many pot-pourris and fantasies, and the more playable paraphrases on operatic airs of which they would have had 'hands-on' experience. Nevertheless, there are echoes: J. Leÿbach's second nocturne ('Fleur de salon') has a touch of Chopin's gentle melodic arching, his use of melodico-rhythmic figures or cells in slightly modified forms, even perhaps one of his melodic fingerprints (marked x in Example 1).[44] Here the harmony is consistent as well and the Italianate sixths, which are also in evidence in Example 2. The fingerprint is even clearer in Example 3, the *Idylle, 'Près du lac'* by Sigismond Lehmeyer, and again the harmonic underlay is of a type common in Chopin, a stretch of tonic with an anticipatory touch of (here) dominant, followed by a cadence on that degree approached by chord vi (occasionally coloured by an augmented sixth).

Example 1   J. Leÿbach, Nocturne No. 2 (*Fleur de salon*)

Ex. 1 (*cont.*)

Example 2   J. Ascher, *Souvenir* Op. 12

Example 3   S. Lehmeyer, *Idylle: Près du lac*

Example 4   A. Linder, *Chant d'amour (Morceau de salon)*

Lacking, however, is that subtle tension between melody and bass line so characteristic of Chopin himself. The long appoggiatura (of which more later) is another
Italianate feature used to great effect by Chopin and also adopted by the salon
composers (see Example 4).

In the case of dance pieces, the influences are often clearer, if only because many
of the defining characteristics were, in a sense, established by Chopin himself.
The results are often very foursquare, as the Redowa ('Spirit of the Night') by
Carlo Minasi shows (see Example 5), or stilted, as in the first of Berthold Tours'
Deux mazurkas (see Example 6). J. Ascher's Mazurka Op. 11 is also Chopinesque
(see Example 7) and the *Mazurka de salon* ('Phoebe') (see Example 8) by W. Mason
from the *Musical Budget* issued during the 1880s draws on the hemiola rhythms of
pieces like the Mazurkas Opp. 24 No. 2 and 17 No. 1. Occasionally it is difficult to

Example 5   C. Minasi, *Redowa (Spirit of the Night)*

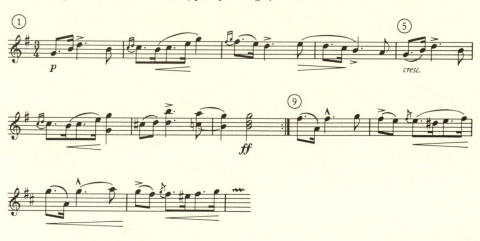

Example 6   B. Tours, No. 1 of *Deux mazurkas*

Example 7   J. Ascher, Mazurka Op. 11

Example 8   W. Mason, *Mazurka de salon (Phoebe)*

stifle the suspicion that a particular Chopin piece has acted as a model. The opening bars of the *Valse impromptu* by J. Trousselle, the *National Schottisch* No. 1 by Charles d'Albert and the *Allegretto con tenerezza* of Adolph Gutmann (Examples 9, 10 and 11) are reminiscent of the 'Minute' Waltz, the first Ecossaise and the Nocturne Op. 27 No. 2, respectively; the last two are even in the same keys as their suspected models.[45]

Example 9   J. Trousselle, Valse Impromptu

Example 10   C. D'Albert, National Schottisch No. 1

Example 11   A. Gutmann, *Allegretto con tenerezza*

Decorative additions and extensions of a kind often found in Chopin are widespread in the salon repertory, although they usually lack his complexity and technical difficulty. They range from the simplest chromatic appoggiaturas to widespread acciaccaturas and octave displacements (often dissonant), as in the central *animato* section of the first of Tours' *Deux mazurkas* (see Example 12). The use of decoration as a variational technique is common, as in Leÿbach's Nocturne *Fleur de salon*, and C. Tasca's *Mélodie: rêve de la jeunesse*.

Example 12   B. Tours, No. 1 of *Deux Mazurkas*

Decorative harmony also features in the salon repertory, although it is usually of a rudimentary kind. It is not surprising that of all the traits recognised and remarked on by commentators, Chopin's harmony should prove least susceptible to reproduction and that attempts to capture it in any way other than as a veneer are comparatively rare and difficult to detect in isolation. A general liking for third relationships is certainly in evidence: it is common for the mid-section of a piece to drop a third, and very often to the flattened sixth (or equivalent) below – C. M. Meyer's *Morceau de salon* 'Chant d'amour' in Db major goes to A major – and this may be compounded, as in the *Warsaw Mazurka* by Charles Coote, which is in C major, but with sections following in A minor and F major. This relationship also occurs in the more immediate context of a dominant being replaced by a mediant, but the supertonic is common as a dominant substitute, also (see *A Little Story for Pianoforte* by Berthold Tours), and on occasion both are used at close quarters, as in the *Grand morceau de concert en forme d'une polonaise*, Ernst Lubeck's Op. 14. Chopin's love for chromatic substitution was not lost on the salon composers, especially at its most basic, the use of the Neapolitan and augmented sixth chords, and could be associated with a decorative climactic flourish (see Example 13, *The Gnome's Rêverie* by Antonio Mora) or as part of a sequence (see Example 14, the *Entrata* to *Valse de grâce* by Carlo Minasi).

Example 13   A. Mora, *The Gnome's Rêverie*

Example 14   C. Minasi, *Valse de grâce*

This last instance shows perhaps the most common use of Chopinesque harmony, the use of diatonic or, more usually, chromatic chords and progressions to add interest to a basic progression or sequence, very often grounded in stepwise melodic and/or harmonic movement. Coming across such passages as those in Example 15 from Alexander MacFadyen's Nocturne Op. 20 No. 1, and in Example 16 from Ravina's *La Douleur* ('Pensée expressive'), Op. 67, one has more than a feeling of *déja vu*. This particular gambit approaches the status of a harmonic leitmotiv in the works of Sir Alexander C. Mackenzie, as in the two extracts in Examples 17 and 18. It may well have been figures such as Mackenzie, Alexander Charles

Example 15   A. MacFadyen, Nocturne Op. 20 No. 1

Example 16   H. Ravina, *La douleur* (*Pensée expressive*) Op. 67

Example 17   A. C. Mackenize, *Valse sérieuse* Op. 15 No. 1

Ex. 17 *(cont.)*

becoming:

Example 18   A. C. Mackenzie, Nocturne Op. 15 No. 2

[Allegretto amorevole]

Macfarren and other British composers whose names, at least, are still recognised (including the young Elgar) who were the cause of Ernest Walker's remark of 1907, about 'prominent composers' writing 'vulgar music. . .with their eyes open, purely for the sake of money' (see footnote 13 below).

Among the more idiomatic echoes of Chopin to be found in salon music might be included the tendency to split a single line into two strands of textural counterpoint. The *poco animando* section of J. Ascher's *Souvenir* from Op. 12 (see Example 19), and his namesake F. Ascher's *Aux fonds du bois* (see Example 20) are characteristic. The converse – the employment of two separate linear elements to achieve what might be called a one-dimensional melodic effect – is also to be found, in the *Pensée romantique* 'Murmuring Shells' by E. H. Bailey, and in the *Mazurka de salon* 'Florence' by Ernest Hensel (see Example 21). These textural borrowings are often concerned with particular registers of the piano (such as 'bass' and 'tenor' melodies), as can be seen in Example 22, the third of Six Compositions for the Pianoforte, Op. 20, and MacFadyen, whose Prelude Op. 18 No. 3 in G minor (Example 23) shows that he was not unfamiliar with Chopin's in

Example 19   J. Ascher, *Souvenir* Op. 12

Example 20   F. Ascher, *Aux fonds du bois (Rêverie)* Op. 135

Example 21   E. Hensel, *Florence* (*Mazurka de salon*)

Example 22   A. C. Mackenzie, *Reminiscence* (No. 3 of 6 Compositions for the Pianoforte Op. 20)

Example 23   A. MacFadyen, Prelude Op. 18 No. 3

Ex. 23 (*cont.*)

Example 24   S. Moniuszko, *Polonaise caractéristique*

Example 25   M. Moszkowski, Valse Op. 8 No. 1

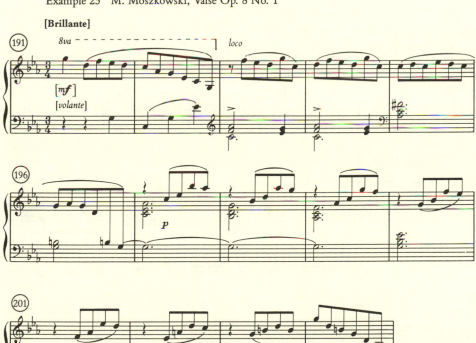

B minor. Even clearer influence is evidenced by Moniuszko, in a rather neat compacting of the opening ideas of the third of the Opp. 6 and 7 Mazurkas to open his own *Polonaise caractéristique* (Example 24) and it would be very odd indeed if Moszkowski had not also imbibed something of his great compatriot's piano-writing style (see Example 25 and the second of his *Valses* Op. 8).

Another feature that is by no means uncommon in drawing-room music of the period is one that is difficult to define, or even describe, but is quite easy to discern. It is a kind of Chopinesque 'gesture', a thumbprint in which a number of musical elements – melody, harmony, technique – seem to coalesce. Some of these are illustrated in Examples 26 (the second of Mackenzie's Six Compositions), 27 (Scherzo

Example 26   A. C. Mackenzie, *Ritornello* (No. 2 of 6 Compositions for the Pianoforte Op. 20)

Example 27   H. Ravina, Scherzo

Example 28   A. Gutmann, Mazurka Op. 14 No. 1

Example 29   C. Mora, *La belle Americaine*

by Henri Ravina) and 28 (from Gutmann's Mazurka Op. 14 No. 2), showing Chopin's habit of using repeated dominant-tonic cadences to underline a (usually local) tonality prior to destroying it. Similarly, Example 29 (from the first of *Deux Mazurkas elégants* ('La belle Americaine') by (Baron) Carlo Mora) is an instance in imitation of a common gesture that appears in many forms in his music, best known from the A major Polonaise, but also found in the Op. 53, the Third Ballade, the Second Scherzo, the Fantaisie, and the E minor Piano Concerto. The slow movement of this last-mentioned work is likely to have been in Mackenzie's mind when he included, in the last of his *Trois Morceaux* ('Ballade') a brooding 'declamando, quasi Recit' which has strong echoes of the younger Chopin.

It seems not unreasonable to conclude that these composers' understanding of Chopin's music was fairly superficial for the most part. By the same token, the range of pieces with which they were familiar seems a very narrow one, confined largely to the mainstream works in the already popular genres mentioned earlier as being typical of drawing-room music in general. This is, of course, speculation, and the chicken-and-egg relationship of this market's supply and demand makes it impossible to be more definite. Any assessment of reception in a past era is coloured by reception at the time of the assessment itself. Nevertheless, the view of Chopin as composer and figure in this particular musical *milieu* does come across as extraordinarily narrow. It was to remain so for some considerable time after the Victorian age itself had passed, as, indeed, the attitudes and values associated with that age have themselves lingered on in many spheres of life and in various guises.

12　*Chopin's influence on the* fin de siècle *and beyond*

ROY HOWAT

While Chopin's influence permeates many countries and traditions, this chapter concentrates mostly on his adopted country of France. In addition to the direct effect of his own compositions, Chopin left an enormous influence there through his piano teaching. To take a few examples, Saint-Saëns, Bizet, Fauré, Debussy and Dukas were all immediate recipients of the 'Chopin tradition' through teachers or close musical contacts.[1]

Fauré, Debussy and Ravel in particular are regarded as Chopin's natural musical heirs, being fundamentally pianistic composers and innovators. Support appears to come from the genres of nocturne, barcarolle, ballade, impromptu and prelude (and a single mazurka) taken over by Fauré, plus the piano Mazurka, Ballade and Nocturne of Debussy's early years, as well as his later Preludes and Etudes. On closer inspection, though, the title connections yield limited musical insights. Indeed, Fauré had little interest in those genre titles, which were often pressed on him by publishers.[2] Debussy's early Chopinesque titles often conceal different sources,[3] his later Lisztian use of picturesque titles is quite different from Chopin's practice, and with Ravel such titular connections are almost non-existent. From that point of view it could well be argued that all these composers grew farther from Chopin as they matured. Yet their music tends to tell the opposite story, as we shall see, with the most potent links lying under the surface of their mature music, and in less obvious contexts.

Paul Dukas, in 1910, pointed out succinctly that Chopin's main legacy to musical posterity was his unprecedented harmonic freedom and mobility.[4] This, combined with his equally unprecedented rhythmic mobility, is the foundation of his musical inventiveness, allowing a piece to move instantly and effortlessly from one genre to another (such as the short mazurka sections within nocturnes or polonaises), or to sound both slow and fast within the same basic tempo, as in the E major Nocturne, Op. 62 No. 2. An even more dramatic example of contrasting tempos within a constant beat is the way a 'fast' tempo is gradually woven into the unchanging 4/4 metre in the central part of the C minor Nocturne,

Op. 48 No. 1. On the broadest scale, this accounts for Chopin's apparently effort-less fluidity of form, most notably in large works like the Fourth Ballade and the *Polonaise-fantaisie*, whose astonishing breadth and sense of balance defy formal classification. Ravel was acutely aware of this, and Debussy's mature music reflects it in some very exact ways.

Gabriel Fauré's music bespeaks a temperament in some ways similar to Chopin's, in other ways different. Unlike Chopin he was a prolific song writer, and his first mature songs and chamber works owe more to French song tradition, or to Mendelssohn and Schumann, than to Chopin. Underneath this difference, though, Fauré and Chopin have an important feature in common. Even their purely in-strumental music, however rich or polyphonic in texture, is basically a song and accompaniment. Chopin was the first to blend simplicity and richness in this way at the keyboard, and it inevitably formed the basis of Fauré's piano writing, whether inspired directly by Chopin's music or at one remove through Fauré's teacher Saint-Saëns. Much of the difference in flavour between Fauré and Chopin probably lies simply in the more Polish (or sometimes Italian) origin of Chopin's melody.

One might also say that they share a way of cradling their melody, as it were, in air or water. Chopin was aware of this quality when he once evoked the character of his A♭ major Etude, Op. 25 No. 1, for a pupil by describing a shepherd sheltering in a cave from an approaching storm, gently playing a melody on his flute while in the distance rushed the wind and rain. Those who heard him play were inspired to similar metaphors – for example, Alfred Hipkins: 'the arpeggios in the bass...swelled or diminished like waves in an ocean of sound.'[5] Even while laughing at the way English (or Scottish) ladies persistently described his music as 'leik [*sic*] water',[6] Chopin must have been aware of the qualities that attracted such comments. In brief, Chopin was the first composer whose music so frequently evoked that analogy, and its spiritual and technical influence reveals itself in the existence of the same quality in virtually all of Fauré's and Debussy's music, as well as in a certain amount of Ravel's.

Fauré's closest contact with the Chopin tradition came through Chopin's pupil and protégée Pauline Viardot and, at one more remove, through Saint-Saëns, who knew Viardot well and later published some of her recollections of Chopin's teach-ing and playing.[7] This contact doubtless helped confirm Fauré's classical sense, one that demands playing his music with suppleness but simply and in time, without grandiose or exaggerated effects. In that respect Fauré's aesthetic was always nearer to Chopin's than to that of his own teacher, Saint-Saëns, and as his musical language became more individual, like Chopin he never lost the priorities of grace, conciseness and clarity.

For all that, Fauré's early piano works reveal an urbane but capricious side to his character that is more in the tradition of Mendelssohn and Saint-Saëns than of

Chopin – unmistakably in works like his Second Impromptu. This nimbleness never left him, but it was combined increasingly with a Chopinesque rhythmic flexibility and breadth of phrase. The closest literal approaches to Chopin appear in Fauré's earlier works, often standing out against less Chopin-like surrounding material. For example, Robert Lortat observed passages in Fauré's First and Third Nocturnes that recall respectively Chopin's 'Raindrop' Prelude (Op. 28 No. 15) and Nocturne in E♭, Op. 9 No. 2.[8] The latter similarity (see Example 1), with the

Example 1   (a) Fauré, Third Nocturne, Op. 33 No. 3

(b) Chopin, Nocturne, Op. 9 No. 2

shared rising melodic sixth and similar textures (and Fauré's Chopinesque cross-rhythm), is in fact exceptional, for Fauré rarely made such a close approach to Chopin's writing. Even his Fourth Nocturne of 1884, more Chopinesque in overall character than the Third, is already stamped more individually by its syncopated bass, a pianistic 'fingerprint' that remained with Fauré right to his Thirteenth Nocturne of almost forty years later.

Jean-Michel Nectoux, probing the subject of Chopin's influence further, points to a mixture of textural and rhythmic suppleness and an increasingly sophisticated use of arpeggio figuration.[9] His examples include those observed by Lortat, plus passages from Fauré's Ballade, First Impromptu, Second Nocturne and Fourth Barcarolle. Yet even here it is revealing that the Chopinesque suggestions in Fauré's

Fourth Barcarolle recall for the most part the least typical of Chopin's Nocturnes, Op. 37 No. 2 in G major, a barcarolle in all but name (see Example 2). By the Eighth Barcarolle of 1908, we can hear how distinctly Fauré makes a basic Chopin gesture his own (see Example 3), through his different tonal setting (note the key signature!).

Example 2   Fauré, Fourth Barcarolle, Op. 44, bar 17

Chopin, Nocturne, Op. 37 No. 2

Example 3   Chopin, Third Ballade, Op. 47, bar 126

Fauré, Eighth Barcarolle, Op. 96, bar 30

Ex. 3 *(cont.)*

In sum, as Fauré's piano music became more individual, its underlying breadth and sophistication began to show deeper affinities with the mature Chopin. Later on it will be seen that this was the case also with Debussy: these two composers seem to have assimilated Chopin's techniques to the full once they had learnt a comparable mastery of line and expression. Like Chopin, Fauré learnt how to take the listener by stealth, introducing bold ideas in graceful guise, as with the repeated F♯–C bass progression in his Fifth Barcarolle of 1894 (see Example 4a). Isolated from its setting, the bass progression sounds more like Mussorgsky than Fauré; in context it is no more harsh than exactly the same progression near the end of Chopin's Barcarolle (see Example 4b). Fauré introduces the figure much earlier in his Barcarolle, and at the final reprise (the point equivalent to Example 4b) he dramatically changes the C to B (see Example 4c), preparing a strong tonic cadence by descending fifths and then an augmented dominant bass progression. The exact bass line is Fauré's own, but for the logic of its strength we can look again to the equivalent place in Chopin's Barcarolle (in the bars following Example 4b, including again a sequence of descending fifths).

Example 4   (a) Fauré, Fifth Barcarolle, Op. 66, bar 12

(b) Chopin, Barcarolle Op. 60, bar 96

Ex. 4 (*cont.*)

(c) Fauré Fifth Barcarolle, Op. 66, bar 110

Those links are the more interesting since the two barcarolles share a powerful breadth of phrase and structure, the key of F♯ and a similarly passionate mood. In many ways the two pieces are quite differently put together (the opening minor mode and a melodic allusion to Brahms set Fauré's Barcarolle apart immediately), but two more strategic parallels stand out. The central episode of each barcarolle begins with an abrupt minor third modulation away from its tonic F♯, over a rocking static bass (to A major in Chopin, at bar 39, and to E♭ major in Fauré as seen in Example 5). And in the closing pages of both pieces the momentous intensity of the principal climax tumbles over into a marvellous series of unexpected subsidiary reprises and waves of intensity.

The Fifth Barcarolle also illustrates Fauré's increasing mastery of transition. As with Chopin, transitions between sections are more frequent and more masked than in earlier works, sounding more like gateways than like divisions. Fauré created his own virtuoso variety of this with his penchant for sudden transitions, usually at a point of dramatic focus, that effortlessly spin the music round the tightest corners as if nothing had happened. Characteristic examples can be heard in the Fifth Barcarolle and the Thirteenth Nocturne (see Example 5). In each case the music starts a clean slate, but with all the preceding dramatic tension effortlessly to hand. Again the nearest precedent – even if the character is different – comes from Chopin, as in the effortless-sounding reprise of the Nocturne in F♯, Op. 48 No. 2.

Example 5   Fauré, Fifth Barcarolle, bar 59

Thirteenth Nocturne, Op. 119, bar 39

Chopin, Nocturne Op. 48 No. 2, bar 97

Another progressive theme in both Chopin's and Fauré's later writing is imitative polyphony. Chopin brings this to something of a summit in his last works, often intensified by chromatic contrary motion. An equivalent can be heard near the beginning of Fauré's Sixth Nocturne, marking out four real voices (see Example 6). Fauré's texture not only produces contrary motions similar to those in Chopin, but does it with cross-rhythms akin to the rubato often written into Chopin's counterpoint, as in his Fourth Ballade (Example 7 – see also the cross-rhythm of his F minor Etude, Op. 25 No. 2). The techniques are by then thoroughly Fauré's own, far from mere imitation of Chopin. The same goes for a characteristic piece of contrapuntal imitation in his Eighth Barcarolle, whose melodic fragment comes straight from Chopin's Third and Fourth Ballades (see Example 8).

Example 6   Fauré, Sixth Nocturne, Op. 63, bar 8

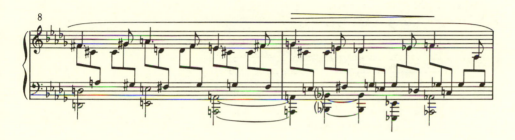

(four-part realisation)

Example 7   Chopin, Fourth Ballade, Op. 52, bar 175

Example 8   Fauré, Eighth Barcarolle, bar 26

Chopin, Third Ballade, bar 95

Fourth Ballade, bar 135

Debussy's affinity with Chopin seems to have taken early root but not to have emerged fully until years later. In 1871 the nine-year-old Debussy received his first piano lessons from a Mme Mauté de Fleurville, who claimed to have been a pupil of Chopin. While her claim has never been proved (or disproved), Debussy appeared to accept it, and his comments more than forty years later, in 1915, indicate the intense impressions she left on him:

> It's a pity that Madame Mauté de Fleurville, to whom I owe the little I know about the piano, is not alive. She knew many things about Chopin. . .
> What Saint-Saëns says about pedalling in Chopin isn't – despite my regard for his great age – quite accurate, for I have very precise memories of what Mme Mauté de Fleurville told me. [Chopin] insisted on practising without the pedal, and [in performance] it was not to be held on except in very rare cases.[10]

It speaks especially well for Mme Mauté that Debussy's memories of her were not swamped by those of his next piano teacher, Antoine Marmontel, whose association with Debussy spanned a much longer period at the Paris Conservatoire. Although not a Chopin pupil, Marmontel was enormously influenced by having frequently heard Chopin play. We may guess the effect on the adolescent Debussy of a piano teacher in the late 1870s and early 1880s – the heyday of the 'Impressionist' painters – who published the following lines in 1878:

> If we draw a parallel between Chopin's sound effects and certain techniques of painting, we could say that this great virtuoso modulated sound much as skilled painters treat light and atmosphere. To envelop melodic phrases and ingenious arabesques in a half-tint which has something of both dream and reality: this is the pinnacle of art; and this was Chopin's art.[11]

The lasting effect of all this can be read in Marguerite Long's memoirs of her intensive work with Debussy in 1914 and 1917:

> Chopin, above all, was a subject he never tired of. He was impregnated, almost *inhabited*, by [Chopin's] pianism. His own playing was an exploration of all he felt were the procedures of that master to us all.
> [Debussy] played nearly always in half-tints, but with a full, intense sonority without any hardness of attack, like Chopin, and was preoccupied by the latter's phrasing. . .
> 'Chopin is the greatest of them all,' [Debussy] used to say, 'for through the piano alone he discovered everything.'[12]

At the Paris Conservatoire, Debussy's musical education was based much more on romantic piano repertoire than was Fauré's education at the Ecole Niedermeyer. Paradoxically, it may have been this that made the piano the last medium in which Debussy found his mature voice – the keyboard probably led his fingers too easily into well-worn grooves. His way round the problem for some time was to follow a more purely French tradition: while the titles of some piano pieces from around 1890, particularly 'Mazurka', 'Ballade' and 'Nocturne', superficially suggest Chopin, other titles, like *Valse romantique*, point more accurately to Chabrier, Delibes and Massenet. In addition the pieces, in fairly static sectional forms, lack Chopin's harmonic mobility and therefore his formal flexibility and sense of direction. If the Chopinesque titles suggest Debussy's admiration, he still had to find this mobility.

Debussy's intent listening to Javanese gamelan, first in 1889 and again in 1900, almost certainly helped him find his mature way of writing for the piano: it is surely no accident that in 1901 he started his piano *Images* with 'Reflets dans l'eau', which ends in a sequence of gong and bell sonorities,[13] or that in 1903 he issued his *Estampes*, opening with the gamelan-like textures and oriental evocations of 'Pagodes'. As a result, where Fauré's music has a more western melodic surface than Chopin's, Debussy's often has a more eastern one, drawing on his attraction to exotic modes and gamelan-like layered textures – a characteristic gradually assimilated into even his orchestral writing.

With his piano writing thus set free, the influence of Chopin becomes more active, no longer posing a threat to Debussy's integrity. Passing details of Debussy's mature piano writing recall Chopin so often as to suggest how ingrained Chopin's music was in Debussy's ears (and fingers). The same key, it seems, could sometimes suffice to set off remarkably similar ideas, even in different contexts – or perhaps more significantly, *especially* when a different context ensured the integrity of Debussy's version. Example 9 shows two brief examples, from 'Pagodes' of 1903 and from the italianate prelude of 1909, 'Les collines d'Anacapri', both recalling moments of Chopin's *Polonaise-fantaisie*. (Compare also bars 214–5 of the *Polonaise-fantaisie* with bars 54–5 of Debussy's 'Hommage à Rameau'.)

Example 9   Chopin, *Polonaise-fantaisie*

Debussy, 'Pagodes' (*Estampes*)

Chopin, *Polonaise-fantaisie*, bar 153

Ex. 9 (*cont.*)

Debussy, 'Les collines d'Anacapri, bar 50

One of Debussy's constant favourites was Chopin's Barcarolle, as noted by one of his piano pupils around 1900;[14] the finale of his Violin Sonata confirms its enduring effect on him as late as 1917 (see Example 10).[15] But a more pervasive influence from Chopin's Barcarolle shows itself in Debussy's whole manner of piano writing in *L'isle joyeuse* of 1903–4 (see Example 11a), with the barcarolle rhythm and irregular left hand groups. Example 11b reinforces this with a suggestion of where Debussy may have found inspiration, consciously or not, for the opening of the same piece.

Example 10   Chopin, Barcarolle, bar 110

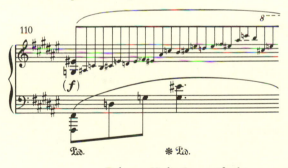

Debussy, Violin Sonata (finale)

Example 11   (a) Chopin, Barcarolle, bar 78

Debussy, *L'isle joyeuse*, bar 67

(b) Chopin, Barcarolle, bar 70

Debussy, *L'isle joyeuse*. bar 1

Christian Goubault observes one of Debussy's most exact echoes of Chopin in the *Prélude à l'après-midi d'un faune* (see Example 12).[16] The affinity extends to the work's intensely fluid form, something then new to Debussy's instrumental music, since the *Prélude* dates from the early 1890s. Ravel was especially struck by this, remarking in 1922 that 'in the *Prélude à l'après-midi d'un faune*, where [Debussy] achieved perfection, it was impossible to say how it had been built up.'[17]

Example 12   Chopin, Nocturne Op. 27 No. 2

p dolce

Debussy, *Prélude à l'après-midi d'un faune*

p expressif et très soutenu   *mf*   *p*

Ravel's comment is equally revealing about Chopin, Debussy and himself, as he made the remark to qualify his criticism that Debussy otherwise

> had shown a *négligence de la forme*; he had achieved through intellectual perception what Chopin had done from inspiration or intuition. Thus, in the larger forms [Debussy] showed a lack of architectonic power.[18]

Whether or not one agrees with Ravel's verdict, Ravel evidently observed that Debussy's structures and formal sections – however unorthodox – are often much more visible than Chopin's, Fauré's or his own.[19]

L'isle joyeuse throws more light on this question, since, consciously or not, Debussy appears to have looked to Chopin for help in solving the problems posed by its length and structural complexity. Under its surface, *L'isle joyeuse* closely matches the formal layout of its contrasting companion piece *Masques*, even to the extent of equivalent transitions arriving at the same points, proportionally, of each piece's architecture.[20] That relationship ends, as musically it must, at the beginning of the final crescendo sequence in *L'isle joyeuse* (bar 186) – at which point *L'isle joyeuse* takes up a course parallel to that of Chopin's third Ballade, as shown in Table 1 and in Example 13.

Example 13   Chopin, Third Ballade, bar 182

Ex. 13 (*cont.*)

Debussy, *L'isle joyeuse*, bar 185

The coincidence extends to the detail that Debussy launches his parallel structure by taking over Chopin's ostinato figure of a bass octave with appoggiatura. This, seen together with the close affinity between Chopin's Third Ballade and his Barcarolle, adds tellingly to the connections already noted between the Barcarolle and *L'isle joyeuse*. A later remark of Debussy's adds implicit comment: 'If [Chopin's] formal freedom has fooled his critics, we nonetheless must recognize the degree to which everything is in its place and carefully organized.'[21]

Might Ravel have been aware of those connections when he made his comments about Debussy's and Chopin's forms? The question arises because the ostinato of Example 13 recurs four years after *L'isle joyeuse*, in Ravel's 'Scarbo' (*Gaspard de la nuit*), here again beginning a long crescendo sequence towards the piece's final climax (see Example 14).[22] Ravel may have observed that of the three pieces which share this stratagem, *L'isle joyeuse* has the most discernible formal seams.

Table 1. Formal parallels between *L'isle joyeuse* and Chopin's Third Ballade

Chopin: bar 185 (183)	bar 213	bar 222	bar 231	end
long crescendo: bass ostinato, rising tonal sequences and thematic compression *ff*	tonic arrival with one of the piece's main themes	tonal interruption	più mosso: tonic reaffirmed with the other main theme	(descending flourish with added sixth)
Debussy: bar 186	bar 220	bar 236	bar 244	end

Example 14   Ravel, 'Scarbo', bar 475

Debussy's forms became both more fluid and more robust as he learned, like Chopin, to contrast musical speeds within the same basic tempo. A simple example is the ternary form of probably the most Chopinesque of Debussy's *Etudes*, 'Pour les sixtes', recalling the contrasts noted earlier within Chopin's C minor and E major Nocturnes. A more sophisticated example occurs in the two consecutive piano *Images* 'Hommage à Rameau' and 'Mouvement', which at first sight appear to be a slow piece followed by a very fast one. Only closer inspection reveals that the underlying minim tempo – like some rhythmic and melodic detail – is virtually identical across the two pieces (see Example 15). (The melodic line common to both extracts in Example 15, incidentally, is surely an echo of the central part of the scherzo from Chopin's B minor Sonata, Op. 58.) Indeed, the outer sections of 'Mouvement' have even slower harmonic motion than 'Hommage à Rameau', in dramatic contrast to the rapid motion (but with identical minim pulse) in the central part of 'Mouvement' (see Example 16). In passing, the initial harmony of Example 16, especially over the F♯ bass pedal, again suggests how attached Debussy was to Chopin's Barcarolle (cf. Example 10).

Both Debussy and Chopin often bring out such contrasts within a basic tempo by juxtaposing harmonically static periods and sudden tonal mobility. In this respect Debussy's long tonic pedal points in works like *La mer*, or the piano pieces 'Pagodes', *L'isle joyeuse*, 'Mouvement' and 'Des pas sur la neige', have often been remarked, and his attachment to bass drones has elsewhere been related at least partly to his interest in Indian music.[23] A source of equal importance must be the bass drones favoured by Chopin (see Example 17). When this occurs in such a

Example 15   Debussy, 'Hommage à Rameau', bar 14

'Mouvement', bar 30

Example 16   Debussy, 'Mouvement', bar 89

Example 17   Chopin, Barcarolle, bars 15, 39

Ex. 17 (*cont.*)

Nocturne Op. 27 No. 1

modally exotic setting as the Nocturne in C♯, Op. 27 No. 1 (see Example 24b below), one is left wondering if Chopin, too, had been affected by Indian music. No answer is known, though some Indian music could certainly be heard in Paris during his lifetime.[24] Chopin's left-hand figurations in these and other similar examples may simply be pianistic realisations of eastern European bagpipes or drones, yet their similarity to the Indian *tāmbūra* with its reiterated bass fourths or fifths is very striking.

The closest genre connection between Debussy and Chopin obviously lies in Debussy's twenty-four Preludes (published as two books of twelve in 1910 and 1913) and his twelve Etudes of 1915. Outwardly the Etudes have the closest connection of all, being dedicated to the memory of Chopin, whose piano music Debussy edited for his publisher, Durand, in 1915.[25] Debussy's last etude, 'Pour les accords', reflects this, its basic material coming straight from the scherzo of Chopin's B♭ minor Sonata, Op. 35 (see especially bars 51–3, 73–6 and 261ff. of the latter). But obvious musical links between Debussy's and Chopin's etudes are scarce, beyond two passages in Debussy's 'Pour les sixtes' that clearly point to Chopin's A♭ major *Nouvelle étude* (see Example 18), a piece on which Debussy apparently claimed to have 'worn down his fingers'.[26] Debussy's etudes are also generally longer and more formally developed than Chopin's, and contain echoes of other composers, particularly Schumann and Chabrier.[27]

Example 18   Chopin, Etude in A♭, bar 13

Debussy, 'Pour les sixtes', bar 38

Chopin, Etude in A♭, bar 29

Debussy, 'Pour les sixtes', bar 43

To that it has to be added that Debussy's dedication to Chopin was decided only after long hesitation between Chopin and Couperin, '*ces deux maîtres, si admirables "devineurs"*'.[28] A truer influence is likely to have been less literal but more creative, from Debussy's simultaneous editing of Chopin's works, and from the special consideration that task involved of not only Chopin's way of writing but also pianism more generally. Those questions – which prompted Debussy's memories of Madame Mauté already quoted – emerge from his letters to Jacques Durand in 1915, in which he discusses the editorial project in terms of combining accuracy, clarity and comprehension of Chopin's notation.[29] By mid-1915 his comments about the Chopin editing are usually juxtaposed with progress reports on his own études, lending weight to the idea that, deliberately or not, Debussy was writing into his études – which have little to do with visible virtuosity and everything to do with sonority, colour and rhythmic clarity – his musical feelings on what still remained to be cultivated in piano playing, despite Chopin's contribution. In that respect the avoidance of surface similarity makes them appear all the more a creative response to Chopin.

Similarly, Debussy's preludes avoid the most immediate characteristic of Chopin's (or Bach's), a succession through all the keys. Yet Chopin's preludes emerge unmistakably – if transformed – from the opening bars of Debussy's Book 1 (see Example 19): the opening chord of 'Danseuses de Delphes' even takes an exact cue from Chopin's unusual voicing of the same chord in Op. 28 No. 21. (The *subito forte* chord at the close of 'Danseuses de Delphes' also comes straight from the end of the first movement of Chopin's B♭ minor Sonata, Op. 35 – a relationship perhaps most discernible through the pianist's fingers).

Probably the strongest structural thread in Debussy's first book of Preludes comes from the Chopinesque chromatic contrary motion in the first two chords of 'Danseuses de Delphes' (from B♭ to A and B♮). Various developments of this device culminate in the sixth prelude, 'Des pas sur la neige'. Beginning with a complete æolian mode on D, the piece's first musical paragraph goes on similarly to split its initial B♭ to A and B♮ (at bar 5), and then subtly introduces the remain-

Example 19   Chopin, end of Prelude Op. 28 No. 21

Ex. 19 (*cont.*)

Debussy, beginning of 'Danseuses de Delphes'

Chopin, beginning of Prelude Op. 28 No. 1

ing semitones of the chromatic octave in a continued sequence of rising fifths
(F♯, C♯/D♭, A♭ and E♭, leading back to B♭).[30] The analogy to the key sequence of
Chopin's preludes needs no labouring.

If Chopin's key sequence is seen qualitatively as C major (or diatonicism)
progressively coloured by the remaining notes and keys, the connection becomes
even clearer, not just to 'Des pas sur la neige' but also to Debussy's second book
of preludes. A persistent thread in the second book is the tonal motive of C major
(or diatonicism) being progressively overlaid by chromaticism: this begins with
the first bar of the first prelude, 'Brouillards', and is completed on the final page of

the last prelude, 'Feux d'artifice', where a final attempt to reinstate C major – in the form of 'La Marseillaise', the old order *par excellence* – crumbles in the face of a quietly conclusive Db. Again Debussy's response to Chopin's sequence, conscious or not, is a creative one beyond mimicry.

One other underlying motive of Chopin's preludes may have been intuitively carried over into Debussy's. Jean-Jacques Eigeldinger observes the virtually un-stated, but extremely pervasive melodic shape of Example 20a (in various transpo-sitions) running through the motives and voicing of Chopin's preludes.[31] Debussy's preludes end with 'Feux d'artifice', dominated by exactly this motive (see Example 20b). Whatever we make of that, one of its chromatic variants (see Example 20c) also suggests the textures of the 'Revolutionary' Etude Op. 10 No. 12.

Ravel's relationship to Chopin, as his comments above suggest, is a subtly intui-tive one, often harder to trace technically than Debussy's. Like Chopin, Ravel reached early musical maturity, and his most daring innovations similarly are often innocently hidden under a more explicit concern for clarity of expression and perfection in taste and form, leaving no seams visible. Several harmonic and tonal links between Ravel and Chopin are discussed below, and Arbie Orenstein has observed Ravel's close approach to Chopin's Berceuse in the similarly ethereal recapitulation of the slow movement of the G major Piano Concerto, his last large-scale work.[32] To that we may add the figurations of his piano prelude of 1913 (rising left hand arpeggios with rests on the main beats), reminiscent of Chopin's lone prelude of Op. 45.

Example 20   (a) melodic shape pervading Chopin's Preludes (Eigeldinger)

(b) Debussy, 'Feux d'artifice' principal motive, bar 82

Ex. 20 (*cont.*)

(c) 'Feux d'artifice', bar 35

As we might expect, some of the most striking similarities to Chopin occur in Ravel's water evocations, most obviously in 'Ondine' from *Gaspard de la nuit*, relative to Chopin's Etude Op. 25 No. 1 (see Example 21). The coincidence is more than momentary, for Chopin's etude – whose attached story of a shepherd in a

Example 21   Chopin, Etude Op. 25 No. 1, bar 30

Ex. 21 (*cont.*)

Ravel, 'Ondine' (*Gaspard de la nuit*)

storm has already been mentioned – has a remarkably similar shape to Ravel's piece, building inexorably to an *appassionato* climax before evaporating, just like Ravel's Ondine, in a final flurry of arpeggios suggestive of laughter and a shower of spray.

Ravel was also interested in the Chopin research of Edouard Ganche and eventually became vice-president of Ganche's Société Frédéric Chopin.[33] His main commentary on Chopin is a series of impressions penned in 1910, culminating in – once again – the Barcarolle, which for Ravel

> sums up the sumptuously expressive art of this great slav of Italian education. . . [In this piece] Chopin made real all that his predecessors managed to express only imperfectly.[34]

Musical comment on that comes from Ravel's *Ma mère l'Oye* of the same year, whose penultimate movement ends by exquisitely tracing out (a semitone lower) the conclusive cadence of Chopin's Barcarolle (Example 22; cf. Example 10).[35]

Ravel's other direct contact with Chopin's music remains mysterious, since we no longer know which of Chopin's works Ravel orchestrated in 1913–14 for Nijinsky's new version of the ballet *Les sylphides*. Only a few tantalising indications

Example 22   'Les entretiens de la Belle et de la Bête'. from *Ma mère l'Oye*, bar 166

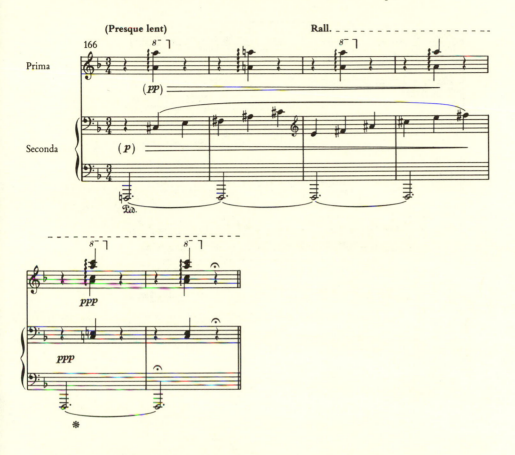

lie in some sketches among Ravel's papers for orchestrations of Chopin's Etude Op. 10 No. 11, a mazurka and a barcarolle.[36]

If this chapter has concentrated so far on musical aspects other than basic harmonic language, it is partly because a whole chapter could not completely cover Chopin's effect in that field. Moreover, much of Chopin's harmonic influence reached French and other music through his enormous effect on Liszt and thence on Wagner. Debussy's strong harmonic links with Wagner frequently reach back to Chopin, as do Ravel's rarer Wagnerian moments. For example, if *Tristan und Isolde* appears an obvious source for the sumptuous texture and half-diminished chord at the central climax of the dawn scene in *Daphnis et Chloë* (Example 23a), an even closer relationship in terms of exact spacing can be seen to Chopin's First Ballade (see Example 23b). It helps us sense how Ravel was wont to explain daring touches in his music with disarming comments like 'this harmony was used by Chopin.'[37]

Example 23   (a) *Daphnis et Chloë*, dawn scene (vocal score)

(b) Chopin, first ballade, bar 124

In other ways Chopin's harmonic influence is most discernible on different composers in tandem. Debussy's *Prélude à l'après-midi d'un faune* of 1894 provides a revealing example, at rehearsal figure 3 (see Example 24a). This piquant harmony is easily traced back to Chopin, either as a variant of Example 10 (with a dominant

C♯ instead of a tonic F♯ underneath), or as a transposition (by a fourth or fifth) from Chopin's Nocturne Op. 27 No. 1 (Example 24b). It gives some indication of how unconsciously ideas can be picked up from other composers, that Ravel in 1903 regarded a closely related passage in Debussy's 'La soirée dans Grenade' as a theft from his own two-piano 'Habanera' of 1895 (see Example 24c), evidently overlooking Example 24a, plus that fact that they really both owed the harmony to Chopin. (The second bar of the Ravel example, incidentally, makes explicit the connection with Example 10.) Another of Debussy's settings of this harmony – still in the same key – in the prelude of 1912 'La terrasse des audiences du clair de lune', turns the G♮ into appoggiatura F×s, recalling a different intermediate link, Fauré's Seventh Nocturne of 1897 (Example 24d). With their emphasis on shifting melody over the C♯ bass, both passages in turn look back to Chopin's Nocturne Op. 15 No. 2 (Example 24e) – an interesting confluence of three nocturnal settings in the same key using this musical idea.

Example 24   (a) Debussy, *Prélude à l'après-midi d'un faune* (reduction)

(b) Chopin, Nocturne Op. 27 No. 1, bar 13

(c) Debussy, 'La soirée dans Grenade', bar 23

Ex. 24 (*cont.*)

(c) Ravel, 'Habanera', bar 13

(d) Debussy, 'La terrasse des audiences du clair de lune', bar 16

Fauré, Seventh Nocturne, Op. 74, bar 84

Ex. 24 (*cont.*)

(e) Chopin, Nocturne Op. 15 No. 2, bar 25

Doppio movimento

Chopin was also something of a pioneer with the octatonic scale (of alternating tones and semitones), as can be seen in Example 25. (An octatonic sequence similar to Example 25c can be found at bars 161–4 in the finale of the Cello Sonata, Op. 65.) Debussy and Ravel are more often credited as innovators in this field, yet one of Debussy's clearest octatonic passages, in 'Jardins sous la pluie' of 1903 (see Example 26), is essentially just Example 25a in reverse.

It is with Ravel that these relationships reach farthest. Even a non-octatonic setting like Example 27, with its initial four-note spring, suggests that passages like

Example 25   Octatonic occurrences

(a) Nocturne Op. 15 No. 3, bar 77

Ex. 25 (*cont.*)

(b) *Polonaise-fantasie*, bar 128

(c) *Polonaise-fantasie*, bar 238

(d) Sonata in B♭ minor, Op. 35, first movement, bar 91

Ex. 25 (*cont.*)

(e) Fourth Ballade, bar 223

Example 26   Debussy, 'Jardins sous la pluie' (*Estampes*), bar 37

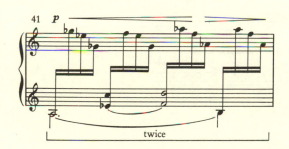

Example 27   Ravel, G major Piano Concerto, first movement

Example 25b were well ingrained in Ravel's ears. Chopin's octatonic runs are answered more closely in Ravel's 'Scarbo', where the bass line descends to the piece's final climax through the octatonic octave A–G♯–F♯–F♮–E♭–D–C–B (bars 556–63). This example is the more striking because it completes the crescendo passage set in motion by Example 14, the ostinato taken from Chopin's Third Ballade.

Examples 25 and 26 show the octatonic scale's obvious origin as diminished sevenths with passing notes. But by Examples 25d and 25e Chopin has gone beyond this, strategically placing the passing notes to produce clashes of major against minor, as well as abrupt juxtapositions of diatonically distant keys. Not until the twentieth century were the implications of this followed through in any systematic way, notably in Ravel's *Gaspard de la nuit* (even before Stravinsky's ballets and Debussy's preludes). Example 28 shows an especially mordant example from 'Le gibet'; yet comparison reveals this, to a large extent, to be a strategic re-ordering, in the same key, of the notes from Example 25d.

Example 28   Ravel, 'Le gibet', bar 23

Whether Ravel consciously devised it thus or not, that analogy is the more striking in the light of other affinities of mood and material between *Gaspard* and Chopin's B♭ minor Sonata. If their most obvious link is the tolling B♭ shared by their funereal slow movements, one of the dominating harmonies of *Gaspard de la nuit*, most evident in the main motive of 'Scarbo' (E♭ major harmony with F♭), can also be found in the Sonata's first movement (particularly at bars 151–2, with the G♭ clash against F major). Bars 37–49 of the Sonata's scherzo suggest a precursor of Ravel's famous sequence of chromatically undulating chords in 'Scarbo' (bar 448 onwards, on the fifth last page of the Durand edition), and bars 50–4 of the scherzo, if examined closely, provide the harmonic basis for Ravel's famous descending sequence at bar 25 of 'Le gibet'.

To be seen in perspective, Chopin's effect on Fauré, Debussy and Ravel has to be balanced with other pianistic influences, especially from Schumann, Liszt and Chabrier – even if some of these loop back to Chopin. For example, the Chopinesque allusions in *L'isle joyeuse* are matched by an accompanying figuration (bar 7 onwards) taken almost verbatim from Liszt's "Les Jeux d'eaux à la Villa d'Este"[38] and Debussy's preludes also quote clear fragments from sources including Brahms, Liszt, Wagner, Chabrier, Ravel, Stravinsky, Stephen Foster, popular tunes and national anthems! Chabrier's, Schumann's and Liszt's influences are just as discernible in Ravel's music, often by Ravel's own admission, and Schumann's especially in Fauré.

Chabrier is probably the most complementary influence to Chopin, more vividly orchestral in his thinking, more formally open and more purely French, looking back to the *clavecinistes*. Nonetheless Dukas twice singles out Chopin as a special influence on Chabrier, too.[39] Certainly the characteristic C–F♯ chord of Chabrier's *Bourrée fantasque* (see Example 29), which Ravel so often quoted in the same key, provides a link between Examples 10 and 24 above. Likewise the evocative bass ostinato on the last two pages of 'Sous bois' (from Chabrier's *Pièces pittoresques*) is basically another offspring of Example 13 (and can be found note for note in the scherzo of Chopin Cello Sonata). Example 30 also speaks for itself in suggesting the pianistic origin of the textures and harmonic sideslips at the end of 'Mélancolie' (from the *Pièces pittoresques*).

Example 29   Chabrier, *Bourrée fantasque* (central episode)

Example 30   Chabrier, 'Mélancolie'

Ex. 30 (*cont.*)

Chopin, Barcarolle

Chopin, Prelude Op. 28 No. 21, bar 39

If we look briefly at other countries, to try describing Chopin's influence on the piano writing of Rachmaninov or Skryabin might risk hammering the obvious. Skryabin's early works possibly make the closest approach of any other composer to Chopin's pianistic writing, if with a more Russian flavour. But his later music went in virtually the opposite direction, led by aesthetic and esoteric theories that invited exploration of grandiose effects and length.

Bartók yields some surprising links to Chopin, again increasing in later years. These may have come partly indirectly through Bartók's strong interest in Debussy and Ravel, and partly through the pianistic diet of his student days. After the romantic flush of his youth, Bartók in the 1920s tended to bracket Chopin with Liszt as influenced more by popular art music than by true folk music; his accompanying misgivings about Chopin's musical sentiment probably owed much to the sickroom interpretation of Chopin then still prevalent.[40] In later years his view of Chopin seems to have broadened with his view of Liszt, as Chopin became an essential part of Bartók's piano teaching and a more regular part of his concert repertoire. His performances of Chopin, widely disliked at the time for not being 'romantic' enough,[41] were probably too intelligent for their audiences' expectations of Chopin: the one surviving recording of Bartók playing Chopin – interestingly

the most eastern-sounding of the nocturnes, Op. 27 No. 1 – shows classical outlines, a broad tempo, little rubato (except his habitual slight left hand anticipation), innate warmth and extreme sensitivity to the piece's modal colours.[42]

Bartók's three piano Etudes of 1918 (Op. 18) naturally invite comparison with
Chopin, and the *Polonaise-fantaisie* immediately suggests a stimulus for Bartók's
first etude (see Example 31). Chopin's chromatic filling-in of motives here and
elsewhere, especially in the *Polonaise-fantaisie,* directly anticipates Bartók's 'modal
chromaticism'. In this respect and others, the opening motive of Bartók's Sonata
for Two Pianos and Percussion of 1937 again relates directly to Chopin (see Example 32).

Example 31   Bartók, *Etude* Op. 18 No. 1

Chopin, *Polonaise-fantaisie,* bar 132

Example 32   Bartók, Sonata for Two Pianos and Percussion, first movement, bar 2

Ex. 32 (*cont.*)

Chopin, Polonasie in F minor, Op. 44

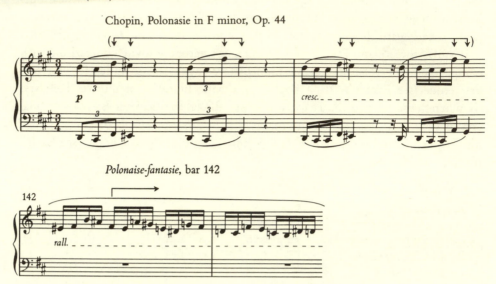

Polonaise-fantasie, bar 142

The basic motive of Example 32 can also be found embedded in the finale of Chopin's B♭ minor Sonata, Op. 35, at bars 2–3, just a few bars before the repeated occurrence of an even more Bartókian 'thumbprint' (bracketed in Example 33). Two of Bartók's other hallmarks, chromatic contrary motion and octatonicism, have already been noted in Chopin (one case of the latter, Example 25b, leads directly into the passage just quoted in Example 31). In summing up, we could hardly find more vivid illustration of Chopin's daring than the fact that his musical discoveries were still causing shock in the modern music of a century later.

Example 33   Sonata in B♭ minor, finale, bars 9, 11

Appendix

A HISTORICAL SURVEY OF CHOPIN ON DISC

James Methuen-Campbell

This selection of pianists and their recordings lists material considered to be of significant musicological value, although ultimately the choice is a subjective one. So as to preserve a historical perspective the pianists have been arranged in chronological sequence according to their dates of birth. Information about recent reissues of performances is given at the end of each entry, where applicable; the contents of these reissues are denoted by numbers in brackets after the relevant works in the text. Releases that are currently available in the UK are indicated with an asterisk. Details of unpublished discs and piano rolls have been excluded. For further reading see Armand Panigel, *L'œuvre de Frédéric Chopin: discographie générale* (Paris, 1949); F. Clough and G. J. Cuming, *The World's Encyclopaedia of Recorded Music* (London, 1952, with three supplements); James Methuen-Campbell, *Chopin Playing* (London, 1981) and *Catalogue of Recordings by Classical Pianists vol. 1* (Oxford, 1984); Józef Kański, *Dyskografia Chopinowska* (Warsaw, 1986).

Francis Planté (1839–1934) French pianist who had a number of contacts with pupils of Chopin; he played in a trio with the cellist Auguste Franchomme.
Etudes, Op. 10 Nos. 4 in c♯, 5 in G♭ and 7 in C, and Op. 25 Nos. 1 in A♭, 2 in f, 9 in G♭ and 11 in a (Columbia 78rpm discs, rec. 1928) all on Pearl OPAL 832 (LP)*

Louis Diémer (1843–1919) Celebrated French teacher; his pupils included Risler, Cortot and Lazare-Lévy.
Nocturne, Op. 27 No. 2 in D♭ (G&T 78rpm disc, rec. 1903) on Symposium 1020 (LP)*

Vladimir de Pachmann (1848–1933) Russian pianist, considered by many to have been the pre-eminent Chopin player of the period 1885–1920.
Ballade No. 3 in A♭, Op. 47 (**1**); Barcarolle, Op. 60 (**2**); Ecossaise, Op. 72 No. 5 in D♭; Etudes, Op. 10 No. 5 in G♭ (**1, 2**) and No. 12 in c, Op. 25 No. 3 in F (**2**), No. 5 in e (**1**) and No. 9 in G♭ (**1**); Impromptus, No. 1 in A♭, Op. 29 (**2**), and No. 2 in F♯, Op. 36 (**2**);

Mazurkas, Op. 24 No. 4 (2), Op. 33 Nos. 3 (2) and 4, Op. 50 No. 2 (2), Op. 59 No. 3, Op. 63 No. 3 and Op. 67 Nos. 1 and 4 (2); Nocturnes, Op. 9 No. 2 in E♭ (2), Op. 15 No. 1 in F (1), Op. 27 No. 2 in D♭ (2), Op. 32 No. 1 in B, Op. 37 No. 2 in G (1, 2), Op. 55 No. 1 in f and Op. 72 No. 1 in e; Polonaise, Op. 26 No. 1 in c♯; Preludes, Op. 28 Nos. 3, 6, 15 (2), 22 (2), 23 (2) and 24 (2); Sonata No. 2 in b♭, Op. 35 (funeral march) (1); Sonata No. 3 in b, Op. 58 (Scherzo) (2); Waltzes, Op. 64 Nos. 1 in D♭ (1), 2 in c♯ (1) and 3 in A♭, Op. 70 No. 1 in G♭ (G&T, Gramophone Co., Columbia, Victor and HMV 78rpm discs, rec. 1911–28) on Pearl GEMM 103 (LP) (1)* Pearl OPAL 9840 (CD) (2)*

Xaver Scharwenka (1850–1924) Polish-German pianist and teacher. Co-editor with Karl Klindworth of influential Chopin editions.
Fantaisie-impromptu, Op. 66; Waltz, Op. 34 No. 1 in A♭ (Columbia 78rpm discs, rec. 1911)

Aleksander Michałowski (1851–1938) Polish pianist and teacher; he had considerable advice from Chopin's pupil, Karol Mikuli.
Berceuse, Op. 57; Impromptu No. 1 in A♭, Op. 29; Nocturne, Op. 15 No. 2 in F♯; Op. 63 No. 3; Nocturnes, Op. 9 No. 2 in E♭ and Op. 15 No. 2 in F♯; Polonaise, Op. 40 No. 1 in A; Prelude, Op. 28 No. 16; Scherzo No. 1 in b, Op. 20; Sonata No. 2 in b♭, Op. 35 (funeral march); Waltzes, Op. 64 Nos. 1 in D♭ and 2 in c♯ (G&T, Favorit, Gramophone Co., Columbia and Syrena 78rpm discs, rec. *c.* 1905–33)

Raoul Pugno (1852–1914) French pianist, especially as partner of the violinist Eugene Ysaÿe; pupil of Chopin's disciple Georges Mathias.
Berceuse, Op. 57; Impromptu No. 1 in A♭, Op. 29; Nocturne, Op. 15 No. 2 in F♯; Waltz, Op. 34 No. 1 in A♭ (G&T 78rpm discs, rec. 1904) all on Pearl OPAL 836*

Nathalie Janotha (1856–1932) Polish pianist; pupil of Chopin's disciple Princess Czartoryska and of Clara Schumann. She owned the MS of the Fugue in a minor, Op. posth.
Fugue, Op. posth. in a (G&T 78rpm disc, rec. 1904)

Ignacy Jan Paderewski (1860–1941) World-famous pianist, statesman and minor composer; pupil of Leschetizky.
Berceuse, Op. 57; Etudes, Op. 10 Nos. 3 in E, 5 in G♭, 7 in C and 12 in c and Op. 25 Nos. 1 in A♭, 2 in f, 6 in g♯, 7 in c♯, 9 in G♭ and 11 in a; Mazurkas, Op. 17 No. 4, Op. 33 No. 2, Op. 59 Nos. 2 and 3, Op. 63 No. 3; Nocturnes, Op. 9 Nos. 2 in E♭ and 3 in B and Op. 15 Nos. 1 in F and 2 in F♯; Polonaises, Op. 26 No. 2 in e♭, Op. 40 No. 1 in A and Op. 53 in A♭; Preludes, Op. 28 Nos. 15 and 17; Waltzes, Op. 18 in E♭, Op. 34 No. 1 in A♭, Op. 42 in A♭, Op. 64 No. 2 in c♯ (Gramophone Co., Victor, HMV 78rpm discs, rec. 1911–38) on Pearl IJP 1 (5 LP box with one performance of each of the above titles)

Moriz Rosenthal (1862–1946) Polish pianist; pupil of Mikuli and Liszt.
Berceuse, Op. 57 (1); Etudes, Op. 10 Nos. 1 in C (1) and 5 in G♭ (1, 2), Op. 25 No. 2 in f (2); Concerto No. 1 in e, Op. 11 (1); Mazurkas, Op. 24 Nos. 3 (2) and 4 (1), Op. 33

Nos. 1 (2), 2 (2) and 4 (2), Op. 50 No. 2 (2), Op. 63 Nos. 1 (2) and 3 (1), Op. 67 No. 1 (1, 2); Nocturnes, Op. 9 No. 2 in E♭ (2) and Op. 27 No. 2 in D♭ (2); Preludes, Op. 28 Nos. 3 (2), 6 (2), 7 (2), 11, 13 (2) and 23; Sonata No. 3 in b, Op. 58 (3); Tarantelle, Op. 43 (3); *Trois nouvelles études*, Op. posth. No. 3 in A♭; Waltzes, Op. 42 in A♭ (2), Op. 64 No. 2 in c♯ (1, 2), Op. posth. in e (1, 2) (Parlophone, Edison, Victor, HMV 78rpm discs, rec. 1929–37) on Pearl GEMM 9339 (CD) (1)* APR 7002 (2LPs) (2)* RCA VIC 1209 (3)

Emil von Sauer (1862–1942) German pianist; pupil of Nikolai Rubinstein and Liszt.
Berceuse, Op. 57; Etudes, Op. 10 No. 3 in E (1), Op. 25 Nos. 7 in c♯ and 12 in c; *Fantaisie-impromptu*, Op. 66; Impromptus, No. 1 in A♭, Op. 29, and No. 2 in F♯, Op. 36; Waltzes, Op. 34 Nos. 1 in A♭ and 3 in F, Op. 42 in A♭ (1), Op. posth. in e (Vox, Parlophone, Pathé 78rpm discs, rec. 1925–40) on Pearl OPAL 824/5 (2LPs)

Arthur de Greef (1862–1940) Belgian pianist; pupil of Liszt.
Nocturne, Op. 15 No. 2 in F♯; Sonata No. 2 in b♭, Op. 35; Waltzes, Op. 18 in E♭ and Op. 42 in A♭ (HMV 78rpm discs, rec. 1925–7)

Eugen d'Albert (1864–1932) Scottish-born pianist and composer resident in Germany; pupil of Liszt.
Berceuse, Op. 57; Etudes, Op. 25 Nos. 2 in f (1) and 9 in G♭ (1); Nocturne, Op. 15 No. 2 in F♯ (1); Polonaise, Op. 53 in A♭; Waltzes, Op. 42 in A♭ (1) and Op. 64 No. 2 in c♯ (Odeon, Vox, DG 78rpm discs, rec. *c.* 1912–23) on Symposium 1046 (CD) (1)*

Ferruccio Busoni (1866–1924) Major Italian pianist and composer.
Etudes, Op. 10 No. 5 in G♭ and Op. 25 No. 5 in e; Nocturne, Op. 15 No. 2 in F♯; Prelude, Op. 28 No. 7 (Columbia 78rpm discs, rec. 1922) all on Pearl GEMM 9347 (CD)*

José Vianna da Motta (1868–1948) Portuguese pianist; pupil of Scharwenka, Liszt and von Bülow.
Polonaise, Op. 53 in A♭ (Pathé 78rpm disc, rec. 1928) on International Piano Library IPL 108

Zofia Rabcewicz (1870–1947) Polish pianist; pupil of Anton Rubinstein.
Ballade No. 2 in F, Op. 38; Mazurkas, Op. 56 No. 2, Op. 63 No. 3; Waltz, Op. 64 No. 2 in c♯ (Polish Columbia/Syrena 78rpm discs, rec. *c.* 1930)

Leopold Godowsky (1870–1938) Polish pianist and composer, active in Europe and latterly in the USA. His rewritings of Chopin's etudes are notoriously difficult.
Berceuse, Op. 57; Etudes, Op. 10 No. 5 in G♭ and Op. 25 Nos. 1 in A♭ (2), 2 in f, 3 in F and 9 in G♭; *Fantaisie-impromptu*, Op. 66 (2); Impromptu No. 1 in A♭, Op. 29; Nocturnes (1), Op. 9 Nos. 1 in b♭ and 2 in E♭, Op. 15 Nos. 1 in F and 2 in F♯, Op. 27 Nos. 1 in c♯ and 2 in D♭, Op. 32 No. 1 in B, Op. 37 Nos. 1 in g and 2 in G, Op. 48 No. 2 in f♯, Op. 55 No. 1 in f, Op. 72 No. 1 in e; Polonaises, Op. 26 No. 1 in c♯, Op. 40

No. 1 in A, Op. 53 in A♭; Preludes, Op. 28 Nos. 15, 21 and 23; Scherzos, No. 2 in b♭, Op. 31, and No. 4 in E, Op. 54 (**2**); Sonata No.2 in b♭, Op. 35 (**1**); Waltzes, Op. 18 in E♭, Op. 34 No. 1 in A♭ (**2**), Op. 42 in A♭ (**2**), Op. 64 No. 2 in c♯ (**2**), Op. 70 No. 1 in G♭, Op. posth. in e on APR 7010 (2 CDs or LPs) (**1**)* APR 7011 (2CDs or LPs) (**2**)*

Joaquin Malats (1872–1912) Catalan pianist.
Waltz, Op. 64 No. 2 in c♯ (privately recorded cylinder, 1903) on International Piano Archives IPA 109 (LP)

Carl Friedberg (1872–1955) German pianist; pupil of Clara Schumann.
Ballade No. 3 in A♭, Op. 47; Impromptu No. 3 in G♭, Op. 51; Nocturne, Op. 15 No. 2 in F♯ (from public performances, 1949) all on International Piano Archives Maryland IPAM 1102/3 (2LPs)*

Sergei Rachmaninov (1873–1943) Russian pianist and composer.
Ballade No.3 in A♭, Op. 47; Mazurkas, Op. 63 No. 3, Op. 68 No. 2; Nocturnes Op. 9 No. 2 in E♭ and Op. 15 No. 2 in F♯; Scherzo No. 3 in c♯, Op. 39; Sonata No. 2 in b♭, Op. 35; Waltzes, Op. 18 in E♭, Op. 34 No. 3 in F, Op. 42 in A♭, Op. 64 Nos. 1–3 in D♭, c♯ and A♭, Op. 69 No. 2 in b, Op. 70 No. 1 in G♭, Op. posth. in e (Edison, Victor 78rpm discs, rec. 1919–30)

Konstantin Igumnov (1873–1948) Russian pianist and teacher; two of his pupils – Lev Oborin and Bella Davidovich – won first prize at the Warsaw Chopin Competition.
Mazurka, Op. 56 No. 1; Sonata No. 3 in b, Op. 58 (previously unissued 78rpm disc, rec. 1935; Sonata from concert of 1947) on Melodya 33s 10-05519-26 (4 LP box) M10-42483-86 (2 LP album)

Edouard Risler (1873–1929) French pianist; famed as a Beethoven interpreter.
Etude, Op. 10 No. 5 in G♭; Mazurka, Op. 17 No. 4; Nocturne, Op. 15 No. 2 in F♯ (**1**); Waltz, Op. 64 No. 2 in c♯ (**1**) (Pathé 78rpm discs, rec. 1917) on Symposium 1020 (LP) (**1**)*

Marguerite Long (1874–1966) French pianist and teacher; pupil of Antonin Marmontel.
Barcarolle, Op. 60; Fantaisie, Op. 49; Concerto No. 2 in f, Op. 21 (orch. Messager); Mazurka, Op. 59 No. 3; Scherzo No. 2 in b♭, Op. 31; Waltzes, Op. 64 No. 3 in A♭ and Op. 70 No. 3 in D♭ (Columbia 78rpm discs and LP, rec. 1928–55)

Josef Lhévinne (1874–1944) Russian pianist; emigrated to the USA.
Etudes, Op. 10 No. 11 in E♭, Op. 25 Nos. 6 in g♯, 9 in G♭, 10 in b and 11 in a; Polonaise, Op. 53 in A♭; Preludes, Op. 28 Nos. 16 and 17 (Victor 78rpm discs, rec. 1935–6) all on Novello NVLCD 902 (CD)*

Josef Hofmann (1876–1957) Polish pianist; pupil of Moszkowski and Anton Rubinstein. He emigrated to the USA and became Director of the Curtis Institute in Philadelphia.
Andante spianato and grande polonaise brillante, Op. 22 (**4**); Berceuse, Op. 57 (**1, 2**); Con-

certos No. 1 in e, Op. 11 and No. 2 in f, Op. 21; Etude, Op. 25 No. 9 in Gb (4); *Fantaisie-impromptu*, Op. 66; Nocturnes, Op. 9 Nos. 2 in Eb (1, 4) and 3 in B (3), Op. 15 No. 2 in F# (2, 4), Op. 27 No. 2 in Db, Op. 55 No. 1 in f; Polonaises, Op. 26 No. 2 in eb (3), Op. 40 No. 1 in A (1, 2); Scherzo No. 1 in b, Op. 20 (1); Sonata No. 3 in b, Op. 58 (1st movement); Waltzes, Op. 18 in Eb (3), Op. 34 No. 1 in Ab (1), Op. 42 in Ab (4), Op. 64 Nos. 1 in Bb (4) and 2 in c# (2), Op. posth. in e (G&T, Brunswick, Columbia, Victor 78rpm discs, public performances, rec. 1904–38) on Pearl OPAL 819/20 (2LPs) (1) International Piano Archives IPA 103 (2), IPA 5007/8 (2LPs) (3) and IPA 5001/2 (2LPs)(4)

Alfred Cortot (1877–1962) French pianist and teacher; pupil of Decombes, a Chopin disciple, and of Diémer. Cortot was the first pianist to record sets of Chopin's works.
4 Ballades (2); Barcarolle, Op. 60 (1); Berceuse, Op. 57 (1, 2); 24 Etudes, Opp. 10 and 25; Fantaisie, Op. 49; 4 Impromptus (1); Concerto No. 2 in f, Op. 21; Nocturnes, Op. 9 No. 2 in Eb, Op. 15 Nos. 1 in F and 2 in F#, Op. 27 No. 1 in c#, Op. 55 Nos. 1 in f and 2 in Eb; Polonaise, Op. 53 in Ab; *Polonaise-fantaisie*, Op. 61; 25 Preludes, Opp. 28 (1, 2) and 45; Sonatas, No. 2 in bb, Op. 35, and No. 3 in b, Op. 58; Tarantelle, Op. 43; *Trois nouvelles études*, Op. posth.; 14 Waltzes (Gramophone Co., HMV 78rpm discs and public performances, rec. 1926–54) on EMI References H7 61050-2 (CD) (1)* Music & Arts CD 317 (CD) (2)*

Mark Hambourg (1879–1960) Russian pianist; pupil of Leschetizky.
Ballades No. 1 in g, Op. 23, and No. 3 in Ab, Op. 47; Berceuse, Op. 57; Etudes, Op. 10 Nos. 5 in Gb and 6 in eb, Op. 25 Nos. 1 in Ab, 2 in f and 3 in F; Nocturnes, Op. 9 No. 2 in Eb, Op. 37 No. 2 in G, Op. 55 No. 1 in f, Op. 62 No. 2 in E; Polonaises, Op. 40 No. 1 in A and Op. 71 No. 2 in Bb; Preludes, Op. 28 Nos. 3, 6, 7 and 15; Waltzes, Op. 34 Nos. 2 in a and 3 in F and Op. 64 Nos. 1 in Db and 2 in c#, Op. 69 No. 2 in b and Op. 70 No. 1 in Gb (Gramophone Co., HMV 78rpm discs, rec. 1910–33)

Rosina Lhévinne (1880–1976) Russian pianist and teacher, wife of Josef Lhévinne; she was on the staff of the Juilliard School, New York.
Concerto No. 1 in e, Op. 11 (LP, rec. 1962)

Ignaz Friedman (1882–1948) Polish pianist and arranger; pupil of Leschetizky.
Ballade No. 3 in Ab, Op. 47; Berceuse, Op. 57; Etudes, Op. 10 Nos. 5 in Gb, 7 in C and 12 in c, Op. 25 Nos. 6 in g# and 9 in Gb; Impromptu No. 2 in F#, Op. 36; Mazurkas, Op. 7 Nos. 1–3, Op. 24 No. 4, Op. 33 Nos. 2 and 4, Op. 41 No. 1, Op. 50 No. 2, Op. 63 No. 3, Op. 67 Nos. 3 and 4, Op. 68 No. 2; Nocturne, Op. 55 No. 2 in Eb; Polonaises, Op. 53 in Ab, Op. 71 No. 2 in Bb; Preludes, Op. 28 Nos. 15, 19 and 23; Sonata No. 2 in bb, Op. 35 (funeral march and finale); Waltzes, Op. 34 No. 2 in a and Op. 64 No. 1 in Db (Columbia 78rpm discs, rec. 1923–36) all on Danacord DACO 141/6 (6LP box)*

Percy Grainger (1882–1961) Australian pianist and composer.
Etudes, Op. 25 Nos. 10 in b and 12 in c; Polonaise, Op. 53 in Ab (1); Prelude, Op. 28 No. 17 (1); Sonatas, No. 2 in bb, Op. 35, and No. 3 in b, Op. 58; Waltz, Op. 42 in Ab (Columbia 78s, rec. 1922–7) on Pearl GEM 143 (1)

Wilhelm Backhaus (1884–1969) German pianist; pupil at the Leipzig Conservatory.
Ballade No. 1 in g, Op. 23; Berceuse, Op. 57; 24 Etudes; *Fantaisie-impromptu*, Op. 66;
Mazurkas, Op. 24 No. 4, Op. 30 No. 3, Op. 33 No. 3; Polonaises, Op. 40 No. 1 in A,
Op. 53 in A♭; Sonata No. 2 in b♭, Op. 35: Waltzes, Op. 18 in E♭, Op. 34 No. 1 in A♭,
Op. 42 in A♭, Op. 64 No. 1 in D♭, Op. 70 No. 1 in G♭ and Op. posth. in e (Gramophone
Co., HMV, Decca 78rpm discs and LPs, rec. 1908–51)

Józef Turczyński (1884–1953) Polish pianist and teacher; he was co-editor of the
Paderewski edition of Chopin's complete works.
Scherzo No. 1 in b, Op. 20 (Syrena 78rpm disc, rec. *c.* 1930)

Raoul Koczalski (1885–1948) Polish pianist; pupil of Chopin's disciple Mikuli.
4 Ballades; Berceuse, Op. 57; Concerto No. 2 in f, Op. 21 (**1**); 3 Ecossaises, Op. 72 (**1**);
24 Etudes; *Fantaisie-impromptu*, Op. 66 (**1**); Impromptus, No. 1 in A♭, Op. 29, and No. 2
in F♯, Op. 36; Mazurkas, Op. 33 No. 4, Op. 68 Nos. 2 and 3; Nocturnes, Op. 9 No. 2 in
E♭ (with authentic variants), Op. 15 No. 2 in F♯, Op. 27 No. 2 in D♭, Op. 32 No. 1 in B,
Op. 48 No. 1 in c, Op. 62 No. 1 in B; Polonaises, Op. 40 No. 1 in A and Op. 53 in A♭;
25 Preludes, Opp. 28 and 45; Scherzo No. 2 in b♭, Op. 31; Sonata No. 2 in b♭, Op. 35
(funeral march); Tarantelle, Op. 43; *Trois nouvelles études*, Op. posth.; Waltzes, Op. 18 in E♭,
Op. 34 Nos. 1 in A♭, 2 in a (**1**) and 3 in F (**1**), Op. 42 in A♭, Op. 64 Nos. 1 in D♭ (**1**), 2 in
c♯ and 3 in A♭ (**1**), Op. 69 No. 1 in A♭, Op. 70 No. 1 in G♭, Op. posth. in e (Polydor,
Mewa 78rpm discs, rec. 1920–47) on Replica RPL 2462 (LP from public performances) (**1**)

Artur Rubinstein (1887–1982) Polish pianist; pupil of Heinrich Barth in Berlin.
Recordings include virtually the complete works of Chopin, excluding rondos, variations,
other early works and the *Allegro de Concert*, Op. 46 (HMV, RCA 78rpm discs and LPs,
rec. 1928–66). The majority of these performances are available in CD format*

Irene Scharrer (1888–1971) English pianist; pupil of Tobias Matthay.
Etudes, Op. 10 Nos. 5 in G♭, 9 in f, 11 in E♭ and 12 in c, Op. 25 Nos. 1 in A♭, 2 in f,
6 in g♯, 9 in G♭, 11 in a, 12 in c; *Fantaisie-impromptu*, Op. 66; Impromptu No. 1 in A♭,
Op. 29; Nocturne, Op. 48 No. 1 in c; Prelude, Op. 28 No. 8; Scherzo No. 2 in b♭, Op. 31;
Sonata No. 2 in b♭, Op. 35 (funeral march); *Trois nouvelles études*, Op. posth. Nos. 1 in
f and 2 in D♭; Waltzes, Op. 64 No. 1 in D♭, Op. posth. in e (HMV, Columbia 78rpm
discs, rec. 1916–37)

Heinrich Neuhaus (1888–1964) Russian pianist and teacher; pupil briefly of Michałowski,
and of Godowsky.
Barcarolle, Op. 60; Berceuse, Op. 57; Concerto No. 1 in e, Op. 11; Fantaisie, Op. 49;
Impromptu No. 3 in G♭, Op. 51; Mazurkas, Op. 6 No. 4, Op. 7 No. 2, Op. 41 No. 1,
Op. 59 Nos. 1–3, Op. 63 Nos. 1–3, Op. 68 No. 4; Nocturnes, Op. 9 No. 3 in B, Op. 15
No. 2 in F♯, Op. 27 No. 1 in c♯, Op. 32 No. 1 in B, Op. 55 No. 1 in f and Op. 62 No. 2
in E; *Polonaise-fantaisie*, Op. 61; Rondo in E♭, Op. 16; Sonata No. 3 in b, Op. 58; *Trois
nouvelles études*, Op. posth. (Melodya 78s and LPs, some from public performances, rec.
1948–55)

Benno Moiseiwitsch (1890–1963) Russian-born pianist, resident in the UK; pupil of Leschetizky.
4 Ballades (No. 3 on **1**); Barcarolle, Op. 60; Berceuse, Op. 57; Etudes Op. 10, Nos. 4 in c# (**1**), 10 in Ab (**1**) and 11 in Eb (**1**), Op. 25 No. 3 in F (**1**); *Fantaisie-impromptu*, Op. 66; Impromptu No. 1 in Ab, Op. 29 (**1**); Mazurka 'à Emile Gaillard', Op. posth.; Nocturnes, Op. 9 No. 2 in Eb, Op. 37 No. 2 in G, Op. 62 No. 2 in E and Op. 72 No. 1 in e; 24 Preludes, Op. 28; 4 Scherzos (No. 2 on **1**); Waltzes, Op. 64 No. 2 in Db, Op. 70 No. 1 in Gb and in e Op. posth. in e (**1**) (HMV 78rpm discs and LPs, rec. 1925–53) on APR 7003 (2LPs) (**1**)*

Mieczysław Horszowski (b.1892) Polish pianist and teacher active in the USA; studied with his mother (a pupil of Mikuli) and Leschetizky.
Concerto No. 1 in e, Op. 11; 4 Impromptus; Nocturnes, Op. 15 No. 2 in F# (**1**) and Op. 27 No. 2 in Db (**1**) (Vox, Nonesuch LPs, rec. 1950–84) on Nonesuch 979160-1 (CD & LP)*

Nikolai Orlov (1892–1964) Russian pianist.
Etudes, Op. 10 Nos. 4 in c# and 8 in F: *Fantaisie-impromptu*, Op. 66; Impromptu No. 1 in Ab, Op. 29; Mazurkas, Op. 7 No. 3 and Op. 50 No. 3; Waltz, Op. 34 No. 3 in F (Decca 78s, 1946)

Arthur Loesser (1894–1969) American pianist and teacher; pupil of Sigismund Stojowski.
Mazurka, Op. 59 No. 3; Nocturne, Op. 9 No. 3 in B (public performances, 1967) on International Piano Library IPL 5003-4

Rosita Renard (1894–1949) Chilean pianist; pupil of Martin Krause in Berlin.
Etudes, Op. 10 Nos. 2 in a, 3 in E, 4 in c# and 11 in Eb, Op. 25 Nos. 2 in f, 3 in F, 4 in a, 5 in e and 8 in Db; Mazurkas, Op. 30 No. 4, Op. 59 No. 3 (public performances, 1949) on International Piano Archives IPA 120-1 (2LPs)

Guiomar Novaes (1895–1979) Brazilian pianist; pupil of Isidor Philipp.
Ballades, No. 3 in Ab, Op. 47, and No. 4 in f, Op. 52; Barcarolle, Op. 60; Berceuse, Op. 57; Concertos, No. 1 in e, Op. 11, and No. 2 in f, Op. 21; 3 Ecossaises, Op. 72; 24 Etudes; Fantaisie, Op. 49; Impromptu No. 2 in F#, Op. 36; Mazurkas, Op. 17 No. 4, Op. 24 Nos. 2 and 4, Op. 33 Nos. 2–4, Op. 41 No. 1, Op. 56 No. 2, Op. 59 No. 2, Op. 63 No. 1, Op. posth. in a; 20 Nocturnes; Polonaises, Op. 44 in f# and Op. 53 in Ab; 24 Preludes, Op. 28; Sonatas, No. 2 in bb, Op. 35, and No. 3 in b, Op. 58; 15 Waltzes (Vox, Brunswick, Vanguard LPs, rec. 1950–68)

Clara Haskil (1895–1960) Rumanian pianist.
Concerto No. 2 in f, Op. 21 (LP, 1955) on Philips ABL 3340

Stefan Askenase (1896–1985) Polish pianist; pupil of Sauer.
Ballade No. 3 in Ab, Op. 47; Barcarolle, Op. 60; Berceuse, Op. 57; Concertos No. 1 in e, Op. 11, and No. 2 in f, Op. 21; 4 Impromptus; Mazurkas, Op. 41 Nos. 1–4 and Op. 50

No. 3; 20 Nocturnes; Polonaises, Op. 26 No. 2 in eb, Op. 40 Nos. 1 in A and 2 in c, Op. 44 in f#, Op. 53 in Ab, Op. 71 No. 2 in Bb; *Polonaise-fantaisie*, Op. 61; 24 Preludes, Op. 28; *Rondo à la Krakowiak*, Op. 14; Scherzos, No. 2 in bb, Op. 31 and No. 3 in c#, Op. 39; Sonatas, No. 2 in bb, Op. 35 and No. 3 in b, Op. 58; 14 Waltzes (DG LPs, rec. 1952–72)

Mischa Levitzki (1898–1941) Polish-born pianist active in the USA.
Ballade No. 3 in Ab, Op. 47 (**1**); Etudes, Op. 10 No. 5 in Gb and Op. 25 No. 1 in Ab; Nocturnes, Op. 15 No. 2 in F# and Op. 48 No. 1 in c (**1**); Polonaise, Op. 53 in Ab; Preludes, Op. 28 (**1**) Nos. 1, 7 and 23; Scherzo No. 3 in c#, Op. 39; Waltzes, Op. 64 No. 3 in Ab (**1**), Op. 70 No. 1 in Gb (**1**), Op. posth. in e (**1**) (HMV, Columbia 78rpm, discs, rec. 1923–33) on International Piano Archives IPA 114 (LP) (**1**)

Henryk Sztompka (1901–64) Polish pianist; pupil of Paderewski.
Discs include: 58 Mazurkas; Nocturnes, Op. 9 Nos. 1 in bb, 2 in Eb and 3 in B, Op. 27 Nos. 1 in c# and 2 in Db (Muza LPs, rec. 1960)

Solomon (1902–88) British pianist; pupil of Mathilde Verne.
Ballade No. 4 in f, Op. 52; Berceuse, Op. 57; Etudes, Op. 10 Nos. 3 in E, 8 in F and 9 in f, Op. 25 Nos. 1 in Ab, 2 in f and 3 in F; Fantasy, Op. 49; Mazurka, Op. 68 No. 2; Nocturnes, Op. 9 No. 2 in Eb and Op. 27 No. 2 in Db; Polonaises, Op. 40 No. 1 in A and Op. 53 in Ab; Waltzes, Op. 42 in Ab and Op. posth. in e (HMV 78rpm discs, rec. 1934–46)

Claudio Arrau (1901/03–91) Chilean pianist; pupil of Martin Krause in Berlin.
With the exception of the mazurkas and polonaises and various juvenile works, Arrau recorded virtually the complete Chopin *œuvre*, including the works with orchestra. These discs have been made for a number of companies, such as Brunswick, Columbia and Philips. Philips (CDs)*

Vlado Perlemuter (b.1904) French pianist and teacher; pupil of Cortot.
4 Ballades; Barcarolle, Op. 60; Berceuse, Op. 57; 24 Etudes; Fantaisie, Op. 49; Mazurkas, Op. 17 No. 4, Op. 30 No. 4, Op. 50 No. 3; Nocturnes, Op. 9 No. 3 in B, Op. 15 Nos. 1 in F, 2 in F# and 3 in g, Op. 27 Nos. 1 in c# and 2 in Db, Op. 48 Nos. 1 in c and 2 in f#, Op. 55 No. 2 in Eb and Op. 62 No. 1 in B; Polonaise, Op. 44 in f#; *Polonaise-fantaisie*, Op. 61; Sonatas, No. 2 in bb, Op. 35, and No. 3 in b, Op. 58; Tarantelle, Op. 43; *Trois nouvelles études*, Op. posth. on several Nimbus CDs*

Grigori Ginzburg (1904–61) Russian pianist.
Ballade No. 4 in f, Op. 52; 12 Etudes, Op. 25; 4 Impromptus; Mazurkas, Op. 17 No. 4, Op. 24 Nos. 1, 3 and 4, Op. 68 No. 1, 'Notre temps' in a, Op. posth. in C; Polonaises, Op. 26 No. 2 in eb, Op. 40 No. 1 in A, Op. 53 in Ab and Op. 71 No. 2 in Bb; Rondo in c, Op. 1; Waltzes, Op. 34 Nos. 1 in Ab and 2 in a, Op. 42 in Ab and Op. 64 No. 2 in c# (Melodya 78rpm discs and LPs, rec. 1949–57)

Vladimir Horowitz (1904–90) Russian pianist, resident in USA.
Andante spianato and grande polonaise brillante, Op. 22; Ballades No. 1 in g, Op. 23 (**1, 4**), No. 3 in A♭, Op. 47, and No. 4 in f, Op. 52 (**2**); Barcarolle, Op. 60; Etudes, Op. 10 Nos. 3 in E (**3, 4**), 4 in c♯ (**3**), 5 in G♭ (**3, 4**), 8 in F (**4**) and 12 in c (**3, 4**), and Op. 25 Nos. 3 in F, 7 in c♯ (**6**) and 10 in b; Impromptu No. 1 in A♭, Op. 29; Mazurkas, Op. 7 No. 3 (**3, 7**), Op. 17 No. 4 (**3, 8**), Op. 24 No. 4, Op. 30 Nos. 3 (**3**) and 4, Op. 33 Nos. 2 (**3**) and 4 (**4, 6**), Op. 41 Nos. 1 and 2 (**3**), Op. 50 No. 3 (**6**), Op. 59 No. 3 (**3**), Op. 63 Nos. 2 and 3; Nocturnes, Op. 9 Nos. 2 in E♭ and 3 in B, Op. 15 Nos. 1 in F and 2 in F♯, Op. 27 No. 1 in c♯, Op. 55 No. 1 in f (**3, 4**), Op. 72 No. 1 in e (**6**); Polonaises, Op. 40 No. 1 in A (**3**), Op. 44 in f♯ (**4, 6**), Op. 53 in A♭ (**3, 5, 8**); *Polonaise-fantaisie*, Op. 61 (**1, 6**); Prelude, Op. 28 No. 6 (**3**); Rondo in E♭, Op. 16; 4 Scherzos (No. 1 on **3, 8**); Sonata No. 2 in b♭, Op. 35 (**6**); Waltzes, Op. 34 No. 2 in a (**3**), Op. 64 No. 2 in c♯ (**3**), Op. 69 No. 1 in A♭ (**2**) (HMV, RCA 78rpm discs, RCA, CBS, DG LPs, rec. 1928–84) on RCA RD 84572 (CD) (**1**)* RCA RCD 14585 (CD) (**2**)* CBS MK 42306 (CD) (**3**)* CBS 44681 (CD) (**4**)* CBS MK 42305 (CD) (**5**)* CBS 42412 (CD) (**6**)* DG 419 499-2GH (CD) (**7**)* DG 419 045-2GH (CD) (**8**)*

Shura Cherkassky (b.1911) Russian pianist; pupil of Josef Hofmann.
Andante spianato and grande polonaise brillante, Op. 22 (**2**); Ballades; Barcarolle, Op. 60; Concerto No. 2 in f, Op. 21 (**5**); 24 Etudes; Fantaisie, Op. 49 (**3**); Mazurkas, Op. 7 No. 3, Op. 33 Nos. 2 and 4, Op. 59 No. 3; Nocturnes, Op. 9 No. 3 in B, Op. 27 No. 2 in D♭ (**2**), Op. 55 No. 1 in f, Op. 62 No. 2 in E (**2**), Op. 72 No. 1 in e (**2**); 7 Polonaises; Preludes, Op. 28 Nos. 4, 6, 7, 10, 13, 15, 17, 20 and 23; Scherzos, No. 1 in b, Op. 20 (**4**), No. 2 in b♭, Op. 31, and No. 3 in c♯, Op. 39; Sonata No. 3 in b, Op. 58 (**2**); *Trois nouvelles études*, Op. posth.; Variations on 'Là ci darem la mano', Op. 2 (**1**); Waltz, Op. 18 in E♭ (HMV, RCA, DG, Tudor, Decca, Nimbus LPs and CDs, rec. 1950s–80s) on Nimbus N 15091 (CD) (**1**)* N 15044 (CD) (**2**)* Menu 160013-2 (CD) (**3**)* N15043 (CD) (**4**) Menuet 160013-2 (CD) (**5**)*

Nikita Magaloff (b.1912) Russian-born pianist, a Swiss citizen; pupil of Isidor Philipp. Complete works for solo piano; Concerto No. 1 in e, Op. 11; *Rondo à la Krakowiak*, Op. 14 (mainly Philips LPs, rec. 1960–78) on Philips 6708067 (16LPs)

Dinu Lipatti (1917–50) Rumanian pianist; pupil of Cortot.
Barcarolle, Op. 60 (**1**); Concerto No. 1 in e, Op. 11; Etudes, Op. 10 No. 5 in G♭ and Op. 25 No. 5 in e; Mazurka, Op. 50 No. 3 (**1**); Nocturne, Op. 27 No. 2 in D♭ (**1**); Sonata No. 3 in b, Op. 58 (**1**); 14 Waltzes (Columbia 78rpm discs and LPs, rec. 1947–50) on EMI References H7 69802-2 (CD) (**1**)*

William Kapell (1922–53) American pianist, killed in an air crash.
Mazurkas, Op. 6. No. 2, Op. 7 Nos. 2 and 5, Op. 17 Nos. 2 and 3, Op. 24 No. 1, Op. 30 No. 3, Op. 33 Nos. 1, 3 and 4, Op. 41 Nos. 1 and 2, Op. 50 Nos. 2 and 3, Op. 56 No. 3, Op. 59 No. 2, Op. 63 Nos. 2 and 3, 'Notre temps' in a, Op. 67 Nos. 3 and 4, Op. 68 Nos. 3 and 4, Op. posth. in b; Sonata No. 3 in b, Op. 58 (RCA Victor LPs, rec. *c.* 1951)

Adam Harasiewicz (b.1932) Polish pianist; winner of the first prize at the 1955 Chopin Competition in Warsaw.

Harasiewicz's Chopin recordings include both piano concertos and virtually the complete solo piano *œuvre*, with the exception of the *Allegro de concert*, Op. 46, and the majority of the mazurkas (Epic, Philips, Muza LPs, rec. 1955–68)

Vladimir Ashkenazy (b.1937) Russian pianist; pupil of Lev Oborin, winner of the first Chopin Competition in Warsaw, 1927.

The complete solo piano works and Concerto No. 2 in f, Op. 21 (Decca LPs, rec. 1964–1980s) all on Decca CDs*

Martha Argerich (b.1941) Argentinian pianist; winner of 1965 Chopin Competition in Warsaw.

Andante spianato and grande polonaise brillante, Op. 22; Barcarolle Op. 60 (**2**); Etudes, Op. 10 Nos. 1 in C and 10 in A♭; Concertos, No. 1 in e, Op. 11 (**3**) and No. 2 in f, Op. 21; Mazurkas, Op. 59 Nos. 1–3; Polonaise, Op. 53 in A♭; *Polonaise-fantaisie*, Op. 61; 26 Preludes (**2**); Scherzos, No. 2 in b♭, Op. 31 (**2**), and No. 3 in c♯, Op. 39 (**1**); Sonatas, No. 2 in b♭, Op. 35 and No. 3 in b, Op. 58 (**1**) (DG LPs, rec. 1965–78) on DG 419 055-1GGA (CD) (**1**)* DG 415 836-2GGA (CD) (**2**)* DG 415 061-2GH (CD) (**3**)*

Daniel Barenboim (b.1942) Argentinian-born pianist and conductor.

Barcarolle, Op. 60 (**1**); Berceuse Op. 57 (**1**); Fantaisie, Op. 49 (**1**); 20 Nocturnes (**2**); *Polonaise-fantaisie*, Op. 61 (**1**); *Souvenir de Paganini*, Op. posth. (**1**); Variations, Op. 12 (**1**) (HMV, DG LPs, rec. 1973–81) on EMI EMX 2117 (LP) (**1**)* DG 423 916-2GGA2 (CD) (**2**)*

Maurizio Pollini (b.1942) Italian pianist; winner of the first prize at the 1960 Chopin Competition in Warsaw.

Ballade No. 1 in g, Op. 23 (**1**); Concerto No. 1 in e, Op. 11 (**1**); 24 Etudes (**3**); Nocturnes (**1**), Op. 15 Nos 1. in F and 2 in F♯; 7 Polonaises (**4**; Op. 53 in A♭ also on **1**); 24 Preludes, Op. 28 (**5**); Sonatas, No. 2 in b♭, Op. 35, and No. 3 in b, Op. 58 (**2**) (HMV, DG LPs, rec. 1960–84) on EMI M7 69004-2 (CD) (**1**)* DG 415 346-2GH (CD) (**2**)* DG 413 794-2GH (CD) (**3**)* DG 413 795-2GH (CD) (**1**)* DG 413 796-2GH (CD) (**5**)*

Murray Perahia (b.1947) American pianist.

Barcarolle, Op. 60 (**2**); Berceuse, Op. 57 (**2**); Concerto No. 1 in e, Op. 11 (**2**); Fantaisie Op. 49 (**2**); 26 Preludes; Sonatas, No. 2 in b♭, Op. 35, and No. 3 in b, Op. 58 (**1**) (CBS LPs and CDs, rec. 1974–85) on CBS 76242 (CD) (**2**)* CBS MK 42400 (CD) (**2**)*

Krystian Zimerman (b.1956) Polish pianist; winner of the first prize at the 1975 Chopin Competition in Warsaw.

Andante spianato and grande polonaise brillante, Op. 22; 4 Ballades (**1**); Barcarolle, Op. 60 (**1**); Concertos (**2**), No. 1 in e, Op. 11, and No. 2 in f, Op. 21; Fantaisie, Op. 49 (**1**); Mazurkas, Op. 6 Nos. 1, 2 and 4; Preludes, Op. 28 Nos. 17 and 18; Scherzo No. 4 in E, Op. 54; 14

Waltzes (DG LPs, rec. 1975–85) on DG 423 090-2GH (CD) (1)* DG 419 054-2GGA (CD) (2)* DG 415 970-2GH (CD) (3)*

Yevgeny Kissin (b.1973) Russian pianist.
Concertos, No. 1 in e, Op. 11, and No. 2 in f, Op. 21 (public performances, rec. 1984) on Olympia OCD 149 (CD)*

Notes

Myth and reality: a biographical introduction

1 The terminology here is adapted from literary theory, notably that of Roman Ingarden.

2 Adam Harasowski, *The Skein of Legends around Chopin* (Glasgow, 1967).

3 The term is Hans-Georg Gadamer's.

4 In Hubert Wellington, ed., *The Journal of Eugène Delacroix* (London, 1951).

5 *The Athenaeum*, 27 January 1842.

6 James William Davison, quoted in Charles Reid, *The Music Monster* (London, 1984), p. 173.

7 Consider the criticism of Chorley, who views Chopin's 'modernism' favourably, and of Rellstab, who deplores it.

8 Doris Leslie, *Polonaise: A Romance of Chopin* (London, 1943), p. 54.

9 These letters, evidencing a passionate affair between the composer and Countess Potocka, were produced (as photographs) in considerable numbers by Paulina Czernicka from 1945 onwards. Most have been demonstrated to be forgeries, but there is still a constituency for the view that some of the first letters produced by Czernicka were genuine. See the Ordway Hilton Report in G. Marek and M. Gordon-Smith, *Chopin: A Biography* (New York, 1978).

10 See Olgierd Pisarenko, 'Chopin and his contemporaries. Paris 1832–1860', in *Studies in Chopin*, ed. D. Żebrowski (Warsaw, 1973), pp. 30–48.

11 Quoted in Pisarenko, 'Chopin and his contemporaries', p. 34.

12 Pisarenko, 'Chopin and his contemporaries', p. 43.

13 A rare exception is Juliusz Zarębski (1854–85), notably in his Piano Quintet and his piano piece *Les Roses et les Épines*.

14 One of the very few attempts to explore Chopin's music in intimate relation to his life is the extended entry on the composer by Mieczysław Tomaszewski in the *Encyklopedia Muzyczna*, ed. Elżbieta Dziembowska, vol. 2 (Cracow, 1984), pp. 108–92. Tomaszewski's approach is loosely a kind of phenomenological analysis which divides Chopin's life into multiple periods and relates his creative output to them.

15 Mirka Zemánova, ed., *Janáček's Uncollected Essays on Music* (London and New York, 1989), p. 72.

1 *Piano music and the public concert 1800–1850*

1 For information on Vienna as a centre of piano playing and piano making, see Arthur Loesser, *Men, Women and Pianos* (New York, 1954), pp. 118–49. Information on pianists prominent in Viennese concert life is provided in Eduard Hanslick, *Geschichte des Concertwesens in Wien*, 2 vols. (Vienna, 1869), vol. 1, pp. 120–30, 208–27.

2 From a review of Chopin's first concert there, in *Allgemeine Theaterzeitung*, 11 August 1829 (reproduced in Robert Bory, *La vie de Frédéric Chopin par l'image* (Geneva, 1951), p. 63).

3 Translations of reviews from Chopin's Viennese concerts are included in William G. Atwood, *Fryderyk Chopin. Pianist from Warsaw* (New York, 1987), Appendix B, pp. 200–04.

4 *Allgemeine Theaterzeitung*, 1 September 1829 ('*Er ist ein junger Mann, der auf eigentümlichem Wege geht. . .*') quoted in translation in Atwood, *Chopin*, p. 204. This view was echoed by the Parisian critic Fétis after Chopin's first public appearance in Paris (see *Revue musicale* 12 (1832), pp. 38–9, quoted in translation in Atwood, *Chopin*, p. 218).

5 Chopin intended to perform the *Rondo à la Krakowiak* for the first concert, but problems in rehearsing the orchestral parts prevented this. For his account of the concert, see *Correspondance de Frédéric Chopin. L'aube 1816–1831*, trans. B. E. Sydow in collaboration with S. and D. Chainaye (Paris, [1953–60]), pp. 104–5.

6 For the most part, these differences were welcomed: the modest and unassuming nature of Chopin's playing, and his absorption in the music itself, rather than in technical display for its own sake, were seen as signs of the true musician. The softness of his touch and the absence of brilliance in his playing were, however, regarded as areas in need of further development.

7 Moscheles, in his diary for 1829, reflected this view when he wrote that artists regarded their concerts as the means of producing their 'newest works before large musical audiences, and subjecting them, year after year, to the ordeal of criticism at the hands of competent judges'. (See *Life of Moscheles, with selections from his diaries and correspondence, by his wife*, adapted from the original German by A. D. Coleridge, 2 vols. (London, 1873), vol. 1, p. 228).

8 See J.-J. Eigeldinger, *Chopin: pianist and teacher as seen by his pupils*, trans. Naomi Shohet, *et al.* (Cambridge, 1986), pp. 4–5.

9 In general references to pianists in this chapter, the male pronoun is used. However, the early nineteenth century was a period in which the number of women pianists appearing in public increased significantly. Brief comment on one aspect of their influence is provided on pages 30–31 and in notes 42 and 71.

10 See note 4 above.

11 *Vollständige theoretische-praktische Pianoforteschule* (Vienna, [1838–39]). Translated by J. A. Hamilton as *Complete Theoretical and Practical Pianoforte School*, Op. 500, 3 vols (London, [1838–39]).

12 *Musical World* 25 (1850), p. 417. The concert was given by Alexandre-Philippe Billet, a French pianist who had settled in London. For information on Billet, see François-

Joseph Fétis, *Biographie universelle des musiciens*, 2nd edn, 8 vols. (Paris, 1860–65), vol. 1, pp. 414–15. This was the last in a series of seven such concerts which Billet gave during the 1850 season. Vocal items were also included in the programme.

13 During the eighteenth and early nineteenth centuries, concerts were often held on those days when, for religious reasons, the theatres would otherwise have been closed, or when it was convenient to provide a concert to complement the entertainment.

14 For information on these societies, see Jeffrey Cooper, *The Rise of Instrumental Music and Concert Series in Paris, 1828–1871*, in Studies in Musicology No. 65 (Ann Arbor, 1983); Arthur Dandelot, *La Société des concerts du Conservatoire de 1828 à 1897* (Paris, 1898); Alfred Dörffel, *Geschichte der Gewandhausconcerte zu Leipzig vom 25. November 1781 bis 25. November 1881* (Leipzig, 1884); Antoine Elwart, *Histoire de la Société des concerts du Conservatoire impérial de musique* (Paris, 1860); Miles Birket Foster, *History of the Philharmonic Society of London: 1813–1912* (London, 1912); Alice Hanson, *Musical Life in Biedermeier Vienna* (Cambridge, 1985).

15 See Simon McVeigh, 'The professional concert and rival subscription series in London, 1783–1793', in *The Royal Musical Association Research Chronicle* 22 (1989), pp. 3–5.

16 See William Weber, *Music and the Middle Class. The Social Structure of Concert Life in London, Paris and Vienna* (London, 1975), p. 11.

17 William Weber, 'Mass culture and the reshaping of European musical taste, 1770–1870', *International Review of the Aesthetics and Sociology of Music* 8/1 (1977), pp. 6–7; and Ivo Supičič, 'Early forms of musical "mass" culture', in *Music in the Classic Period. Essays in Honor of Barry S. Brook*, ed. Allan W. Atlas, Festschrift Series No. 9 (New York, 1985), pp. 254–55.

18 In his book on Chopin, Liszt ascribed to him the comment, 'I am not fitted to give concerts. The public frightens me, I feel suffocated by its panting breath, paralysed by its curious glance, mute before those unknown faces.'

19 In German-speaking cities, the term *musikalische Akademie* was sometimes used. Originally associated with concerts given for charity, its use was extended to include concerts mounted for the benefit of individual artists. Throughout this chapter, however, the term 'concert' is used in the modern, generic sense.

20 Quite a number of works for piano published at this time were advertised as designed for performance in solo, piano duo or accompanied versions, with accompaniment suitable for performance by quartet as well as by full orchestra.

21 The absence of a full orchestra is implied by the lack of reference to orchestral forces and by the inclusion in the programme of a string quintet, an oboe solo and a work by Kalkbrenner for six pianos. Among the musicians who attended the concert were Friedrich and Clara Wieck, whose accounts of the event make no reference to an orchestral group.

22 See, for example, Nancy Reich, *Clara Schumann. The Artist and the Woman* (Ithaca and London, 1985), p. 249; *Life of Moscheles*, vol. 2, pp. 22–3; and Alan Walker, *Franz Liszt. The Virtuoso Years, 1811–1847* (London, 1983), pp. 356–7.

23 For a comprehensive account see Rosamond E. M. Harding, *The Piano-Forte. Its History Traced to The Great Exhibition of 1851*, 2nd edn (Old Woking, Surrey, 1978).

24 *A Complete Theoretical and Practical Course of Instructions on the Art of Playing the Piano Forte*, 3 parts (London, [1828]), Part 3, p. 64.

25 For discussion of the style, see Czerny, *Pianoforte School*, vol. 3, p. 100. Concert tours by these pianists did much to spread knowledge of the 'brilliant style'. For comment on the influence of Moscheles, see *Harmonicon* 8 (1830), p. 115.

26 See Atwood, *Chopin*, p. 202.

27 Parisian critics, in particular, were initially opposed to the piano on these grounds. For contemporary criticisms of the instrument, see Adélaïde de Place, *Le piano à Paris entre 1760 et 1822* (Paris, 1986), pp. 156–8.

28 Chopin gave five concerts in Warsaw in 1829–30. The four that took place between March and October 1830 were held in the National Theatre. Reviews of these concerts can be found in Atwood, *Chopin*, pp. 204–16.

29 See Atwood, *Chopin*, pp. 201–3 *passim*. It was this work which Schumann hailed in a review with the phrase 'Hats off, gentlemen – a genius'. For comment on this review, see Leon B. Plantinga, *Schumann as Critic* (New Haven, 1967), pp. 227–8.

30 For examples of the responses of Chopin's Warsaw audiences to items based on Polish folk melodies, see Atwood, *Chopin*, pp. 211–16 *passim* and Humphrey Searle, 'Miscellaneous pieces', in *Frédéric Chopin*, ed. Alan Walker (London, 1966), p. 214.

31 *Gazette musicale* 2/15 (1835), p. 130.

32 For details of Beethoven's concert appearances as pianist, see *Thayer's Life of Beethoven*, rev. and ed. Elliott Forbes (Princeton, 1964), pp. 254–5, 270, 328–9, 416; and Hanslick, *Geschichte*, pp. 208–10. For concertos performed by London-based pianists in the 1790s, see Thomas B. Milligan, *The Concerto and London's musical culture in the late eighteenth century*, in Studies in musicology No. 69 (Ann Arbor, 1983), pp. 298–364 *passim*. For Dussek, see Howard Allen Craw, 'A Biography and thematic catalogue of the works of J. L. Dussek (1760–1812)' (Ph.D. Diss., University of Southern California, 1964), pp. 106–94 *passim*.

33 See Leon B. Plantinga, *Clementi* (London, 1977), pp. 69–116 *passim*. For early nineteenth-century examples of the accompanied sonata, and discussion of attitudes to the genre, see William S. Newman, 'Concerning the accompanied clavier sonata', *Musical Quarterly* 33/3 (1947), pp. 348–9. This convention lasted well into the nineteenth century. It is noticeable that Chopin does not appear to have performed any of his three piano sonatas in public; only the Cello Sonata was performed, and that in the last of his Paris concerts, in 1848.

34 For a late eighteenth-century example of the type of reservations about the 'respectability' of the piano concerto which continued to colour attitudes until well into the nineteenth century, see William Jackson, 'Observations on the present state of music in London, 1791', quoted in *Harmonicon* 4 (1826), p. 47. For observations on practice in Vienna, see Hanson, *Biedermeier Vienna*, p. 94.

35 Foster, *Philharmonic Society*, pp. 4–5.

36 Ibid., pp. 8–42 *passim*.

37 *Revue musicale* 2 (1828), p. 211.

38 Foster, *Philharmonic Society*, p. 82.

39 For comment on the work, see Frederick Niecks, *Frederick Chopin as a man and musician*, 2 vols. (London, 1888), vol. 2, p. 244. For the full programme of this concert, see Elwart, *Société des concerts*, p. 172.

40 See, for example, Schumann's comments (in Plantinga, *Schumann*, pp. 203–4).

41 Niecks, *Chopin*, vol. 1, p. 253. (Hiller's concert took place in 1833, not 1832, as given by Niecks: cf. *Le Pianiste* 1 (1834), p. 42.)

42 Some pianists requested themes from members of the audience at the concert itself. This practice is sometimes ascribed particularly to Liszt but concert programmes and reviews make clear that the custom was more general than this (see, for example, the programme of the Hummel concert reproduced in Fig. 1).

It seems to have been generally accepted that women pianists did not include improvisations in their concert programmes: Friedrich Wieck singled out his daughter, Clara, as differing from other female pianists in her ability to improvise. The tendency for women pianists not to improvise may have been a further factor which contributed to their early acceptance of the interpretative role of the pianist.

43 Reviews of a private concert given in 1841 include reference to Chopin improvising (see Atwood, *Chopin*, pp. 237–8).

44 But by the 1830s even the improvisations of Hummel were being questioned by some critics (see, for example, *Revue musicale* 3 (1828), p. 262).

45 See Czerny, *Pianoforte School*, vol. 3, pp. 87, 116–23.

46 Foster, *Philharmonic Society*, pp. 131–218 *passim*.

47 See, for example, performances at orchestral society concerts by Thalberg, Liszt and Doehler from 1836. It was in large measure the performances of Thalberg during the mid 1830s which first drew attention to the possibilities of solo piano performance: in 1836, it was Thalberg who broke with convention by performing solo works – fantasies of his own composition – rather than works with orchestral accompaniment, when appearing at the concerts of leading orchestral societies in Paris, London and Vienna (see Hanslick, *Geschichte*, p. 331).

48 Joel Sachs, *Kapellmeister Hummel in England and France*, Detroit Monographs in Musicology No. 6 (Detroit, 1977), pp. 22, 49, 63. Of the septets, the earlier, in D minor, quickly became a frequently-heard concert item: it was one of the few works that by the late 1830s had already achieved the status of standard repertoire for pianists.

49 Concerts given by the violinist, Baillot, in Paris from 1814 were prominent among these (see Cooper, *Instrumental Music*, pp. 66, 221–2).

50 Among the series that had a marked effect on patterns of concert-giving were The Musical Union in London and the Société Alard-Franchomme in Paris (see Cooper, *Instrumental Music*, pp. 52–4).

51 Programme reproduced in Bory, *Chopin*, p. 180.

52 Programmes reproduced in Bory, *Chopin*, pp. 150–51, 186, 189; reviews in Atwood, *Chopin*, pp. 231–60. For comment on these programmes, see Alfred Cortot, 'Les concerts de Chopin', in *Aspects de Chopin* (Paris, 1949), pp. 186–95; and Niecks, *Chopin*, vol. 2, pp. 89–93.

53 Bory, *Chopin*, pp. 150–51; Eigeldinger, *Chopin*, p. 293, note 40.

54 Atwood, *Chopin*, p. 247; Bory, *Chopin*, p. 186.

55 See Susan Bradshaw, *Concerning Chopin in Manchester*, 1st edn [Manchester, 1937].

56 Cooper, *Instrumental Music*, p. 240. From the 1840s, Gewandhaus concerts were arranged in 'historical order', with each concert 'dedicated to some great composer' (see *Revue et Gazette musicale de Paris* 8 (1841), p. 165; Dörffel, *Geschichte*, p. 95).

57 And it is unlikely that his audiences would have wanted this, so great was the desire to hear Chopin perform.

58 See *Athenaeum* (1837), pp. 146–7, 180, 220; and *Life of Moscheles*, vol. 2, pp. 22–3. The programme for the first of the series is given in Harding, *Piano-Forte*, p. 88.

59 *Revue et Gazette musicale de Paris* 4 (1837), pp. 36–91 *passim*; Thérèse Marix-Spire, *George Sand et la musique* (Paris, 1955), pp. 539–40. Vocal music was retained in both series (i.e., that of Moscheles and that of Liszt), although substantially reduced in prominence.

60 *Life of Moscheles*, vol. 2, pp. 34–6; *Revue et Gazette musicale de Paris* 5 (1838), pp. 62–4; *Musical World* 8 (1838), pp. 71–215 *passim*.

61 *Athenaeum* (1842), p. 460. This became a constant theme: after one of his London concerts in 1848, a critic, while praising Thalberg's positive qualities, expressed his regret that he left his audiences 'without the ability to judge of his powers as the [*sic*] interpreter of classical music' (*Musical World* 23 (1848), p. 170).

62 *Musical Examiner* (1844), p. 681. Doehler (1814–1856), a pupil of Czerny, toured extensively in Europe from the mid 1830s to the mid 1840s.

63 *Musical Examiner* (1843), p. 303.

64 See, for example, *Life of Moscheles*, vol. 2, pp. 52–3.

65 James Methuen-Campbell, *Chopin Playing from the Composer to the Present Day* (London, 1981), pp. 33–5. Although the catalogue Liszt compiled of works that he played in public between 1838 and 1848 (see Walker, *Liszt*, pp. 445–8) includes some of the larger works, programmes for his major concerts suggest it was the shorter character pieces that he played most often (cf. George Kehler, *The Piano in Concert*, 2 vols. (Metuchen, N.J., and London, 1982), vol. 1, pp. 759–68).

66 In 1844, a London reviewer referred to Chopin's studies as being 'more in vogue now than those of any other master' and 'a sine qua non in the education of all pianistes [*sic*] who aspire to public display' (*Musical Examiner* (1844), p. 87, quoting a reviewer in *The Morning Post*).

67 *Musical World* 18 (1843), p. 231; *Musical Examiner* (1843), pp. 237–9, 261–3, 266.

68 *Musical Examiner* (1843), pp. 250–64 *passim*.

69 Pamela Susskind Pettler, 'Clara Schumann's recitals, 1832–50', *19th Century Music* 4/1 (1980), pp. 72–4.

70 Methuen-Campbell, *Chopin*, pp. 37–8.

71 Clara Schumann did include works of her own in concert programmes (see Reich, *Schumann*, pp. 263–6; and Pettler, 'Recitals', pp. 72–4), as did certain other women pianists.

72 Pettler, 'Recitals', pp. 72–3.

73 Berthold Litzmann, *Clara Schumann. Ein Künstlerleben nach Tagebüchern und Briefen*, 3 vols. (Leipzig, 1910), vol. 3, pp. 616–19.

74 Although evident in the tone and content of other publications that emerged around 1850, mid-century thinking on the subject of the pianist's repertoire is demonstrated particularly clearly in the Appendix to Czerny's *Art of Playing* (pp. 159–86). This comprises a 'List of the best and most useful works for the Pianoforte, by the most esteemed composers from Mozart to the present day' which Czerny offered in order to 'assist pianists in making a selection for study, as well as for Teachers and Pupils'.

75 *Revue musicale* 12 (1832), pp. 38–9. In this review (given in translation in Atwood, *Chopin*, p. 218–20) Fétis differentiates between 'music for the piano' and 'music for pianists'. It is the latter that he associates with Chopin.

2 The nocturne: development of a new style

1 I am indebted to Jeffrey Kallberg for sending me a copy of his paper 'Understanding genre: a reinterpretation of the early piano nocturne', delivered to the International Musicological Society in Bologna, 1987.

2 François-Joseph Fétis, 'Etat actuel de la musique en France', *L'Europe Littéraire* 69 (1833), p. 277.

3 Letter of Madame Pleyel to Ignaz Pleyel quoted in Gottfried Müller, *Daniel Steibelt* (Leipzig, 1933), p. 92.

4 The numbering of Field's nocturnes follows that in the Breitkopf & Härtel and Peters editions.

5 Carl Czerny, *School of Practical Composition: Complete Treatise on the Composition of All Kinds of Music, Opus 600*, trans. John Bishop (London, 1848), vol. 1, pp. 97–8 (German original 1839).

6 François Henri Joseph Castil-Blaze, *Dictionnaire de Musique Moderne* (Paris, 1821), article 'Nocturne'.

7 See, for example, the entry 'Nocturne' in *The New Grove Dictionary of Music and Musicians*, ed. Stanley Sadie (London, 1980), and most of the rest of the literature that discusses the origins of the style.

8 François-Joseph Fétis, *Dictionnaire des Mots* (Paris, 1834), article 'Nocturne'.

9 Czerny, *School of Practical Composition*, vol. 1, p. 99.

10 Pièrre Larousse, *Grand Dictionnaire Universel du XIXe Siècle* (Paris, 1864–90), article 'Nocturne'.

11 For a detailed examination of pedalling techniques see David Rowland, 'Pianoforte pedalling in the eighteenth and nineteenth centuries' (Ph.D. Diss., Cambridge, 1985) and 'Early pianoforte pedalling', *Early Music*, 13/1 (1985), pp. 5–17.

12 John Field, *Nocturnes*, edited by Franz Liszt, preface trans. Theodore Baker (New York, 1902), p. v.

13 Kallberg, 'Understanding genre'.

14 Jim Samson, *The Music of Chopin* (London, 1985), pp. 92–3.

15 Jim Samson, ed., *Chopin Studies* (Cambridge, 1988), p. 164.

3   The twenty-seven etudes and their antecedents

1 The piano etude was a nineteenth-century phenomenon, though it had obvious prece-
dents in earlier didactic keyboard genres: see J. Brian Brocklehurst, 'The studies of
J. B. Cramer and his predecessors', *Music & Letters* 39/3 (1958), pp. 256–64; and Peter
Ganz, 'The development of the etude for pianoforte' (Ph.D. Diss., Northwestern
University, 1960), chaps. 1 and 2, pp. 8–67.

2 Donald Tovey, 'Observations on Chopin's etudes', in *Essays in Musical Analysis: Chamber Music* (London, 1944), pp. 155–6.

3 Of course, this does not make him unique, even as a composer of etudes. Debussy's
Douze études of 1915 (these were dedicated to Chopin) are similarly remarkable for their
ingenuity and use of resources. Tovey cites Schumann's *Etudes Symphoniques* (1837)
and Brahms's *Paganini Studien* (1866) as the only nineteenth-century etudes comparable
in quality to Chopin's, prior to discounting them as 'variations first and Etudes afterwards' (a view with which one might legitimately take issue); see 'Observations on
Chopin's etudes', p. 156. And although Tovey displays a perplexingly negative attitude
towards Liszt, there can be little doubt about the expressive quality and technical finish
of a study such as 'Feux follets' (No. 5 of the *Douze études d'exécution transcendante* of
1852), achieved by means of a 'transcendent' and very un-Chopinesque blend of chromaticism and virtuosity.

4 Gerald Abraham, *Chopin's Musical Style* (London, 1939), 'Introduction', p. x.

5 Jim Samson, *The Music of Chopin* (London, 1985), p. 59.

6 *Neue Zeitschrift für Musik* 4 (1836), pp. 45–6.

7 Schumann cites 'Exercises Op. 1, 6 volumes, and Op. 2' by Bach. He is referring here
to a contemporary Peters edition of the *Clavierübung*: the '6 volumes' are actually the
six partitas that constitute the original first volume. See Leon Plantinga, *Schumann as
Critic* (London, New Haven, 1967), pp. 146–7. Bach's significance in the context of
nineteenth-century piano etudes will be appraised later in this chapter.

8 Tovey, 'Observations', p. 157.

9 Subsequent reference to works in the checklist will be made to composer and opus
number or, where there is no opus number, to an English translation of the title.
Cramer's first two collections, Op. 39 and Op. 40, were later published together as
Les célèbres études pour le piano (eighty-four pieces in all). These will be referred to in
this combined version (i.e. *Eighty-four Studies*, No. 1, No. 2, etc.).

10 The close similarity between these two passages highlights what was undoubtedly
the strongest influence on Chopin of any living composer. This and various other comparisons are illustrated in Richard Davis's article, 'The music of J. N. Hummel. Its
derivations and development', *The Music Review* 26 (1965), pp. 169–91. See also David
Branson, *John Field and Chopin* (London, 1972), p. 156.

11 Interestingly, the seeds of another technical idea, this one later developed in a study
by Moscheles, can be found in the same movement of Hummel's A minor concerto.
A version of the figure appearing at bar 431 – a chromatic scale punctuated by double
notes in the right hand over staccato broken chords in the left – turns up as the main
idea in Moscheles's Op. 70 No. 3. The latter piece is frequently, and misleadingly, cited

as a precursor of Chopin's Op. 10 No. 2, although few works could better illustrate the differences between the two composers. No. 14 of Maria Szymanowska's *Twenty Preludes and Exercises* approximates much more closely to the technical requirements of the Chopin etude, though a more interesting precedent for both works relates to the fingering patterns, which resemble those used for scale passages before Bach's time; see Hugo Leichtentritt, *Analyse der Chopinschen Klavierwerke*, 2 vols. (Berlin, 1921–2), vol. 2, p. 90.

12 See William Weber, *Music and the Middle Class* (London, 1975), p. 41.

13 Adolph Kullak, *The Aesthetics of Pianoforte-Playing*, trans. T. Baker (New York, 1893), pp. 22–3; the original German word 'Form' in 'Die Etüde ist herrschende Form', might be better rendered in English using the term 'style'. See also Lajos Hernádi, 'Einige charakteristische Züge in dem Chopinschen Klaviersatz', in *The Book of the First International Congress Devoted to the Works of Frederick Chopin*, ed. Zofia Lissa (Warsaw, 1963), pp. 168–75; on p. 172 there is a striking illustration of Kullak's point about turning ornament into figuration (Hernádi's Examples c and d).

14 See his Op. 78 Nos. 3 and 11 (neither cited by Schumann).

15 Moscheles's Op. 70 Nos. 19 and 22, for instance, seem to have been designed to take advantage of the new double escapement action patented by Pierre Erard in 1821. In a diary entry of 1 June 1825, Moscheles describes the action as being 'of priceless value for the repetition of notes' (see *Life of Moscheles*, ed. Charlotte Moscheles and trans. A. D. Coleridge, 2 vols. (London, 1873), vol. 1, p. 108).

16 Robert Collett makes this point in his chapter on the 'Studies, preludes and impromptus', in *Frédéric Chopin. Profiles of the Man and the Musician*, ed. Alan Walker (London, 1966), pp. 120–21.

17 Zofia Chechlińska, 'The nocturnes and studies: selected problems of piano texture', in *Chopin Studies*, ed. Jim Samson (Cambridge, 1988), p. 145.

18 John Gillespie, *Five Centuries of Keyboard Music* (Belmont, CA, 1965), p. 224.

19 Compare Zofia Chechlińska's remarks on texture: 'Such specific devices of piano technique as octave sequences and trills are not in themselves texture. It is only when these devices are inserted into a musical fabric, or indeed when a specific musical fabric is woven from them, that they constitute texture.' See 'The nocturnes and studies', p. 143.

20 This quotation and those that follow are from Oscar Bie, *History of the Pianoforte and Pianoforte Players*, trans. E. E. Kellett and E. W. Naylor (London, 1899), pp. 204–7.

21 The expression is borrowed from Alfredo Casella, *Il Pianoforte* (Rome, Milan, 1939), p. 79.

22 See, for example, *Neue Zeitschrift* 7 (1837), p. 39, and 27 (1847), p. 91. In the latter, a review of several works by Dreyschock including the *Romance en forme d'étude* Op. 49, Schumann summed up his feelings with the acid sentence 'Er hat kein Talent zur Composition.'

23 *Neue Zeitschrift* 14 (1841), p. 175.

24 Compare Leichtentritt's observation that the accompaniments to several of Schubert's songs have the appearance of etudes, in *Analyse* vol. 2, p. 79. Peter Ganz notes that problems may arise even when there is a melody, as in Czerny's Op. 299 No. 10, where

'the melody is purely incidental; it seems written to fit the accompaniment' ('The development of the etude', p. 184).

25 The quotation is from J. Cuthbert Hadden's discussion of Chopin's etudes in *Chopin* (London, 1903), p. 230.

26 This remark is not intended to be controversial, though I am aware that it goes against the grain of traditional wisdom. There are several effective and useful etudes among the *Gradus ad Parnassum*, but they make up a small proportion of the total. The various canons, fugues, rondos, sonata movements and so on that constitute the majority of the *Gradus* are really studies in different forms and styles of keyboard music as distinct from specific techniques.

There is no need here to go into the dispute that arose between Clementi and Cramer over Cramer's alleged plagiarism and the question of which of them first thought of writing a 'studio' for the piano. Those interested in the details of this lively altercation should consult issues of the *Quarterly Musical Magazine and Review* from 1820 and 1821. The matter was raised again in two recent articles: Alan Tyson, 'A feud between Clementi and Cramer', *Music & Letters* 54/3 (1973), pp. 281–8; and Jerald Graue, 'The Clementi–Cramer dispute revisited', *Music & Letters* 56/1 (1975), pp. 47–54.

27 Charles Rosen, *Sonata Forms* (London, New York, 1980), pp. 110–18.

28 Czerny, *School of Practical Composition or Complete Treatise on the Composition of All Kinds of Music* Op. 600, 2 vols. (London, 1839), vol. 1, pp. 91–3. For a discussion of Czerny's analytical ideas, see Ian Bent, 'Analytical thinking in the first half of the nineteenth century', in *Modern Musical Scholarship*, ed. Edward Olleson (London, 1980), pp. 151–66.

29 See, for example, Kessler's Op. 20 No. 9 in A♭, where the presentation of the figure assumes some strange and contradictory harmonic contexts (e.g. G major, C♯ minor). The background shape which emerges from this piece is difficult to interpret because it fails to accommodate its own harmonic activity within a cogent structure and because it does not resolve or explain the progressions at the musical surface. The figuration and texture superficially resemble those of Chopin's Op. 25 No. 1. But in the latter the iridescent harmonic colourings are brought exquisitely into focus by the large-scale structure; the contexts introduced by Kessler's modulations, on the other hand, remain indistinct, colourless and indecipherable throughout.

30 Czerny, *School of Practical Composition*, vol. 1, p. 114; his emphasis.

31 Compare Chopin's similar exploitation of harmonic detail in bars 11, 25 and 71 of Op. 10 No. 8.

32 It would take too long to delve into the apparent problems of nomenclature raised by this and other titles. The terms 'etude', 'exercise' and 'prelude' were all used inconsistently and somewhat interchangeably by composers and publishers of the period. Even now they overlap to a degree. Suffice it to say that the majority of these *Exercises and Preludes* purport to be etudes in the sense in which the genre is now understood. The same is true of those by Müller, to be discussed shortly. For an elucidation of what 'prelude' may have meant to Chopin, see Jean-Jacques Eigeldinger, 'Twenty-four Preludes Op. 28: genre, structure, significance', in *Chopin Studies*, pp. 167–93.

33 George Golos, 'Some Slavic predecessors of Chopin', *Musical Quarterly* 46 (1960), p. 443.

34 Fétis provides a biographical sketch of Müller's life: see the *Biographie Universelle des Musiciens*, 2nd edn (Paris, 1870–75), vol. 6, p. 257. A lengthy obituary was published in the *Allgemeine musikalische Zeitung* 29/17 (1827), pp. 294–6.

35 See, in particular, Walter Wiora, 'Chopins Préludes und Etudes und Bachs Wohltemperiertes Klavier', in *The Book of the First Congress*, pp. 73–81.

36 Allen Forte and Stephen Gilbert, *Introduction to Schenkerian Analysis* (New York, London, 1982), pp. 188–90 (in the chapter entitled 'Elaborated chorales: instrumental preludes and studies'). See also Czerny, *School of Practical Composition*, vol. 1, pp. 93 and 114.

37 Leichtentritt, *Analyse*, vol. 2, pp. 84–5.

38 Samson, *The Music of Chopin*, p. 66. Samson also points to an interesting nineteenth-century precedent for Chopin's opening chord sequence: No. 60 of Clementi's *Gradus*, likewise in Eb minor.

39 Abraham, *Chopin's Musical Style*, p. 76; Alan Walker, 'Chopin and musical structure', in *Frédéric Chopin*, ed. Walker, p. 238.

40 Leichtentritt, *Analyse*, vol. 2, p. 165.

41 Felix Salzer, 'Chopin's Etude in F major, Opus 25, No. 3. The scope of tonality', in *The Music Forum*, ed. William Mitchell and Felix Salzer, 3 (New York, 1973), p. 283.

42 Ibid. p. 287. Salzer's analytical method is placed under a certain amount of stress during the course of these arguments, particularly by his insistence on a rigid hierarchical interpretation of every musical event in the work. Putting his analysis another way, we are asked to believe that the B major statement is a false recapitulation in the foreground, entirely subordinate to the foreground voice-leading that prolongs a superordinate whole-tone descent that is in turn a prolongation of the structural dominant at the middleground level, the whole process being finally reducible to a background $\hat{3}$–$\hat{2}$–$\hat{1}$/I–V–I *Ursatz*, divided through interruption. This does not so much explain the B major section as explain it away.

43 Salzer, ibid. p. 286.

44 See Zdisłas Jachimecki's comments on this piece in *Frédéric Chopin et son œuvre* (Paris, 1930), p. 120.

45 This is the term used by Józef Chomiński to describe the rhythmic texture of this piece. See 'La Maîtrise de Chopin Compositeur', *Annales Chopin* 2 (1958), p. 193.

46 *Méthode des méthodes de piano ou traité de l'art de jouer cet instrument* by Fétis and Moscheles, 2 vols. (Paris, 1840). Vol. 2 contains a selection of etudes contributed by various composers.

4 Tonal architecture in the early music

1 Dates in this chapter are taken from Jim Samson, *The Music of Chopin* (London, 1985), pp. 235–8 and *passim*. I provide a detailed 'working chronology' of the early music in 'The evolution of Chopin's "structural style" and its relation to improvisation' (Ph.D. Diss., Cambridge, 1989), pp. 57–8.

2 See for instance Józef Chomiński, 'Die Evolution des Chopinschen Stils', in *The Book of the First International Musicological Congress Devoted to the Works of Frederick Chopin*, ed. Zofia Lissa (Warsaw, 1963), p. 45; Gerald Abraham, *Chopin's Musical Style* (London, 1939), p. xi; and Frederick Niecks, *Frederick Chopin as a Man and Musician*, 3rd edn, 2 vols. (London, 1902), vol. 1, p. 199.

3   I asked [Chopin] what establishes logic in music. He made me feel what counterpoint and harmony are; how the fugue is like pure logic in music, and that to know the fugue deeply is to be acquainted with the element of all reason and all consistency [*conséquence*] in music. . . . Art is. . .[not] what the vulgar think it to be, that is, some sort of inspiration which comes from nowhere, which proceeds by chance, and presents no more than the picturesque externals of things. It is reason itself, adorned by genius, but following a necessary course and encompassed by higher laws. This brings me back to the difference between Mozart and Beethoven. As he said to me, 'Where the latter is obscure and seems lacking in unity, the cause is not to be sought in what people look upon as a rather wild originality, the thing they honor him for; the reason is that he turns his back on eternal principles; Mozart never. Each of the parts has its own movement which, while still according with the others, keeps on with its own song and follows it perfectly; there is your counterpoint, "*punto contrapunto*".' He told me that the custom was to learn the harmonies before coming to counterpoint, that is to say, the succession of the notes which leads to the harmonies.

The Journal of Eugene Delacroix, trans. Walter Pach (New York, 1948), pp. 194–5.

4 Schenker's embrace of Chopin is discussed by Ian Bent in 'Heinrich Schenker, Chopin and Domenico Scarlatti', *Music Analysis* 5/2–3 (1986), pp. 131–49.

5 Samson, *The Music of Chopin*, p. 155.

The main premise of Schenkerian theory is that masterpieces of tonal music are based on a hierarchy of interdependent structures ranging from the 'fundamental structure' (*Ursatz*) and the 'background' level (in which a simple harmonic progression (I–V–I) in the bass accompanies a contrapuntal linear descent in the treble) to increasingly complex elaborations or prolongations of this remote structure at 'middleground' and 'foreground' levels. According to Schenker, this multi-layered foundation is the principal source of unity and coherence in a work.

Most of the examples ('graphs') in this chapter draw freely upon Schenkerian analytical principles, presenting simplified sketches of the underlying tonal structure in various compositions. Essential structural harmonies and/or melodic (contrapuntal) structures are shown; the graphs should be compared with the scores. When two or more structural levels are depicted (as in Example 12), these can be read either from bottom to top (thus approximating one's *analytical* procedure, i.e. inferring from the score the hypothetical foreground structure on which the music is built by removing nonstructural melodic and harmonic embellishment, and repeating such 'reduction' through the middleground and background all the way to the *Ursatz*), or from top to bottom (a process more consistent with Schenkerian *theory*, which claims that simple structures give rise through embellishment to more elaborate ones at lower structural levels).

For further discussion of Schenkerian analysis, see Jonathan Dunsby and Arnold Whittall, *Music Analysis in Theory and Practice* (London, 1988); Ian Bent, *Analysis* (London, 1987); Nicholas Cook, *A Guide to Musical Analysis* (London, 1987); and

Oswald Jonas, *Introduction to the Theory of Heinrich Schenker*, trans. and ed. John Roth-geb (New York, 1982). Examples of Schenker's analyses of Chopin can be found in Heinrich Schenker, *Free Composition*, trans. and ed. Ernst Oster (New York, 1979), and *Five Graphic Music Analyses* (New York, 1969). See also my chapter 'The *Barcarolle*: *Auskomponierung* and apotheosis', and Carl Schachter, 'Chopin's Fantasy op. 49: the two-key scheme', in *Chopin Studies*, ed. Jim Samson (Cambridge, 1988), pp. 195–219 and 221–53 respectively.

6 Other studies of Chopin's 'apprenticeship' providing a broader context for this investigation of tonal architecture include Samson, *The Music of Chopin*; Chomiński, 'Die Evolution', and *Fryderyk Chopin*, trans. Bolko Schweinitz (Leipzig, 1980); Gastone Belotti, 'Le prime composizioni di Chopin', *Rivista Italiana di Musicologia* 7/2 (1972), pp. 230–91; Abraham, *Chopin's Musical Style*; and Niecks, *Frederick Chopin*.

7 For a more exhaustive catalogue of Chopin's early music, see Krystyna Kobylańska, *Rękopisy utworów Chopina*, 2 vols. (Cracow, 1977).

8 Abraham, *Chopin's Musical Style*, p. 36; Donald Francis Tovey, *Essays in Musical Analysis*, vol. 3: 'Concertos' (London, 1936), p. 103; and Samson, *The Music of Chopin*, pp. 40 and 55.

9 Charles Rosen, *Sonata Forms* (New York, 1980), p. 319.

10 *The Music of Chopin*, p. 55.

11 William S. Newman (*The Sonata since Beethoven*, 3rd edn (New York, 1983), pp. 484–5) suggests that when Chopin wrote Op. 4, which he dedicated to Józef Elsner, his teacher at the Warsaw Conservatory, he '. . .may have been driven into a more academic stance by the very title "sonata". . . ', reflecting not only the early-Romantic attitude in general toward the sonata but Chopin's own last concessions to formal training'.

12 Samson, *The Music of Chopin*, p. 31.

13 Niecks, *Frederick Chopin*, vol. 1, p. 54.

14 Ibid., vol. 1, p. 55.

15 Example 20 in Rink, 'The evolution of Chopin's "structural style"' shows how the subsidiary harmonies function in the overall tonal scheme.

16 Abraham, *Chopin's Musical Style*, p. 15.

17 See his letter dated 27 December 1828 to Tytus Woyciechowski in Poturzyń.

18 Abraham, *Chopin's Musical Style*, p. 27. The D section is typically the most complex part of Chopin's early polonaises.

19 'Mazurkas, Waltzes, Polonaises', in *Frédéric Chopin: Profiles of the Man and the Musician*, ed. Alan Walker, (London, 1966), p. 96.

20 *The Music of Chopin*, p. 41.

21 Ibid., pp. 12–13.

22 The 'lydian' sequential descent towards the end of Op. 5 (see Example 1) is typical of these cadential expansions in the Warsaw repertoire.

   Extensions of the 'final' cadence in Chopin's 'brilliant' works originally had a practical purpose. Like most compositions written in the prevailing virtuoso manner, Chopin's large-scale showpieces usually conclude with bravura finales designed to inspire applause from the '*claqueurs*'. (See Samson, *The Music of Chopin*, p. 44.)

By elaborating the cadence ending the main body of the work, Chopin signals that the virtuosic coda is about to start.

23 See Edward T. Cone, *Musical Form and Musical Performance* (New York, 1968), *passim*, and William Rothstein, 'Phrase rhythm in Chopin's nocturnes and mazurkas', in *Chopin Studies*, pp. 115–41.

24 See Wojciech Nowik, 'Autografy muzyczne jako podstawa badań źródłowych w Chopinologii', *Muzyka* 16/2 (1971), pp. 65–84.

25 For a discussion of the seemingly arbitrary endings and 'paratactic' structures in Op. 6 and Op. 7 see Jeffrey Kallberg, 'The problem of repetition and return in Chopin's mazurkas', in *Chopin Studies*, pp. 1–23. Note also his comment (p. 22) that '. . .given the inherent formal ambiguity in Op. 7, the printed versions here cannot really exert any authority over the various manuscript versions'.

26 The linking passage in Op. 7 No. 4 is not entirely without precedent in Chopin's mazurkas. Cf. bars 39–42 in the first version of the D major Mazurka (published as *Anhang 2* in the Henle edition), which similarly joins the trio to the first section's reprise. (This version may be inauthentic, however: see the Paderewski edition, x: 217.)

27 'Mazurkas, Waltzes, Polonaises', p. 79.

28 See Abraham, *Chopin's Musical Style*, p. 45.

29 'Mazurkas, Waltzes, Polonaises', p. 89.

30 Chopin fools the listener at the start of section E, where he briefly modulates to Gb major and thereby suggests the next phase of the sequence – ♭III – although it is not until section G that Gb major is definitively reached. This harmonic reference nevertheless succeeds in heightening structural momentum by planting the anticipated ♭III in the listener's ear, if only for a few bars.

31 See Samson, *The Music of Chopin*, p. 123.

32 Ibid., p. 59.

33 In bars 37–8 Chopin uses material similar to that in 25–6 to suggest an imminent cadence on Gb major, but in 39 the music suddenly turns away from ♭VII towards the dominant. Note that the cadential approach in 40–2 is extended by one bar (cf. 25–6 and 37–8) to delay and thus stress the impending arrival of V.

34 Consider for instance the Eb–Fb–Eb neighbour-note motions in the treble (bars 43–4 and 44–5) and the bass (spanning bars 49, 54 and 55), which derive from the peak of the melodic arch heard throughout section A, i.e. the high eb^3–f^3–eb^3 motion in bar 2 *et seq*. Cf. also bars 63 and 65–7, where the reiterated melodic figure f^3–fb^3–eb^3 in the right hand recalls these neighbour-note motions, and bars 75–6, where the Eb–Fb–Eb figure is suggested in an inner voice just before the etude ends.

35 See Rink, 'The evolution of Chopin's "structural style"' for detailed analyses of the remaining Op. 10 etudes.

5   Extended forms: the ballades, scherzos and fantasies

1 See chapter 4 of the present volume.

2 The term 'brilliant style', originally used to describe a manner of playing, was applied by late eighteenth-century theorists to a particular component of compositional prac-

tice. The term was later used to describe an entire repertory which had a sharply defined and widely recognised individual profile in contemporary perceptions. The concertos and bravura solos of Daniel Steibelt were among the main antecedents of the style, and it was given its finest expression in the 'public' works of Hummel, Weber and early Chopin.

3 These three areas are the basic subject matter of chapters 2, 3 and 4 of the present book.

4 It is worth noting that Liszt drew very different formal conclusions from the materials of early nineteenth-century piano virtuosity, elaborating a form of virtuoso embellishment of melodic substance which plays only a limited role in Chopin's music.

5 The earlier date sometimes given for the genesis of the ballade (1831) is based entirely on evidence from Maurice Schlesinger, whose reliability is demonstrably shaky. There is evidence from the paper of the autograph that 1835 is a more likely date. There is a consensus among current Chopin scholars that – on stylistic grounds – the scherzo was almost certainly coeval (or nearly so) with the ballade, but there is no supporting documentary evidence.

6 The *Fantasy on Polish Airs*, Op. 13, uses the term in a rather different, but no less common, meaning, referring to a chain of variations on a well-known theme, or to a 'pot-pourri' of several themes. The only other use of the title in Chopin's work is the *Fantaisie-impromptu*, where the 'fantasy' title was supplied not by Chopin but by Julian Fontana.

7 For a discussion of the interaction of norms and deviations in the definition of genre see Jim Samson, 'Chopin and genre', *Music Analysis* 8 (1989), pp. 213–31.

8 See Jeffrey Kallberg, 'Chopin's Last Style', *Journal of the American Musicological Society* 38/2 (1985), pp. 264–315.

9 Noted, for instance, in Whistling's *Handbuch der musikalischen Literatur* (Leipzig, 1817).

10 In a paper, 'The Scherzo as a genre: selected problems', read to the Second International Musicological Symposium devoted to the works of Fryderyk Chopin, Warsaw, 1989.

11 For a detailed discussion of this link see Jim Samson, *The Music of Chopin* (London, 1985), pp. 169–70.

12 This pattern of a single deviation in a generic class of four holds with the scherzos, ballades and impromptus. I argue the case for the impromptus in 'Chopin and genre'.

13 In a paper, 'Ballade und Drama', read to the Chopin Symposium, Warsaw 1989 (see note 10).

14 Edward T. Cone drew attention to Chopin's apotheotic reprises in *Musical Form and Musical Performance* (New York, 1968), p. 84.

15 For an analytical discussion see Samson, *The Music of Chopin*, p. 191.

16 Leonard Ratner, *Classic Music: Expression, Form and Style* (New York and London, 1980).

17 The term is from a review by Fétis of Chopin's first Paris concert.

18 For a fuller discussion of this issue see William Kinderman, 'Directional tonality in Chopin', in Jim Samson, ed., *Chopin Studies* (Cambridge, 1988), pp. 59–76.

19 See in particular Harald Krebs, 'Alternatives to monotonality in early nineteenth-century music', *Journal of Music Theory* 25 (1981), pp. 14–15.

20 See Kinderman, 'Directional tonality in Chopin'.

21 Harald Krebs in a conference paper, 'Dyadic unification in tonally deviating works', read to the conference *Alternatives to Monotonality*, University of Victoria (Canada), 1989.

22 The connotative values here are exemplified not only in any number of contemporary French and Italian operas, but in many nineteenth-century piano pieces, most obviously the pastoral rondos which were popular at the time.

23 In 'Chopin and genre' I outline frames of reference for the 'march' and the 'prelude' of Op. 49. See pp. 226–7.

24 The case is made above all by Chomiński and Eigeldinger, but is challenged by Kallberg. For a discussion, including references, see Kallberg's chapter in the present volume.

25 Lew Mazel, 'Fantazja F-Moll Chopina', in *Studia Chopinowskie* (Krakow, 1965), pp. 17–218.

26 Carl Schachter, 'Chopin's Fantasy Op. 49: the two-key scheme', in Samson, ed., *Chopin Studies*, pp. 221–53.

27 Kallberg, 'Chopin's Last Style'.

28 Ibid.

6   Small 'forms': in defence of the prelude

1 The quotation comes from Arnold Whittall's interesting article on 'Form' in *The New Grove Dictionary of Music and Musicians*, ed. Stanley Sadie (London, 1980), vol. 6, p. 709.

2 For all but Koch, I cite from the translations in *Music and Aesthetics in the Eighteenth and Early-Nineteenth Centuries*, ed. Peter le Huray and James Day (Cambridge, 1981): Kant, p. 219; Schelling, p. 280; Michaelis, p. 228; Nägeli, p. 398; Schilling, pp. 464–6; and Kahlert, pp. 561, 563.

  The Koch translation is my own; it derives from the 1981 Hildesheim reprint of the 1807 Leipzig original, p. 156.

3 Władysław Tatarkiewicz distinguishes at least five different meanings of *form* in the history of aesthetics; see 'Form in the history of aesthetics' in *The Dictionary of the History of Ideas*, ed. Philip P. Wiener, 5 vols. (New York, 1973), vol. 2, p. 216.

  For an exemplary analysis of the history of form in the first half of the nineteenth century, see Carl Dahlhaus, 'Eduard Hanslick und der musikalische Formbegriff', *Die Musikforschung* 20 (1967), pp. 145–53.

4 Cited and translated in *Music and Aesthetics*, p. 343.

5 The truly 'essential' [*wesentlich*] concept for Koch was not *Form* but *Anlage*, or 'plan', a mental construct in which the inner character and effect of the whole composition was revealed to the composer in a moment of inspiration. On Koch's 'Anlage', see Dahlhaus, 'Eduard Hanslick', pp. 150–51, and Nancy Kovaleff Baker, 'The aesthetic theories of Heinrich Christoph Koch', *International Review of the Aesthetics and Sociology of Music* 8 (1977), pp. 183–209.

6 The quotations come from *Music and Aesthetics*, p. 276.

    A further comment is necessary on Schelling's use of *form*. His discussion makes clear that, unlike the other aestheticians cited, he understood form in the platonic sense of 'eternal and absolute archetype', a pure concept normally at some level of remove from the art work itself. ('Philosophy, like art, does not generally deal with tangible phenomena; it deals only with their forms or eternal essences.' [ibid., p. 280]) The attraction of music for Schelling, though, lay precisely in the way in which it expressed, through rhythm and harmony, pure form of the platonic variety ('music brings before us in rhythm and harmony the form of the motions of physical bodies; it is, in other words, pure form liberated from any object or from matter' [ibid., p. 280]). As le Huray and Day observe, this claim closely anticipates Schopenhauer's famous assertion that listening to music brings us into contact not with an image of the will, but with the will itself (ibid., p. 275).

7 Something of this broadly aesthetic understanding of form still remains with us today: it is a common reflex for critics who define form to state that it embraces more than design or morphology. But ordinarily these other categories – pitch, duration, and so forth – are made to serve the understanding of morphology or design, rather than being allowed to stand as form independent of plan as could be the case in Chopin's day.

8 My thoughts on the relationship between form and genre were stimulated by Laurence Dreyfus's 'Matters of kind: genre and subgenre in Bach's Well-Tempered Clavier, Book I', a paper read (in a somewhat different version) at the 1986 Annual Meeting of the American Musicological Society. In this paper, Dreyfus attempts to make the case that form, rather than having acted as a synonym for genre before the mid-nineteenth century, instead was understood as a metaphor for it. As should be clear, my reading of the philosophical and musical evidence differs from Dreyfus's, who I think too restrictively equates form in its theoretical usages with shape.

9 Review of Chopin's Mazurkas Op. 17, *Gazette musicale de Paris* 1 (29 June 1834), p. 210. Henceforth, all translations in this article are my own, unless otherwise indicated.

10 *Allgemeine musikalische Zeitung* 48 (4 February 1846), col. 74.

11 On the notion of genre in Chopin, see my 'The rhetoric of genre: Chopin's Nocturne in G Minor', *19th-Century Music* 11 (1988), pp. 238–61, and Jim Samson, 'Chopin and genre', *Music Analysis* 8 (1989), pp. 213–31.

12 'Matters of Kind'.

13 Discussions of structural form sometimes occurred in instrumental treatises. But normally these cropped up in connection with advice on how to improvise, a situation in which the instrumentalist essentially functioned as a composer.

14 See the translation in Hector Berlioz, *Fantastic Symphony*, ed. Edward T. Cone (New York, 1971), pp. 220–48, and especially pp. 230–31.

15 Maurice Bourges, 'Lettres à Mme la Baronne de *** sur quelques morceaux de piano moderne', *Revue et Gazette musicale de Paris* 9 (17 April 1842), p. 171. In the paragraph that follows the excerpt, Bourges discusses Chopin's Prelude Op. 45, hence the example in the last clause of the quotation.

16 It is possible that Chopin may have used some kind of formal analysis as a pedagogical tool. An anonymous Scottish pupil of his reported the following reminiscence in 1903: 'My next lesson began with the Sonata [Beethoven, Op. 26]. He called my attention to its structure, to the intentions of the composer throughout [. . .] From the Sonata he passed to his own compositions. [. . .] He would sit patiently while I tried to thread my way through mazes of intricate and unaccustomed modulations, which I could never have understood had he not invariably played to me each composition – Nocturne, Prelude, Impromptu, whatever it was – letting me hear the framework (if I may so express it) around which these beautiful and strange harmonies were grouped.' (I cite the translation found in Jean-Jacques Eigeldinger, *Chopin: Pianist and Teacher As Seen by his Pupils*, trans. Naomi Shohet with Krysia Osostowicz and Roy Howat (Cambridge, 1986), p. 59; the ellipses are mine).

Two problems cloud the assessment of this reminiscence. First, it is not clear that her terms 'structure' and 'framework' refer to form in the structural sense under discussion here; they seem rather to concern explanations of unusual modulatory passages. And second, if she did mean to allude to morphological form, that her recollection was recorded more than a half-century after the fact raises the possibility that the Scottish lady interpreted in a contemporary, early twentieth-century structural sense what had been a different meaning of form in her actual lessons with Chopin in 1846.

17 In 'Criticism, faith, and the *Idee*: A. B. Marx's early reception of Beethoven', *19th-Century Music* 13 (1990), pp. 183–92, Scott Burnham persuasively argues that Marx's programme was only to a limited degree motivated by contemporary philosophical thought such as Hegel's. But other unambiguously Hegelian music theorists like Krüger nonetheless took Marx to be one of their own. For this reason, in my view, it remains reasonable to number Marx amongst the Hegelians.

18 *Music and Aesthetics*, p. 535.

19 See Charles Rosen and Henri Zerner, *Romanticism and Realism: the Mythology of Nineteenth-Century Art* (New York, 1984), pp. 38–48.

20 *Neue Zeitschrift für Musik* 2 (12 June 1835), pp. 189–91.

21 Ibid., p. 190–91.

22 From a review of the Nocturnes Op. 37, the Ballade Op. 38 and the Waltz Op. 42 in *Neue Zeitschrift für Musik* 15 (2 November 1841), p. 141. My translation differs in several important respects from that offered by Paul Rosenfeld in Robert Schumann, *On Music and Musicians*, ed. Konrad Wolff (New York, 1946), pp. 142–3.

23 Indeed, he had already adumbrated his position in an earlier review of the Etudes Op. 25: 'It is unfortunately true, however, that our friend writes little at present, and no works at all of greater compass. The distracting Paris may be partly to blame for this.' *Neue Zeitschrift für Musik* 7 (22 December 1837), p. 200.

24 *Neue Zeitschrift für Musik* 11 (19 November 1839), p. 163.

25 *Revue et Gazette musicale de Paris* 8 (2 May 1841), p. 246. The 'great contemporary poet' to whom Liszt referred was presumably Lamartine, whose 'Les préludes' was published in 1823. Perhaps then it was also the Preludes that inspired the claim of another anonymous reviewer of the same concert that 'to hear Chopin is to read a strophe of Lamartine' (*Le ménestrel* 8 [2 May 1841]).

26 The reviewer for the *Allgemeine musikalische Zeitung* 40 (25 December 1839), col. 1040, partially shared Schumann's reaction, faulting numbers 1, 2, 5, 7 and 23 of Op. 28 for being too short.

27 *Notes sur Chopin* (Paris, 1948), p. 32.

28 Carl Czerny, *A Systematic Introduction to Improvisation on the Pianoforte, Opus 200*, ed. and trans. Alice L. Mitchell (New York, 1983), p. 6.

29 Ibid., p. 17.

30 'Twenty-four Preludes, Op. 28: genre, structure, significance', in *Chopin Studies*, ed. Jim Samson (Cambridge, 1988), p. 177.

31 Others who have argued along somewhat similar analytical lines – though with differing degrees of subtlety – for the musical unity of the set include Józef M. Chomiński in *Preludia Chopina* (Cracow, 1950), pp. 300–33; Charles J. Smith in 'On hearing the Chopin Preludes as a coherent set', *In Theory Only* 1/5 (1975), pp. 5–16; Judith Becker in 'On defining sets of pieces', *In Theory Only* 1/6 (1975), pp. 17–19 (see also Charles J. Smith's reply to Becker, ibid., pp. 19–20); Lawrence Kramer, *Music and Poetry: the Nineteenth Century and After* (Berkeley and Los Angeles, 1984), pp. 99–103; and Anselm Gerhard, 'Reflexionen über den Beginn in der Musik: Eine neue Deutung von Frédéric Chopins *Préludes* Opus 28', *Deutsche Musik im Wegekreuz zwischen Polen und Frankreich*, ed. Christoph-Hellmut Mahling (in press).

In addition to the historical and formal arguments I will make below, I would also fault on methodological grounds the positions of those who argue for unity on the basis of motivic repetition (this applies also to Kramer, who lobbies for a harmonic process as the determining feature that assures the coherence of the set). Briefly stated, the reductive methods used to draw the motives out of generally rather complex textures are highly suspect: critics identify pitches as being motivically significant only when they suit the analytical purpose at hand. The assumption of unity governs which notes are selected; in this circumstance, one could show any group of pieces to be 'unified'. And even if one grants that a motive recurs in several preludes, this scarcely insures 'unity'. Rather the varied contexts of the motives can equally well accentuate the dissimilarity of the different preludes.

On these methodological points, see Leonard B. Meyer, *Explaining Music* (Berkeley and Los Angeles, 1973), pp. 59–79.

32 Not surprisingly, this practice apparently took hold around the turn of the century. James Huneker mentioned approvingly that the Russian pianist Arthur Friedheim played all of Op. 28 through in concert (*Chopin: the Man and his Music* [New York, 1900; repr. edn 1966], p. 131). And James Methuen-Campbell cites Cortot and Busoni as responsible for popularising performances of the complete set (*Chopin Playing: From the Composer to the Present Day* (London, 1981), p. 23). Pianists apparently mirrored the actions of composers, who at this time seemed particularly concerned to articulate motivic connections across large expanses of music.

33 The key word, 'individual', is curiously missing in the translations of both Paul Rosenfeld (in Schumann, *On Music and Musicians*, p. 138) and Edward Lowinsky (in Frédéric Chopin, *Preludes, Opus 28*, ed. Thomas Higgins (New York, 1973), p. 91).

34 Here too the most commonly cited English translation quite tellingly reveals recent

attitudes. Thomas Higgins (Chopin, *Preludes*, pp. 91–2) renders Liszt's 'ce ne sont pas seulement. . .des morceaux destinés à être joués en guise d'introduction à d'autres morceaux' as 'they are not merely. . .introductions to other *morceaux*'. In addition to misguidedly paraphrasing the last portion of the quotation, Higgins's 'merely' imputes an unduly negative connotation to Liszt's remarks: it is modern critics who would scorn the 'merely' functional aspects of the prelude, not critics of Chopin's day.

35 Léon Escudier, in *La France musicale* 4 (2 May 1841), p. 155.

36 Friedrich Kalkbrenner, in his *Traité d'harmonie du pianiste: Principes rationnels de la modulation, pour apprendre à préluder et à improviser* (Paris, n.d. [1849]), p. 39, may have reinforced this perceptual model when he named Chopin (along with Mozart, Beethoven, Moscheles, Mendelssohn and others) as the 'most distinguished improvisers that have existed', in a context where 'improvisation' also meant 'preluding'.

37 The programme is reproduced in *Chopin na obczyźnie*, ed. Maria Mirska and Władysław Hordyński (Cracow, 1965), p. 302.

38 Chopin commenced his recital in Edinburgh on 4 October 1848 with the same 'Andante et Impromptu', and a review in the *Edinburgh Evening Courant* of 7 October 1848 may further support the case for the 'Andante' being Op. 28 No. 8. The reviewer wrote 'The first piece was an 'Andante et Impromptu'; the opening movement being in three parts, with the theme standing out in alto relievo, as it were, from the maze of harmony with which it was surrounded' (I cite from the reprint of the review in William G. Atwood, *Fryderyk Chopin: Pianist from Warsaw* (New York, 1987), p. 256). The reviewer's description of the theme better fits the prelude, where the theme sounds amidst a flurry of rapid fioriture, than the *Andante spianato*, where the theme constitutes the top voice in normal pianistic treble-dominated homophony. And the prelude can be heard as 'three-part', in the sense of statement–departure–return, whereas the *Andante spianato* is, properly speaking, not laid out in three-part form.

39 I would recommend in particular Rose Rosengard Subotnik, 'Romantic music as post-Kantian critique: Classicism, Romanticism, and the concept of the semiotic universe', in *On Criticizing Music*, ed. Kingsley Price (Baltimore, 1981), pp. 74–98; Kramer, *Music and Poetry*, pp. 91–124; Jim Samson, *The Music of Chopin* (London, 1985), pp. 73–80 and 142–58; Kramer, 'Impossible objects: apparitions, reclining nudes, and Chopin's Prelude in A Minor', in his *Music as Cultural Practice 1800–1900* (Berkeley and Los Angeles, 1990), pp. 72–101; and Eigeldinger, 'Twenty-four Preludes, Opus 28', pp. 167–79.

40 My discussion of closure is indebted in many respects to V. Kofi Agawu's excellent 'Concepts of closure and Chopin's Opus 28', *Music Theory Spectrum* 9 (1987), pp. 1–17.

41 'Concepts of Closure', p. 12.

42 Lawrence Kramer, in *Music and Poetry*, pp. 91–124, frames a discussion of these aesthetic issues as they manifest themselves in Chopin and Shelley in terms of his provocative concept of the 'transit of identity'.

7 *Beyond the dance*

1 Weddings in Poland traditionally included dances for the various stages of the celebrations (cf. Stravinsky's *Les noces*) and on 10 September 1832 Chopin responded to news

of a wedding by sending the happy couple 'a polonaise and a mazur, so that you can hop about and be really gay and that your souls may rejoice' (*Chopin's Letters*, ed. H. Opieński, trans. E. L. Voysick (New York, 1931), p. 170). The polonaise is a stately, processional dance, whereas the mazurka is livelier, with characteristic features such as the gliding step, kneeling figures, the circling of pairs lightly holding one another and quick running passages.

2 See *Saltus Polonici, Polonoises, Lengjel Tántzok*, ed. Z. Stęszewska (Cracow, 1970), p. xxxviii, n. 4.

3 The principal collection of compositions from this period, with a commentary in English, is *Music of the Polish Renaissance*, ed. J. M. Chomiński and Z. Lissa (Cracow, 1955). An example here of the 'Volta polonica' (p. 88) comes from Fuhrmann's tablature *Testudo gallo-germanica* (1615).

4 The 'Wyrwany' included in *Music of the Polish Renaissance* (p. 91) is clearly of the *mazur* family in its rhythmic, melodic and cadential patterns. The gait and tempo of the *chodzony* indicates its kinship with the *polonez*.

5 Collections from 1729, 1742 and 1757 (surviving in Hungary, Czechoslavakia and Rumania) chart these transitional developments. See *Saltus polonici*.

6 A keyboard realisation of this melody is included in a collection of Polish polonaises, *Z polonezów polskich*, ed. K. Hławiczka (Cracow, 1978), vol. 1, no. 1, p. 5. The collection is recorded by Elżbieta Stefańska-Łukowicz on Polskie Nagrania, Muza SX 1718.

7 K. Hławiczka, ed., *Polonezy ze zbiorów Anny Marii Saskej*, 3 vols. (Cracow, 1967, 1968, 1971).

8 For a detailed discussion of this feature and related matters, see K. Hławiczka, 'Ein Beitrag zur Verwandtschaft zwischen der Melodik Chopins und der polnischen Volksmusik', in *The Book of the First International Musicological Congress Devoted to the Works of Frederick Chopin, 1960*, ed. Z. Lissa (Warsaw, 1963), pp. 176–84.

9 See O. Kolberg, in *'Pieśni ludu polskiego'* ('Polish folk song') (Cracow, 1857), reprinted 1974 in *Dzieła Wszystkie* (Collected Works), vol. 1, no. 240, p. 382 (from Wilanów, nr. Warsaw).

10 Realised as no. 21 in *Z polonezów polskich*, vol. 1, pp. 28–9.

11 The term *duma* is Ukrainian, denoting in this period a ballad song. The Ukraine was part of Poland during the seventeenth and eighteenth centuries and the use of this title is a fairly sure indication of the composition being by a Polish hand.

12 For eighteenth-century ensemble polonaises, see K. Hławiczka, *Polonezy z XVIII Wieku na zespoły instrumentalne* (Cracow, 1967), which includes anonymous polonaises for ensembles ranging from three parts (2 violins and cello) to seven (2 violins, 2 flutes or oboes, 2 horns and cello). The collection also includes six polonaises for larger groupings by Prince Maciej Radziwiłł (*c.* 1751–1800), most colourfully *La chasse* (for 2 violins, viola, cello, bassoon, timpani, 2 clarinets, 2 horns), with its additional hunting horn (Polnisch Horn) and detailed programmatic text written into the score.

13 The *oberek*, a fast cousin of the mazurka, is a quick round dance, with refrains and cries, and most eye-catchingly the *hołubiec* (heel-clicking leap) for the male dancers. It originated in Chopin's home region of Mazowsze, in central Poland. The *krakowiak*, as its name suggests, comes from the Cracow (Kraków) region, and is a spirited and syncopated dance in duple metre.

14 This polonaise and a keyboard reduction of Miechodmuch's aria from Act II of *Krakowiacy i Górale* are included in *Z polonezów polskich*, vol. 2 (Cracow, 1977). Ogiński, who had participated in the heroic Kościuszko Uprising of 1794 (commemorated by the famous *Polonez Kościuszki*), fled to Paris, anticipating later emigrations by his compatriots.

15 N. Davies, *God's Playground: A History of Poland* (Oxford, 1981), vol. 2, p. 8.

16 Occasionally he participated in the popular pastime of variations on operatic arias, hence the embellishment, in the trio of the Polonaise in B♭ minor (1826), of 'Vieni fra queste braccia', Gianetta's Act I cavatina from Rossini's *La gazza ladra*, and his Variations Op. 2 (with its finale 'Alla Polacca') on 'Là ci darem la mano' from Mozart's *Don Giovanni*. He also extemporised frequently, as on themes from Rossini's *Moses in Egypt* (23 August 1829, Cieplic) or Auber's *La muette de Portici* (8 November 1830, Wrocław).

17 Jadwiga Sobieska deals with these and other possible citations in her chapter 'Problem cytatu u Chopina' in *Polska muzyka ludowa i jej problemy*, ed. J. and M. Sobiescy (Cracow, 1973), pp. 410–19.

18 The words come from *Laura i Filon*, a pastoral love-ballad which became very popular at the end of the eighteenth century, although there are a number of different melodies to which this text is sung. The author, Franciszek Karpiński (1741–1825), also penned the well-known carol in mazurka rhythm, 'Bóg się rodzi' (God is born). (In a further example of borrowing from existing sources, another carol, 'Lulajże Jezuniu' (Lullay, little Jesus), appears as the second theme in the Scherzo No. 1 in B major).

19 The kujawiak, from the central region of Kujawy, is a lyrical, moderately paced dance involving supported lifts and leaps as well as other movements characteristic of its (usually) faster cousins, the mazurek and oberek. For folk transcriptions of this theme, see Kolberg, 'Mazowsze' (Mazovia), (Cracow, 1867, reprinted 1978 in *Dzieła Wszystkie*, vol. 4), no. 130, recorded in Służew, near Warsaw; and U. Brzozowska, *Pieśni i Tańce Kujawskie* (Songs and Dances from Kujawy, 1890–1910) (Cracow, 1950), no. 91, recorded in Głuszyn, near Piotrków Kujawski.

20 This is one of several versions of this popular tune in Kolberg, vol. 6, *Krakowskie* (From around Cracow) (Cracow, 1873, reprinted 1977 in *Dzieła Wszystkie*, vol. 6), nos. 620–23. It is better known as 'Albośmy to jacy jacy chłopcy krakowiacy', which may be freely translated as 'We're just Cracow boys'. See Z. Jachimecki, *Chopin* (Cracow, 1957), p. 274, and H. Feicht, 'Ronda Fr. Chopina', part 3, *Kwartalnik Muzyczny* (1948), no. 24, p. 10.

21 Letter of 27 December 1828 in Opieński, *Letters*, p. 47.

22 Quoted in Kolberg, vol. 6, p. 367; see also L. Bielawski, 'Problem krakowiaka w twórczości Chopina' in First International Congress report, pp. 100–03.

23 Chopin's frequent dance improvisations no longer survive (except in isolated instances, such as the two mazurkas in B♭ and G, 1825–6), so the nature of his celebrated improvisation in Vienna on 11 August 1829 on the Polish bride-capping song 'Chmiel' (Hops) remains a mystery. The original triple-time melody is in two parts, slow-fast: two modal versions are printed in Opieński, *Letters*, p. 54. Alternatively, Sobieska (in *Polska muzyka ludowa*, pp. 409–10) gives four perceptibly different versions of the

'Chmiel' melody which Chopin could have known and used: the simplest and best-known (purely pentatonic, also given in the entry for Polonaise in *The New Grove Dictionary of Music and Musicians*, 20 vols., ed. S. Sadie (London, 1980)), and three modal versions, from the Mazowsze and Kujawy regions and from his local district around Łowicz.

24 In chronological order: A♭ (1821), G♯ minor (1824[?]), Op. 71 No. 1 (1824–5), Op. 71 No. 3 (1825–6[?]), B♭ minor 'Adieu' (1826), Op. 71 No. 2 (1828), G♭ (1830[?]).

25 Letter of 25 August 1841 in Opieński, *Letters*, p. 235.

26 Jachimecki, *Chopin*, p. 134, associates this with Alexander I, who had died in 1825, to be succeeded that year by his son Nicholas.

27 It is not surprising, then, that within a few years of regaining national independence after World War I, Polish Radio adopted the opening idea from Op. 40 No. 1 as its national call-signal. On the other hand, musical ears have often been offended by being regaled with just the first 4 1/2 beats, ignoring the balance created by the answering 1 1/2 beats in the bass register.

28 For an alternative interpretation, see J. Samson, *The Music of Chopin* (London, 1985), p. 108.

29 Letters of 26 January and July 1831 in Opieński, *Letters*, pp. 137 and 147.

30 Letter of 18 July 1834, ibid. p. 174.

31 Letter of 20 July 1845, ibid. p. 284.

32 The mazurka influence may be traced, *inter alia*, in the Waltzes Op. 34 Nos. 1–3, Op. 42, Op. 64 Nos. 2–3, Op. 69 No. 1 and Op. 70 No. 2 (the 'Sostenuto' Waltz in E♭ of 1840 is more a ländler than a slow mazurka). Equally, several nocturnes show a similar influence, including Op. 9 No. 1, Op. 15 Nos. 1 and 3 and Op. 48 No. 2. Among the songs of Op. 74, 'Życzenie' (The Wish), 'Hulanka' (Drinking Song) (with its classic ABB four-bar structure), 'Precz z moich oczu!'(Out of my sight!), 'Moja pieszczotka' (My Sweetheart), 'Pierścień' (The Ring) and 'Leci liście z drzewa' (Leaves are falling from the tree) draw on this source. Chopin's only apparently unac-companied song, 'Jakież kwiaty, jakie wianki' (Which flowers, which wreaths) is a reminder that the *mazur* is founded in sung dance. Fifteen of the keyboard mazurkas were sung with texts in Chopin's lifetime, and he heard Pauline Viardot sing several in England in 1848. For a full list, see Jachimecki, *Chopin*, p. 156. There is even the suggestion, in J. Prosnak, *Siedem wieków pieśni polskiej* (Seven Centuries of Polish Songs) (Warsaw, 1986), p. 87, that the teenage Chopin wrote the well-known mazurka melody for the underground student song of the 1820s 'Witaj, majowa jutrzenko' (Hail, May dawn), published in 1831.

33 Letter of 19 April 1847 in Opieński, *Letters*, p. 325. In fairness to Kolberg, it should be pointed out that what Chopin saw were not the original notations but versions with added piano accompaniments, intended for domestic consumption: *Pieśni ludu polskiego* (Poznań, 1842–5), reprinted in *Dzieła Wszystkie*, vols. 67/1 and 67/2, as *Pieśni i melodie ludowe* (Folk songs and melodies) (Cracow, 1986 and 1989).

34 M. E. J. Brown, in *Chopin: An Index of his Works in Chronological Order* (London, 1960), p. 35, traces the melody back to the folk-tune 'Oj Magdalino'.

35 Up to and including the Op. 6 and Op. 7 sets, we may discern some mazurkas for dancing. Op. 7 No. 5, for example, has the simplest sixteen-bar structure drawn direct

from folk models (one-bar motivic units in the pattern *a a b c, a a b c*, first in C major, then in G), the whole marked *Dal segno, senza fine*, leaving the performer to decide when the dance is exhausted.

36 See entries for kujawiak, mazurka, oberek and Poland (II. Folk music) in *The New Grove* for concise information on rhythmic and phrase patterns and their syllabic folk origins. One of many Polish handbooks to dance movements is *Tańce Harnama: Polonez, Mazur, Oberek, Kujawiak,* ed. J. Hryniewicka (Warsaw, 1961), in which non-technical choreographic patterns and line and photographic illustrations give a practical guide to these dances.

37 H. Windakiewiczowa, *Wzory ludowej muzyki polskiej w mazurkach Fryderyka Chopina* (Cracow, 1926), p. 22.

38 Letter from August 1839, in Opieński, *Letters,* p. 204.

39 W. Paschałow, *Chopin a polska muzyka ludowa* (Cracow, 1951), pp. 91–5.

40 The pianist Jan Ekier, editor of *Wydanie Narodowe Dzieł Fryderyka Chopina* (The National Edition of the Complete Works of Chopin), comments on editorial problems (raised by musicological research since the publication of the 'Paderewski' Edition) in the Introduction, vol. 1 (Cracow, 1974).

41 Jachimecki, *Chopin,* pp. 157–8.

42 7a is a wedding song from Sadlno, in Kujawy (Kolberg, vol. 3, 'Kujawy', no. 99); in 7b, from the Warsaw district of Błonie, a girl puts a playful curse on her faithless seducer (Kolberg, vol. 1, no. 428).

43 See Samson, *The Music of Chopin,* p. 114. An even closer parallel is given in Windakie-wiczowa, *Wzory ludowej muzyki,* p. 39 and Sobiescy, *Polska muzyka,* p. 421.

44 In a number of significant cases, the wave shape is preceded by repeated uni-directional phrases, usually descending, a characteristic of Polish folk music and one that empha-sises the melancholic nature of many of the mazurkas (see the trio of Op. 17 No. 4 and the relentless downward momentum of Op. 30 No. 2, a momentum that is barely rescued by the eventual rising answer and a final cadence in the dominant key).

8 The sonatas

1 See, for example, Gerald Abraham, *Chopin's Musical Style,* 2nd edn (London, 1941), p. 44, and *A Hundred Years in Music,* 2nd edn (London, 1949), pp. 33, 42, 48; Joan Chissel, *Schumann,* 2nd edn (London, 1956), p. 118, and *Schumann Piano Music,* 3rd edn (London, 1971), p. 7.

2 Jean-Jacques Eigeldinger, *Chopin: Pianist and Teacher* (Cambridge, 1986), pp. 59, 61.

3 *Analyse der Chopin'schen Klavierwerke* (Berlin, 1921), vol. 2.

4 See, for example, Rudolph Réti, *The Thematic Process in Music* (London, 1951), pp. 298–310; Rudolf Klein, 'Chopins Sonatentechnik', *Österreichische Musikzeitschrift,* 1967; Leo Mazel, *Issledovaniya o Chopine* (Moscow, 1971), pp. 126–131; Alan Walker, 'Chopin and Musical Structure', in *Frédéric Chopin,* ed. Alan Walker (London, 1967), pp. 239–42.

5 See Anatole Leikin, 'The Dissolution of Sonata Structure in Romantic Piano Music (1820–1850)', (Ph.D. Diss., University of California at Los Angeles, 1986).

6 Actually, the identical sixth, F–D♭, taken as a harmonic interval in the outermost voices and based on the dominant, is latent already in bar 3. Chopin compensates for the tonal ambiguity of the opening interval by a gradual and thorough-going resolution: first to F–D♭ on the dominant (bar 3) and then to the identical, but melodic, sixth within the tonic (bar 5).

7 This aspect of the sonata reprise was first discussed in my article 'Osnovnye faktory stanovleniya sonatnoy normy', in *Voprosy muzykalnogo analiza*, ed. Z. Glyadeshkina, (Moscow, 1976).

8 D. F. Tovey, 'Franz Schubert', in *The Main Stream of Music and Other Essays* (New York, 1959), p. 124.

9 *Sonata Forms* (New York, 1972), p. 319.

10 Joachim Hermann, *Jósef Elsner und die Polnische Musik* (Delp, 1969), p. 25.

11 *Jósef Elsner*, p. 24.

12 This ascending bass line figures prominently in the motivic matrix of the movement. It incorporates (in bars 17 and 33) the rising semitone E–F from the slow introduction. In the introduction, and the principal and transitional sections this bass semitone is combined contrapuntally with the inverted treble semitone, D♭–C (Examples 1, 8).

13 Romantic art had an indisputable fascination with tragic love affairs. Gustave in *Valérie* by Madame de Krüdener dies of consumption; Werther in Goethe's *The Sorrows of Young Werther* shoots himself; Huldbrand in *Undine* by de La Motte Fouqué is embraced to death by Undine; the Poet in Shelley's *Alastor* descends to an untimely grave.

14 Walker, 'Chopin and Musical Structure', p. 242.

15 Jim Samson, *The Music of Chopin* (London, 1985).

16 Walker, 'Chopin and Musical Structure', p. 244.

17 Liszt also used this type of mirror reprise in his *Concerto pathétique* for two pianos. Its exposition contains an E-minor principal and a G-major subsidiary group; in the recapitulation both groups retain their keys, but they appear in reverse order.

18 See, for example, Rudolf Klein, 'Chopins Sonatentechnik', *Österreichische Musikzeitschrift*, 1967; Leo Mazel, *Issledovaniya*, pp. 126–31; Walker, 'Chopin and Musical Structure', pp. 251–4; Samson, *The Music of Chopin*, pp. 133–6.

19 'K voprosu o rasshirenii ponyatiya odnoimennoy tonalnosti' (Expanding the Concept of Parallel Keys), *Sovetskaya muzyka* No. 2 (1957).

20 Samson, *The Music of Chopin*, pp. 137–8.

21 Ibid., pp. 138–9.

9 Chopin in performance

1 See Jean-Jacques Eigeldinger, *Chopin: Pianist and Teacher*, trans. Naomi Shohet (Cambridge, 1986), pp. 52, 74, 77–9.

2 Ibid. p. 26.

3 Ibid. pp. 275–6.

4 Ibid. p. 276.

5 William G. Atwood, *Fryderyk Chopin: Pianist from Warsaw* (New York, 1987), p. 246.

6 Hector Berlioz, *Memoirs*, trans. David Cairns (London, 1970), p. 537.

7 See Eigeldinger, *Chopin*, pp. 173–4.

8 Ibid. p. 97.

9 Ibid. p. 79.

10 *Hanslick's Music Criticisms*, trans. Henry Pleasants (London, 1950; repr. New York, 1988), pp. 49–50.

11 Reginald Gerig, *Famous Pianists and Their Technique* (Devon, 1976), p. 208.

12 Alice M. Diehl, *Musical Memories* (London, 1897), p. 247.

13 *Selected Correspondence of Fryderyk Chopin*, ed. Arthur Hedley (London, 1962), p. 117.

14 Wilhelm von Lenz, *Great Piano Virtuosos of Our Time*, trans. Philip Reder (London, 1971), p. 24.

15 Ibid. p. 59.

16 *Shaw's Music*, ed. Dan H. Laurence (London, 1981), vol. 2, p. 831.

17 *Hanslick's Music Criticisms*, p. 230.

18 Frederick Niecks, *The Life of Chopin* (London, 1888, 2nd edn 1973), vol. 2, p. 103.

19 James Gibbons Huneker, *Mezzotints in Modern Music* (London, 1900), p. 212.

20 Alfred Cortot, *Aspects de Chopin* (Paris, 1949).

10   Chopin reception in nineteenth-century Poland

1 Adaszewska-Czerniakowska, 'Recepcja Chopina w Warszawie w pierwszej połowie XIX w.' (typescript, Warsaw University, Institute of Musicology); D. Pistonne, 'Chopin i Paryż w drugiej połowie XIX w.', *Rocznik Chopinowski*, vol. 17 (1985); O. Pisarenko, 'Wyraz muzyczny dzieł Chopina w opinii jego współczesnych', *Z badan nad Chopinem*, vol. 3 (Warsaw, 1973); J. Ludvova, 'Twórczość Chopina w dziewięt-nastowiecznej Pradze', *Rocznik Chopinowski*, vol. 18 (1986); M. Tomaszewski, *Kompozytorzy polscy o Chopinie* (Cracow, 1959); I. Poniatowska, 'Chopin – paradigmaty interpretacji', *Rocznik Chopinowski*, vol. 16 (1984), and 'Twórczość Chopina w świetle pierwszych monografii', in *Chopin Studies*, vol. 4 (Warsaw, in press).

2 According to T. Kneif the socio-functional aspect is one of the three criteria for assessing a work, along with the historical and aesthetic aspects: see T. Kneif, 'Zur Deutung des musikalischen Geschmacks', in *Über das Musikleben des Gegenwart* (Berlin, 1968).

3 See *Pamiętnik Warszawski*, vol. 10 (1818): '*I na naszej ziemi powstają geniusze.*' (Geniuses are born in our country, too.)

4 The quotation is from *Dziennik Powszechny Krajowy*, 24 September 1830. For evidence of the warm reception given the earlier works mentioned, see, for examples, *Dziennik Powszechny Krajowy*, no. 63 (4 March 1831), p. 306; *Kurier Warszawski*, no. 80 (23 March 1830), p. 40, no. 181 (9 July 1830) and no. 274 (12 October 1830); *Flora*, no. 87 (30 August 1830).

5 *Gazeta Polska*, no. 81 (26 March 1830); *Gazeta Korespondenta Warszawskiego i Zagranicznego*, no. 66 (19 March 1830).

6 The edition of lithographed scores (except for the Polonaise in G minor, all Chopin's pieces published in Warsaw were lithographed) did not exceed 150–200 copies; the

edition of engraved scores (e.g. the Polonaise in G minor) may have been greater, but was often significantly smaller, about 100 copies. It is highly unlikely that the 'Wunderkind's' first published work had a large print run. See W. Tomaszewski, *Warszawskie edytorstwo muzyczne w latach 1722–1865* (Warsaw, in press).

7 See, for example, *Kurier Polski*, no. 103 (18 and 22 March 1830); *Gazeta Korespondenta Warszawskiego*, no. 66 (19 March 1830); *Dziennik Powszechny Krajowy*, no. 78 (20 March 1830), p. 382.

8 *Dekameron Polski*, no. 9 (31 March 1830), p. 369–70.

9 *Kurier Polski*, no. 103 (18 March 1830).

10 Ibid. no. 110 (26 March 1830).

11 F. Liszt, *Frederick Chopin* (Paris, 1852).

12 It is difficult to ascertain whether or to what extent Chopin aimed consciously to impart a national character to his music. Such intent is highly probable, however, since he had been brought up in an atmosphere that sought to 'nationalise' art. This is confirmed by a remark in his letter of 25 December 1831 to Tytus Woyciechowski: 'You know how much I wanted to feel our national music, and now I've partly managed to do so.' (B. E. Sydow, *Korespondencja Fryderyka Chopina* (Warsaw, 1955), vol. 1, p. 210.

13 *Kurier Warszawski*, no. 274 (12 October 1830).

14 *Gazeta Korespondenta Warszawskiego*, no. 66 (1830).

15 *Kurier Polski*, no. 103 (18 March 1830).

16 See, for example, *Dziennik Powszechny Krajowy*, no. 78 (20 March 1830), p. 382, and no. 265 (24 September 1830), p. 1312.

17 See *Dziennik Powszechny Krajowy*, no. 78 (20 March 1830), p. 382.

18 Ibid. no. 63 (4 March 1830), p. 306.

19 Ibid.

20 *Pamiętnik Muzyczny Warszawski*, no. 5 (1836); see also W. Żywny's letter to Chopin in Sydow, *Korespondencja*, vol. 1, p. 257–8.

21 *Tygodnik Literacki*, no. 10 (1842), p. 76.

22 M. Chopin's letter to his son dated 13 April 1833, in Sydow, *Korespondencja*, vol. 1, p. 225.

23 An undated letter of 1835 from the composer's sister, in Sydow, *Korespondencja*, vol. 1, p. 252.

24 An undated letter of 1836 from M. Chopin to his son, in Sydow, *Korespondencja*, vol. 1, p. 282.

25 Letter of 7 December 1833, in Sydow, *Korespondencja*, vol. 1, p. 230.

26 In a letter to Chopin his sister, Ludwika Jędrzejowiczowa, described a concert given at her home in which Józef Brzowski (a Warsaw composer) and his daughter Jadwiga (a pianist) played compositions by Chopin (letter of 9 January 1841 in Sydow, *Korespondencja*, vol. 2, p. 15); Józef Damse (a popular Warsaw composer) wrote to Chopin: 'My younger daughter fêtes me with your nocturnes' (letter of 2 June 1842 in Sydow, *Korespondencja*, vol. 2, p. 64).

27 In describing the new editions of Chopin's pieces, M. A. Szulc wrote of the Mazurka in A minor from 'notre temps': 'we shall not describe it more fully here as everyone more or less knows Chopin's mazurkas' (*Tygodnik Literacki*, no. 11 (1842), p. 83).

28 Chopin's sister wrote to the composer: 'Your mazurka, the one with the third section going Bam, boom, boom, (nota bene seems to be creating a furore here, particularly in the theatre. . .with full orchestra); they played it all evening at the Zamoyski ball and Barciński [Chopin's brother-in-law] who heard it there said they loved dancing to it. What do you feel about such profanity? — your music's really for listening to. . . now you can hear it [this mazurka] everywhere' (undated letter of 1835 in Sydow, *Korespondencja*, vol. 1, pp. 252–3).

29 See B. Wilczyński's article on Chopin in *Gazeta Muzyczna i Teatralna*, no. 8 (1865), p. 3.

30 In Warsaw alone the press cited over fifty public performances of this polonaise in the second half of the nineteenth century.

31 This sonata was performed in Warsaw by Aleksander Zarzycki, the outstanding Polish pianist and composer. A reviewer at the time described the piece as 'a work full of inspiration and difficulty. . .the high-point of the concert' (*Gazeta Muzyczna i Teatralna*, no. 17 (1866), p. 2).

32 A contemporary reviewer wrote:

> In the alteration of several purely pianistic passages to make them more suitable for the violin the work lost nothing, and definitely gained in fame and popularity. Its performance by Mr. Bilse's orchestra left one wanting for nothing, and this was confirmed by the audience's rapture. (*Ruch Muzyczny*, no. 20 (1857), p. 154).

33 J. Kleczyński, *Chopin w celniejszych swoich utworach* (Warsaw, 1886, new edn Cracow, 1959), p. 123.

34 Ibid., p. 130; see also M. A. Szulc, *Fryderyk Chopin i utwory jego muzyczne* (Poznań, 1873; new edn Cracow, 1986), p. 176.

35 See Szulc, *Fryderyk Chopin*, p. 169.

36 Kleczyński, *Chopin w celniejszych*, p. 106.

37 J. Kleczyński, *O wykonywaniu utworów Chopina* (Warsaw, 1879; new edn Cracow, 1959), p. 38.

38 See F. Niecks, *Frederick Chopin as a Man and Musician* (London, 1888).

39 H. Leichtentritt, *Analyse der Chopinschen Klavierwerke* (Berlin, 1921).

40 See H. Barbedette, *Chopin – Essai de critique musicale* (Paris, 1861), p. 48.

41 L. Rellstab was for a number of years a reviewer for the Berlin journal *Iris im Gebiete der Tonkunst*, where his reviews of Chopin's works were famed for their negative appraisal. Rellstab published the first review of Chopin (Mazurkas Opp. 6 and 7, Nocturnes Op. 9 published in Leipzig) in the issue of 12 July 1833.

42 After the first concert in Paris, which took place on 26 February 1832, Fétis praised Chopin as an original composer who would bring about, if not a complete, then at least a partial renaissance in piano music. However, after the concert of 20 May 1832 a critical appraisal of the first movement of the Concerto in F minor appeared. See O. Pisarenko, 'Recepcja Chopina we Francji w latach 1830–1860' (typescript, Warsaw University, Institute of Musicology).

43 *The Musical Magazine*, July 1835, p. 111.

44 Quoted after T. Uppström, *Pianister i Sverige* (Stockholm, 1973), p. 212; for longer fragments of this review see pp. 29–30.

45 See Szulc, *Fryderyk Chopin*; Kleczyński, *O wykonywaniu* and *Chopin w celniejszych*; Wilczyński in *Gazeta Muzyczna i Teatralna*, no. 8.

46 See Kleczyński, *O wykonywaniu*, p. 38.

47 Kleczyński, *Chopin w celniejszych*, p. 116.

48 Szulc, *Fryderyk Chopin*, p. 77.

49 M. A. Szulc, article about Chopin in *Orędownik naukowy*, no. 26 (17 June 1841).

50 See Szulc, *Fryderyk Chopin*; S. Tarnowski, 'Kilka słów o Chopinie', in *Przegląd Polski*, vol. 11 (1871); Kleczyński, *Chopin w celniejszych*, pp. 129–30.

51 E.g. bluster, delicacy, feelings of sorrow, sympathy, warmth: see Kleczyński, *Chopin w celniejszych*, p. 116.

52 J. Kenig, 'Z powodu wydania pośmiertnych dzieł Chopina', *Gazeta Warszawska*, no. 121 (1856), quoted from S. Jarociński, *Antologia polskiej krytyki muzycznej XIX i XX w.* (Cracow, 1955), p. 133.

53 J. Sikorski, 'Album Towarzystwa Muzycznego we Lwowie', in *Pamiętnik Muzyczno-Teatralny*, no. 32 (1862).

54 Letter to his family dated 19 April 1847, in Sydow, *Korespondencja*, vol. 2, p. 193.

55 Letter to Tytus Woyciechowski dated 25 December 1831, in Sydow, *Korespondencja*, vol. 1, p. 210.

56 E.g. I. F. Dobrzyński, Nocturne in G minor.

57 See D. Pistonne, 'Chopin i Paryż', and E. Öhrström, *Borgerliga kvinnors musicerande i 1800-tals Sverige* (Göteborg, 1987), p. 148 onwards.

58 See, for example, the review in *Ruch Muzyczny*, no. 23 (1858), p. 182, where a waltz by H. Koman is compared to one by Chopin, and no. 45 (1858), p. 355, where an analogy is found between the polonaises of a mediocre composer (Madeyski) and the polonaises in A major, Op. 40, and A♭ major, Op. 53, by Chopin.

59 See Z. Chechlińska, 'Chopin a impresjonizm', in *Szkice o kulturze muzyczej XIX w.* (Warsaw, 1973).

60 C. Debussy, *Monsieur Croche antidilettante* (Paris, 1926; Polish trans. Cracow, 1961), p. 13.

11 Victorian attitudes to Chopin

1 John Old, 'Correspondence', *Monthly Musical Record*, (London, March 1875), p. 37.

2 See Cyril Ehrlich, *The Piano: A History* (London, 1976).

3 Cyril Ehrlich, *The Music Profession in Britain since the Eighteenth Century: A Social History* (Oxford, 1985), pp. 104–7.

4 Rev. Peter Maurice, DD, *What Shall we Do with Music? A letter to the Rt. Hon. Earl of Derby, Chancellor of the University of Oxford* (Oxford, 1856). Quoted in Ehrlich, *The Music Profession*, p. 42.

5 C. L. Graves, 'Edward Dannreuther', in Graves, *Post-Victorian Music with Other Studies and Sketches* (London, 1911), p. 60.

6 Ehrlich, *The Music Profession*, p. 74.

7 Graves, 'Musical England', in Graves, *Post-Victorian Music*, p. 356.

8 Graves, 'Charles Santley', in Graves, *Post-Victorian Music*, pp. 116–17.

9   Sir W. H. Hadow, *Studies in Modern Music. Second Series* (Eleventh Impression, London, 1926), pp. 81–2.

10   Letter from Mrs. Gaskell to Anne Robson (her sister-in-law), dated 1 September 1851, quoted in Winifred Gérin, *Elizabeth Gaskell: A Biography* (Oxford, 1976), p. 144.

11   Ehrlich, *The Music Profession*, pp. 119–120.

12   Hadow, *Modern Music*, p. 30.

13   Ernest Walker, in his *History of Music in England* (Oxford, 1907), writes that while '[the British] are very far from having a monopoly of vulgar music . . . in no other country, perhaps, have prominent composers written such with their eyes open, purely for the sake of money, nor has this kind of thing elsewhere hampered the real progress of the art to anything like so considerable and extent,' (p. 356).

14   Walker, referring to Elgar, in *History of Music in England*, pp. 305–6.

15   The early twentieth-century composer and critic W. D. Browne suggests that the general training of musicians in the late nineteenth century was responsible for this basically harmonic approach, harmony being taught first, and counterpoint second. (Quoted in Stephen Banfield, *Sensibility and English Song: Critical Studies of the Early 20th Century*, vol. 1 (Cambridge, 1985), p. 106.)

16   Adolf Weissmann, *The Problems of Modern Music*, trans. M. M. Bozman (London, 1925), p. 30. (First published in German in 1922.)

17   Hadow, *Modern Music*, p. 147.

18   Ibid., p. 155.

19   Waldo Selden Pratt, *The History of Music* (New York, 1907), p. 530.

20   Hadow, *Modern Music*, p. 158.

21   Pratt, *History of Music*, p. 529.

22   John Old, 'Correspondence', *Monthly Musical Record* (London, March 1875), p. 38.

23   Hadow, *Modern Music*, p. 169.

24   Weissmann, *Modern Music*, p. 161.

25   Hadow, *Modern Music*, p. 155.

26   Pratt, *History of Music*, p. 531.

27   A 'German critic', quoted in Charles S. Wilkinson, *Well-Known Piano Solos: How to Play them with Understanding, Expression and Effect*, second series (London, 1909), p. 22.

28   For example, in Percy Scholes, *Listener's History of Music: A Book for any Concert-Goer, Gramophonist or Radio Listener Providing also a Course of Study for Adult Classes in the Appreciation of Music*, vol. 2 (London, 1929), the author speaks of Chopin tending 'at the extreme towards effeminacy, even morbidity' (p. 119). This remains unaltered in the fourth edition (1954) and its subsequent reprints in 1956, 1960 and 1963. See also Oscar Bie, *A History of the Pianoforte and Pianoforte Players* (English trans. pub. New York, 1966), pp. 255–6.

29   Bie, *A History of the Pianoforte*, pp. 255–6.

30   Hadow, *Modern Music*, p. 160–62.

31   J. S. Shedlock, 'Correspondence', *Monthly Musical Record* (London, February 1875), p. 23.

32   John Old, 'Correspondence', *Monthly Musical Record* (London, March 1875), p. 37.

33   Weissmann, *Modern Music*, pp. 16–17.

34 Hadow, *Modern Music*, pp. 169.

35 Pratt, *History of Music*, p. 530.

36 J. S. Shedlock, *The Pianoforte Sonata: its Origin and Development* (Da Capo repr. edn, New York, 1964), p. 209. (First published London, 1895).

37 Hadow, *Modern Music*, p. 151.

38 Ibid., p. 154.

39 Ibid., p. 157.

40 Sir Hubert Parry, *The Art of Music*, 5th edn (London, 1909), p. 299.

41 Kenneth Young, in his book *Music's Great Days in the Spas and Watering-Places* (London, 1968) quotes from the reminiscences of the conductor J. Sidney Jones describing the 'rare specimen of the amateur snob' who criticises the orchestra in concerts such as those Jones conducted. 'Usually he is a pianist who can play some Chopin, a Grieg sonata or even a Liszt rhapsody' (Young, p. 50).

42 Ethel Newcomb, *Leschetizky as I knew him* (Da Capo repr. edn, New York, 1967), p. 37. (First published New York & London, 1923).

43 Wilkinson, *Well-Known Piano Solos*, pp. 54–5.

44 See Jim Samson, *The Music of Chopin* (London, 1985), p. 87.

45 Of interest here is the fact that Gutmann had been a pupil of Chopin.

12   Chopin's influence on the fin de siècle and beyond

1 For details see Jean-Jacques Eigeldinger, *Chopin: Pianist and Teacher* (Cambridge, 1986), pp. 129–30, 170, 188 and *passim*. (Dukas was taught piano by Chopin's pupil Georges Mathias.) Thanks are extended to Jean-Jacques Eigeldinger, Jean-Michel Nectoux, Arbie Orenstein, Malcolm Gillies and Deborah Crisp for providing useful information or documentation for this chapter, and to Wendy Hiscocks for perceptive musical comments.

2 Philippe Fauré-Fremiet, *Gabriel Fauré* (Paris, 1957), p. 139; corroborated by Robert Lortat, 'Gabriel Fauré', *Conférencia* 16–17 (5 and 19 August, 1929), p. 191.

3 Debussy's orchestral Nocturnes, for example, take the title from Whistler's paintings, and his one early piano nocturne shows mostly Russian influence.

4 'A propos du monument Chopin', in *Les écrits de Paul Dukas sur la musique* (Paris, 1948), pp. 514–15.

5 Both stories are reported in Eigeldinger, *Chopin*, pp. 65 and 69. Alfred Cortot, who must have known the shepherd story, conveys its atmosphere wonderfully in his various recordings of Op. 25 No. 1.

6 *Selected correspondence of Fryderyk Chopin*, ed. Arthur Hedley (London, 1962), p. 348.

7 Camille Saint-Saëns, 'Quelques mots sur l'exécution des oeuvres de Chopin', *Le courrier musical*, 13/10 (1910), pp. 386–7; 'Etudes des variantes', in Cortot and Ganche, *Trois manuscrits de Chopin* (Paris, 1932), pp. 19–26. Viardot's contributions to these texts are quoted in Eigeldinger, *Chopin*, pp. 49, 54, 58–9 and 65–6.

8 Lortat, 'Gabriel Fauré'.

9 Jean-Michel Nectoux, *Gabriel Fauré* (Paris, 1990). pp. 73–4; Eng. trans. Cambridge, 1991, p. 49.

10 Letters to Jacques Durand dated 27 January and 1 September 1915, printed in *Lettres de Claude Debussy à son éditeur, publiées par Jacques Durand* (Paris, 1927), pp. 131 and 150. Debussy's reference to Saint-Saëns may well be to the latter's dubious assertion in 1910 that 'the reason Chopin indicated the pedal so frequently is that he wanted it to be used only where he had indicated it, and nowhere else' ('Quelques mots sur l'exécution des oeuvres de Chopin', p. 387). Mme Mauté is briefly discussed, relative to Chopin, in Eigeldinger, *Chopin*, p. 129n.

11 Antoine Marmontel, *Les pianistes célèbres* (Paris, 1885), pp. 4–5; quoted in Eigeldinger, *Chopin*, p. 275.

12 Marguerite Long, *Au piano avec Claude Debussy* (Paris, 1960), pp. 25–6, 36–7 and 74. (An English translation is published as *At the piano with Debussy* (London, 1972).)

13 Although the first series of *Images* was not published until 1905, Ricardo Viñes noted in his diary that Debussy played him early versions of 'Reflets dans l'eau' and 'Mouvement' in December 1901. (Quoted in Nina Gubisch, 'La vie musicale à Paris entre 1887 et 1914 à travers le journal de R. Viñes', *Revue internationale de la musique française*, 1/2 (June, 1980), p. 224.)

14 Madame Gérard de Romilly, 'Debussy professeur, par une de ses élèves (1898–1908)', *Cahiers Debussy*, nouvelle série 2 (1978), p. 6: 'The way in which he explained and analysed this piece was something special.'

15 Debussy doubtless also observed Chopin's use of the same harmonic combination, in the same key, in the First Scherzo and the *Polonaise-fantaisie*.

16 Christian Goubault, *Claude Debussy* (Paris, 1986), p. 138.

17 Interview published in the *Morning Post*, London, 10 July 1922, quoted in Arbie Orenstein, *Ravel, man and musician* (New York, 1975), p. 127.

18 Ibid.

19 This is amply attested to by the mountain of existing analytical literature on Debussy beside the comparative molehill on the other three composers. For more discussion of this aspect of Debussy see Roy Howat, *Debussy in Proportion* (Cambridge, 1983).

20 For details of this relationship see Roy Howat, 'Debussy, *Masques, L'isle joyeuse* and a lost Sarabande', *Musicology Australia* 10 (1987), pp. 16–30. As this title suggests, the two pieces were initially intended as the outer parts of a triptych.

21 Preface to F. Chopin, *Oeuvres complètes pour le piano*, révision par Claude Debussy (Paris, 1915), *Valses*, p. ii.

22 Example 14's slight disparity from Chopin's figuration in Example 13 can be traced, incidentally, to the finale of Chopin's B minor Sonata, Op. 58 (bars 189–90). Ravel may also have found this exact figuration in Chabrier's two-piano arrangement of *España*, where it again begins the piece's culminating crescendo. Chabrier is discussed again later in this chapter.

23 Roy Howat, 'Debussy et les musiques de l'Inde', *Cahiers Debussy* 12–13 (1988–9, joint volume), pp. 141–52.

24 In the course of some patronising remarks about the Indian music he heard at the London Great Exhibition in 1851, Hector Berlioz mentions in passing the Indian musicians 'who accompanied the Calcutta dancing-girls in Paris a few years ago' (*Evenings in the orchestra* (London, 1963), p. 223). Berlioz's own negative reaction partly

reflects the adverse conditions in which the music was performed, and in any case need not speak for Chopin, who had very different tastes.

25 This edition was prompted by the wartime unavailability of German editions.

26 M. Long, *Au piano avec Debussy*, p. 37.

27 Roger Nichols has pointed out (in conversation) that the strongest allusion of all in 'Pour les sixtes' is to Schumann's Fifth Novelette (bars 222ff.).

28 *Lettres de Claude Debussy à son éditeur*, pp. 141, 146 and 148.

29 Ibid., pp. 130–50.

30 For detailed documentation of this see Roy Howat, 'Modes and semitones in Debussy's Preludes and elsewhere', *Studies in music* 22 (1988), pp. 81–104.

31 J.-J. Eigeldinger, 'Twenty-four Preludes Op. 28: genre, structure, significance', in *Chopin Studies*, ed. Jim Samson (Cambridge, 1988), pp. 181–93.

32 Orenstein, *Ravel*, p. 205.

33 See Maurice Ravel, *Lettres, écrits, entretiens* (Paris, 1989), p. 520.

34 'Les Polonaises, les Nocturnes, les Impromptus, la Barcarolle: impressions', in *Lettres, écrits, entretiens*, p. 293. This text is to be read nonetheless with some reserve, as Ravel complained after its first publication in 1910 that it had been brutally edited (*Lettres, écrits, entretiens*, p. 576).

35 Ravel had earlier used this chord in a distinctly less exquisite context, for the opening of 'Scarbo'. If any debt is owed there, however, it is more probably to the same harmony in Debussy's 'Mouvement' (see Example 16 above). Ravel was certainly aware of the harmony's ancestry, with a further twist: the late Arthur Hoérée related (in conversation) that Ravel once showed him where it could be found in the first movement of Beethoven's 'Moonlight' Sonata – an observation doubtless made with an ironic twinkle, given Ravel's usual disdain for the composer he used to call *le grand sourd*.

36 Orenstein, *Ravel*, pp. 242–3. Ravel's arrangement was made to replace the earlier *Les sylphides* devised by Diaghilev. Disastrously, Ravel's autograph score seems to have been either thrown out from a London warehouse during the 1914–18 war (see Bronislav Nijinska, *Early memoirs* (New York, 1981), p. 508) or else stolen in a later burglary from Bronislav Nijinska's home.

37 Orenstein, *Ravel*, p. 119.

38 In 1936 Béla Bartók opined that Debussy's and Ravel's mature piano music would be 'unimaginable' without the influence of this particular piece by Liszt: see *Béla Bartók Essays*, ed. Benjamin Suchoff (London, 1976), p. 505.

39 *Ecrits de Paul Dukas*, pp. 205 and 517.

40 *Béla Bartók Essays*, pp. 317–23 and 451.

41 See, for example, the memoirs of Julia Székely in Malcolm Gillies, *Bartók remembered* (London, 1991), pp. 137–8.

42 Fragment only (bars 1–83), recorded in January 1939; issued on Hungaroton LPX 12335 (Bartók Record Archives, vol. 2, Budapest, 1981).

Chopin's works

The chronology of Chopin's music is anything but well-established. The present list is based largely on Chomiński and Turło, *Katalog Dzieł Fryderyka Chopina* (Krakow, 1990), which differs in numerous ways from Jan Ekier's *Wstęp do wydania narodowego*. Several changes from the Chomiński/Turło chronology have been made, based either on my own research or on Jeffrey Kallberg's dating of autograph manuscripts as reported in John Rink, 'The Evolution of Chopin's "Structural Style" and its Relation to Improvisation' (PhD dissertation, Cambridge, 1989).

1 Original Opus numbers

	Opus title	Date of composition	Date of publication
1	Rondo, c; pf	1825	1825
2	Variations on 'Là ci darem la mano', Bb; pf, orch.	1827	1830
3	*Introduction and Polonaise Brillante*, C; vc, pf	1829–30	1831
4	Sonata, c; pf	1827–8	1851
5	*Rondo à la mazur*, F; pf	1826	1828
6	Four Mazurkas, f#, c#, E, Eb; pf	1830–2	1832
7	Five Mazurkas, Bb, A, F, Ab, C; pf (1st version of No. 4, 1825)	1830–32	1832
8	Piano Trio, g	1828–9	1832
9	Three Nocturnes, bb, Eb, B; pf	1830–32	1832
10	Twelve Etudes, pf	1830–32	1833
11	Concerto No. 1, e; pf, orch.	1830	1833
12	*Variations brillantes*, Bb; pf	1833	1833
13	*Fantasy on Polish Airs*, A; pf, orch.	1828	1834
14	*Rondo à la krakowiak*, F; pf, orch.	1828	1834
15	Three Nocturnes, F, F#, g; pf	1830–32	1833
16	*Introduction and Rondo*, c, Eb; pf	1832–3	1834
17	Four Mazurkas, Bb, e, Ab, a; pf	1833	1834

Opus	title	Date of composition	Date of publication
18	Waltz, Eb; pf	1831–2	1834
19	Bolero, C/A; pf	*c.*1833	1834
20	Scherzo, b; pf	*c.*1835	1835
21	Concerto No. 2, f; pf, orch.	1829	1836
22	*Andante spianato and Grande Polonaise brillante*, G; pf, and Eb; pf, orch.	1830–35	1836
23	Ballade, g; pf	*c.*1835	1836
24	Four Mazurkas, g, C, Ab, bb; pf	1833	1836
25	Twelve Etudes, pf	1835–7	1837
26	Two Polonaises, c#, eb; pf	1835	1836
27	Two Nocturnes, c#, Db; pf	1835	1836
28	Twenty-four Preludes, pf	1838–9	1839
29	Impromptu, Ab; pf	*c.*1837	1837
30	Four Mazurkas, c, b, Db, c#; pf	1837	1838
31	Scherzo, Db; pf	1837	1837
32	Two Nocturnes, B, Ab; pf	1837	1837
33	Four Mazurkas, g#, D, C, b; pf	1838	1838
34	Three Waltzes		1838
	Ab	1835	
	a	*c.*1834	
	F	1838	
35	Sonata, bb; pf (slow movement 1837)	1839	1840
36	Impromptu, F#; pf	1839	1840
37	Two Nocturnes, g, G; pf	1838–9	1840
38	Ballade, F/a; pf	1839	1840
39	Scherzo, c#; pf	1839	1840
40	Two Polonaises, A, C; pf	1838–9	1840
41	Four Mazurkas, e, B, Ab, c#; pf	1838–9	1840
42	Waltz, Ab; pf	1840	1840
43	Tarantelle, Ab; pf	1841	1841
44	Polonaise, f#; pf	1841	1841
45	Prelude, c#; pf	1841	1841
46	*Allegro de concert*, pf	*c.*1834–41	1841
47	Ballade, Ab; pf	1841	1841
48	Two Nocturnes, c, f#; pf	1841	1841
49	Fantaisie, f/Ab; pf	1841	1841
50	Three Mazurkas, G, Ab, c#; pf	1842	1842
51	Impromptu, Gb; pf	1842	1843
52	Ballade, f; pf	1842–3	1843
53	Polonaise, Ab; pf	1842–3	1843
54	Scherzo, E; pf	1842–3	1843

Opus title		Date of composition	Date of publication
55	Two Nocturnes, f, E♭; pf	1842–4	1844
56	Three Mazurkas, B, C, c; pf	1843–4	1844
57	Berceuse, D♭; pf	1844	1845
58	Sonata, b; pf	1844	1845
59	Three Mazurkas, a, A♭, f♯; pf	1845	1845
60	Barcarolle, F♯; pf	1845–6	1846
61	*Polonaise-fantaisie*, A♭; pf	1846	1846
62	Two Nocturnes, B, E; pf	1846	1846
63	Three Mazurkas, B, f, c♯; pf	1846	1847
64	Three Waltzes, D♭, c♯, A♭; pf	1847	1847
65	Sonata, g; vc, pf	1845–6	1847

2 Published posthumously with Opus numbers by Fontana

Opus title		Date of composition	Date of publication
66	*Fantaisie-impromptu*, c♯; pf	*c*.1834	1855
67	Four Mazurkas, pf		1855
	G	*c*.1835	
	g	1848–9	
	C	1835	
	a	1846	
68	Four Mazurkas, pf		1855
	C	*c*.1830	
	a	*c*.1827	
	F	*c*.1830	
	f	*c*.1846	
69	Two Waltzes, pf		1855
	A♭	1835	
	b	1829	
70	Three Waltzes, pf		1855
	G♭	1832	
	f	1842	
	D♭	1829	
71	Three Polonaises, pf		1855
	d	1827–8	
	B♭	1828	
	f	1828	
72	Three Ecossaises, D, g, D♭; pf	*c*.1829	1855
73	Rondo, C; 2 pfs (originally solo pf)	1828	1855
74	17 Songs		1857
	1 'Życzenie' (Witwicki)	*c*.1829	
	2 'Wiosna' (Witwicki)	1838	
	3 'Smutna rzeka' (Witwicki)	1831	

Opus title	Date of composition	Date of publication
4 'Hulanka' (Witwicki)	1830	
5 'Gdzie lubi' (Witwicki)	*c*.1829	
6 'Precz z moich oczu' (Mickiewicz)	1827	
7 'Posel' (Witwicki)	1831	
8 'Śliczny chlopiec' (Zaleski)	1841	
9 'Melodia' (Krasiński)	1847	
10 'Wojak' (Witwicki)	1831	
11 'Dwojaki koniec' (Zaleski)	1845	
12 'Moja pieszczotka' (Mickiewicz)	1837	
13 'Nie ma czego trzeba' (Zaleski)	1845	
14 'Pierścień' (Witwicki)	1836	
15 'Narzeczony' (Witwicki)	1831	
16 'Piosnka litewska' (Witwicki)	1831	
17 'Leci liście z drzewa' (Pol)	1836	

3 Works without Opus number (K. =Kobylanska, Katalog)

	Date of composition	Date of publication
Polonaise, B; pf (K. 1182–3)	1817	1834
Polonaise, g; pf (K. 889)	1817	1817
Polonaise, A♭; pf (K. 1184)	1821	1908
Introduction and Variations on a German air ('Der Schweizerbub'), E; pf (K. 925–7)	1824	1851
Polonaise, g♯; pf (K. 1185–7)	1824	1850–60?
Mazurka, B♭; pf (K. 891–5)	1825–6	1826
Mazurka, G; pf (K. 896–900)	1825–6	1826
Variations, D; pf 4 hands (K. 1190–2)	1826	1865
Funeral March, c; pf (K. 1059–68)	*c*.1826	1855
Polonaise, b♭; pf (K. 1188–9)	1826	1881
Nocturne, e; pf (K. 1055–8)	1827	1855
Souvenir de Paganini, A; pf (K. 1203)	1829	1881
Mazurka, G; pf (K. 1201–2)	1829	1879
Waltz, E; pf (K. 1207–8)	*c*.1829	1867
Waltz, E♭; pf (K. 1212)	1830	1902
Mazurka, G; voice (K. 1201–2)	1829	1879
Waltz, A♭; pf (K. 1209–11)	1830	1902
Waltz, e; pf (K. 1213–4)	1830	1850–60
Czary, voice, pf (K. 1204–6)	1830	1910
Polonaise, G♭; pf (K. 1197-1200)	1829	1850–60
Lento con gran expressione, c♯; pf (K. 1215–22)	1830	1875
Grand Duo concertant on themes from Meyerbeer's 'Robert le Diable', E; vc, pf (K. 901–2)	1831	1833
Mazurka, B♭; pf. (K. 1223)	1832	1909

Opus title	Date of composition	Date of publication
Mazurka, D; pf (K. 1224, 1st version K. 1193–6)	1832	1880
Mazurka, C; pf (K. 1225–6)	1833	1870
Cantabile, B♭; pf (K. 1230)	1834	1931
Mazurka, A♭; pf (K. 1227–8)	1834	1930
Prelude, A♭; pf (K. 1231–2)	1834	1918
Variation No. 6 in *Hexameron*, E; pf (K. 903–4)	1837	1839
Trois Nouvelles Etudes, pf (K. 905–17)	1839–40	1839
Canon, f; pf (K. 1241)	*c.*1839	
Mazurka 'Notre Temps', a; pf (K. 919–24)	*c.*1839	1842
Sostenuto (Waltz), E♭; pf (K. 1237)	1840	1955
Dumka, voice, pf (K. 1236)	1840	1910
Fugue, a; pf (K. 1242)	*c.*1841	1898
Moderato, E; pf (K. 1240)	1843	1910
Two Bourrées, g, A; pf (K. 1403–4)	1846	1968
Largo, E♭; pf (K. 1229)	1847	1938
Nocturne, c; pf (K. 1233–5)	1847	1938
Waltz, a; pf (K. 1238–9)	1847	1955

Bibliographical note

Information on the manuscript and printed sources for Chopin's music is available in several major catalogues: Krystyna Kobylańska, *Rękopisy Utworów Chopina: Katalog* (2 vols.), Kraków, 1977; Krystyna Kobylańska, *Frédéric Chopin: Thematischbibliographisches Werkverzeichnis*, ed. Ernst Herttrich, trans. Helmut Stolze, Munich, 1979; Józef Chomiński and Dalila Turło, *Katalog Dzieł Fryderyka Chopina*, Kraków, 1990. Also useful is Jan Ekier, *Wstęp do wydania naradowego*, Warsaw, 1974. Although these are not in English they can be used fairly easily by the English reader and supersede in every way Maurice Brown's earlier study, *Chopin: An Index of his Works in Chronological Order*, London, 1960, rev. 1972. Bibliographical information is available in Kornel Michałowski, *Bibliografia Chopinowska (1849–1969)*, Krakow, 1970 (updated in several issues of the specialist journal *Rocznik Chopinowski*). Selections from this journal are now published in English as *Chopin Studies*, of which three volumes have appeared. Two collections of Chopin's letters are available in English: Arthur Hedley, *Selected Correspondence of Fryderyk Chopin*, London, 1962, and Henryk Opienski, *Chopin's Letters*, New York, 1931, rev. 1971.

Biographical studies in English are legion, but the following may be recommended: Frederick Niecks, *Chopin as a Man and a Musician* (2 vols.) London, 1888, repr. 1973; James Huneker, *Chopin: the Man and his Music*, New York, 1900, repr. 1966; Arthur Hedley, *Chopin*, London, 1947; Camille Bourniquel, *Chopin*, Paris, 1957, Eng. trans. 1960; Adam Harasowski, *The Skein of Legends about Chopin*, Glasgow, 1967; Ruth Jordan, *Nocturne: A Life of Chopin*, London, 1978; George Marek and Maria Gordon-Smith, *Chopin: A Biography*, New York, 1978; Adam Zamoyski, *Chopin: A Biography*, London, 1979.

More specialised studies of Chopin as a pianist and teacher include E. J. Hipkins, *How Chopin Played*, London, 1937; Jean-Jacques Eigeldinger's path-breaking study *Chopin: Pianist and Teacher* (originally *Chopin vu par ses élèves*), Cambridge, 1986; James Methuen-Campbell, *Chopin Playing*, London, 1981, and William Attwood, *Fryderyck Chopin: Pianist from Warsaw*, New York, 1987. Among the studies of his music in English are G. C. Jonson, *A Handbook to Chopin's Works*, London, 1905; Gerald Abraham, *Chopin's Musical Style*, London, 1939; Alan Walker (ed.), *Frederic Chopin: Profiles of the Man and the Musician*, London, 1966; D. Żebrowski (ed.), *Studies in Chopin*, Warsaw, 1973; Jim Samson, *The Music of Chopin*, London, 1985, and (ed.), *Chopin Studies*, Cambridge, 1988. For those inclined to probe further there are two excellent PhD dissertations: Jeffrey Kallberg, 'The Chopin Sources: Variants and Versions in Later Manuscripts', University of Chicago, 1982, and John Rink, 'The Evolution of Chopin's "Structural Style" and its Relation to Improvisation', University of Cambridge, 1989.

Index